DK INDIA

Editor Priyanjali Narain
Senior art editor Mahua Sharma
Assistant art editor Garima Agarwal
Picture researcher Surya Sankash Sarangi
Jacket designer Suhita Dharamjit
Senior DTP designer Harish Aggarwal
DTP designers Nand Kishor Acharya,
Jaypal Chauhan
Pre-production manager Balwant Singh
Production manager Pankaj Sharma
Managing editor Rohan Sinha
Managing art editor Sudakshina Basu

DK UK

Project editor Sarah MacLeod
Art editor Chrissy Barnard
Jacket editor Emma Dawson
Jacket designer Akiko Kato
Jacket design development manager Sophia MTT
Producer, Pre-production Jacqueline Street-Elkayam
Senior producer Mary Slater
Picture research manager Martin Copeland
Managing editor Francesca Baines
Managing art editor Philip Letsu
Publisher Andrew Macintyre
Art director Karen Self
Design director Phil Ormerod
Associate publishing director Liz Wheeler
Publishing director Jonathan Metcalf

FIRST EDITION

Senior editor Julie Ferris
Senior designer Stefan Podhorodecki
Project editors Francesca Baines, Hazel Beynon
Designers Katie Knutton, Hoa Luc, Smiljka Surla, Nihal Yesil
Editors Steven Carton, Jenny Finch, Niki Foreman, Fran Jones, Andrea Mills
Additional design Jim Green, Spencer Holbrook, Phil Letsu,
Johnny Pau, Marilou Prokopiou, Jacqui Swan

Managing editor Linda Esposito
Managing art editor Diane Thistlethwaite

Commissioned photography Dave King
Creative retouching Steve Willis
Picture research Nic Dean

Publishing manager Andrew Macintyre
Category publisher Laura Buller

DK picture researchers Lucy Claxton, Rose Horridge
Production editor Andy Hilliard
Production controller Pip Tinsley

Jacket design Jacqui Swan, Akiko Kato
Jacket editor Mariza O'Keeffe
Design development manager Sophia M Tampakopoulos Turner
Development team Natasha Rees, Yumiko Tahata

This edition published in 2019
First published in Great Britain in 2008 by
Dorling Kindersley Limited,
80 Strand, London, WC2R 0RL

Copyright © 2019, 2008 Dorling Kindersley Limited
A Penguin Random House Company
10 9 8 7 6 5 4 3 2 1
001–312860–Apr/2019

A CIP catalogue record for this book is available from the British Library
ISBN: 978-0-24136-435-2

Printed and bound in Dubai

A WORLD OF IDEAS:
SEE ALL THERE IS TO KNOW

www.dk.com

WOW!

the visual encylopedia of everything

Contributors and consultants:
Chris Barker, Hazel Beynon, Kim Bryan, Laura Buller,
Jack Challoner, Peter Chrisp, Mike Goodman, Derek Harvey, Andrea
Mills, Simon Mumford, Kristina Routh, Giles Sparrow, Carole Stott,
Richard Walker, Claire Watts, Jon Woodcock, John Woodward

3

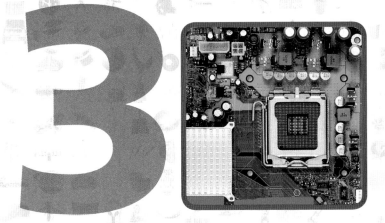

4

Contents

5

Earth

6

People and places

7

8

ALBATROSS COLONY
Every year, black-browed albatrosses return to the Falkland Islands in the Atlantic Ocean to breed. This albatross colony is one of the largest in the world, with more than 500,000 birds. Each pair produces a single egg.

Nature

❶ GERMINATION

A bean plant begins life as a seed with two halves, called cotyledons. In spring when the weather is mild, the seed starts to absorb water through a minute hole in its outer coating (the testa). The seed swells and about three days later a root grows to hold the plant in place, and a shoot appears above the ground. This process is called germination.

❷ ROOTS

The plant's roots absorb water from the soil. The water is used by the leaves to make food. The water also contains dissolved mineral salts, such as nitrates and phosphates, which are essential for growth.

❸ STEM

The strong stem of the plant supports its leaves in the sunlight. It also contains bundles of tubes or veins. These allow water containing dissolved nutrients to flow up from the roots to the leaves, and also carry sugary food from the leaves to other parts of the plant.

PLANTS

All green plants use the energy of sunlight to make sugary carbohydrate food from water and carbon dioxide in the air. This is why they grow well only in sunlit, moist places. The food fuels growth and is used to make cellulose – the tough, fibrous tissue that helps support all the various parts of the plant, from its stems and leaves to its flowers.

❹ LEAVES

The leaves are the plant's food factories. They act like solar panels, as the green chlorophyll enables the plant to absorb the energy of sunlight and use it for photosynthesis – the process in which the plant takes carbon dioxide from the air, and combines it with water drawn up by the roots to make sugar. Oxygen is also produced in the process and released into the air.

❺ TRANSPIRATION

As sunlight warms a plant, water in the leaves is lost as water vapour, through pores called stomata. The leaves then take in water from the stem, which in turn draws more water up into the plant from the roots. The water carries nutrients from the soil with it.

Strong ribs kept rigid by water pressure support the thin, delicate leaf tissue

More leaves are produced as the plant continues to grow

Cotyledons become the first leaves of the plant, once above the ground

Seed is covered by a hard coat called the testa, which protects it from fungi and bacteria

Shoot sprouts from the testa to form a root, with two seed leaves, called cotyledons, at its tip

New leaves sprout from buds that form at the tips of shoots

Green chlorophyll in leaves absorbs solar energy and uses it for photosynthesis

5

Growing point of bean plant is at top of main stem, between leaf stalks

Leaves make sugar, which mixes with water to make sap that flows to other parts of plant

4

Stem is kept upright at first by water pressure, but is gradually stiffened with tough cellulose

Cotyledons contain food that fuels early growth, but fall off after true leaves form

Soil provides the plant with anchorage, and is the main source of water and nutrients

3

Root network anchors plant in the soil as well as absorbing water and nutrients

TREES

Trees are the tallest, heaviest, and oldest of all living things. The Californian giant sequoia known as General Sherman weighs approximately 6,000 tonnes – 30 times as much as the biggest animal, the blue whale. The oldest living bristlecone pine tree, which also grows in California, is nearly 5,000 years old. Yet even these ancient giants can still produce tiny seeds that grow into new trees.

LEAVES

Like all green plants, trees absorb sunlight through their leaves and use its energy to turn air and water into sugar. A tree's leaves are its food factories.

Japanese maple

NEEDLES AND SCALES

Thin leaves make food efficiently, but they are easily damaged by hot sunshine or frost. So many trees that grow in very hot or cold places have thicker, tougher needles or scales.

Robina has a pinnate compound leaf

Horse chestnut has a palmate compound leaf

COMPOUND LEAVES

Most trees have simple leaves of various shapes, but some have compound leaves, made up of many leaflets. These either sprout from a long stalk (pinnate) or fan out from a single point (palmate).

Holly

Hawthorn flowers

English oak

Blue Atlas pine needles

A monkey puzzle tree has leathery, sharp-pointed scales

Arolla pine needles

Oak leaves

Acorns are oak seeds

FRUIT

The flowers of some trees turn into juicy fruits that contain seeds. If birds eat the fruit, the seeds pass through them unharmed and are scattered far away.

Apple blossom

Yew berries

FLOWERS

All trees produce flowers, but some may not be obvious because they do not have colourful petals. Other trees, however, such as apples, have showy flowers that attract insects.

Apples are big, fleshy fruits

Magnolia trees bear some of the biggest flowers

TREE RINGS

Every year a tree adds a layer of new wood to its trunk. If the tree is cut down, each year's growth shows as a visible ring, so the number of rings gives its age.

Closed pine cone

Nutmeg spice is a seed

Pine cone seeds

CONES

Coniferous trees such as pines have woody cones that contain small papery seeds. When the cones open up in the sun, the seeds fall out and blow away.

Open pine cone

SEEDS AND NUTS

Some trees have tiny seeds, but others produce the bigger seeds we call nuts. Animals eat them, but also bury and forget them, so they grow into new trees.

Horse chestnut

DECIDUOUS LEAVES

Many trees lose their leaves in winter, and grow new ones in spring. Before they fall, the old leaves lose their green colour and turn yellow, brown, or even red.

Sycamore seeds

Red maple

FLOWERS

Many plants produce beautiful flowers, often vividly coloured and fragrant. These intricate structures form the reproductive parts of plants, and have evolved so that they attract insects and birds to sip the sugary nectar at the flower's centre. While feeding, the insect or bird is dusted with pollen, which is produced by the stamens and contain the male sex cells. The pollen is deposited on the sticky stigma of another flower. This is pollination. A pollen tube then grows down the style to the ovary and fertilizes an ovule. This is fertilization. Some plants, such as grasses and many types of trees, rely on the wind to carry their pollen, and their flowers do not need showy petals or fragrant nectar to attract animals. Since this is a less efficient system, they must produce far more pollen, which can fill the air and cause hay fever.

❶ FLOWER STRUCTURE

A typical flower develops inside a bud at the end of a stalk. When the bud opens, it reveals a ring of petals, each of which secretes nectar from its base. At the centre of the flower lie the male structures that produce pollen. These surround the female structures that hold the ovules, or egg cells. An outer ring of green sepals may protect the flower when it is in bud.

Petals unfurl when the flower opens, but fall away once it is fertilized

Bright reds and pinks are more attractive to birds than insects, because not all insects can see the colour red

Stamen is made up of an anther and a filament

❷ CARPEL

An ovary, a style, and a stigma form the main parts of a carpel. At the heart of the flower lie the ovules, enclosed in a case called an ovary. The top of each ovary extends into a style that carries a sticky pad called a stigma. The flowers of some plants have many carpels, each with their own stigma, but this lily has just one.

❸ STAMEN

The tiny, dust-like pollen grains that contain the male cells are produced by stamens. These usually form a ring around the central carpel or carpels. Each stamen has a long filament, which supports a club-like anther that produces the pollen.

Sticky stigma traps pollen carried to flower by insects and birds

Anther is loaded with minute pollen grains containing male cells

Style

4 2

Bright line at base of petal guides the insect or bird towards the nectar

Filament

5

Ovary at base of carpel contains ovules that will become seeds if fertilized

❹ TRANSFERRING POLLEN

Insects such as butterflies often drink nectar from one type of flower. Hummingbirds do the same, because their bills are the right shape to reach the nectar. The bird and the insect get dusted with pollen in the process, and carry it directly to another flower of the same type.

❺ FERTILIZATION

If a hummingbird sips nectar from this lily, it will pick up pollen on its breast feathers. If the bird visits another lily, the sticky central stigma may pick up the pollen. Each pollen grain then sprouts a long tube that grows down through the carpel to reach an ovule. The male cell moves down the tube to fertilize the ovule so it can develop into a seed.

15

FRUITS

All plants produce fruits that contain their seeds. Some fruits are dry husks, but others are juicy and tasty. These attract animals, which eat them and carry the seeds in their stomachs. The tough-skinned seeds are not digested, but are scattered far away from the parent plant in the animals' droppings, and grow into new plants. The fruits shown here are cultivated types that have been specially bred for their size and flavour.

Bananas

Papayas

Tough skin encloses soft flesh

Dragon fruit

Pomelo

Watermelons

Dates

Oranges

Lemons

Limes

Kiwis

Blueberries

Passionfruit

Cantaloupe melon

Sweet granadilla

Strawberries

Raspberries

Honeydew melon

Blackberries

Figs

Redcurrants

Starfruit

Tamarillos

Nuts

❶ ORANGE

An orange has very soft juicy flesh contained in many segments, which are enclosed by a hard rind. Each segment usually contains a seed, or pip. An orange is technically a type of berry, which develops over the winter from the single ovary of an orange flower. Green at first, it turns orange as it swells to full size.

❷ BANANA

The bananas that are cultivated in the tropics have been bred to be seedless, but the wild bananas of southeast Asia have small fruits containing many big, hard seeds. They grow in bunches on large plants with huge leaves that sprout straight from the ground.

❸ NUTS

All nuts are large seeds, which the plant has equipped with a store of concentrated plant food. This ensures that the seedlings get a good start in life. The nut is surrounded by a hard shell, which is technically a fruit, but tough and fibrous rather than soft and juicy.

❹ DURIAN

To attract fruit-eating mammals, many fruits are fragrant. The southeast Asian durian fruit is famous for its strong aroma, which some people like and others hate. Animals such as forest pigs and orang-utans seem to love both its smell and taste.

Grapes

Mango

Pineapple

Pomegranates

Coconut

❺

Sharon fruit

❻

Guavas

Cucumber

Durian

Peaches

Tomatoes

❽

Prickly pears

Plums

Physalis

Pumpkins

Butternut squash

Rambutans

Peppers

Red kuri squash

Aubergine

Quinces

Broad beans

Baby aubergines

Fruit forms pod, protecting big seeds

Chilli peppers

Apples

❼

❺ GRAPES

Some fruits such as grapes grow as clusters of soft, edible, thin-skinned berries. Each berry has several seeds embedded in its flesh, although many cultivated varieties of grapes are seedless. Berries are often vividly coloured to attract birds, which have excellent colour vision.

❻ PEACH

The juicy flesh of a peach, plum, or cherry encloses a hard "stone" that contains a single seed. This type of fruit is called a drupe. The fleshy part is meant to be eaten, so animals spread the seeds, but some animals such as parrots can crack the stones and eat the seeds, too.

❼ BROAD BEAN

The edible part of a broad bean plant is its seeds, and its fruit is the entire pod. The wild ancestors of such beans do not attract animals. Instead, their pods dry up and split open with explosive force, so the seeds shoot out and are scattered on the ground.

❽ TOMATO

Not all fruits are edible. Some of the wild relatives of tomatoes are extremely poisonous. They include deadly nightshade, which is lethal to humans, although some animals can eat the berries without coming to harm. Tomatoes are also related to chilli peppers.

FUNGI

The mushrooms and other fungi that can appear overnight in damp places are not plants. They belong to a completely separate group of living things that feed on dead or living plants and animals. Each fungus forms a hidden network of slender stems called a mycelium, and the visible part is just the "fruiting body" that sprouts like an apple on a tree to spread the spores that grow into new fungi.

❶ OAK BOLETE
A typical mushroom has radiating gills beneath its cap that produce millions of spores. Other fungi, like the oak bolete, have spongy undersides that release spores from tiny holes, or are covered with spore-producing tufts.

Inocybe geophylla

Beechwood sickener

Birch brittlegrill

Oak bolete

Cortinarius rickenianus

Orange birch bolete

Lepiota cristata

Sulfur tuft

Death cap

Inocybe sindonia

Sheathed woodtuft

Pearly webcap

Mealy funnel

False chanterelle

Yellow ramaria

Turkeytail

White saddle

Felt saddle

Omphaliaster asterosporus

❷ TURKEYTAIL
Fungi are vital to life because they break down and recycle dead organisms. The turkeytail grows on dead wood, rotting it down so the nutrients it contains can be used by growing plants.

❸ DEATH CAP
Some fungi are extremely poisonous if they are eaten. The well-named death cap has probably been responsible for 90 per cent of all known deaths from mushroom poisoning.

❹ SAFFRON MILK CAP
Many fungi grow around the roots of certain plants, and provide them with plant foods in exchange for sugars. The saffron milk cap, for example, always grows with pine trees.

❺ PARASOL MUSHROOM

Some fungi, like the penny bun and parasol mushroom, are good to eat. But if you are not an expert at identifying them, you could be poisoned by a killer like the death cap.

❻ FLY AGARIC

The fly agaric is one of the best-known "toadstools" – a word often used for inedible or poisonous fungi. The white scales on its red cap are the remains of a thin veil that covered the growing fungus.

The ring is part of the veil that covered the cap of the young mushroom

The tough stem and cap contain chitin, which also forms the wings of insects

Bloodred webcap

Rosso coral

Parasol mushroom

Grooved bonnet

Fly agaric

Bearded milk cap

Green brittlegill

Persistent waxcap

Penny bun

Russula maculata

Hare's ear

Chanterelle

❼ PENNY BUN

The root-like fibres attached to the stem are just a tiny part of the penny bun's mycelium. This can cover huge areas. The mycelium of a single honey fungus can extend 150,000 sq m (1.6 million sq ft).

Pholiota adiposa

Saffron milk cap

Collared earthstar

Stump puffball

❽ STUMP PUFFBALL

Puffballs are named for the way the ripe fungi puff clouds of dust-like spores when they are kicked or hit by rain. Just one giant puffball can contain an amazing 7 trillion (7,000,000,000,000) spores.

ANIMAL KINGDOM

All living things fall into one of five categories, or "kingdoms" – bacteria and protists (single-celled organisms), fungi, plants, and animals. The animal kingdom is made up of many groups of invertebrates (animals without backbones, such as insects) and a few groups of vertebrates, such as mammals. They all share the ability to move and sense their surroundings, and the need to find food.

❶ INSECTS

Small animals with hard external skeletons, all insects have six legs when adult and, in most cases, two pairs of wings. They include creatures such as butterflies, wasps, flies, and beetles. Many are very attractive, but some can sting, bite, and carry deadly diseases.

This silver-washed fritillary butterfly has bright wing markings

❷ WORMS

There are many types of worms. They include tapeworms, which live inside other animals, flatworms, and roundworms. Most familiar are segmented worms like the earthworms that burrow in soil, marine worms that live on tidal shores, and leeches.

❸ AMPHIBIANS

Soft-skinned amphibians, such as frogs and toads, lose body moisture easily. To avoid drying out, nearly all frogs live in damp places, often near a pond. Most lay their eggs in water or other damp places, and these hatch into fish-like young, such as tadpoles.

Sticky pads on the frog's toes

❹ BIRDS

These highly specialized, warm-blooded vertebrates are superbly equipped for flight, and some may stay airborne for most of their lives. They are the only animals with feathers, which stop them losing body heat, enable them to fly, and are often brightly coloured.

❺ MAMMALS

Like birds, mammals are warm-blooded, meaning they can control their body temperature. The females feed their young on milk. Most eat plants, but some, such as lions, are meat eaters. Humans belong to the mammal group.

❻ ARACHNIDS

The spiders, scorpions, ticks, and their relatives are eight-legged invertebrates with hard external skeletons but no wings. Spiders kill their prey with venomous fangs, and scorpions have stings in their tails, some of which are powerful enough to kill a human.

The red-kneed tarantula has eight legs for walking and two chelicerae (mouthparts) to hold its prey

A leech lives by sucking the blood of its victims

● **MOLLUSCS**

Most molluscs are soft-bodied animals that live in water and have protective shells. They include mussels, clams, and whelks. The only molluscs able to live on land are the snails and slugs. Octopuses and squids are also molluscs, but they are highly evolved, with well-developed brains and eyes.

Lion's paw has soft pads for running and sharp, retractable claws

Suckers on each arm help the octopus move around and grab prey

● **CRUSTACEANS**

Like insects, crustaceans have hard external skeletons with several segments, and strong jointed legs. All are aquatic, apart from woodlice. They include tough-shelled animals like crabs and lobsters, as well as more delicate shrimps and water fleas.

The powerful claws of this lobster can seize and crush prey

● **MIRIAPODS**

Named for their many legs, miriapods have long bodies divided into segments. Centipedes have a single pair of legs on each segment, while millipedes have two pairs. Some millipedes have more than 90 segments, and more than 180 pairs of legs. Millipedes eat mainly dead material, but centipedes are speedy hunters.

A millipede's legs are moved by a wave-like action of the body

● **FISH**

Fish were the first vertebrates, and the ancestors of all amphibians, reptiles, mammals, and birds. They are perfectly adapted for life in water, which supports their bodies and provides them with vital oxygen. There are two main fish groups: those with bony skeletons, and the sharks and rays, which have skeletons of flexible cartilage.

● **ECHINODERMS**

Sea urchins, starfish, feather stars, and sea cucumbers are echinoderms, meaning "spiny skinned". Their bodies tend to be wheel-shaped, with a central mouth. Feather stars trap food that floats through their feathery arms, but most search for food on the seabed.

● **REPTILES**

Although cold-blooded like amphibians, reptiles such as snakes and lizards have waterproof, scaly skins that allow them to live in dry places such as deserts. Most are active hunters, and some snakes have powerful venom, which they use to kill their prey and for defence, if threatened.

Like other reptiles, snakes have scaly skin

21

PLANKTON

The sunlit surface waters of many oceans teem with life, most of it microscopic, that drifts with the currents. The whole drifting community is called the plankton. It is made up of plant-like phytoplankton, which use the energy of sunlight to make food from carbon dioxide and water, and zooplankton – animals that feed on both the phytoplankton and each other. This image shows the plankton in a splash of seawater, magnified more than 25 times.

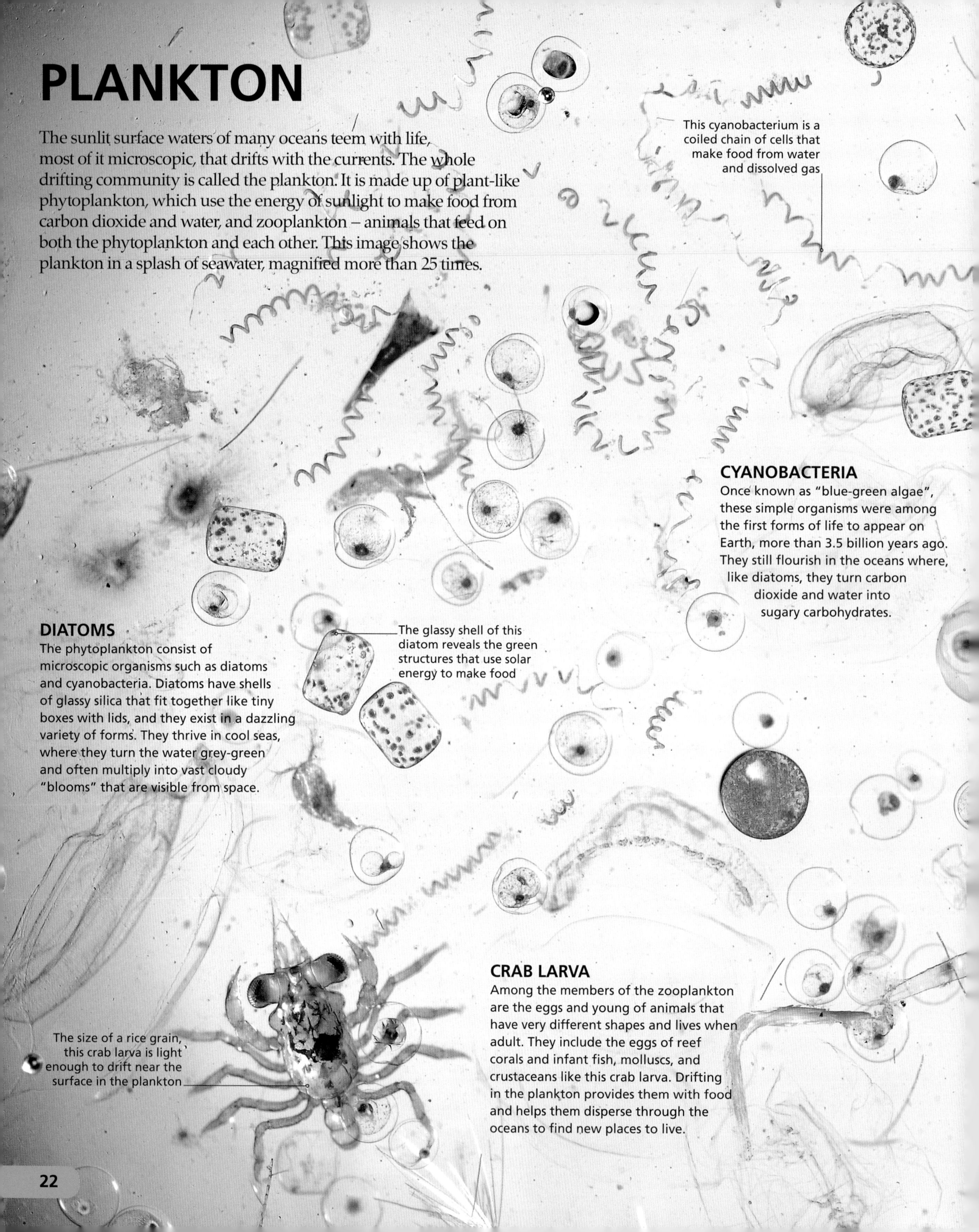

This cyanobacterium is a coiled chain of cells that make food from water and dissolved gas

CYANOBACTERIA

Once known as "blue-green algae", these simple organisms were among the first forms of life to appear on Earth, more than 3.5 billion years ago. They still flourish in the oceans where, like diatoms, they turn carbon dioxide and water into sugary carbohydrates.

DIATOMS

The phytoplankton consist of microscopic organisms such as diatoms and cyanobacteria. Diatoms have shells of glassy silica that fit together like tiny boxes with lids, and they exist in a dazzling variety of forms. They thrive in cool seas, where they turn the water grey-green and often multiply into vast cloudy "blooms" that are visible from space.

The glassy shell of this diatom reveals the green structures that use solar energy to make food

CRAB LARVA

Among the members of the zooplankton are the eggs and young of animals that have very different shapes and lives when adult. They include the eggs of reef corals and infant fish, molluscs, and crustaceans like this crab larva. Drifting in the plankton provides them with food and helps them disperse through the oceans to find new places to live.

The size of a rice grain, this crab larva is light enough to drift near the surface in the plankton

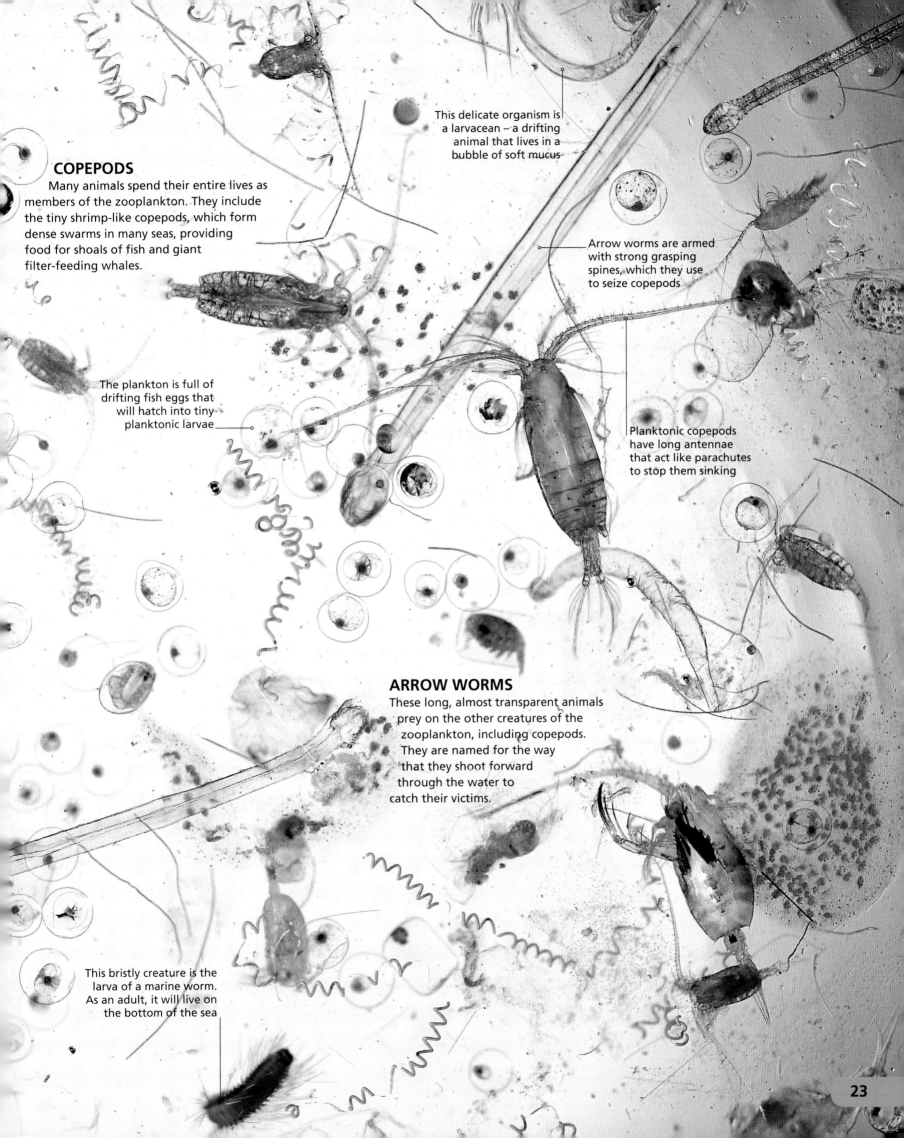

This delicate organism is a larvacean – a drifting animal that lives in a bubble of soft mucus

COPEPODS

Many animals spend their entire lives as members of the zooplankton. They include the tiny shrimp-like copepods, which form dense swarms in many seas, providing food for shoals of fish and giant filter-feeding whales.

Arrow worms are armed with strong grasping spines, which they use to seize copepods

The plankton is full of drifting fish eggs that will hatch into tiny planktonic larvae

Planktonic copepods have long antennae that act like parachutes to stop them sinking

ARROW WORMS

These long, almost transparent animals prey on the other creatures of the zooplankton, including copepods. They are named for the way that they shoot forward through the water to catch their victims.

This bristly creature is the larva of a marine worm. As an adult, it will live on the bottom of the sea

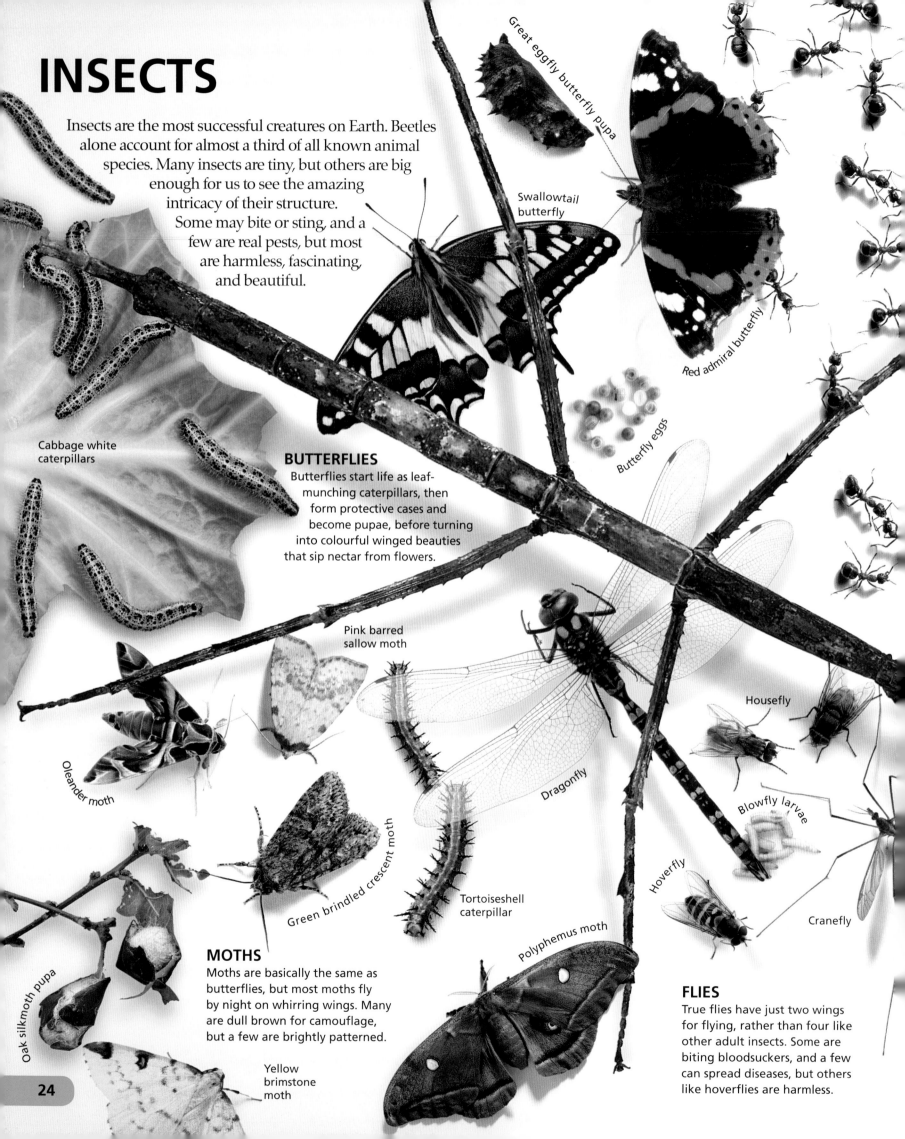

INSECTS

Insects are the most successful creatures on Earth. Beetles alone account for almost a third of all known animal species. Many insects are tiny, but others are big enough for us to see the amazing intricacy of their structure. Some may bite or sting, and a few are real pests, but most are harmless, fascinating, and beautiful.

Great eggfly butterfly pupa

Swallowtail butterfly

Red admiral butterfly

Butterfly eggs

Cabbage white caterpillars

BUTTERFLIES
Butterflies start life as leaf-munching caterpillars, then form protective cases and become pupae, before turning into colourful winged beauties that sip nectar from flowers.

Pink barred sallow moth

Dragonfly

Housefly

Oleander moth

Blowfly larvae

Green brindled crescent moth

Tortoiseshell caterpillar

Hoverfly

Cranefly

Oak silkmoth pupa

MOTHS
Moths are basically the same as butterflies, but most moths fly by night on whirring wings. Many are dull brown for camouflage, but a few are brightly patterned.

Polyphemus moth

FLIES
True flies have just two wings for flying, rather than four like other adult insects. Some are biting bloodsuckers, and a few can spread diseases, but others like hoverflies are harmless.

Yellow brimstone moth

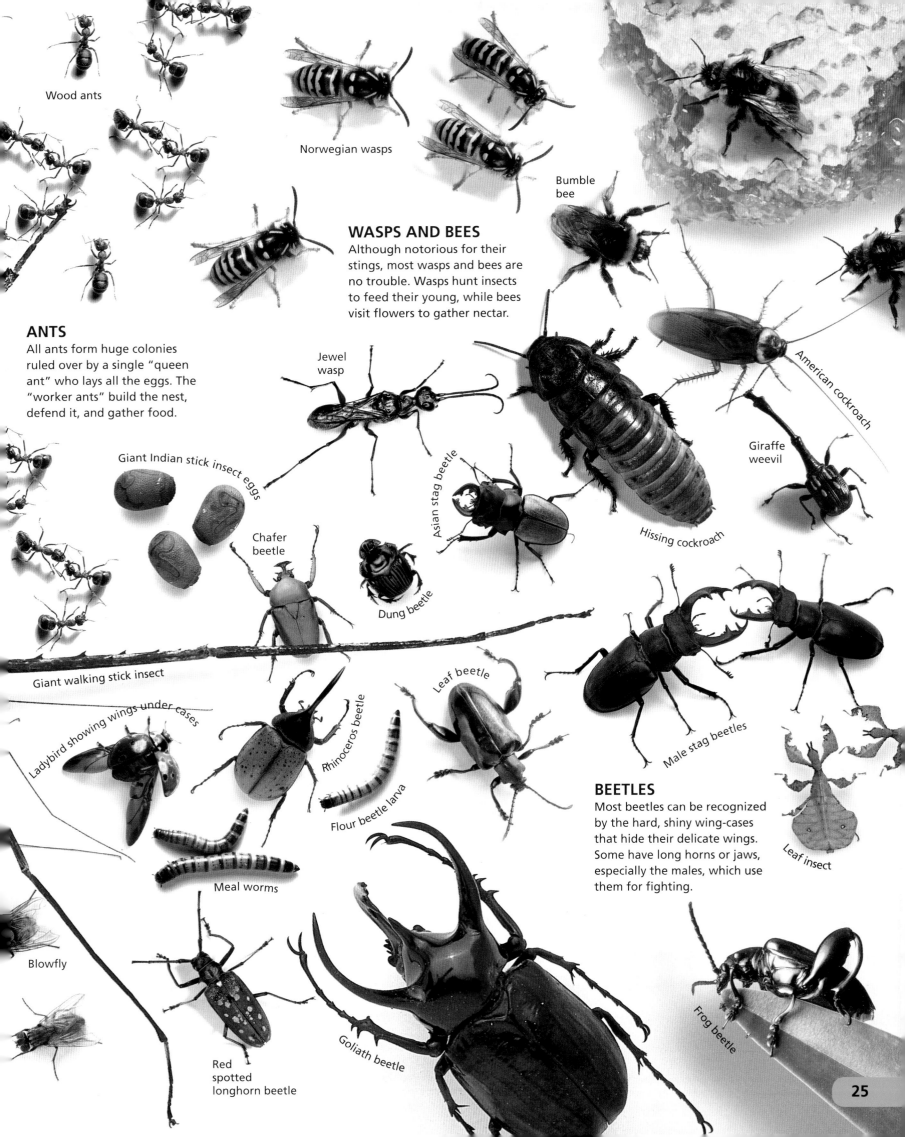

Wood ants

Norwegian wasps

Bumble bee

WASPS AND BEES
Although notorious for their stings, most wasps and bees are no trouble. Wasps hunt insects to feed their young, while bees visit flowers to gather nectar.

ANTS
All ants form huge colonies ruled over by a single "queen ant" who lays all the eggs. The "worker ants" build the nest, defend it, and gather food.

Jewel wasp

American cockroach

Giraffe weevil

Giant Indian stick insect eggs

Chafer beetle

Asian stag beetle

Dung beetle

Hissing cockroach

Giant walking stick insect

Ladybird showing wings under cases

Rhinoceros beetle

Leaf beetle

Male stag beetles

Leaf insect

BEETLES
Most beetles can be recognized by the hard, shiny wing-cases that hide their delicate wings. Some have long horns or jaws, especially the males, which use them for fighting.

Flour beetle larva

Meal worms

Blowfly

Red spotted longhorn beetle

Goliath beetle

Frog beetle

INSECT ANATOMY

Many insects start life as soft-skinned grubs, or larvae, but eventually they all turn into adults with hard, segmented bodies and six jointed legs. Their skin is toughened with a substance called chitin, which is rather like hard plastic, so it acts as an external skeleton. It is often shiny and brightly coloured, but it can look furry or scaly. Most adult insects like this wasp also have wings made from sheets of chitin, powered by muscles inside their bodies.

❶ ANTENNAE

An insect's long antennae help it feel its way, but they are mainly used to detect scent. They are covered with sensitive nerve endings that pick up chemical signals. The antennae of some moths can detect scents from more than a kilometre (0.6 miles) away.

❸ EYES

Like many other insects, an adult wasp has two large compound eyes. Each has hundreds of tiny lenses that see the world as a mosaic of coloured dots. A wasp also has three small simple eyes, which are called ocelli, on the top of its head.

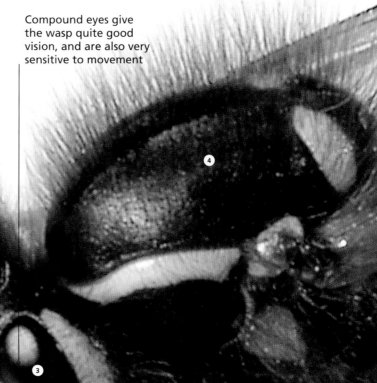

Each of the three simple eyes has just one lens that can sense light but cannot form an image

Compound eyes give the wasp quite good vision, and are also very sensitive to movement

Fine, touch-sensitive bristles on the insect's body detect vibrations and air movements

Long, jointed antennae are vital sense organs

The antenna of a female wasp has 12 segments, while the male antenna has 13

The sensory antennae of this wasp enable it to recognize food and other members of its colony

HEAD

THORAX

Mandibles, or mouth parts, are used to slice vegetation or prey

❷ HEAD

An insect's head contains its brain and carries most of its sense organs. It is also equipped with mouthparts that are specialized to deal with its diet. A mosquito has a sharp needle for sucking blood, while this wasp has stout jaws for chewing other insects.

❹ THORAX

The legs and wings of an insect are attached to the front section of its body, the thorax. This is packed with wing muscles, which power the wings rather like someone in a rowing boat using a pair of oars. It also contains the insect's crop, used to store food.

❻ WINGS
The wings of an insect like this wasp are thin, transparent plates of chitin. Butterfly and moth wings are similar, but covered with coloured scales. Most insects have two pairs of wings for flight, but flies have just one pair.

The thin, flexible membranes that form the wings are supported by stiff ribs, called veins

Delicate wings are strong enough to lift the weight of the wasp

Slender waist linking thorax and abdomen allows wasp to curl body

❼ STING
Most insects are harmless, but some may bite or sting. This wasp has a sting in its tail that can inject a painful venom. It uses it to defend itself and its nest, and to kill insect prey.

Dramatic black and yellow markings warn predators that the wasp is venomous

The wasp's sting is a modified egg-laying organ, or ovipositor

ABDOMEN

Each foot has sharp claws, and some insects, such as flies, also have sticky foot pads

❺ ABDOMEN
The flexible abdomen contains most of an insect's internal organs, including its digestive system. Tiny holes lead to a system of tubes that supply air to its organs and muscles. The vivid stripes of this wasp warn other animals that it can sting.

❽ LEGS
All adult insects have six legs. When they walk, they lift three legs while keeping the other three on the ground – like a tripod – so they have no problem with balance. Each leg is a series of stiff tubes, hinged together and powered by muscles inside the tubes.

FISH

Fish were the first animals with backbones to appear on Earth, more than 500 million years ago. They have since evolved into a wonderful variety of forms. From powerful sharks to delicate seahorses, fish now make up more than half of all vertebrate species. Most fish live in the salty oceans, like those shown below, but many – including the fish on the opposite page – live in freshwater lakes and rivers. A few, such as salmon, are able to live in both.

❸ FORCEPS FISH
A type of butterflyfish that lives on the coral reefs of the Indian and Pacific oceans, the forceps fish has a highly elongated snout with a very small mouth at the tip. The fish uses this to pick tiny animals from coral crevices, and from the spines of sea urchins.

❺ PUFFERFISH
Pufferfish defend themselves by inflating their bodies with water so they are hard for predators to swallow. Some species have sharp spines that add to the effect, and many of their internal organs contain lethal poisons.

❶ RAY
Closely related to sharks, with skeletons made of cartilage, rays are flattened fish that swim by using their pectoral (side) fins like wings. They live on the seabed, hunting smaller fish and shellfish.

❷ BOXFISH
The curious boxfish are named for their box-like defensive armour, formed from thick, fused scales. This prevents all body movement, so the fish swim by using their small fins like oars.

❹ SEAHORSE
These strange fish owe their name to their horse-like heads. They live in shallow seas, where they cling to marine plants with their tails. The male "incubates" the female's eggs in a pouch on his belly.

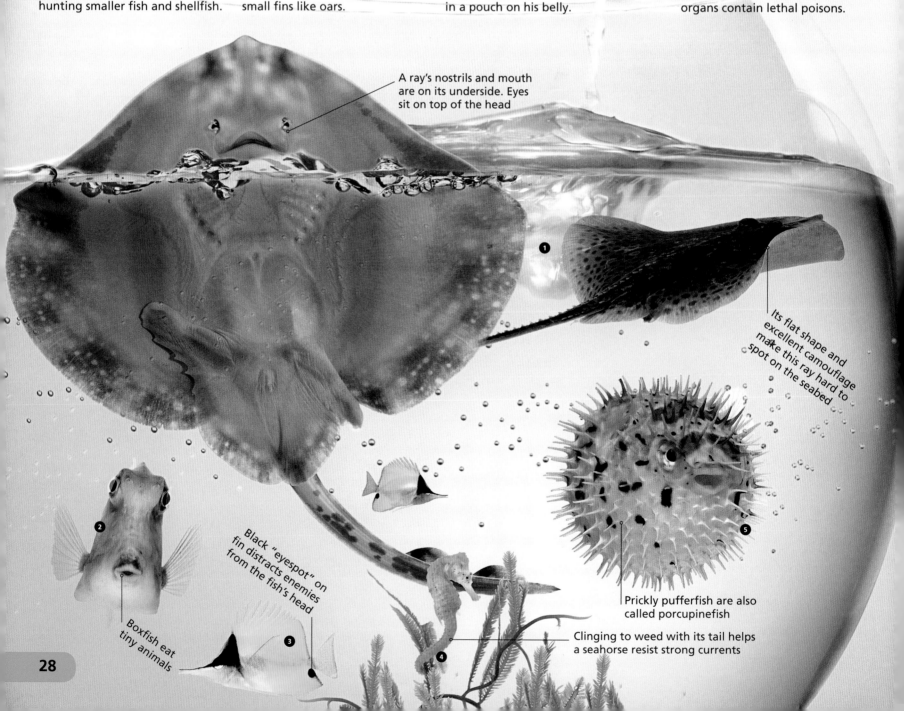

A ray's nostrils and mouth are on its underside. Eyes sit on top of the head

Its flat shape and excellent camouflage make this ray hard to spot on the seabed

Black "eyespot" on fin distracts enemies from the fish's head

Boxfish eat tiny animals

Prickly pufferfish are also called porcupinefish

Clinging to weed with its tail helps a seahorse resist strong currents

❻ SALMON

Big, powerful salmon spend most of their lives at sea, but swim upstream to the shallow rivers with gravelly bottoms where they breed. They have adaptations that allow them to move between fresh and salt water.

❼ CARP

Able to live in water that has very little oxygen, carp are well equipped for life in warm, still lakes and ponds. They feed by using their extendible jaws to root around on the bottom for small animals and aquatic plants.

❽ VELVET CICHLID

Better known by its common name, Oscar, this species lives in slow-flowing South American rivers and digs in the riverbeds for small animals such as worms and freshwater shrimps. There are currently 1,721 species of cichlids known.

❾ STICKLEBACK

This fish gets its name from the sharp spines on its back. It lives in ponds, rivers, and lakes, and some shallow seas. In spring, the male makes a nest of plant fibre, and does a dance to attract females to lay their eggs.

❿ PIKE

This powerful hunter lives in lakes and slow-flowing rivers throughout Europe, northern Asia, and North America. Pike hunt fish and waterbirds by lying in wait among aquatic plants and darting out to seize victims.

⓫ PIRANHA

Notorious for its sharp teeth, this South American predator mainly preys on other fishes, but may strip the meat from larger carcasses of dead animals.

Three sharp spines help to defend the stickleback from bigger predatory fish

Tough, shiny scales help protect the carp's skin from injury and attack by parasites

The colours of this cichlid are variable, changing as the fish grows older

Long, pointed jaws have big, sharp teeth to give the pike a good grip on slippery prey

Piranhas stick together in shoals for safety

FEEDING

All animals get the nutrients they need by eating plants, animals, or other organisms such as bacteria or fungi. Some of these foods are easy to find but hard to digest, like leaves and grass. Others, such as animal prey, can be difficult to find or catch, but are easy to digest and rich in food value. Animals have developed a variety of adaptations for gathering and digesting their food. Some of these are much more specialized than others, and govern the animal's whole way of life.

Gills in long slots at the back of the shark's mouth trap floating food

Sucker surrounds the mouth and sharp teeth

❶ BASKING SHARK

The enormous basking shark has tiny teeth. It feeds by swimming through swarms of tiny drifting organisms with its mouth gaping open, and trapping them in its sieve-like gills. Many whales filter feed in a similar way, as do some birds, such as flamingos.

❷ GIRAFFE

A giraffe's extra-long neck allows it to eat leaves that other animals cannot reach. Like many leaf-eaters and grass-eaters, giraffes have bacteria in their digestive system, which break down the tough plant fibre to release vital nutrients.

❸ LEECH

A parasitic leech clings to a living animal, slices into its skin, and sucks its blood. Some leeches may take up to five times their own weight in blood, but only need to feed once or twice a year.

Parrots often use their feet to grip nuts while they crack into them with their bills

❹ PARROT

Birds need concentrated food that does not weigh them down, so most birds feed on insects, meat, fruit, or seeds. Many parrots eat nuts, cracking the strong shells with their powerful hooked bills, but some have brush-tipped tongues to lap up sugary flower nectar.

❺ LION

Catching large live animals can be difficult and dangerous. A lion relies on its strength and long, sharp canine teeth to kill its prey. It slices the meat into mouthfuls with scissor-like cheek teeth, but swallows it without chewing because meat is easy to digest.

❻ GIANT ANTEATER

Many animals eat insects, but few are so specialized for the job as the giant anteater. It has a long, sticky, worm-like tongue, which it flicks in and out of its long snout up to 150 times a minute to scoop its tiny prey from their nest.

❼ TAPEWORM

This parasite lives in the intestines of another animal – including some people. Since it is surrounded by pre-digested food it does not need a digestive system of its own, or even a mouth, and it just soaks up nutrients through its thin skin.

A housefly can contaminate food by walking on it

❽ EGYPTIAN VULTURE

Many creatures are scavengers that feed on carrion (dead flesh) and other scraps. They include the Egyptian vulture, which clears up remains that would otherwise simply rot. Without scavengers, the world would be a lot less healthy.

❾ HOUSEFLY

Many insects, including all flies, can eat only liquid food. Some suck blood, or gather nectar or plant juices. The housefly can also liquefy some solid foods such as sugar by drenching them with saliva and soaking up the result with its mop-like mouthparts.

❿ BROWN BEAR

Although basically a meat-eater, the brown bear devours many foods ranging from meat and fish to fruit and honey. This means that it is not specialized for any particular way of feeding, and can change its food with the seasons. Humans have the same "omnivorous" (eat-all) diet.

CRUSTACEANS

This varied group of invertebrates includes around 67,000 known species. Crustaceans take their name from the hard, jointed shells, or exoskeletons, that support and protect their bodies. Most crustaceans live in the sea, or in freshwater lakes and rivers, but woodlice and some species of crab live permanently on land. Crustaceans have at least four pairs of jointed legs, gills for breathing underwater, and sensory antennae that they use to feel and smell the things around them.

❶ CRAB

Armed with a pair of powerful claws, and protected by a thick shell, a crab is built for both attack and defence. Crabs can creep forwards very slowly, but they prefer to scuttle sideways because they can move much quicker that way.

❷ BARNACLE

Young barnacles drift in the water like shrimps, but when they become adults they cement themselves to rocks, piers, and even other crustaceans. They feed by extending feathery legs from their shells to catch tiny floating creatures.

❸ LANGOUSTINE

Found in the Atlantic Ocean and North Sea, langoustines are also known as Norway lobsters. They come out at night from their sea-floor burrows to feed on worms and smaller crustaceans. Their muscular tails are eaten as "scampi".

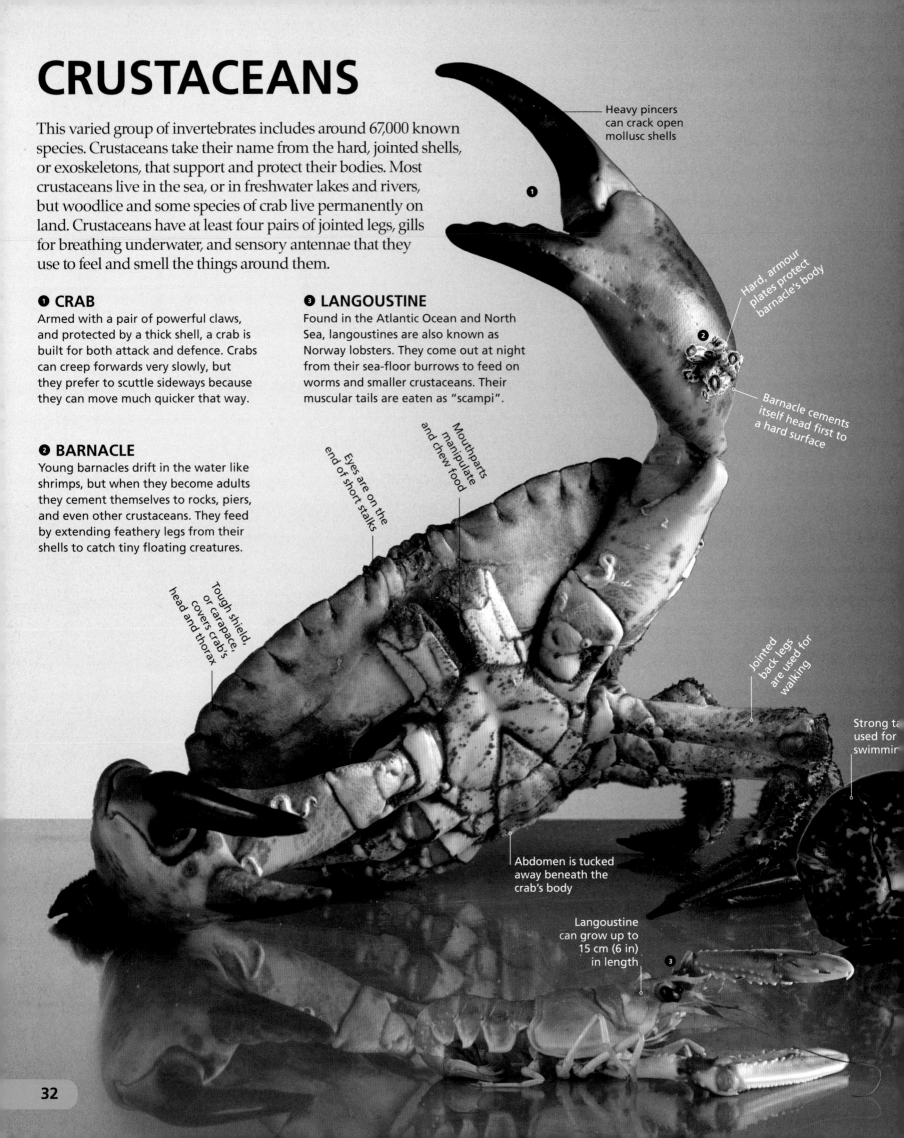

Heavy pincers can crack open mollusc shells

Hard, armour plates protect barnacle's body

Barnacle cements itself head first to a hard surface

Eyes are on the end of short stalks

Mouthparts manipulate and chew food

Tough shield, or carapace, covers crab's head and thorax

Jointed back legs are used for walking

Strong ta used for swimmir

Abdomen is tucked away beneath the crab's body

Langoustine can grow up to 15 cm (6 in) in length

❹ LOBSTER

Weighed down by their heavy shells, lobsters usually walk on the sea floor, but they can swim backwards to escape danger by flipping their tails. Like all crustaceans, they have to moult (shed) their hard exoskeletons several times as they grow.

❺ WOODLOUSE

Woodlice are among the only crustaceans that are completely at home on land, but they must live in damp places. They have seven pairs of legs and some species can roll themselves into a ball if they feel threatened. Despite their name, they do not damage wood.

❻ PRAWN

Many prawns and shrimps swim or drift in the water, but others spend most of their lives searching for food on the sea bed. Some specialize in picking bloodsucking parasites off the fish that live on coral reefs, which queue to be cleaned up.

Toothed crusher claw pulverizes shells

Claws used for gripping and shredding food

Claw curved at end to aid grip

Lobster can regrow claws and legs if they break off

Tough curved plates protect soft parts of the woodlouse's body

Female woodlouse keeps fertilized eggs in a pouch on the underside of her body until they hatch

Long antennae used for sensing surroundings

Prawns use their two large eyes to detect movements in water

Shorter antennae detect odours in the water to help the lobster find food or a mate

Hard carapace covers head and thorax

Fan-shaped tail used for swimming

Transparent exoskeleton

Four pairs of walking legs

33

AMPHIBIANS

Although amphibians look a little like scaly reptiles, they do not have waterproof skin, so cannot live in hot, dry places where they might dry out. Most hide away by day, and emerge only at night. They must also lay their eggs in ponds and other wet places, and many spend their early lives as aquatic tadpoles.

❶ COMMON FROG
All amphibians eat live animals, which they hunt by sight. The frog on the left is leaping through the air to catch a ladybird, which it will snap up and swallow alive.

Common frogs are able to lighten or darken their skins to blend in with their surroundings

European common frog

❼ Mandarin salamander

Colourful lumps and bumps ooze toxic fluids for protection from predators

❹ MIDWIFE TOAD
Most frogs and toads lay their eggs in water, but the male midwife toad wraps the strings of eggs around his legs and looks after them until they are ready to hatch.

Midwife toad

Tinker vine frog

Caecilian

❿

Frog's thin, moist skin can absorb oxygen directly from the air

Australian tree frog

Big eyes help poison dart frogs see well in the dark forest

Poison dart frog

Madagascan tomato frogs

❻ POISON DART FROG
Tiny tree frogs of American tropical forests are protected by powerful poisons on their skin. Some are so deadly that local people use them to make poison darts.

❼ MANDARIN SALAMANDER
Salamanders and newts are rather like frogs with long tails. Some, like the Asian mandarin salamander, have vividly coloured skin that warns enemies that they are poisonous to eat.

❽ AUSTRALIAN TREE FROG
Tree frogs have suckers on the tips of their toes so that they can cling to wet foliage. Most tree frogs only visit pools of water to breed.

❾ TOMATO FROG
Many frogs and toads, like these tomato frogs, defend themselves by inflating their bodies with air so that they are harder to eat.

❷ TADPOLES
Nearly all frogs start life in the water as tadpoles with long tails and no legs. Gradually they grow legs, hop out of the water, and their tails shrivel away.

Froglet with tail

Froglet losing tail

❷

Frogs cannot chew, but they have huge mouths so that they can swallow their prey whole

European common frog

❸

African bullfrog

❸ AFRICAN BULLFROG
A mouse makes a tasty snack for a bullfrog, which will eat almost anything that moves.

Red-eyed tree frog

❺ FOAM-NESTING FROG
Some tree frogs keep their eggs moist by laying them in a nest of wet foam high in the trees.

Foam nesting frog

❺

Covered by tough skin, a caecilian's eyes cannot form clear images but they can detect light

Fire salamander

Asian painted frog

❶

❶❷

Chilean four-eyed frog

Bright yellow spots warn off enemies, even at night

❿ CAECILIAN
Worm-like caecilians burrow in tropical forests by pushing their bony heads through the soil. They have no legs and are almost blind.

⓫ FOUR-EYED FROG
A four-eyed frog has a pair of big eyespots on its back. If attacked, it turns its back and inflates its body so that it looks like a fierce animal.

⓬ FIRE SALAMANDER
Bright patterns warn predators that this salamander can spray a blinding poison up to 4 m (13 ft) through the air.

LIFE CYCLES

All animals pass through different stages of life as they grow into fully developed adults. The first stage is the start of a new life, and for most animals the final phase is when they breed to start the cycle over again. For some animals, such as most mammals, these stages are very similar. For others, such as many insects, every stage is quite different, and involves a complete transformation, or metamorphosis, from the previous stage.

3 After about two weeks, the puppy can see, but its digestive system can still only cope with milk.

4 The older puppy can eat solid food provided by its mother, and begins to learn vital skills through play.

2 For the first two weeks, the puppy cannot see the world around it.

5 Though not able to breed just yet, this young dog can find its own food.

DOG ▶

A dog's life cycle is typical of many mammals, because it starts life as a smaller version of its parents. As it grows bigger, its internal organs develop so it can eat an adult diet, and eventually produce its own young.

1 Blind and helpless, a newborn puppy cannot eat solid food, so it lives on its mother's milk.

6 The fully grown dog now looks to find a mate to produce puppies of its own.

3 Wriggling out of the jelly into the water, the tadpole uses a sticky fluid to cling to an aquatic plant.

4 As the tadpole grows older, it develops back legs, then front legs, and its body starts to look like that of a frog.

Young tadpole has three pairs of feathery gills, which absorb vital oxygen from the water

◀ FROG

Most amphibians, such as frogs, have complex life cycles. A typical frog lays eggs in water, and these hatch out as fish-like tadpoles. The tadpoles develop lungs and legs, and hop out of the water as tiny froglets, eventually becoming fully grown adult frogs.

2 An embryo develops inside the egg and starts to move, using energy supplied by the yolk of the egg.

Tail shrinks to a stump as the froglet learns to use its legs to swim and hop

5 Lungs develop, the tail shrinks, and the new froglet hops out of the water to live on land, where it hunts small animals.

1 An adult frog lays frogspawn containing hundreds of eggs protected by jelly, which swells up in the water.

6 Living mainly on land, the adult frog will return to the water in spring to find a mate and either lay or fertilize eggs.

1 By eating ravenously the baby caterpillar grows fast. It sheds its tough skin several times as it gets bigger.

2

3 The full-grown caterpillar has a fat, soft body full of stored energy, which will fuel its metamorphosis into an adult.

Caterpillar sheds its colourful skin to emerge as a legless, pale-looking pupa

4 The caterpillar stops feeding and becomes a pupa – the stage of its life cycle when it is transformed into a winged adult.

1 An adult female lays her eggs on a carefully chosen plant, and a tiny larva, or caterpillar, hatches from each egg.

Pupa splits open and crumpled butterfly crawls out

6 After emerging, the butterfly feeds on sugary nectar to get the energy it needs to fly, but its main job is to mate and lay eggs.

5 The pupa stays motionless for several weeks while the caterpillar inside is taken apart and rebuilt as a butterfly.

◀ BUTTERFLY

Butterflies, like many insects, have two quite different phases in their life cycle. They hatch as soft-bodied larvae that spend all their time eating and growing. Then they turn into winged adults, which do not grow and may not eat at all.

Baby turtle has well-developed flippers when it hatches

4 The young turtle feeds in the same way as its parents, but takes smaller food items.

3 After struggling out of the egg, the baby turtle heads for the ocean.

TURTLE ▶

Most reptiles, such as turtles, lizards, and snakes, lay eggs. When these hatch, the babies that crawl out are like miniature replicas of the adults. They live in exactly the same way, and often eat the same foods.

5 Growing steadily as it feeds, the turtle does not go through any type of metamorphosis like an amphibian or insect.

2 An embryo develops inside the buried egg, which is abandoned by the mother, but kept warm by the sun.

Sea turtle's long flippers enable it to swim long distances to reach suitable breeding beaches

1 The egg has a soft, leathery skin that stops it from drying out.

6 The mature adult is able to breed, and females come ashore to bury their eggs on sandy tropical beaches.

ATTACK AND DEFENCE

Many animals are hunters that prey on other animals. Catching and killing fast-moving prey is hard, so over time hunters have evolved features and tactics to make the job easier. This has made survival harder for the animals that they hunt, so many have evolved defences that make them difficult, or even dangerous, to catch.

◄ NIGHT HUNTER

Insect-eating bats target their prey using pulses of high-pitched sound. The sounds bounce off the victim, creating a sound image that enables a bat to hunt flying insects in total darkness.

DRIFTING TRAP ►

The long tentacles of the box jellyfish are armed with thousands of tiny stinging cells. The animal simply drifts with the currents and devours any creature that is unlucky enough to come into contact with its tentacles.

▲ AMBUSH

The praying mantis lurks motionless on a plant, waiting for another insect to come within range. Then it shoots out its spiny front limbs to catch its victim, and eats it alive.

◄ VENOM AND CLAWS

Many animals have venomous bites or stings that they can use to kill their prey and to defend themselves. A scorpion normally uses its claws to hunt, and the sting on the end of its tail for defence.

◄ TEAMWORK

Lions are equipped with dagger-like teeth and long claws, but their main weapon is teamwork. They encircle their prey so there is no escape.

CONSTRICTOR ▼

A python coils around its prey, squeezing a little tighter every time the victim breathes out, until eventually it cannot breathe at all. A snake's lower jaws are loosely linked to its skull, so it can swallow its prey whole.

POISON GLANDS ▶

If attacked by a hunter, a toad defends itself by inflating its body with air and oozing poisons from its skin. This makes it hard to eat and also makes it taste unpleasant, so its enemy is likely to leave it alone.

CAMOUFLAGE ▼

The best defence is to avoid being noticed at all. Camouflage makes animals hard to see against their background. This mountain hare turns white in winter to match the snow.

SPINES ▼

Some animals have defensive armour. Others, like this porcupine, bristle with long, sharp spines. This can make them almost impossible to attack, and even dangerous to animals that try.

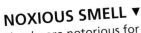

PLAYING DEAD ▼

Many hunters will only eat prey that they have killed themselves. Some animals like this opossum take advantage of this by "playing dead" if threatened. An opossum may keep up the pretence for six hours!

NOXIOUS SMELL ▼

Skunks are notorious for the vile-smelling fluid that they spray from scent glands under their tails if attacked. They can aim accurately for up to 2 m (6.5 ft), often targeting the faces of their enemies.

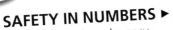

SAFETY IN NUMBERS ▶

Solitary animals make easy targets, so many try to confuse their enemies by living in dense shoals, flocks, or herds. By staying close together, this shoal looks like one big fish rather than lots of little ones.

▼ VENOMOUS LIZARDS

The Gila monster is one of just two species of lizard with a venomous bite. Both live in deserts in Mexico and the United States.

Gila monster

◀ CHAMELEONS

Famous for their ability to change their skin colour, chameleons are slow-moving lizards that hunt by shooting out their very long, sticky tongues to catch insects.

Jackson's chameleon

GECKOS ▶

Special hairs beneath the broad toes of many geckos act like suckers, enabling these active, agile lizards to climb up any surface, including glass, and even run across ceilings.

Madagascan day gecko

IGUANAS ▼

Iguanas are typical lizards – reptiles that usually have four legs, a long tail, and scaly skin. Most lizards eat small animals, but the green iguana is mainly vegetarian.

Green iguana

European glass lizard

Corn snake

▲ PYTHONS

Most of the biggest snakes are pythons – powerful, non-venomous reptiles that kill their prey by coiling around it and squeezing until it cannot breathe.

Ball python

This is the snake's tail, which it uses as a fake head to deceive its enemies if threatened

Much smaller than many pythons, this west African species is a burrowing snake that eats rodents

Calabar ground python

COLUBRIDS ▶

Three-fifths of all snake species belong to the colubrid family. Most are harmless, but some, including the mangrove snake, have venomous fangs at the backs of their mouths.

Mangrove snake

Grass snake

Snakes shed their outer skin at least once a year, emerging with glossy scales and brighter colours

REPTILES

Scaly, creeping, cold-blooded reptiles can seem sinister – especially venomous snakes and snapping crocodiles. Yet many reptiles are glossy, vividly coloured creatures, with fascinating habits. Most are hunters, but since they do not use any energy keeping warm they do not need to eat much. Crocodiles often go for months without eating, and some big snakes can survive for a year on just one big meal.

▼ TUATARA
Found only in New Zealand, the two species of tuatara are the only survivors of a group of reptiles that mostly died out 100 million years ago, during the age of dinosaurs.

Tuatara

▲ CROCODILES
The most powerful of all reptiles, alligators and crocodiles are ferocious predators that ambush, kill, and eat animals as big as zebras.

American alligator

LEGLESS LIZARDS ▶
Some lizards have no legs, so they look and behave like snakes. The European glass lizard has tiny vestiges of legs, showing that its ancestors were like normal lizards.

The red-tailed racer's slender body is adapted for climbing

Rattlesnake

Sensing danger, this grass snake is "playing dead" in the hope that it will be ignored

Red-tailed racer

▼ COBRAS
Among the deadliest of venomous snakes, cobras are armed with a nerve poison that paralyzes their victims so they cannot breathe and they die from suffocation.

VIPERS ▶
Equipped with long poison fangs that hinge forwards when they open their mouths, vipers such as rattlesnakes are extremely dangerous. Luckily, rattlesnakes rattle their tails as a warning.

The grass snake is an excellent swimmer. It ripples its body to move through water in search of frogs to eat

This small turtle has a streamlined shell to help it glide through water

Hermann's tortoise

▲ TURTLES
Instantly recognizable by their shells, turtles and tortoises have existed since the days of the first dinosaurs. Tortoises are famously slow, but turtles can swim quite fast over long distances.

Slider terrapin

Albino monocled cobra

MOLLUSCS

Snails, clams, mussels, and even octopuses are all molluscs – soft-bodied animals that often have strong chalky shells. Some live on land, but most molluscs live underwater or on tidal seashores. A snail or octopus can move about and use its sense organs to find food, but many aquatic molluscs, such as mussels, spend their adult lives in one place. They do not have obvious sense organs or even heads, and their bodies are encased within two shells that can be closed for protection.

Eye at tip of snail's tentacle

Squid's head end has eight arms and two tentacles

Squid can swim faster than any other invertebrat

Whelks grow their shells from chalky deposits extracted from sea water

1 Snail Able to creep about on its muscular foot, a snail can squeeze its soft, boneless body into its coiled shell when it feels threatened.

2 Giant snail A native of tropical Africa, the giant snail can be 30 cm (12 in) long. A gland at the front of the foot produces the slime that enables a snail to slide along.

3 Giant clam The biggest of all molluscs, the giant clam can grow to more than 1 m (3.25 ft) across. It finds a spot in a coral reef and, once there, stays in place for life.

4 Squid Fast-swimming squid can catch fish with their tentacles, change colour, and shoot through water backwards using jet propulsion.

5 Slug Basically snails without shells, slugs can live in places with few of the chalky minerals that other molluscs need to build up their shells as they grow larger.

6 Limpet Able to clamp its strong shell to rocks, the limpet is well equipped to survive the rough and tumble of rocky seashores.

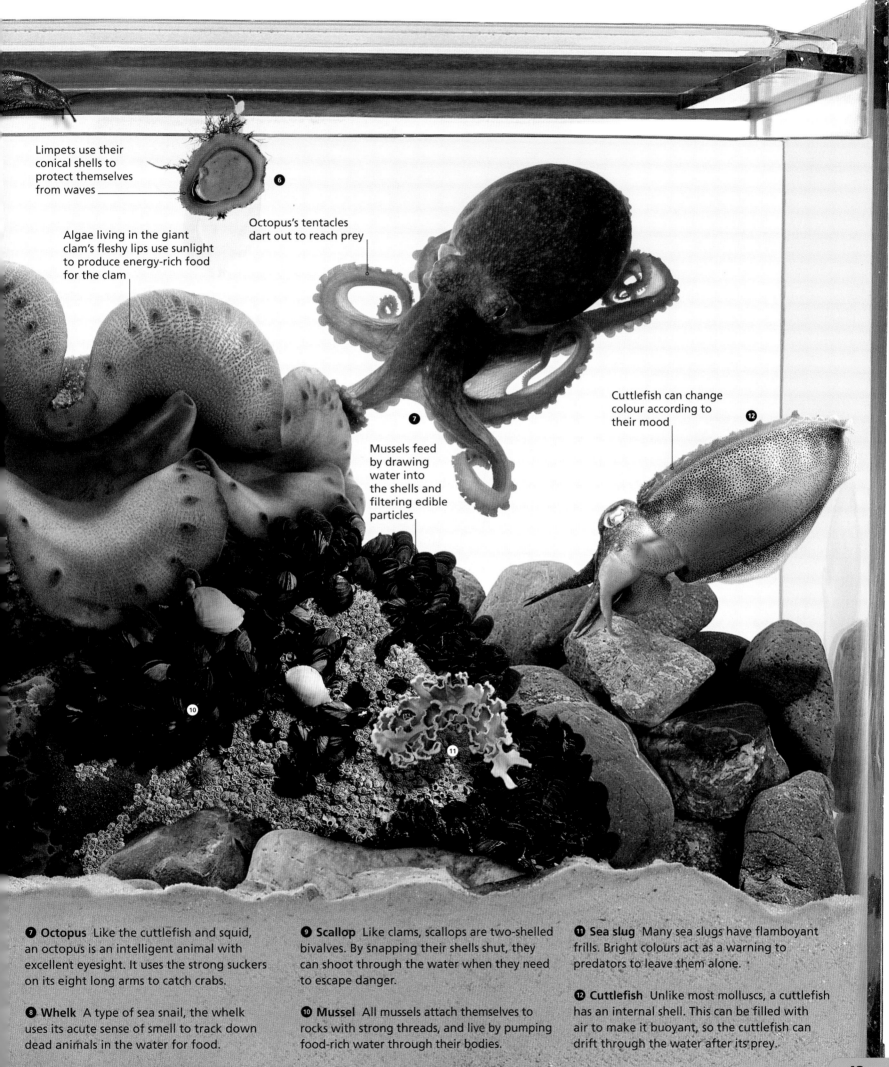

Limpets use their conical shells to protect themselves from waves

Algae living in the giant clam's fleshy lips use sunlight to produce energy-rich food for the clam

Octopus's tentacles dart out to reach prey

Cuttlefish can change colour according to their mood

Mussels feed by drawing water into the shells and filtering edible particles

❼ **Octopus** Like the cuttlefish and squid, an octopus is an intelligent animal with excellent eyesight. It uses the strong suckers on its eight long arms to catch crabs.

❽ **Whelk** A type of sea snail, the whelk uses its acute sense of smell to track down dead animals in the water for food.

❾ **Scallop** Like clams, scallops are two-shelled bivalves. By snapping their shells shut, they can shoot through the water when they need to escape danger.

❿ **Mussel** All mussels attach themselves to rocks with strong threads, and live by pumping food-rich water through their bodies.

⓫ **Sea slug** Many sea slugs have flamboyant frills. Bright colours act as a warning to predators to leave them alone.

⓬ **Cuttlefish** Unlike most molluscs, a cuttlefish has an internal shell. This can be filled with air to make it buoyant, so the cuttlefish can drift through the water after its prey.

SHELLS

The bodies of some creatures are protected by strong shells. They include all kinds of animals ranging from crabs to armadillos, but the most well known are marine molluscs such as winkles, cockles, and clams. These animals absorb chalky minerals from their food or sea water and turn them into beautiful, sculptured, often vividly coloured "seashells". These are sometimes lined with iridescent, gleaming mother-of-pearl.

❶ NAUTILUS
A relative of the octopuses, with big eyes and up to 90 tentacles, the nautilus can retreat into its pearl-lined shell for safety. The inner chambers of the shell act as flotation tanks.

❷ VENUS COMB MUREX
Named for its comb-like appearance, this sea snail of the tropical Indian and Pacific oceans has up to 100 sharp spines that protect it from predators such as shellfish-eating rays.

❸ PAPAL MITRE
This is one of about 800 known species of mitre shells, which all have a pointed form similar to the ceremonial hats worn by bishops and popes. The papal mitre may be up to 15 cm (6 in) long.

❹ CUBAN LAND SNAIL
Some land snails are brightly coloured too, but their colours are usually similar to those of the places where they live. Snails that have noticeably different colours are soon eaten by birds.

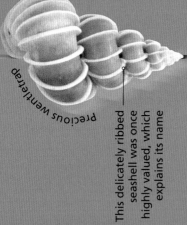

precious wentletrap

This delicately ribbed seashell was once highly valued, which explains its name

Papal mitre

Common distorsio

Distorsio shells are found mainly in tropical waters

Spines are as sharp as needles, and break off easily if they pierce another animal

Venus comb murex

A nautilus can adjust its buoyancy by pumping fluid in and out of gas-filled shell chambers

Cross-section of a nautilus shell

Cowrie shells are glossy where partly covered by the animal's body

5 OYSTER SHELL

Most oysters have shells that are rough outside, but pearly inside. Grains of sand that find their way into oyster shells are smothered with layers of shell material, turning them into pearls.

6 SEA URCHIN TEST

Sea urchins belong to a group of animals called echinoderms. Their "shells" are covered with skin, so they are not true shells like those of molluscs. Known as tests, they are peppered with holes and small knobs where the spines were once attached.

7 SPINY SAND COCKLE

Cockles and clams are molluscs with two shells, called bivalves. A cockle burrows into sand, often on coasts that dry out at low tide, but it can close its shells tightly to keep itself moist until the tide turns.

8 MANUS ISLAND SNAIL

All snails have a shell that is coiled in a spiral, so the coil gets smaller towards the tip. As the snail grows, it adds shell material at the shell mouth, which gets broader all the time.

Tropical sea urchin

8 Manus Island snail

Position of sea urchin's mouth

Tropical sea urchin

6

7

Spiny sand cockle

Cuban land snails

4

The spiny oyster shell is found off California, and is often used in Native American jewellery

Cowries

Spiny oyster shell

5

Black-lipped oyster

Rock pigeon

BIRDS

The only animals with feathers, birds are found in all parts of the world. Many have superb flying skills, with strong chest muscles to power their flapping wings. There is a dazzling diversity of species, from soaring albatrosses and flamboyant peacocks to flightless rheas and tiny hummingbirds.

▲ ZEBRA FINCH

Like many birds, the zebra finch of Australia lives in large flocks that fly and feed together for safety. Its stout bill is adapted for splitting the tough skins of grass seeds to get at their nourishing kernels.

▲ TAWNY EAGLE

Eagles are powerful hunters. They target their prey while soaring high overhead, then swoop down to seize it in their talons. The tawny eagle is also notorious for stealing the victims of other birds of prey.

Immensely strong, sharp-clawed talons are the eagle's main weapons

Penguins' wings are adapted for swimming, not flight

▲ RHEA

As tall as 1.5 m (5 ft), these large flightless birds roam the grassland of South America. They eat plants, nuts, seeds, and fruits, as well as insects and small animals, such as lizards.

Birds spend hours preening their feathers to keep them in good condition

King penguins

Farmyard ducks

Peacock

The male peacock raises its hugely elongated tail feathers to display them

Parrots can crack nuts with their strong bills

Green parakeet

▲ ALBATROSS

The long, narrow wings of an albatross enable it to soar for hours on oceanic winds without moving a muscle. It feeds on marine animals, which it snatches from the ocean with its bill.

Swift

Some swifts can keep flying for many months without landing

SNOWY OWL ▶

Most owls hunt by night, but the snowy owl is active during the almost continuous daylight of the Arctic summer. It uses its acute hearing to locate small animals such as lemmings feeding beneath the snow.

Soft feathers allow owls to fly in complete silence

Hummingbird

Hummingbirds hover on whirring wings to sip flower nectar

◀ WOODPECKER

Woodpeckers use their powerful bills to carve out nesting holes in trees, and many also hack into soft timber to find insects. This green woodpecker catches ants with its extra-long tongue.

Budgerigars

TOUCAN ▶

The enormous bill of the toco toucan is much lighter than it looks, because it is a hollow shell of lightweight horny material supported by criss-crossing internal struts. The toucan uses it for display as well as feeding.

Blue tit

The flamingo's pink colouring comes from pigments in the bird's food

Peacock display

FLAMINGO ▲

Vast wading flocks of flamingos gather tiny animals and algae from warm lakes. Holding their extraordinary bills upside down in the shallows, they use their tongues to pump water through their sieve-like bill fringes to trap food.

Pelicans use the pouch beneath their bills like fishing nets to catch their food

PEAFOWL ▶

The female peafowl, or peahen, looks drab and colourless compared to the dazzling male peacock, with his amazing courtship display of fanned tail feathers.

Webbed feet stop wading birds sinking into mud

Dalmatian pelican

EGGS

All female birds lay eggs. The young grow inside the eggs, which are kept warm by their parents. To hatch, they must chip their way through the eggshell. Some chicks, such as ducklings, can run and walk around soon after hatching, but other baby birds hatch at a much earlier stage in their development when they are naked, blind, and almost helpless.

King penguin

Ostrich chick breaking out of shell

Waxwing

Peregrine falcon

Great auk

Skylark

Golden eagle

Cormorant

Carrion crow

Guillemot

Quail

Sparrowhawk

Elegant crested tinamou

Cuckoo

Curlew

Redshank

Blackcap

Coal tit

❶ GREAT AUK

This beautiful egg is one of the last relics of a big flightless seabird that once lived in the north Atlantic and hunted fish like a penguin. Each pair laid just one egg, and the last known pair was killed in 1844.

❷ GOLDEN EAGLE

A female golden eagle lays two eggs a few days apart. She keeps the first egg warm so it hatches earlier. This chick may be the only one to survive if food is hard to find.

❸ KING PENGUIN

King penguins breed in huge colonies on windswept rocky islands around Antarctica. Each female lays one egg and both parents take turns keeping it warm by supporting it on their feet beneath their warm bellies.

❹ OSTRICH

The ostrich is the world's largest bird, and it lays the biggest eggs. Each one can weigh anything up to 1.9 kg (4 lbs) – the same weight as 27 chicken's eggs.

❺ QUAIL

The quail lays a huge clutch of up to 18 eggs in a nest on the ground. Like many eggs, they have camouflage markings that make them harder to see. The female starts keeping them warm only after she lays the last one. This means they start developing at the same time, so they all hatch at once. The chicks are active as soon as they hatch, just like ostriches.

❻ SPARROWHAWK

In the 1960s, sparrowhawks suffered from poisoning by pesticides used in farming. The poisons thinned their eggshells, so they broke when the birds tried to keep them warm. Most of these pesticides are now banned.

Herring gull

Song thrush

Cetti's warbler

Chough

Great northern diver

Nightjar

Meadow pipit

Emu

❽ Kiwi

❾ Common sandpiper

Chicken

❶❶

Red grouse

Yellowhammer

Ruby-throated hummingbird

❿

Tawny owl

Dunnock

Brushland tinamou

Newly hatched ostrich chick

❼ CUCKOO

Cuckoos lay single eggs in the nests of other birds, and their colour varies to match the host bird's eggs. When the cuckoo hatches, it heaves the other eggs out so it can eat all the food its foster parents collect.

❽ KIWI

A kiwi is 20 times smaller than an emu, yet its eggs are almost the same size. This means that the egg is huge compared to the kiwi that lays it, at up to a quarter of her weight. That's like a human mother giving birth to a three-year-old child.

❾ COMMON SANDPIPER

Sandpipers are shorebirds that lay their eggs in shallow scrapes on the ground near the water. Their pointed shape allows them to be pushed together in a tight clutch to take up less space. The eggs are camouflaged by speckled patterns, and can be hard to see – but if you do find any birds' eggs, remember it is illegal to collect or disturb them.

❿ HUMMINGBIRD

Hummingbirds lay the smallest of all birds' eggs. The bee hummingbird's egg is the size of a pea, because the bird itself is no bigger than a large moth. This ruby-throated hummingbird's egg is bigger, but still tiny compared to the ostrich egg.

❶❶ CHICKEN

The egg that everybody recognizes is laid by the domestic chicken. We eat 1.1 trillion of these eggs every year.

MOVEMENT

The feature that makes animals so different from other living things is their ability to move. Some do not move much – a sea anemone, for example, is sedentary (remains in one place) and catches anything that touches its tentacles. Most animals, however, travel to look for food, find breeding partners, or escape from their enemies. They slither, crawl, walk, hop, run, swim, and fly, sometimes at incredible speed. Some have evolved other amazing ways of getting about, like the insects and spiders that walk on water, and the extraordinary sidewinding rattlesnakes.

❶ GIBBON
Although gibbons can walk well, they usually move through the forest by using their long, powerful arms to swing from the trees. They hurl themselves from branch to branch with astonishing speed, agility, and elegance.

❷ SNAKE
A typical snake slips along by curving its flexible body around plants and stones, and pushing the curves towards its tail. Sidewinders like this desert viper have a more baffling method, looping sideways over the sand like rolling springs.

❸ OCTOPUS
An octopus normally hauls itself over the seabed using its long, elastic arms. But it can shoot away from danger by jet propulsion, drawing water into its body and blasting it out at high pressure. Cuttlefish and squid do the same.

❹ PENGUIN
All penguins are superb swimmers, using their wings to "fly" through the water, but they walk clumsily. On snowy slopes they often prefer to toboggan on their well-padded bellies, pushing themselves along with their stoutly clawed feet.

❺ FISH
Most fish have flexible bodies that allow them to move through the water using their fins for stability and to control their direction. Some fish, such as tunas, propel themselves at high speed using just their tails.

❻ STARFISH
A starfish can curl its arms, but it actually creeps over the seabed using hundreds of tiny "tube feet" on its underside. Each tube foot is pumped full of water, and is extended and moved by changes in water pressure.

❼ SNAIL
The muscles in a snail's foot contract and expand to create a rippling movement that pushes the snail forward. Glands in the foot produce a slimy mucus to make the track slippery. The slime also protects the snail from debris.

❽ POND SKATER

The water molecules at the surface of a pool cling together to form an elastic film, strong enough to support tiny animals like this pond skater. Its special brush-tipped feet just dimple the surface, so it can skate around without sinking.

❾ CHEETAH

The fastest of all land animals, a cheetah can run at an astonishing 95 km/h (60 mph). It achieves this by flexing its back to extend its stride as it bounds forward on its long legs, but it can only keep up this pace for about 40 seconds.

❿ BARN OWL

Birds are the masters of the air. Most, like this barn owl, use their powerful feathered wings to drive themselves forward. Others can travel long distances by soaring on rising air currents like gliders, without beating their wings at all.

⓫ KANGAROO

A leaping kangaroo uses the elastic tendons in the backs of its legs like the springs of a pogo stick. Every time it lands on its long feet the tendons stretch like rubber bands, then spring back again to catapult the kangaroo forward.

LIVING TOGETHER

Animals and plants often rely on other living things for survival. Food, shelter, and pollination are some of the clearest examples of this. However, some animals and plants have much closer relationships. They can be partners, providing things like food or protection for each other. Some tag along with others without providing anything in return. Many do worse, latching on to other organisms as parasites, which can harm or even kill their often helpless hosts.

The microscopic algae that live in partnership with this coral provide its vivid colour **①**

②

This long, tubular flower is a perfect fit for the long bill of the sword-billed hummingbird

③

Ants protect the aphids from their enemies in exchange for sweet, syrupy honeydew

This cuckoo chick has outgrown both the host bird and its nest, but it still cries out for food

④

A strangler vine uses a tree for support, but eventually kills it by competing for food and light

⑤

An impala welcomes the attention of a red-billed oxpecker searching for tasty parasites

A remora clings to a shark's skin using a special sucker on the back of its head

❶ CORAL
Corals trap prey in their stinging tentacles. They pass some of the nutrients from their victims to tiny algae living in their tissues. These use the sun's energy to make sugar, and they pass some of this food back to the corals.

❷ HUMMINGBIRD
Hummingbirds gather flower nectar, and in the process they carry pollen from flower to flower. Some plants have evolved flowers that match the bills of particular hummingbird species, to encourage the birds to visit them and deliver their pollen efficiently.

❸ ANTS AND APHIDS
Aphids are tiny insects that feed on sugary plant sap. They must eat a lot of it to get enough protein, and they excrete the excess sugar as drops of sweet honeydew. Ants love to drink this, so they "farm" the aphids, protecting them from predators, ensuring a constant supply.

❹ CUCKOO
Cuckoos are "brood parasites" – they lay their eggs in the nests of other birds. Each young cuckoo hatches quickly and destroys any other eggs in the nest, so it can eat all the food brought by its foster parents. It soon outgrows its hosts, who often do not seem to notice its massive size.

❺ STRANGLER VINE
Some slender rainforest plants, such as figs, grow by encircling a tree and slowly killing it – a process that can take up to 150 years. They steal the tree's nutrients, and eventually the tree dies and decays, leaving the fig plant standing alone.

❻ OXPECKER
Hoofed grazing animals, such as impalas, are often plagued by tiny bloodsuckers, such as ticks, that they cannot remove by scratching. In Africa, stout-billed birds called oxpeckers do the job for them by picking the parasites off their skin and eating them.

❼ REMORA
Predatory sharks have very sharp teeth that cut their prey to shreds. The scraps are eagerly devoured by fish called remoras, which travel with the sharks by clinging to their skin. They do their hosts no harm, and the sharks seem to ignore them.

MAMMALS

Mammals are warm-blooded creatures that feed their babies on milk until the young are able to eat solid food. Most are furry or hairy, unlike all other vertebrates (animals with backbones). Many eat plants, while others prey on other animals. Some, like humans, eat both plants and meat.

ECHIDNA ▶
The echidna and the equally strange platypus are the only mammals that lay eggs. A baby echidna lives on milk produced by its mother for up to six months. The mother eats food such as earthworms, which she digs from the ground with her long snout.

▲ MOUSE
Nearly half of all mammal species are rodents – a group that includes mice, rats, beavers, porcupines, and squirrels. The house mouse is the only mammal, apart from humans, to live on every continent.

◀ ELEPHANT
Elephants use their sensitive trunks to gather coarse vegetation, which they grind to pulp with their massive teeth. They are the biggest land animals and are very intelligent.

KANGAROO ▶
Marsupials such as kangaroos give birth to tiny young that are only half-formed. The newborn crawls into a pouch on its mother's belly to drink milk and grow into a fully developed baby kangaroo, or joey.

▲ BAT
Bats are mammals that can fly. Some eat fruit, but most species like this long-eared bat catch insects. They are nocturnal (active at night) and locate prey in the dark by emitting high-pitched clicks and listening for echoes from their target.

◀ TIGER
Powerful hunters like the tiger eat other mammals and birds. They have long, dagger-like canine teeth for killing their prey, and scissor-like cheek teeth for slicing through hide and meat.

▲ MOLE
Moles are specially adapted to their underground environment. They have strong claws for digging and very sensitive whiskers, which compensate for their poor eyesight.

▲ KILLER WHALE
Whales and dolphins, like this killer whale, live in the ocean, swimming with up-and-down movements of their powerful tails. They come to the surface to breathe air.

◀ GORILLA
Our closest relatives among the mammals are apes like the gorilla – a plant-eater that lives in the rainforests of tropical Africa.

HIPPOPOTAMUS ▶
The hippopotamus spends most of its time wallowing in rivers and lakes. The massively built plant-eater has the largest mouth of any land mammal.

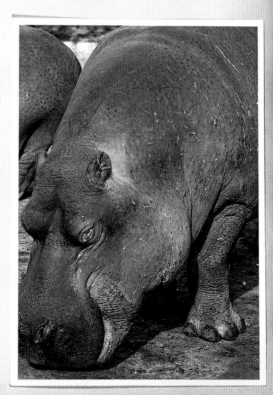

SLEEP

Animals sleep to save energy, rest their muscles, and allow their brains to process the information that they pick up while awake. Some hunting animals sleep a lot, because they devote only a few hours each day to looking for food. Animals that are hunted spend much more of their time awake and alert.

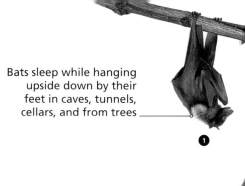

Bats sleep while hanging upside down by their feet in caves, tunnels, cellars, and from trees

1 **Bats** sleep for about 20 hours a day, often in large colonies.

2 **Two-toed sloths** are awake for only four hours a day. Like bats, they can cling to branches with their claws while fast asleep.

3 **Gorillas** like to have about 12 hours of sleep a day.

4 **Horses** need just three hours of sleep a day.

5 **Elephants** stand up for two of the four hours a day they sleep. They have to lie down for the dreaming stage, when their muscles are too relaxed for them to stay on their feet. Large plant-eating animals tend to get less sleep than smaller animals, because they have to spend so much time looking for food and eating.

6 **Seals** often sleep on rocks and beaches, but they can also sleep floating upright at sea, or even underwater, surfacing to breathe without waking up.

7 **Wolves** may sleep for up to 14 hours a day, especially if they have had a big meal after a successful hunt.

8 **Pigs** need eight hours of sleep a day, just like adult humans.

9 **Bears** also clock up about eight hours of sleep a day.

10 **Tigers** sleep for up to 16 hours, since they can catch all the food they need within a very short time.

11 **Sheep** are descended from wild animals that needed to stay awake to escape predators, so they sleep for less than four hours a day.

12 **Kinkajous** are raccoon-like animals that forage for food at night, and sleep all day for about 12 hours.

13 **Armadillos** sleep for 18 hours a day, curled up in their burrows.

Seals sleep for around six hours every day

14 **Human babies** need 15 hours of sleep a day. We sleep less as we get older, so adults sleep for an average of eight hours, and elderly people for less than six hours.

15 **Echidnas** are egg-laying mammals that sleep for about 14 hours a day. Scientists believe they do not have phases of dream sleep like other mammals.

16 **Red foxes** sleep for about 10 hours, mostly during the day. Like many hunters they are more active at night when they track their prey using their sensitive noses and ears.

22 Chinchillas sleep in burrows for about 13 hours a day, high in the mountains of South America.

23 Rabbits sleep for about eight hours, mainly during the day. They prefer to feed at night when they are not so vulnerable to predators.

24 Chimpanzees normally sleep for 10 hours a day, but baby chimps sleep for longer.

25 Baby gorillas need more sleep than their parents, and may sleep or doze for more than 15 hours.

26 Hedgehogs usually sleep for 10 hours during the day. In winter, they hibernate (spend the cold months in a sleep-like, inactive state).

Horses can sleep standing up without toppling over because their legs lock in place

Dogs have similar sleep patterns to humans

17 Koalas eat tough eucalyptus leaves that are hard to digest and provide little energy, so they spend about 15 hours a day sleeping and another five hours dozing.

18 Dogs sleep for 10 hours a day.

19 Red pandas, which are like bamboo-eating raccoons, sleep for about 11 hours a day.

20 Cats often sleep for 15 hours a day. Wild cats are most active during the night.

21 Lions sleep for at least 13 hours. While they sleep, other animals feed near them without risking attack.

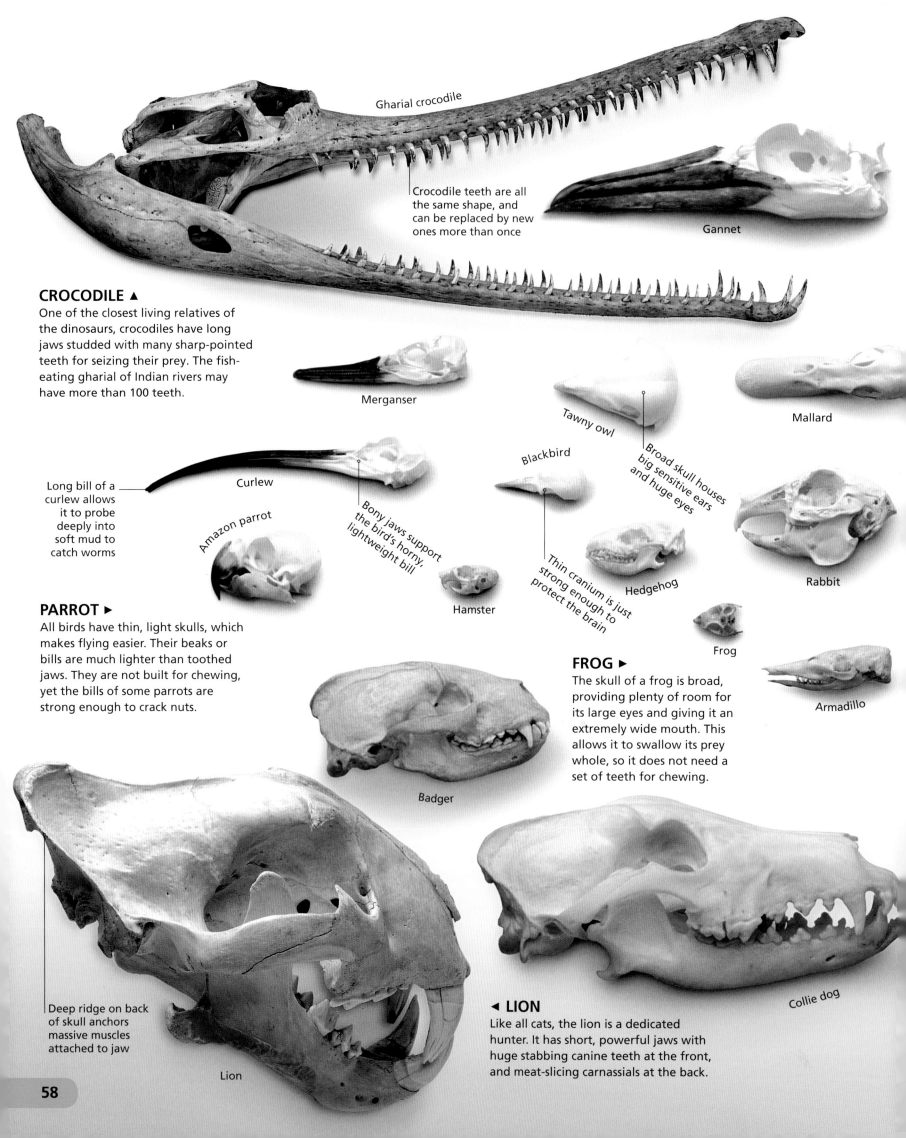

Gharial crocodile

Crocodile teeth are all the same shape, and can be replaced by new ones more than once

Gannet

CROCODILE ▲

One of the closest living relatives of the dinosaurs, crocodiles have long jaws studded with many sharp-pointed teeth for seizing their prey. The fish-eating gharial of Indian rivers may have more than 100 teeth.

Merganser

Tawny owl

Mallard

Broad skull houses big sensitive ears and huge eyes

Blackbird

Long bill of a curlew allows it to probe deeply into soft mud to catch worms

Curlew

Bony jaws support the bird's horny, lightweight bill

Amazon parrot

Thin cranium is just strong enough to protect the brain

Hedgehog

Rabbit

Hamster

PARROT ▶

All birds have thin, light skulls, which makes flying easier. Their beaks or bills are much lighter than toothed jaws. They are not built for chewing, yet the bills of some parrots are strong enough to crack nuts.

Frog

FROG ▶

The skull of a frog is broad, providing plenty of room for its large eyes and giving it an extremely wide mouth. This allows it to swallow its prey whole, so it does not need a set of teeth for chewing.

Armadillo

Badger

Deep ridge on back of skull anchors massive muscles attached to jaw

Lion

◀ LION

Like all cats, the lion is a dedicated hunter. It has short, powerful jaws with huge stabbing canine teeth at the front, and meat-slicing carnassials at the back.

Collie dog

Anteater

Anteaters have long jaws and extremely long tongues, but no teeth at all

The big eyes of this powerful, fast-swimming predator are contained in large sockets

▼ ANTELOPE

Some animals, such as antelope and cattle, have massive horns on their heads for defence and fighting rivals. Male deer grow antlers, which they use to impress females and fight each other, but these antlers fall off at the end of the mating season. Each male grows a new pair every year.

BARRACUDA ▶

Fish have quite strong skulls, but the various parts are not fused together like those of mammals. The jaws of many fish are separate from the brain case, but attached by bones that allow them to be thrust forward to seize prey.

Barracuda

Massive jaws are armed with needle-sharp teeth for a secure grip on prey

Furry skin (velvet) nourishes the antler as it grows, and is shed in the summer

▼ BABOON

Close relatives of humans, baboons have similar skulls, but longer jaws and bigger back teeth. This is because they eat large quantities of grass, which requires a lot of chewing. They also have long, sharp canines, which they use to kill animals for food, and to fight among themselves.

Strong bony cores are sheathed with tough outer layers of ridged horn

Antelope

Deer

Baboon

Eye sockets at front of skull allow the baboon to see things in three dimensions

Nasal cavity contains thin scroll-like bones, which support the membranes that detect scent

Long snout allows antelope to nibble grass while keeping watch for danger

SKULLS

Most vertebrates (animals with backbones) have strong bony skulls. They are made up of cranial bones that protect their brains, jaw bones that support their teeth or beaks, and face bones that contain their eye sockets and nasal cavities. The whole structure can be quite heavy, and is supported by strong neck muscles.

Sharp, blade-like incisor teeth on lower jaw are ideal for cropping grass and gathering leaves

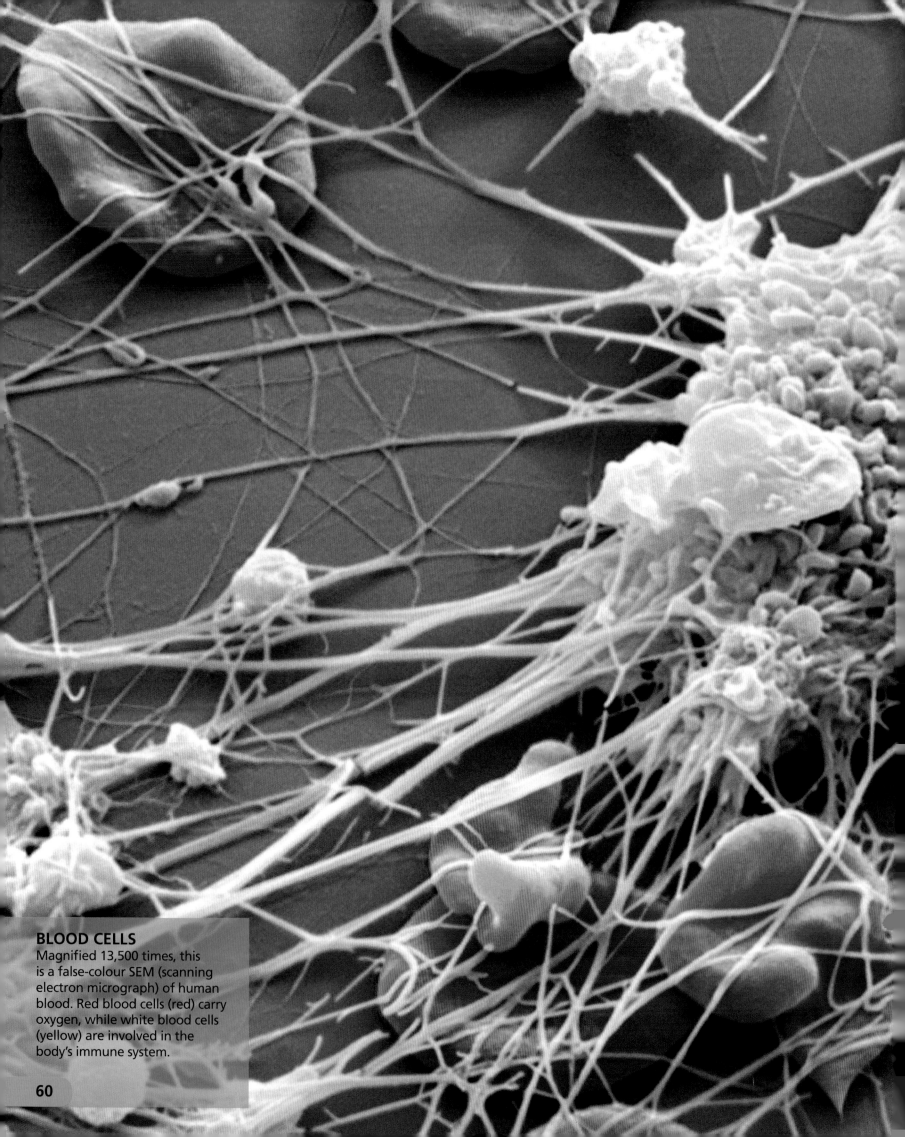

BLOOD CELLS
Magnified 13,500 times, this is a false-colour SEM (scanning electron micrograph) of human blood. Red blood cells (red) carry oxygen, while white blood cells (yellow) are involved in the body's immune system.

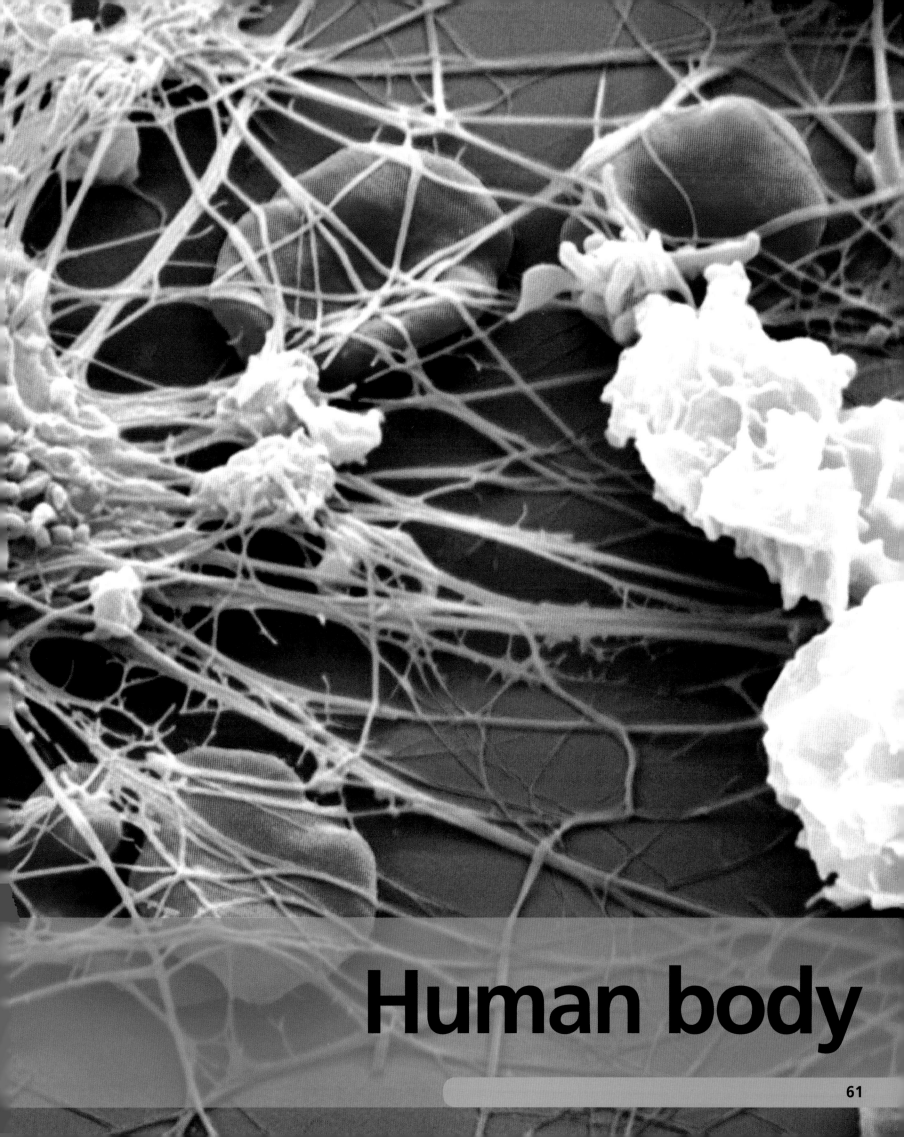

Human body

CELLS

The body is constructed from trillions of tiny living units, known as cells. There are more than 200 different types of cells – and each has its own shape, size, and specific job to do. Typically, cells of the same type work together in units called tissues. Each individual cell is surrounded by a thin membrane that regulates the movement of nutrients and other substances in and out of the cell. Cells multiply by continually dividing into two identical "offspring". This division allows the body to grow and to replace cells that are damaged or worn out.

A macrophage "reaches out" to capture bacteria (blue), which it will then digest

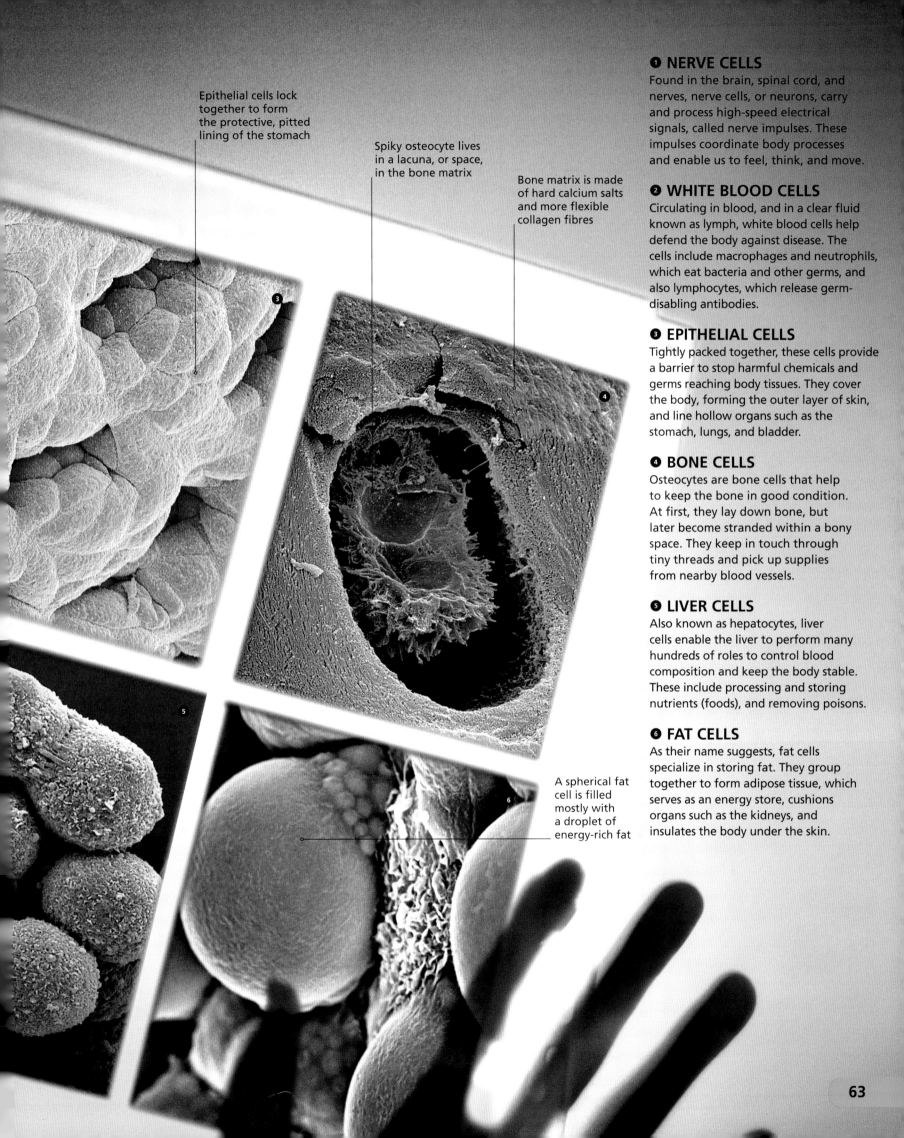

Epithelial cells lock together to form the protective, pitted lining of the stomach

Spiky osteocyte lives in a lacuna, or space, in the bone matrix

Bone matrix is made of hard calcium salts and more flexible collagen fibres

A spherical fat cell is filled mostly with a droplet of energy-rich fat

❶ NERVE CELLS

Found in the brain, spinal cord, and nerves, nerve cells, or neurons, carry and process high-speed electrical signals, called nerve impulses. These impulses coordinate body processes and enable us to feel, think, and move.

❷ WHITE BLOOD CELLS

Circulating in blood, and in a clear fluid known as lymph, white blood cells help defend the body against disease. The cells include macrophages and neutrophils, which eat bacteria and other germs, and also lymphocytes, which release germ-disabling antibodies.

❸ EPITHELIAL CELLS

Tightly packed together, these cells provide a barrier to stop harmful chemicals and germs reaching body tissues. They cover the body, forming the outer layer of skin, and line hollow organs such as the stomach, lungs, and bladder.

❹ BONE CELLS

Osteocytes are bone cells that help to keep the bone in good condition. At first, they lay down bone, but later become stranded within a bony space. They keep in touch through tiny threads and pick up supplies from nearby blood vessels.

❺ LIVER CELLS

Also known as hepatocytes, liver cells enable the liver to perform many hundreds of roles to control blood composition and keep the body stable. These include processing and storing nutrients (foods), and removing poisons.

❻ FAT CELLS

As their name suggests, fat cells specialize in storing fat. They group together to form adipose tissue, which serves as an energy store, cushions organs such as the kidneys, and insulates the body under the skin.

SKELETON

Constructed from 206 bones, the human skeleton is a strong, flexible framework that supports and shapes the body and produces movement when pulled by muscles. The skeleton also protects soft, internal organs, such as the brain and lungs. Bones, which make up 20 per cent of the body's mass, are connected to each other at joints and are held together by strong straps of tissue called ligaments.

❶ SKULL

The bones in the skull protect the brain, provide a framework for the face, and anchor the muscles that produce facial expressions. The skull consists of 22 bones, 21 of which are locked together by immovable joints called sutures. Only the lower jaw (mandible) can move.

Mandible moves to open the mouth for eating, breathing, and speaking

❷ CHEST

The bones of the chest (thorax) consist of the sternum (breastbone), the ribs, and part of the backbone. Together, they form a protective "cage" that protects the lungs and the heart.

Shoulder joint is the most flexible joint in the body

Humerus

❸ FOREARM

The forearm is made up of two parallel bones – the ulna and the radius. The ulna curves round the humerus to form the elbow's point, while the radius forms a joint with the carpals (wrist bones).

Radius is the outer bone of the forearm

Ulna is the inner bone of the forearm

❹ ELBOW

The bones of the upper arm and forearm meet at the elbow. This joint acts like a door hinge allowing the arm to bend or straighten. The forearm bones can rotate at the elbow, enabling the palm of the hand to face upwards or downwards.

Hip joint is where the ball-shaped head of the femur fits into the cup-shaped socket in the hip bone

Sacrum anchors the backbone to the pelvic girdle

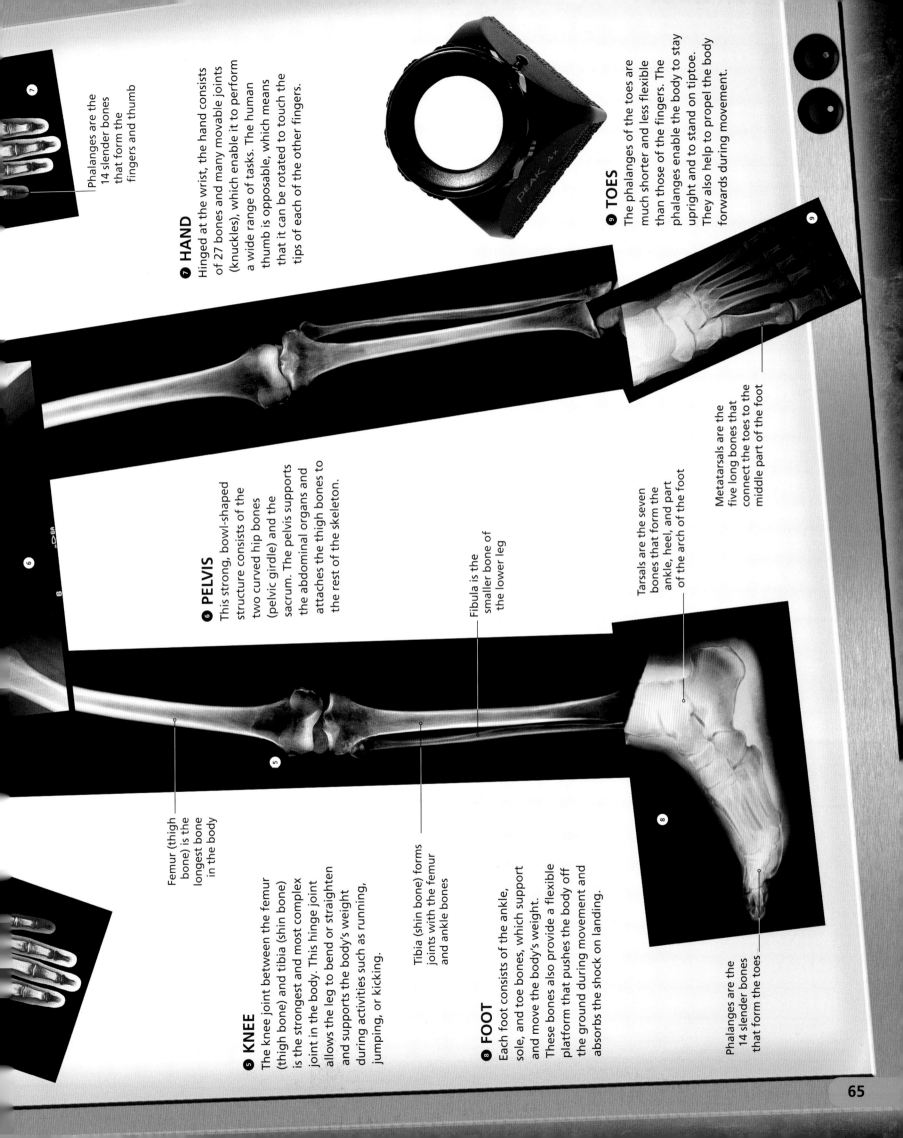

Phalanges are the 14 slender bones that form the fingers and thumb

❼ HAND

Hinged at the wrist, the hand consists of 27 bones and many movable joints (knuckles), which enable it to perform a wide range of tasks. The human thumb is opposable, which means that it can be rotated to touch the tips of each of the other fingers.

❾ TOES

The phalanges of the toes are much shorter and less flexible than those of the fingers. The phalanges enable the body to stay upright and to stand on tiptoe. They also help to propel the body forwards during movement.

Metatarsals are the five long bones that connect the toes to the middle part of the foot

❻ PELVIS

This strong, bowl-shaped structure consists of the two curved hip bones (pelvic girdle) and the sacrum. The pelvis supports the abdominal organs and attaches the thigh bones to the rest of the skeleton.

Fibula is the smaller bone of the lower leg

Tarsals are the seven bones that form the ankle, heel, and part of the arch of the foot

Femur (thigh bone) is the longest bone in the body

❺ KNEE

The knee joint between the femur (thigh bone) and tibia (shin bone) is the strongest and most complex joint in the body. This hinge joint allows the leg to bend or straighten and supports the body's weight during activities such as running, jumping, or kicking.

Tibia (shin bone) forms joints with the femur and ankle bones

❽ FOOT

Each foot consists of the ankle, sole, and toe bones, which support and move the body's weight. These bones also provide a flexible platform that pushes the body off the ground during movement and absorbs the shock on landing.

Phalanges are the 14 slender bones that form the toes

65

MUSCLES

Every body movement, whether it's a leap in the air, a wink of the eye, a rumbling stomach, or a rapid heartbeat, is produced by muscles. Skeletal muscles are attached to bones of the skeleton, which they pull to move us around. Smooth muscle moves food along the intestine. Cardiac muscle keeps the heart pumping. All muscles are made of cells called fibres that contract (get shorter) to produce a pulling force.

❶ SKELETAL MUSCLE

Long, cylindrical muscle fibres run in parallel and can reach up to 30 cm (1 ft) in length. They are bundled together to form muscles that are attached to bones by strong cords called tendons. Skeletal muscles move the body when instructed by the nervous system.

❷ SMOOTH MUSCLE

Tightly packed into layered sheets, smooth muscle fibres are found in the walls of hollow organs, such as the small intestine, along which they push food, and the bladder, from which they expel urine. Smooth muscle contracts slowly and cannot be controlled voluntarily.

❸ CARDIAC MUSCLE

Found solely in the wall of the heart, cardiac muscle fibres form a branching network that contracts automatically, without stopping or tiring, to pump blood around the body. Stimulation by the nervous system increases or decreases heart rate according to the body's demands.

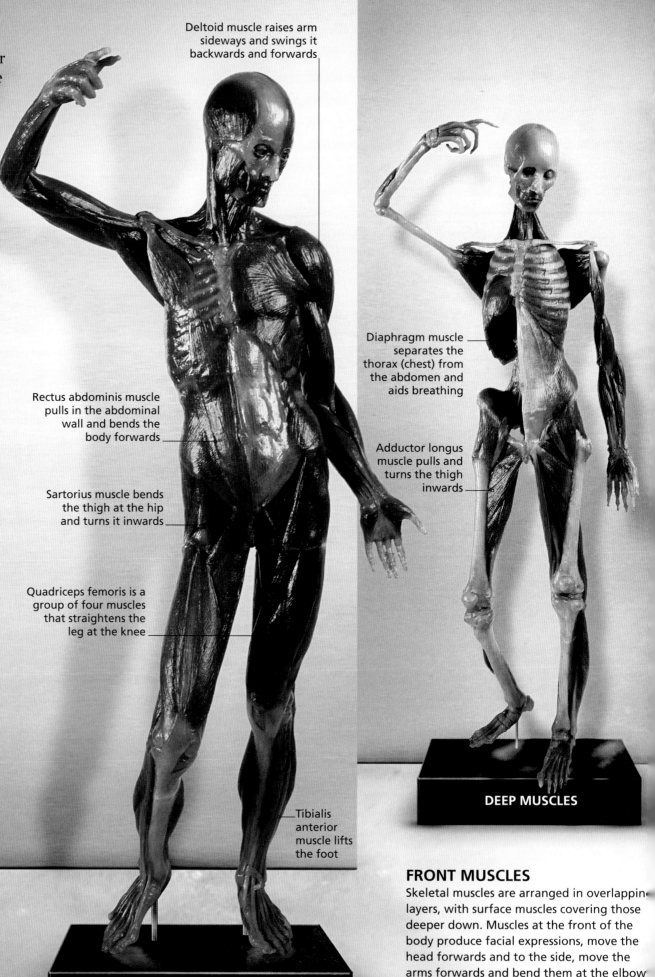

Deltoid muscle raises arm sideways and swings it backwards and forwards

Rectus abdominis muscle pulls in the abdominal wall and bends the body forwards

Sartorius muscle bends the thigh at the hip and turns it inwards

Quadriceps femoris is a group of four muscles that straightens the leg at the knee

Tibialis anterior muscle lifts the foot

SURFACE MUSCLES

Diaphragm muscle separates the thorax (chest) from the abdomen and aids breathing

Adductor longus muscle pulls and turns the thigh inwards

DEEP MUSCLES

FRONT MUSCLES

Skeletal muscles are arranged in overlapping layers, with surface muscles covering those deeper down. Muscles at the front of the body produce facial expressions, move the head forwards and to the side, move the arms forwards and bend them at the elbow, bend the body forwards and to the side, bend the legs at the hip, straighten the knees, and lift the feet upwards.

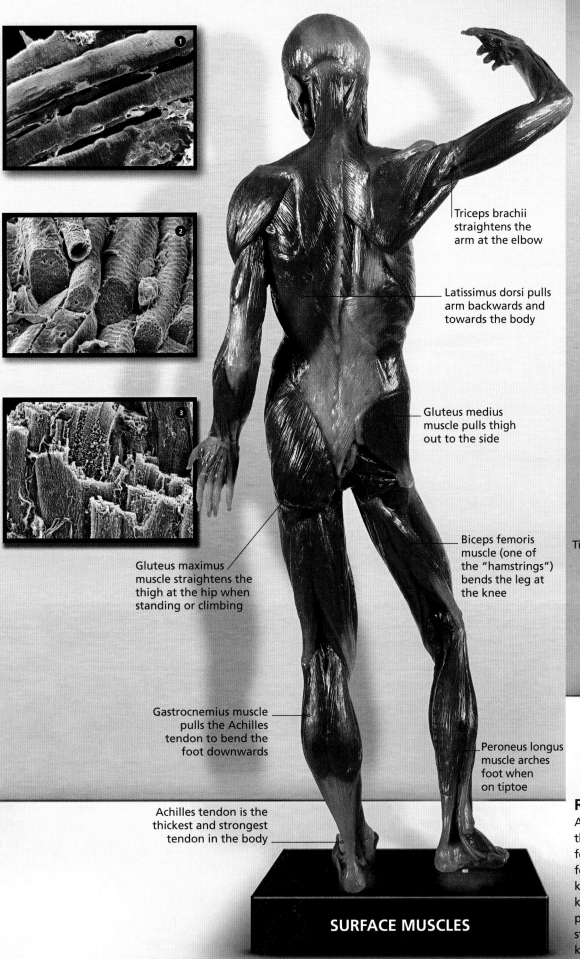

Triceps brachii straightens the arm at the elbow

Latissimus dorsi pulls arm backwards and towards the body

Gluteus medius muscle pulls thigh out to the side

Biceps femoris muscle (one of the "hamstrings") bends the leg at the knee

Gluteus maximus muscle straightens the thigh at the hip when standing or climbing

Gastrocnemius muscle pulls the Achilles tendon to bend the foot downwards

Peroneus longus muscle arches foot when on tiptoe

Achilles tendon is the thickest and strongest tendon in the body

SURFACE MUSCLES

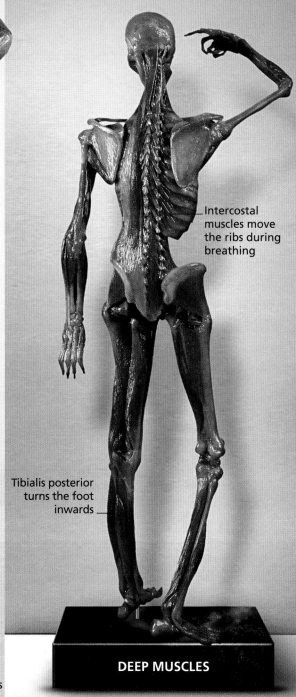

Intercostal muscles move the ribs during breathing

Tibialis posterior turns the foot inwards

DEEP MUSCLES

REAR MUSCLES

All muscles are given Latin names that describe their size, location, shape, action, or other feature. Working downwards from head to feet, skeletal muscles at the rear of the body keep the head upright, steady the shoulders, keep the back upright to maintain posture, pull the arms backwards and straighten them, straighten the thighs at the hip, bend the knees, and point the toes downwards.

BODY SYSTEMS

The body's trillions of cells are highly organized. Cells of the same type are grouped together in tissues. Two or more types of tissue are used to build organs that perform specific roles. Linked organs form different systems that each carry out an essential job, such as digestion. There are 12 body systems that cooperate and interact with each other to form the human body. The organs of six body systems are shown here. The other six systems are the integumental (skin); skeletal (bones); muscular; endocrine (hormones); immune (defence); and reproductive systems.

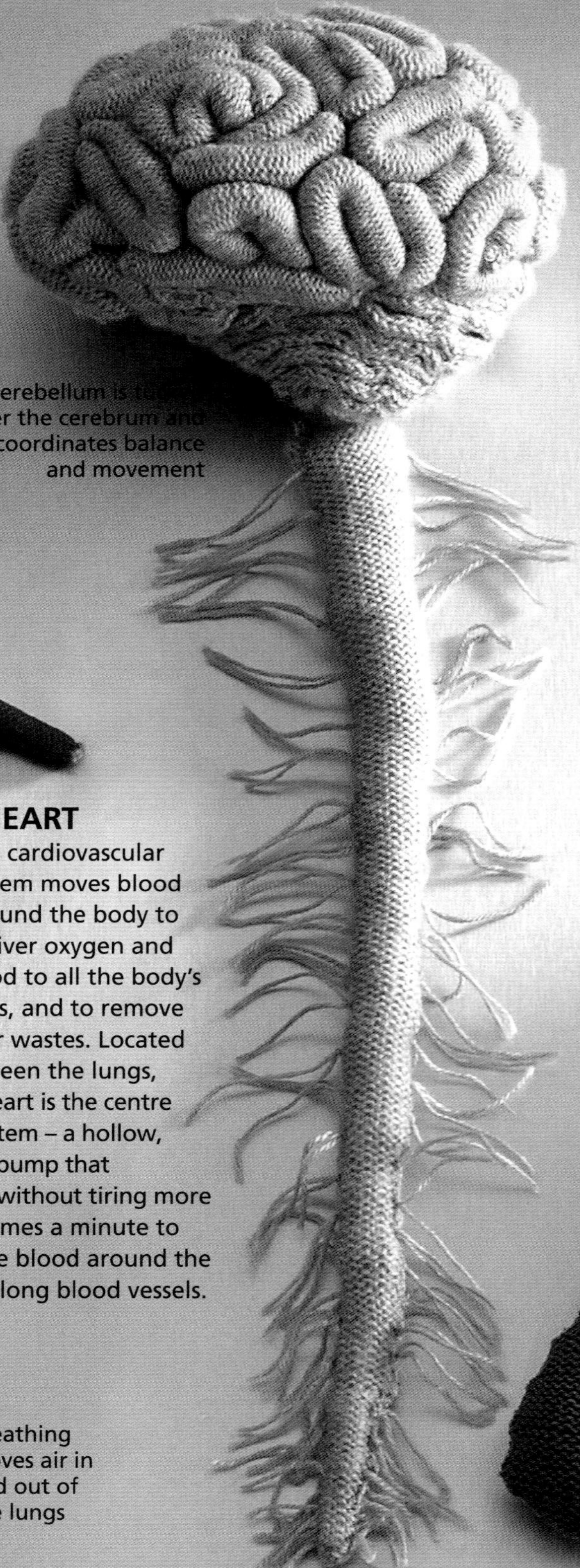

▼ BRAIN

The brain is the centre of the nervous system, which is responsible for controlling body activities. It is dominated by the folded cerebrum that enables us to feel, think, and remember, and instructs the body to move. Other brain parts are the cerebellum, tucked under the cerebrum, and the brain stem, which automatically controls breathing and heart rate and links the brain to the spinal cord.

The cerebellum is tucked under the cerebrum and coordinates balance and movement

◀ SPINAL CORD

An extension of the brain that runs down the back, the spinal cord relays signals between brain and body through the spinal nerves connected to it. It also controls many of the body's automatic reflex actions, such as pulling the hand back if it touches something sharp. Together the brain, spinal cord, and nerves form the nervous system.

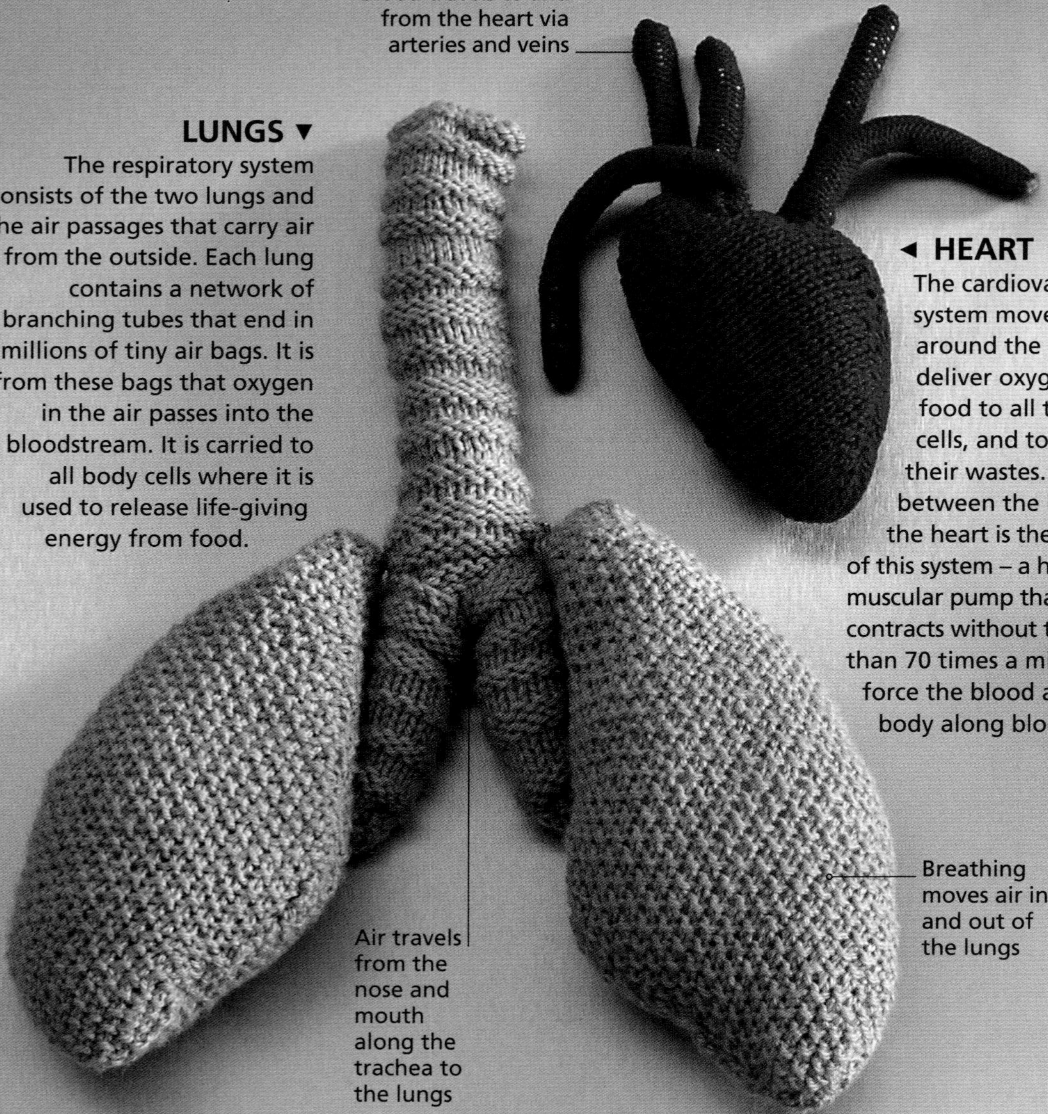

◀ HEART

The cardiovascular system moves blood around the body to deliver oxygen and food to all the body's cells, and to remove their wastes. Located between the lungs, the heart is the centre of this system – a hollow, muscular pump that contracts without tiring more than 70 times a minute to force the blood around the body along blood vessels.

Blood travels to and from the heart via arteries and veins

LUNGS ▼

The respiratory system consists of the two lungs and the air passages that carry air from the outside. Each lung contains a network of branching tubes that end in millions of tiny air bags. It is from these bags that oxygen in the air passes into the bloodstream. It is carried to all body cells where it is used to release life-giving energy from food.

Air travels from the nose and mouth along the trachea to the lungs

Breathing moves air in and out of the lungs

▼ SPLEEN

The spleen is part of the lymphatic system, the body's drainage network. It contains white blood cells, which fight infection by destroying bacteria, and also removes worn-out red blood cells from the blood.

Liver stores excess glucose and releases it when the body needs it

▲ STOMACH

This muscular bag expands as it receives and stores food that has been chewed and swallowed. During storage the stomach's walls churn food into a part-digested "soup", which is released into the small intestine.

The large intestine turns waste into faeces (poo) and pushes them out of the body

The small intestine is a long tube in which most digestion and absorption occurs

◀ LIVER

The largest internal organ, the liver controls the composition of the blood, processing nutrients newly absorbed from the small intestine.

PANCREAS ▶

The pancreas releases chemicals called enzymes into the small intestine to aid digestion, and hormones (chemical messengers) into the blood to control levels of glucose – the body's main fuel – in the blood.

The gall bladder stores bile, a fluid that aids fat digestion

Each kidney contains a million tiny filtering units that process blood to make urine

Ureter has muscular walls that squeeze urine downwards to the bladder

Billions of harmless bacteria digest waste in the large intestine

Bladder is a muscular bag that, when filled, pushes urine out through the urethra

DIGESTIVE SYSTEM ▶

The body needs nutrients for energy, growth, and repair. The digestive system breaks down food to release these essential nutrients. The system consists of the mouth and teeth, the oesophagus (a muscular tube leading from the mouth to the stomach), the stomach, and the small and large intestines. Food is digested using mechanical force, such as chewing, and through chemical digesters called enzymes. Nutrients are then absorbed into the blood and carried to the body's cells.

URINARY SYSTEM ▶

Consisting of the kidneys, ureters, bladder, and urethra, the urinary system makes urine and removes it from the body. The kidneys make urine by removing wastes and excess water and salts from the blood, thereby keeping its composition constant. Urine is stored in the bladder and expelled through the urethra at its base.

RESPIRATION

The body's trillions of cells require an uninterrupted supply of oxygen to release the energy they need to stay alive. They get this by means of a process called respiration. Air containing oxygen is breathed into the body by the respiratory system. Oxygen enters the bloodstream through the lungs and is carried to body cells. Waste carbon dioxide is carried by the blood to the lungs and breathed out.

RESPIRATORY SYSTEM

Located in the head, neck, and chest, the respiratory system consists of the lungs, which fill most of the chest, and the air passages – nasal cavity, throat, larynx, trachea, and bronchi – that carry air. This X-ray shows the parts of the respiratory system located in the chest.

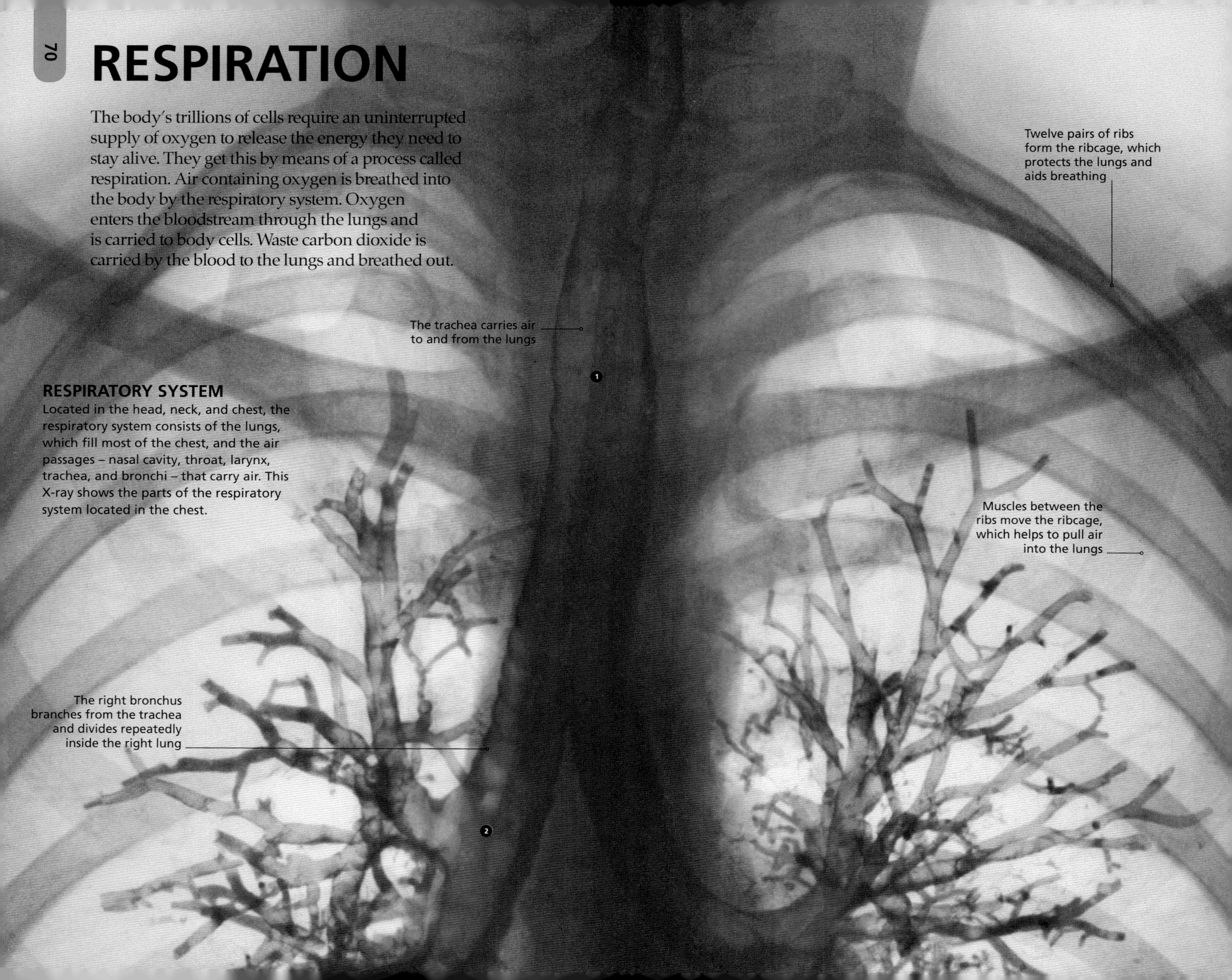

Twelve pairs of ribs form the ribcage, which protects the lungs and aids breathing

Muscles between the ribs move the ribcage, which helps to pull air into the lungs

The trachea carries air to and from the lungs

The right bronchus branches from the trachea and divides repeatedly inside the right lung

Branches of
the smallest
bronchioles
reach the
deepest parts
of the lung

The diaphragm is a domed
sheet of muscle that separates
chest from abdomen

❶ TRACHEA

Also called the windpipe, this flexible tube
carries air between the larynx (voice box)
at the base of the throat and the two
bronchi that arise at its lower end. Up
to 20 C-shaped rings of cartilage that
encircle the trachea hold it open when
you breathe in. Mucus lining the
trachea cleans the incoming air
by trapping dirt and germs, a process
that began in the nasal cavity.

❷ BRONCHIAL TREE

Once inside a lung, each bronchus
divides into smaller bronchi that then
spilt even further. These, in turn, divide
repeatedly to form smaller branches
called bronchioles. This arrangement
is often called "the bronchial tree"
because its structure looks like an
upside-down tree with the trachea
as the trunk, bronchi as branches,
and bronchioles as twigs.

❸ BRONCHIOLES AND ALVEOLI

The narrowest bronchioles end in 300
million air-filled bags called alveoli that
fill most of the lungs and are surrounded
by blood capillaries. Oxygen passes
through the wall of each alveolus into
the bloodstream in exchange for carbon
dioxide, which moves in the opposite
direction. The alveoli provide a large
surface across which this exchange
can take place efficiently.

❹ DIAPHRAGM

Situated just below the lungs, the
diaphragm plays a key role in breathing.
When breathing in, the diaphragm
contracts and flattens as muscles pull
the ribs upwards and outwards. This
increases the space in the chest so that air
is sucked into the lungs. When breathing
out the relaxed diaphragm is pushed
upwards, and the ribs move downwards
and inwards, squeezing air from the lungs.

BLOOD

Flowing all around your body, blood delivers food, oxygen, and other essentials to trillions of cells and removes their wastes. Blood also distributes heat around your body and defends it against infection. Blood is made up of a yellow liquid called plasma in which blood cells float. Red blood cells pick up oxygen in the lungs and deliver it to your body's cells. White blood cells defend the body against disease-causing germs. Blood also contains platelets, which enable it to clot to seal damaged blood vessels. The heart pumps blood around the body along three types of blood vessels. Arteries carry blood away from the heart, while veins return blood to the heart. Microscopic capillaries link arteries and veins and supply blood to cells.

Circulating around the average body are 5 litres (8.8 pints) of blood.

Oxygen-rich blood in arteries is bright red in colour. Oxygen-poor blood in veins is dark purple-red.

Blood is 55 per cent plasma and 45 per cent blood cells.

One drop of blood contains 250 million red blood cells, 375,000 white blood cells, and 16 million platelets.

Plasma is 90 per cent water and contains more than 100 different dissolved substances including food, waste, hormones, and salts.

White blood cells called neutrophils and macrophages eat germs. Lymphocyte white blood cells disable germs by releasing chemicals called antibodies.

Unravelled and stretched out, one adult's blood vessels would encircle Earth twice. Capillaries would make up 98 per cent of the total length.

Each as broad as a thumb, the largest artery and vein (the aorta and vena cava) are 2,500 times wider than a capillary, which is just one-tenth the width of a hair.

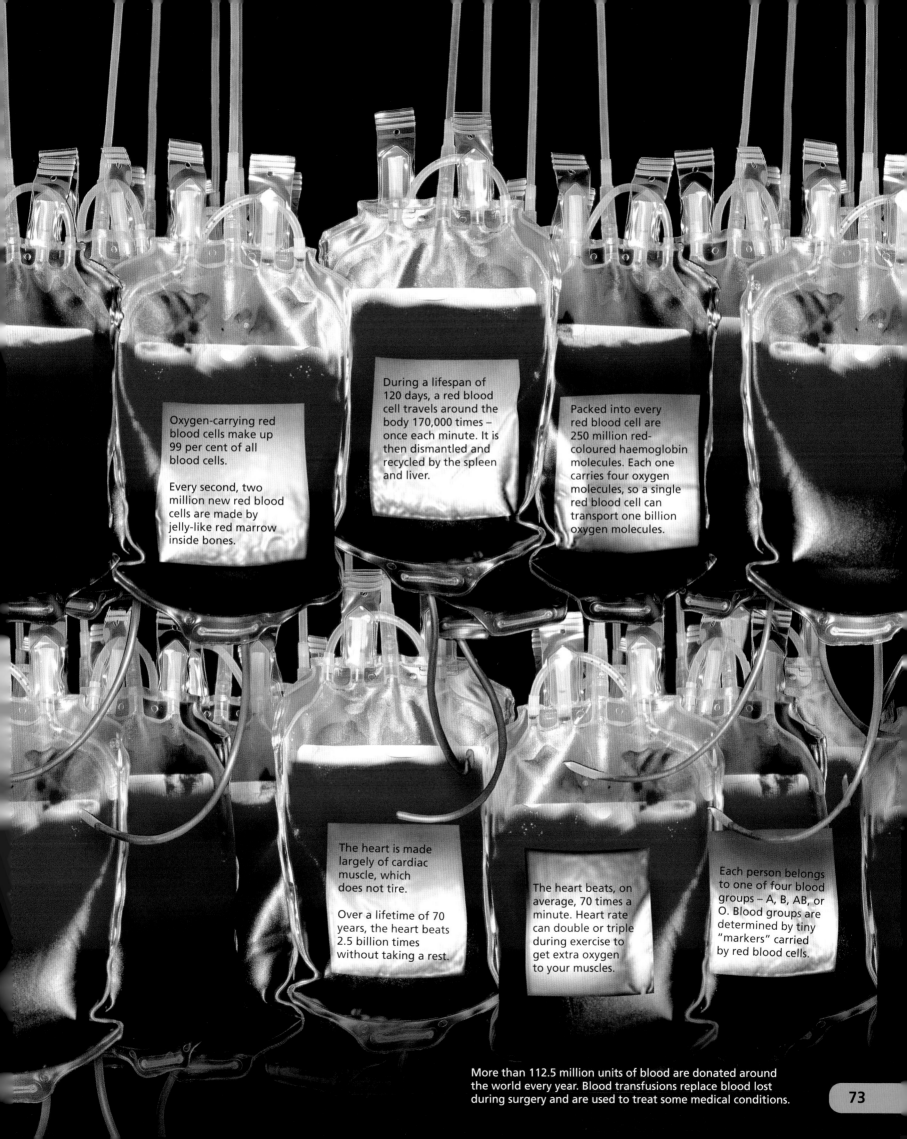

Oxygen-carrying red blood cells make up 99 per cent of all blood cells.

Every second, two million new red blood cells are made by jelly-like red marrow inside bones.

During a lifespan of 120 days, a red blood cell travels around the body 170,000 times – once each minute. It is then dismantled and recycled by the spleen and liver.

Packed into every red blood cell are 250 million red-coloured haemoglobin molecules. Each one carries four oxygen molecules, so a single red blood cell can transport one billion oxygen molecules.

The heart is made largely of cardiac muscle, which does not tire.

Over a lifetime of 70 years, the heart beats 2.5 billion times without taking a rest.

The heart beats, on average, 70 times a minute. Heart rate can double or triple during exercise to get extra oxygen to your muscles.

Each person belongs to one of four blood groups – A, B, AB, or O. Blood groups are determined by tiny "markers" carried by red blood cells.

More than 112.5 million units of blood are donated around the world every year. Blood transfusions replace blood lost during surgery and are used to treat some medical conditions.

SKIN, HAIR, AND NAILS

Skin is the body's protective overcoat, forming a barrier between vulnerable body tissues and the harsh, changing conditions of the outside world. It prevents water loss, blocks invasion by germs, repairs itself when damaged, helps us keep warm, and enables us to sense our surroundings. The uppermost layer of the skin is made from dead cells filled with a tough, waterproof substance called keratin. Hair and nails, both derived from skin, are also made from dead, keratin-filled cells.

The epidermis consists of cells that migrate upwards, dying, flattening, and filling with keratin as they do so

Flat, scaly cells in the upper epidermis are constantly worn away as skin flakes

The dermis contains living cells and fibres that allow skin to stretch and recoil

Cells in the base of the epidermis divide constantly to replace those lost from the surface

Surface of the epidermis on the back of a person's hand

Melanin, along with blood flowing through the dermis, gives the skin its colour

Skin surface is not smooth but covered with ridges into which sweat spreads

Sweat is a watery solution, filtered from blood and containing salts and wastes, that oozes from small openings called pores

❶ SKIN CROSS-SECTION

A section through the skin reveals that it has two parts. The epidermis is a germ-proof, waterproof barrier that protects against harmful rays in sunlight. The thicker dermis contains blood vessels, sensory receptors, and sweat glands.

❷ SWEAT

This salty liquid is produced by sweat glands in the dermis. In hot conditions, sweat is released onto the skin's surface. It then evaporates, cooling the body and helping to maintain a constant body temperature of 37°C (98°F).

❸ SKIN COLOUR

Special cells in the epidermis produce the brown pigment melanin, which filters out harmful ultraviolet rays from sunlight before they can damage skin cells.

Fingernail is formed from layers of dead, flattened cells from the epidermis

Skin covering the fingertips is sensitive because it contains many touch receptors

Hair shaft is made of dead cells packed with keratin, pushed up from the hair bulb

Hair follicle is a hollow space in the skin from which a hair grows

Sebaceous gland secretes oily sebum that keeps hair and skin flexible and soft

Hair bulb, deep in the dermis, contains living, dividing hair cells

❹ FINGERNAIL
Ideal for gripping objects and scratching itches, fingernails are clear plates that protect the sensitive upper parts of the fingertips. The cells that make nails die, flatten, and fill with keratin as they are pushed forward from the nail's root.

❺ HAIR
Millions of hairs grow from the skin covering most body areas. Scalp hairs protect the skin from sunlight and reduce heat loss. Finer, shorter body hairs sense the presence of insects on the skin before they can sting or bite us.

❻ TOUCH RECEPTORS
The dermis contains a range of receptors that respond to soft touch, firmer pressure, and vibrations, and send signals to the brain so we can feel our surroundings. The dermis also has receptors that detect pain, heat, and cold.

BRAIN

Safely inside the skull, the brain allows us to sense, think, learn, remember, and move. It also automatically regulates vital functions such as breathing. The cerebrum, the main part of the brain, has two halves, or hemispheres. The left hemisphere controls the right side of the body and is in charge of language, maths, and problem solving, while the right side controls the body's left side and deals with creativity, music, and art. The cerebrum's many tasks are carried out by its outer layer, or cortex. This has distinct areas that have different roles. Motor areas trigger movement, sensory areas deal with the senses, while association areas interpret information.

❶ PREFRONTAL CORTEX

The most complex part of the cerebrum, the prefrontal cortex makes us what we are. It determines our personality and intellect, and enables us to reason, plan, create, and learn complex ideas, and have a conscience.

❷ BROCA'S AREA

Named after Paul Broca, the 19th-century doctor who discovered it, Broca's area is normally found in the left hemisphere. It plans what a person wants to say and sends instructions to muscles in the throat, tongue, and lips that produce speech.

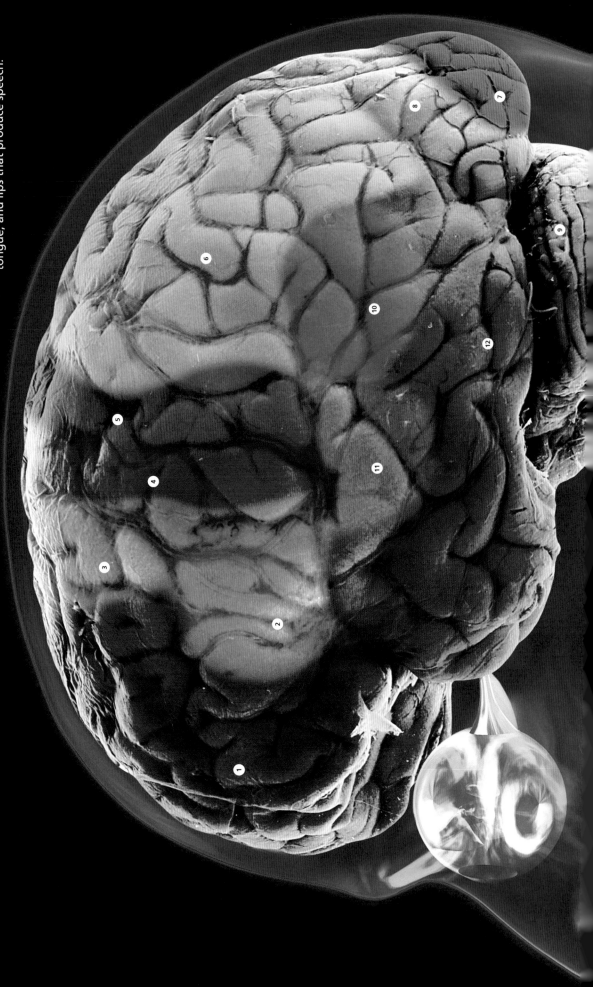

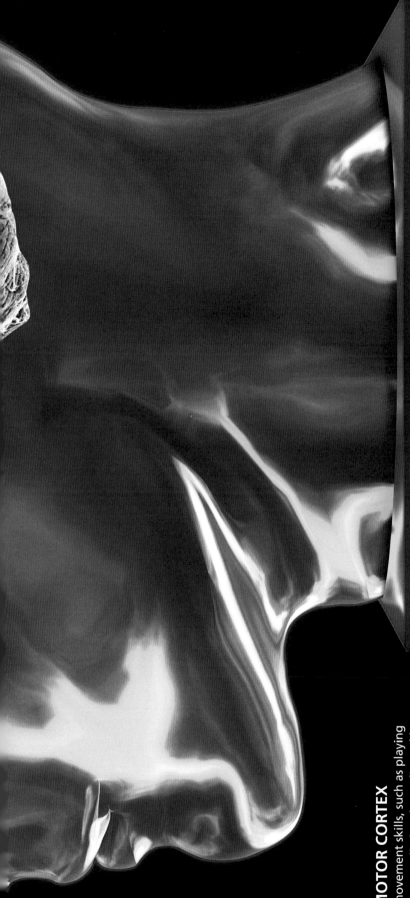

❸ PREMOTOR CORTEX

Learned movement skills, such as playing tennis, are controlled and coordinated by the premotor cortex. It tells specific muscles to contract either through the primary motor cortex or, in some cases, directly.

❹ PRIMARY MOTOR CORTEX

Most movements we make are controlled by the primary motor cortex. Guided by information from the cerebellum and other brain parts, it sends instructions to muscles that move the skeleton instructing them when, and in what sequence, to contract.

❺ PRIMARY SENSORY CORTEX

Receptors in the skin for touch, pressure, vibration, heat and cold, and pain send signals to the primary sensory cortex enabling us to feel those sensations. Our lips and fingertips have high concentrations of receptors, hence their sensitivity.

❻ SENSORY ASSOCIATION CORTEX

Basic information about touch, pressure, and other skin sensations is passed on by the primary sensory cortex to the sensory association cortex. Here sensations are analyzed, stored, and compared with previous experiences. It enables us to identify objects by touch.

❼ PRIMARY VISUAL CORTEX

When light hits the retina at the back of each eye, its light detectors send signals to the primary visual cortex. Here those signals are interpreted as basic shapes, colours, and movements before being passed on to the visual association cortex.

❽ VISUAL ASSOCIATION CORTEX

This is where information from the primary visual cortex about seen objects is interpreted and compared with previous visual experiences. The visual association cortex identifies what we are looking at and where it is in space, enabling us to "see" it.

❾ CEREBELLUM

The cerebellum is responsible for producing smooth, coordinated movements of the body. It analyzes incoming information about the body's current position and movement, then interacts with the primary motor cortex to precisely time muscle contractions.

❿ WERNICKE'S AREA

Usually located in the left hemisphere, Wernicke's area gives meaning to words that have been heard or read. Named after the German doctor Karl Wernicke, it has a direct link to Broca's area enabling us to speak the words we hear or see.

⓫ PRIMARY AUDITORY CORTEX

When sounds are detected by the two ears they send signals to the primary auditory cortex. Here the loudness, pitch (whether high or low), and rhythm of sounds are identified. That information is passed on to the auditory association area.

⓬ AUDITORY ASSOCIATION AREA

Sounds are "heard" in the auditory association area. Using information received from the primary auditory cortex, it pieces together the complete sound, and, by comparing it with sounds stored in memory, identifies it as, for example, music, speech, or thunder.

SENSES

Our senses make us aware of the world around us, and the changes that are happening in it. The eyes detect light waves, and the ears sound waves, enabling us to see and hear. The tongue and nose detect dissolved chemicals so we can taste, smell, and enjoy flavours. The skin allows us to feel the texture and warmth of objects.

Iris controls the amount of light entering the eye

Shapes, colour, and movement are all detected by the sense of vision

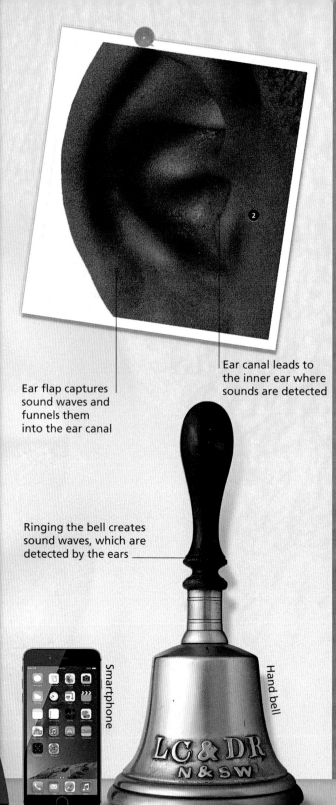

Ear flap captures sound waves and funnels them into the ear canal

Ear canal leads to the inner ear where sounds are detected

Ringing the bell creates sound waves, which are detected by the ears

Smartphone

Hand bell

LC & DR N & SW

Spiky papilla enables the tongue to grip food, but does not house taste buds

Sweets taste sweet because they contain lots of sugar

❶ VISION

Vision is the most important sense, providing the brain with an immense amount of information about the body's surroundings. Light reflected from, or produced by, outside objects is automatically focused onto a layer of light receptors that lines the back of the eye. In response, these receptors send signals to areas at the back of the brain. From there, we can determine what we are looking at and where it is, thus enabling us to "see" moving, 3-D images in colour.

❷ HEARING

The ears detect waves of pressure, called sound waves, that travel through the air. Sound waves are produced by objects, such as a ringing mobile phone or bell, which move or vibrate. The waves pass into the inner ear, which is enclosed in bone on the side of the skull. Here, receptors convert pressure waves into signals. The signals travel to the brain, which identifies the pitch, volume, and direction of the sound.

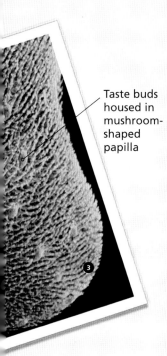

Taste buds housed in mushroom-shaped papilla

❸

❸ TASTE

Small projections on the tongue, called papillae, house taste receptors called taste buds. Food molecules dissolved in saliva are detected by the taste buds. These can distinguish between five basic tastes – sour, sweet, salty, bitter, and umami (savoury and meaty). As well as helping us to enjoy food, our sense of taste enables us to detect foods that may be poisonous.

Citrus fruits

Feathers feel soft and ticklish

❹

Skin ridges in the fingertips help us grip the objects we touch

A cactus spine puncturing the skin stimulates a pain receptor

❹

❺

Some cheeses emit a strong smell

Fresh flowers

Lemons and most other citrus fruits taste sour

❹ TOUCH

The skin acts like a sense organ. It contains several different types of receptors that enable us to "feel" our surroundings. Most are touch receptors that send signals to the brain when the skin comes into contact with objects. Some detect light touch, some heavier pressure, and some vibrations. Other receptors in the skin pick up temperature changes or detect pain.

❺ SMELL

The nose can detect more than 10,000 different smells. When air is breathed into the nose, odour molecules dissolve in watery mucus and are detected by odour receptors high in the roof of the nasal cavity. Together, the senses of smell and taste enable us to detect flavours. Smell is more important, however, which explains why food lacks flavour when we have a blocked nose. Some smells, such as those produced by burning, can warn us of danger.

REPRODUCTION

Human beings have a limited lifespan but are able, through reproduction, to produce a new generation to succeed them. Male and female reproductive systems produce specialized sex cells – called sperm and eggs – that unite during fertilization and combine their genetic instructions to make a new, unique human. After fertilization the embryo – later called a fetus – grows and develops inside its mother's uterus (womb) for the nine months of pregnancy.

FERTILIZATION ▲

Inside a woman's reproductive system, sperm swim towards and surround an egg and attempt to penetrate its outer layer. Eventually one succeeds, loses its tail, and its head fuses with the egg's nucleus, thereby combining two sets of genetic instructions (DNA).

Female egg is large and spherical. It cannot move of its own accord

Male sperm with beating tail penetrates the outer layer of the egg

◄ CELLS MULTIPLY

As the fertilized egg, or pre-embryo, is swept towards the uterus it divides repeatedly, producing first two cells, then four, then eight, and so on. Six days after fertilization it embeds itself in the uterus lining.

72 hours after fertilization the pre-embryo is a ball of 16 cells

The head becomes more erect and the ears, including the organs of balance, develop

The liver makes the embryo's blood cells until bone marrow can take over

Dark retina of a developing eye on the side of the embryo's head

▲ FOUR WEEKS

This pea-sized, four-week-old embryo – its head is on the left – is growing in its mother's uterus. Its tiny heart is beating and the nervous system and vital organs are forming.

▲ FIVE TO SIX WEEKS

The embryo's brain continues to develop, as do other organs, such as the intestines. Its skull and face are taking shape, and limbs, in the form of buds, are starting to grow. The embryo floats within a sac filled with protective fluid.

▲ SEVEN WEEKS

The bones of the grape-sized embryo start to harden and muscles develop and get stronger. Wrists and ankles are now visible and fingers and toes are just starting to appear. Internally, the kidneys start to remove waste to make urine.

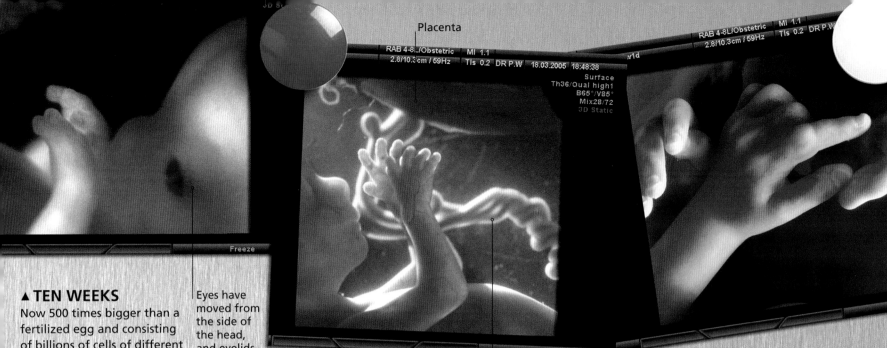

Placenta

RAB 4-8L/Obstetric   MI 1.1
2.8/10.3cm / 59Hz   Tis 0.2 DR P.W 18.03.2005 18:48:38
Surface
Th36/Qual high1
B65°/V85°
Mix28/72
3D Static

RAB 4-8L/Obstetric   MI 1.1
2.8/10.3cm / 59Hz   Tis 0.2 DR P.W

Freeze

Freeze

▲ TEN WEEKS

Now 500 times bigger than a fertilized egg and consisting of billions of cells of different types, the fetus, as it is now called, has all its basic organs in place and is growing rapidly. Its large head accommodates a fast-expanding brain. Fingers have formed and fingernails are growing.

Eyes have moved from the side of the head, and eyelids are forming

▲ TWELVE WEEKS

Since their implantation, the cells have been growing and specializing and the tiny individual they have moulded is now recognizably human. It has facial features, and fingers and toes have separated. The internal organs are in place, and the heart is beating.

The fetus receives food and oxygen through the umbilical cord, which is connected to the mother via an organ called the placenta

▲ TWENTY WEEKS

Fingers and ears clearly visible, the movements of the fetus can be felt by its mother inside her expanding uterus. The fetus blinks and swallows and follows phases of sleeping and waking. The ridges that produce fingerprints appear on its fingertips.

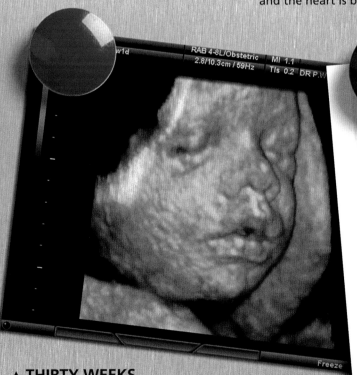

RAB 4-8L/Obstetric   MI 1.1
2.8/10.3cm / 59Hz   Tis 0.2 DR P.W

Freeze

▲ THIRTY WEEKS

Ultrasound scanning, shown here, is a safe method used to monitor the development of a fetus, and can also reveal whether it is a girl or boy. At this stage, the brain is still growing rapidly. The fetus can hear sounds and its eyes respond to light. Its lungs can now potentially breathe air.

NEWBORN

As pregnancy comes to an end, the uterus contracts to push the fully grown fetus into the bright, noisy outside world. The newborn baby takes its first breath and the umbilical cord is cut. In the next phases of its growth and development the baby is completely dependent on its parents for food, warmth, and protection.

GENETICS

Though all humans share the same basic body plan, each of us (apart from identical twins) has a unique mixture of features. That is because the set of instructions – called genes – required to construct a human varies slightly from person to person. Genetics is the study of how the genes we inherit from our parents shape the way we are.

Eye colour is controlled by specific genes, and different versions of those genes produce a range of colours

❷ CHROMOSOMES

A cell's DNA molecules are packaged into 23 pairs of chromosomes, which are found in the nucleus, the cell's control centre. Normally they are long and thin, but when a cell prepares to divide into two new cells, each chromosome shortens – as its DNA coils up – and duplicates, taking on the X-shape shown here.

❸ INHERITANCE

We inherit half of our chromosomes from each of our parents. A set of 23 chromosomes contains about 25,000 genes. Maternal and paternal chromosomes carry matching pairs of each gene – such as the gene that controls eye colour – but not necessarily the same version. If two versions are present, only one – the dominant gene – has an effect.

❶ DNA

Long molecules of DNA (deoxyribonucleic acid) are found in every body cell. When magnified, DNA resembles a twisted ladder with "rungs" made from four types of chemicals called bases (shown in colour). The sequence of bases along a section of DNA forms an instruction – a gene – for making one of the proteins that build and run a cell.

❹ GENETIC SIMILARITY

As brothers and sisters inherit a selection of genes from the same two people, their parents, they are more likely to resemble each other than they would a non-relative. Identical twins share almost identical genes, so they look the same and are of the same sex.

NUTRITION

Eating a balanced diet is an important part of good health. The food we eat supplies the nutrients required to build and repair the body, and to provide it with energy. Most of our nutrition consists of three food types – carbohydrates, proteins, and fats – but vitamins and minerals are also needed in tiny amounts. Water and dietary fibre are other key components. To remain healthy, a person should eat a variety of food in the correct proportion. Carbohydrates, the body's main source of energy, come in two forms – complex carbohydrates and sweet-tasting sugars.

◄ SUGARS

Foods such as sweets, cakes, and biscuits should be eaten sparingly because they contain lots of added sugar. Eating large amounts of sugar gives the body sudden bursts of energy rather than the constant stream it obtains from complex carbohydrates. Sugar that is excess to requirements is stored as fat, causing a person to put on weight.

Good-quality chocolate supplies some useful nutrients, but can also be high in fat and sugar

FATS AND OILS ►

Although fats and oils supply vitamins and are essential to the functioning of the body, they should be consumed in moderation. Plant oils, such as olive oil, contain unsaturated fatty acids (as do oily fish), which are good for health. However, saturated fatty acids, contained in many animal foods and added to processed foods, can clog arteries.

Olive oil, like all unsaturated fats, is liquid at room temperature

PROTEINS AND DAIRY FOODS ►

About 15 per cent of our diet should include proteins needed for growth and repair. Foods rich in proteins include nuts, beans, eggs, fish, and meat. Red meat is also rich in saturated fat, harmful to health if eaten in excess. Dairy foods, such as milk and cheese, supply the bone-building mineral calcium and some protein, but can also be high in fats.

Walnuts are rich in omega 3 fatty acids, which are essential for good health

FRUIT AND VEGETABLES ▶

Fruit is a good source of water, fibre, and vitamins, and the natural sugars that give us a burst of energy. Many also supply antioxidants, which can reduce the risk of some diseases. Vegetables contain vitamins and minerals and are a good source of fibre. Nutritionists recommend we eat at least five portions of fruit and vegetables daily.

Orange, red, and green, peppers are all excellent sources of vitamins A and C

Brown rice is rich in some B vitamins

Wholemeal bread supplies some iron, protein, and fibre

Potatoes are a good source of both vitamins C and B6, as well as some minerals

Bran cereals are rich in fibre, which helps to make digestion more efficient

▲ COMPLEX CARBOHYDRATES

Starch is the main complex carbohydrate in our diet. Foods rich in starch include pasta, cereals, potatoes, bread, and rice. During digestion, starch is broken down to the sugar glucose, the body's main source of energy. Complex carbohydrates should make up about half of our diet.

Pasta is made from wheat flour and is a good source of slow-release energy

HEALTH

A healthy body is one that is fit, strong, supple, and working well. Disease and injury prevent the normal working of the body. While it is not always possible to avoid illness, the chances of developing a disease are reduced by adopting a healthy lifestyle, including taking regular exercise and eating a good, mixed diet of fresh foods. If a person does become ill, a doctor has to work out exactly what the problem is, and then decides on a suitable course of treatment. This might include drugs, surgery, or other means to return the person to full health.

DRUGS

Chemicals that are used to treat and prevent disease, by changing some aspect of the way the body works, are called drugs. Antibiotics, which kill harmful bacteria, and analgesics, which reduce pain, are both examples of drugs. They may be given to a patient in a number of ways – by injection, as pills and syrups that are swallowed, or as a vapour that is inhaled into the lungs.

Cough syrup

Inhaler is used to introduce drugs, such as those that treat asthma, into the lungs

Hypodermic syringe is used to inject drugs into the bloodstream, skin, or a muscle

Pills

Laryngeal mirror is placed in the mouth to check the larynx (voice box)

Thermometer

Otoscope has a lens and a light and is used to look into a patient's ear

Ophthalmoscope enables a doctor to examine the inside of a patient's eye

Stethoscope is used to listen to chest sounds such as breathing and heartbeat

FIRST AID

The initial treatment to a person who is sick or injured is called first aid. It is often carried out by someone who is not medically qualified, but has been trained to use simple yet effective treatments. In more serious cases, first aid may keep a person alive until medical help arrives. A first-aid kit contains essential items such as disposable gloves, scissors, antiseptic cream and wipes, sticking plasters, sterile dressings, and bandages.

Blue plasters are used by caterers as they are easy to spot if they fall in food

DIAGNOSIS

If a person is ill their doctor first needs to determine exactly what is wrong with them. This is called making a diagnosis. The doctor asks about symptoms – the features of the disease or injury the patient has noticed – and considers the patient's medical history. Next, the doctor looks for signs to help identify the illness, for example, using a thermometer to check body temperature. The patient may require further tests, such as blood tests or X-rays.

Training shoes are ideal footwear for running and other exercises that improve fitness

Dumbbell weight

Chicken is a meat that is rich in protein, but low in harmful fats

PREVENTION

Regular exercise, such as running, walking, or playing sport, improves fitness by making the heart and body muscles more efficient. It is also important to eat a balanced diet made up of a wide range of foods – including pasta and rice, fruit and vegetables, lean meat, and oily fish – and low in salt, sugar, and in the unhealthy fats found in red meat. Not only does a healthy diet reduce the risk of becoming overweight, it can also help protect against certain diseases.

Oranges, like all fruits, contain vitamins that are essential for good health

Fish, especially oily fish, contain fatty acids that can reduce the risk of heart disease

Elasticated bandages support joints, limit swelling, and secure dressings that control bleeding

SURGERY

Performed by a doctor called a surgeon, surgery involves cutting into a patient's body to repair, remove, or replace tissue damaged by disease or injury. Surgery takes place in an operating theatre. To reduce the risk of infection, staff wear gowns and masks, and everything is sterile (free of germs). During an operation the patient is given an anaesthetic – a drug or gas that stops them feeling any pain.

Sterile surgical instruments are the "tools" used by a surgeon to perform operations

Scalpel is a sharp blade for cutting through skin and other tissues

Coarse forceps

Fine scissors

Coarse scissors

Probes

Fine forceps are used to grip and lift tissues during an operation

Antiseptic cream

Sterile dressing

Disposable gloves

87

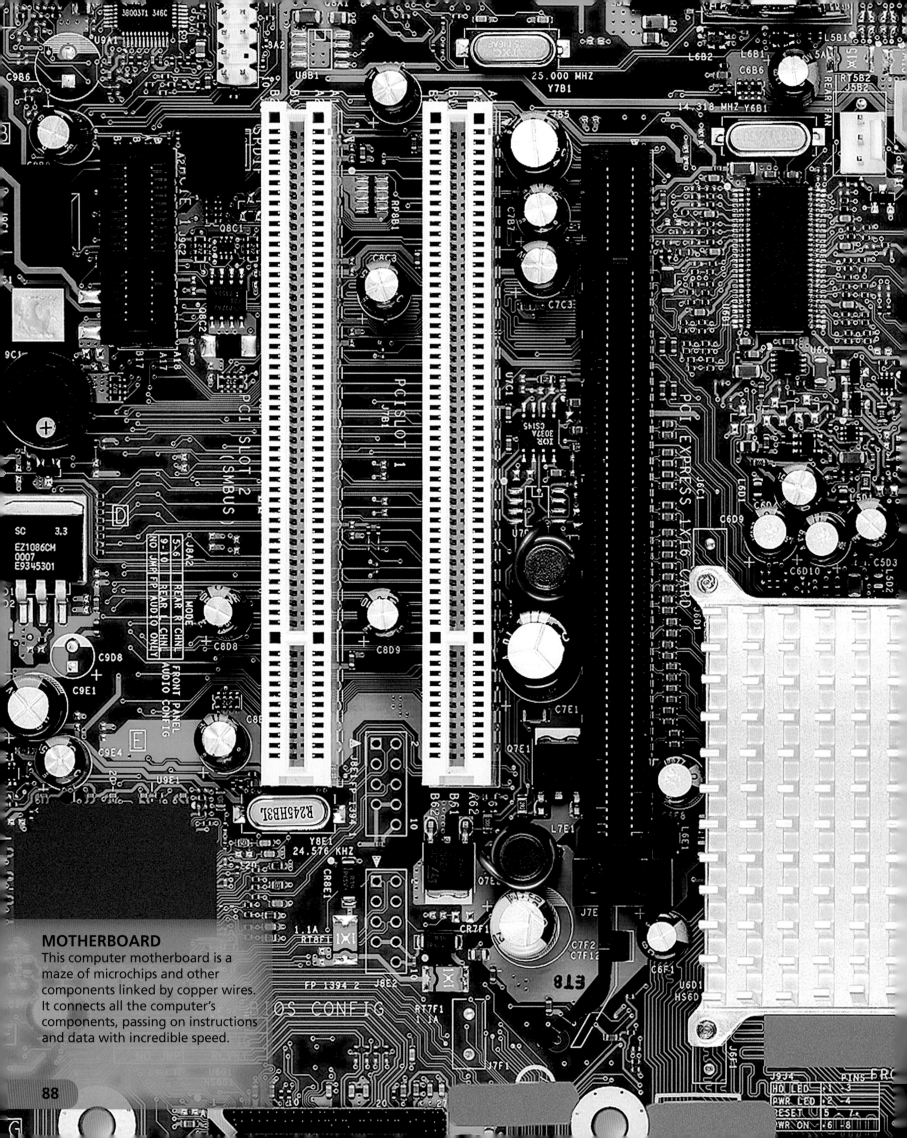

MOTHERBOARD

This computer motherboard is a maze of microchips and other components linked by copper wires. It connects all the computer's components, passing on instructions and data with incredible speed.

Science and technology

ELEMENTS

Everything in the world is made from elements – pure substances that cannot be broken down into anything simpler. Elements can be grouped according to the properties they have in common, such as their appearance, how they conduct electricity, and how they react with other substances. There are nine main groups and the element hydrogen, which is unique.

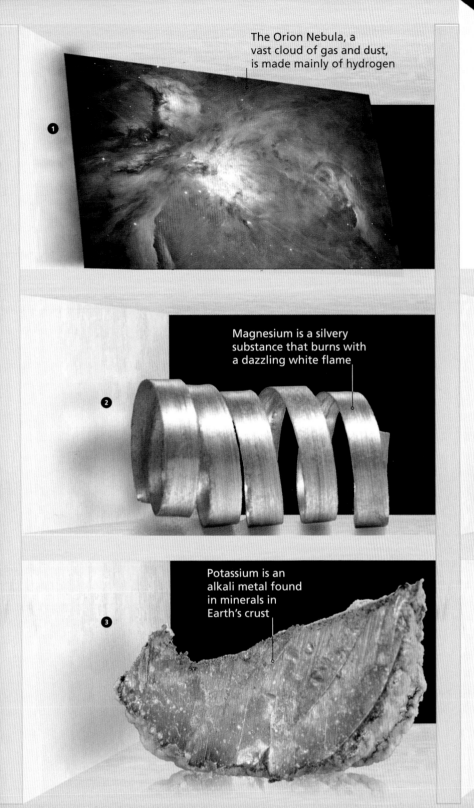

❶ The Orion Nebula, a vast cloud of gas and dust, is made mainly of hydrogen

❷ Magnesium is a silvery substance that burns with a dazzling white flame

❸ Potassium is an alkali metal found in minerals in Earth's crust

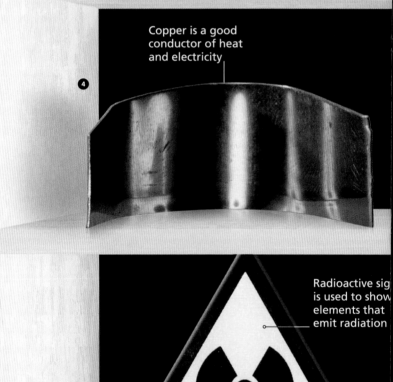

❹ Copper is a good conductor of heat and electricity

❺ Radioactive sig is used to show elements that emit radiation

❶ HYDROGEN

Hydrogen makes up 90 per cent of all the matter in the Universe. Pure hydrogen is an invisible gas on Earth. It is not considered part of any one group. Hydrogen powers the nuclear reactions inside stars, including our Sun, and is found on Earth in the compound H_2O, or water.

❷ ALKALINE-EARTH METALS

Alkaline-earth metals react with water and are found in minerals in Earth's crust. In pure form, they are silvery-white. They are similar to alkali metals, but less reactive. Calcium, found in chalk, milk, and bones, is a member of this group.

❸ ALKALI METALS

Sodium, contained in salt, is an alkali metal. These elements are characterized by their vigorous reaction with water. On contact, they will zoom all over the water's surface or even explode. Alkali metals are not found in a pure form in nature because they react so strongly with water.

❹ TRANSITION METALS

This group is the largest and includes iron, silver, gold, nickel, platinum, and titanium. Transition metals are considered typical metals – they are hard and shiny, conduct electricity and heat well, and have high melting points.

❺ ACTINIDES

The elements in this group are radioactive metals mostly created synthetically in nuclear reactors or nuclear explosions. They have unstable atoms that break up and give out radiation particles. Uranium and plutonium are examples of actinides.

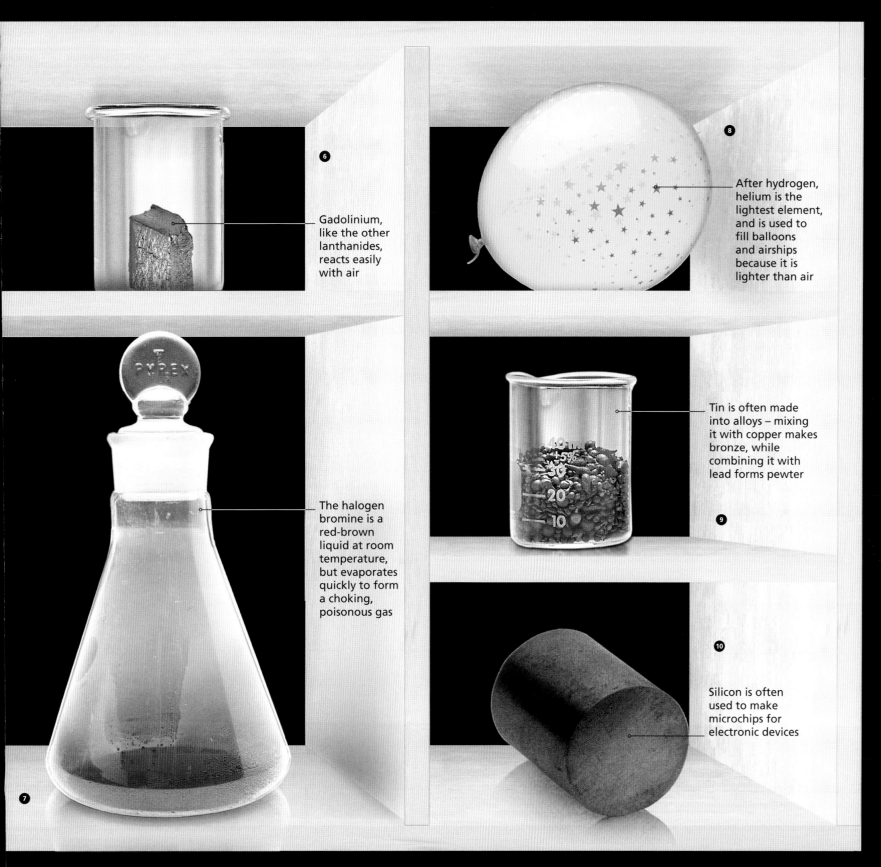

6 Gadolinium, like the other lanthanides, reacts easily with air

8 After hydrogen, helium is the lightest element, and is used to fill balloons and airships because it is lighter than air

The halogen bromine is a red-brown liquid at room temperature, but evaporates quickly to form a choking, poisonous gas

7

Tin is often made into alloys – mixing it with copper makes bronze, while combining it with lead forms pewter

9

10 Silicon is often used to make microchips for electronic devices

6 LANTHANIDES

These soft, reactive metals were known as rare earths, because they were wrongly believed to occur only scarcely in nature. Silvery-white in appearance, they tarnish easily on contact with air. Holmium, the element with the greatest magnetic strength, is in this group.

7 NON-METALS

Around one-sixth of elements are non-metals. They are poor conductors of electricity and melt at low temperatures. Carbon, nitrogen, and oxygen are all examples of non-metals, as are the halogens, a group of highly reactive elements that combine with other elements to form salts.

8 NOBLE GASES

There are seven noble gases – also called rare or inert gases because they do not readily react with anything or combine with other elements to make compounds. They are helium, neon, argon, krypton, xenon, radon, and oganesson, although the latter may be a solid at room temperature.

9 POOR METALS

Metals that are fairly soft and melt easily are known as poor metals. They are readily found as ores (minerals) in Earth and can be very useful, especially when made into alloys (two metals mixed together to make a harder metal). Aluminium and lead are both poor metals.

10 SEMI-METALS

These elements have some properties of metals and some of non-metals. Arsenic, for example, is shiny like a metal, but not a good conductor. Some semi-metals are semiconductors, behaving as conductors or insulators depending on what other substances are added to them.

MOLECULES

An element is a substance made of only one kind of atom. Atoms join, or bond, to other atoms of the same element, or to atoms of other elements. They do this by sharing or exchanging electrons. In many cases, the bonded atoms form groups called molecules. When atoms of one element combine with atoms of other elements, they form compounds.

Oxygen atom

◄ OXYGEN (O₂)

Some elements can bond in several ways to form different substances. Atoms of the element oxygen (O) bond together in pairs to form molecules of oxygen gas. High in the atmosphere, however, oxygen atoms also bond in threes to form the gas ozone.

VITAMIN C (C₆H₈O₆) ►

Like ethanol, vitamin C (ascorbic acid) contains carbon (C), hydrogen (H), and oxygen (O) atoms. However, because the molecule contains different quantities of the elements arranged in a different way it forms an entirely different substance – a compound that is solid at room temperature.

Hydrogen atom

Carbon atom

Oxygen atom

Hydrogen atom

Oxygen atom

Carbon atom

ETHANOL (C₂H₅OH) ▲

Ethanol is a compound with molecules containing two carbon (C) atoms, six hydrogen (H) atoms, and one oxygen (O) atom. At room temperature, it is a colourless liquid used as a disinfectant, preservative, and the alcohol in drinks.

Hydrogen atom

Carbon atom

◄ METHANE (CH₄)

Molecules of the gas methane contain four hydrogen (H) atoms bonded to a carbon (C) atom. Compounds of carbon and hydrogen are called hydrocarbons. They include fuels, such as methane, oil, and coal, and artificial materials, such as polystyrene.

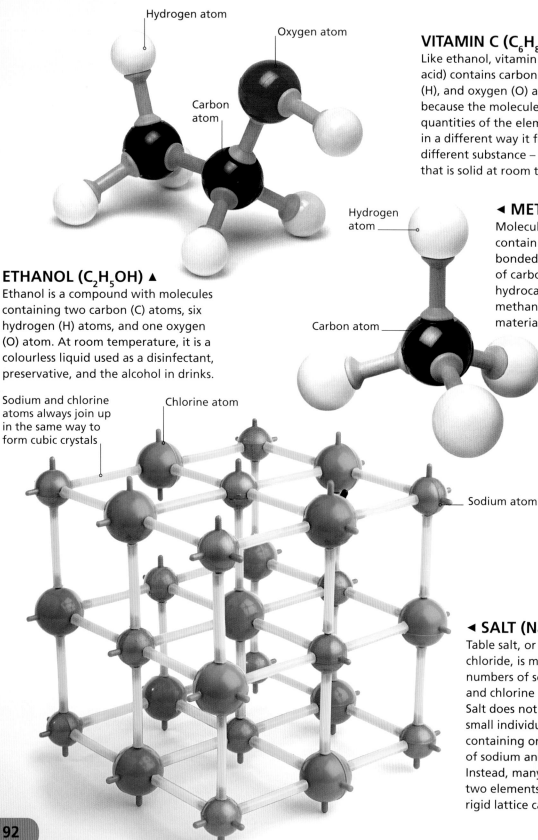

Sodium and chlorine atoms always join up in the same way to form cubic crystals

Chlorine atom

Sodium atom

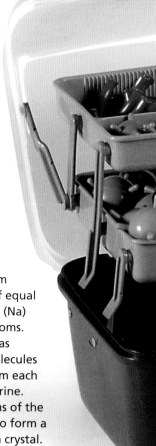

◄ SALT (NaCl)

Table salt, or sodium chloride, is made of equal numbers of sodium (Na) and chlorine (Cl) atoms. Salt does not form as small individual molecules containing one atom each of sodium and chlorine. Instead, many atoms of the two elements link to form a rigid lattice called a crystal.

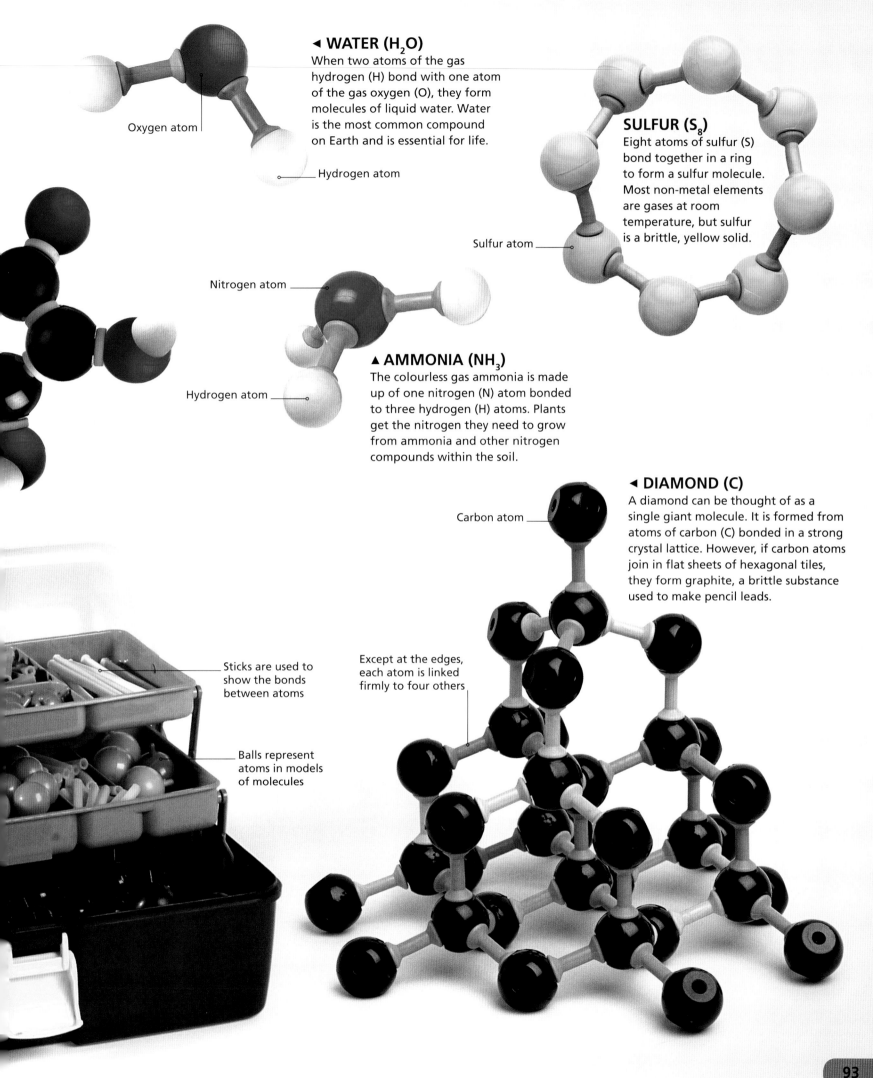

◄ WATER (H₂O)

When two atoms of the gas hydrogen (H) bond with one atom of the gas oxygen (O), they form molecules of liquid water. Water is the most common compound on Earth and is essential for life.

Oxygen atom

Hydrogen atom

SULFUR (S₈)

Eight atoms of sulfur (S) bond together in a ring to form a sulfur molecule. Most non-metal elements are gases at room temperature, but sulfur is a brittle, yellow solid.

Sulfur atom

Nitrogen atom

Hydrogen atom

▲ AMMONIA (NH₃)

The colourless gas ammonia is made up of one nitrogen (N) atom bonded to three hydrogen (H) atoms. Plants get the nitrogen they need to grow from ammonia and other nitrogen compounds within the soil.

◄ DIAMOND (C)

A diamond can be thought of as a single giant molecule. It is formed from atoms of carbon (C) bonded in a strong crystal lattice. However, if carbon atoms join in flat sheets of hexagonal tiles, they form graphite, a brittle substance used to make pencil leads.

Carbon atom

Sticks are used to show the bonds between atoms

Balls represent atoms in models of molecules

Except at the edges, each atom is linked firmly to four others

ACIDS AND BASES

An acid is a substance that produces positively charged particles of hydrogen, called hydrogen ions, when dissolved in water. The more hydrogen ions an acid contains, the stronger the acid is. A base is the chemical opposite of an acid. Bases produce negatively charged particles in water, called hydroxide ions. The more hydroxide ions a base contains, the stronger it is. Bases that dissolve in water are called alkalis.

◄ CITRIC ACID
The sharp taste in citrus fruit such as lemons and grapefruit is due to the citric acid they contain. Citric acid is often artificially added to manufactured foods and drinks to give a tangy sensation that tastes refreshing.

Vinegar is made when bacteria convert the ethanol in alcohol into acetic acid

INDICATOR PAPER ▼
When a strip of indicator paper is dipped into a liquid, the paper changes colour. The colour can be compared to a pH scale to find out the acidity of the solution. pH stands for "potential of hydrogen", and measures how many hydrogen ions the solution contains.

◄ VINEGAR
The sour taste of vinegar comes from the acetic acid it contains. Every step on the pH scale is 10 times less acidic than the previous step, so acetic acid with a pH of 4 is 1,000 times less acidic than hydrochloric acid.

◄ HYDROCHLORIC ACID
The lower the pH value, the stronger the acid. Hydrochloric acid, created when hydrogen chloride gas dissolves in water, has a pH of about 1. It is highly corrosive, capable of eating through metals.

◄ STINGER
When a bee stings, it injects a mild acid into a person's flesh, which causes a stinging sensation. Washing the sting with alkaline soap may relieve the pain by neutralizing the acid.

◄ CHEMICAL HAZARD
Strong acids and bases have to be stored in containers that will not be corroded by the chemical within. These containers are labelled with chemical hazard symbols that show the potential dangers.

All bases tend to feel
slippery like soap

LIQUID SOAP ▶

Soap is a weak base. It is
made by combining a
weak acid with a strong
base, making it only
mildly alkaline with a pH
of about 8. An indicator
paper dipped into liquid
soap turns blue.

LIMESTONE ▶

Calcium carbonate, or
limestone, is a type of rock
formed from the remains of
dead sea creatures over millions
of years. It is an important base,
which is quarried and crushed
to make fertilizers, paints,
ceramics, and cement.

◀ WATER

Pure water is neither acid nor
alkali, but neutral, with a pH of 7.
Rainwater is slightly acidic, with a
pH of 5 to 6, while seawater is slightly
alkaline, with a pH of between 8 and 9.

CLEANING FLUID ▶

The strongest bases have a
pH of 14 or more. Alkaline
solutions with a high pH are
used as cleaning materials as
they dissolve fats. Cleaning fluids
such as bleach and caustic soda
have a pH of around 10.

The pH of tap water is usually
between 6 and 8 depending
on the gases and minerals
that are dissolved in it

HYDRANGEAS ▶

The hydrangea shrub
produces different coloured
flowers depending on the
acidity of the soil. On acid
soils, it produces blue
flowers, on alkaline soils, it
produces pink or purple
flowers, and on neutral soils,
it has creamy white blooms.

Chalk and vinegar fizz vigorously as the acid breaks down the chalk

CHEMICAL REACTIONS

The atoms within a molecule are held together with links called chemical bonds. In a chemical reaction, the bonds between a molecule's atoms break, and the atoms bond in a different way to form new molecules. In some reactions, elements combine to create a compound. In others, compounds break down into elements or simpler compounds. All the atoms from the original substance exist in the changed substance, but in different places.

Silver metal clings to the copper coil

Burning is a non-reversible reaction – the wick cannot be remade from the ash and smoke

The energy produced when sulfur and iron react causes the mixture to glow

The explosion caused by igniting thermite produces a temperature of around 2,400°C (4,350°F)

When chemicals in an apple's cells that contain substances called phenols are exposed to the air, they oxidize and turn brown

❶ REACTION

When vinegar (acetic acid) and chalk (calcium carbonate) are mixed, a chemical reaction takes place. The acidic vinegar breaks down the chalk to release carbon and oxygen as bubbles of carbon dioxide. The starting materials in a chemical reaction are called reactants. The materials that exist after are called products.

❷ DISPLACEMENT

In a displacement reaction, the metal that forms part of a compound is removed and replaced by another metal. When a coil of copper is dipped into a clear solution of silver nitrate, the copper displaces the silver from the solution to form a blue solution of copper nitrate and needles of solid metal silver.

❸ BURNING

When the wick of a candle burns, it is reacting with oxygen in the air to produce ash and smoke. The burning also produces energy in the form of heat and light. In all reactions, energy is used up when bonds between atoms break, and energy is released as new bonds are made.

❹ REACTION RATES

The rate of a chemical reaction is affected by factors such as temperature, pressure, light, surface area, and concentration. It is possible to change the rate of a reaction by varying one of these factors. For example, increasing the concentration of dye in a solution will dye the material more quickly.

❺ REVERSIBLE

A few reactions are reversible. The molecules created by the reaction can be reformed into the original materials. The initial reaction is called the forward reaction and the reverse is the backward reaction. Dinitrogen tetraoxide breaks down into nitrogen dioxide when heated, but reverts when cooled.

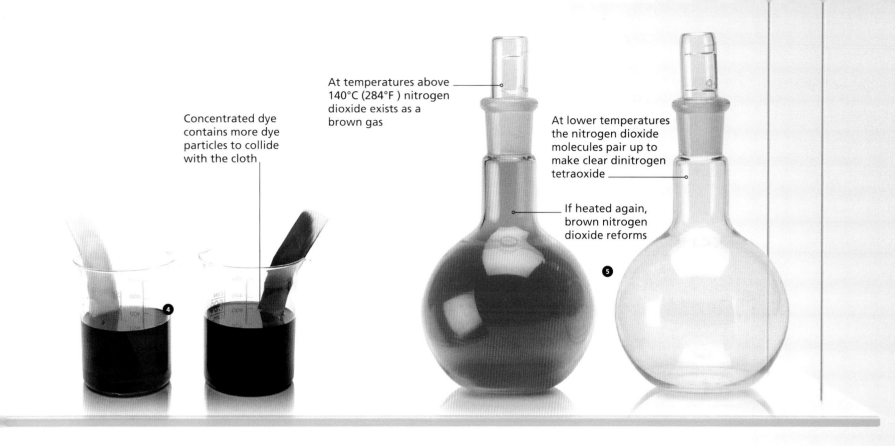

Concentrated dye contains more dye particles to collide with the cloth

At temperatures above 140°C (284°F) nitrogen dioxide exists as a brown gas

At lower temperatures the nitrogen dioxide molecules pair up to make clear dinitrogen tetraoxide

If heated again, brown nitrogen dioxide reforms

As crystals of potassium permanganate begin to dissolve, purple trails spread through the water, until an even purple solution is formed

When a bread dough mixture is left in a warm place, carbon dioxide bubbles appear, making the bread rise

APPLYING HEAT

When a mixture of yellow powder sulfur and silver-grey iron filings is heated to a high temperature, a chemical reaction takes place and iron sulfide is formed. Without heat, the substances would not react with each other. Heat speeds up most reactions, and cold slows reactions down.

❼ EXOTHERMIC

Thermite is a mixture of aluminium and iron oxide. When it is ignited at a high temperature there is an explosion, as the chemical reaction produces a sudden release of energy in the form of light, heat, and noise. Reactions that produce heat are known as exothermic reactions.

❽ OXIDATION

Some chemical reactions happen around us naturally. One of the commonest reactions is oxidation – when substances gain oxygen. Oxidation is happening when metals rust, when wood burns, and when we breathe. In all these reactions, substances are reacting with oxygen from the air.

❾ SOLUTIONS

A solution is a mixture in which the molecules are mixed so evenly and completely that it seems like a single substance. However, in a solution, a chemical reaction has not taken place. Neither the solute (the substance being dissolved) nor the solvent (the substance that it is dissolved in) have changed.

❿ CATALYST

A catalyst is a molecule that helps bring about and speed up a chemical reaction, but does not change itself during the reaction. Natural catalysts are called enzymes. Bread dough rises because enzymes in yeast cause a reaction that produces bubbles of carbon dioxide when it is mixed with water and sugars.

STATES OF MATTER

Everything you can smell, touch, or taste is made from matter, including living things such as yourself, and non-living things such as this book. Matter is made up of atoms and anything that is not made of matter is energy. Heat, light, and sound are forms of energy. You cannot smell, touch, or taste energy, and it is not made from atoms. All matter on Earth exists in one of three states: solid, liquid, or gas.

❶ SOLID

A solid, such as this ice sculpture, has a fixed volume and a shape that is not easy to change. Strong links hold atoms together and do not allow them to move around, as they can in a liquid and in a gas. The atoms in most solids are arranged in regular patterns that form three-dimensional shapes, such as cubes and prisms, called crystals.

❷ GAS

A gas does not have a fixed shape or a fixed volume. It expands to fill all the space around it. Atoms in a gas can move freely in every direction. They whizz around far too fast to ever stick together.

Unlike most substances, water expands when it freezes (rather than contracting) because its molecules move further apart when locked into the rigid structure of a solid

❹ STATE TO STATE

Matter changes from one state to another when it is heated or cooled. Heating melts solids into liquids and boils liquids to form gases. Cooling condenses gases to form liquids and freezes liquids into solids. As matter changes from one state to another, the atoms within it remain the same but become arranged differently.

❺ CHANGING SHAPE

Solids do not always have a fixed shape. Some solids, such as ice or glass, are brittle and will break if you hammer or crush them. Other solids, such as rubber or metals, are malleable and can be hammered, stretched, or squashed into different shapes without breaking.

Most gases are invisible. Even steam cannot be seen until it condenses into a mist of droplets as it mixes with cooler air

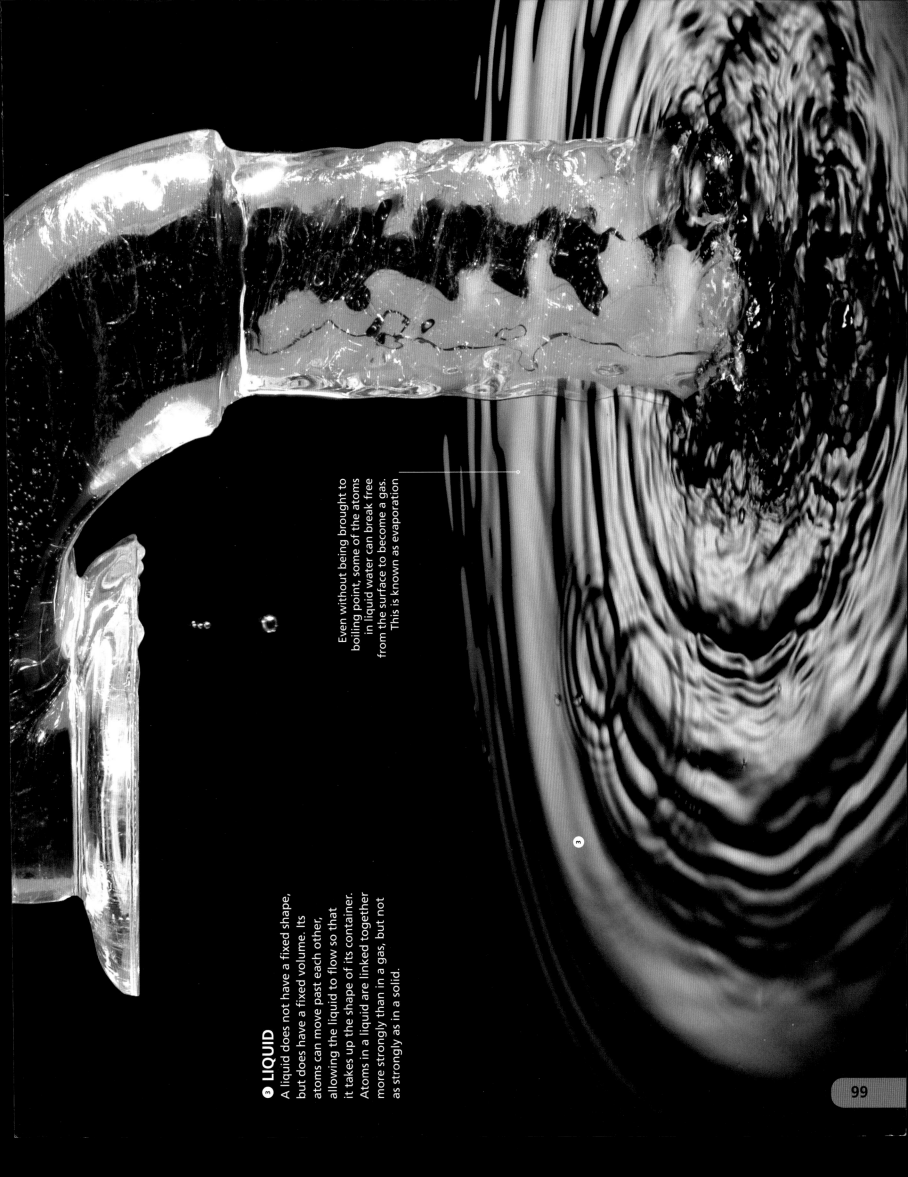

❸ LIQUID

A liquid does not have a fixed shape, but does have a fixed volume. Its atoms can move past each other, allowing the liquid to flow so that it takes up the shape of its container. Atoms in a liquid are linked together more strongly than in a gas, but not as strongly as in a solid.

Even without being brought to boiling point, some of the atoms in liquid water can break free from the surface to become a gas. This is known as evaporation

WATER

Water is a tasteless, odourless liquid. Although it appears to be colourless, in fact it is very pale blue. Each molecule of water is made up of two hydrogen atoms and one oxygen atom, giving it the chemical formula H_2O. Water is Earth's most common compound, found everywhere, from the oceans that cover 71 per cent of the planet to each cell of every living organism.

• Unlike most compounds, water can exist in all three states of matter, solid, liquid, and gas, within Earth's normal range of temperatures.

• At sea level, water is liquid between 0 and 100°C (32–212°F), but below 0°C (32°F), it solidifies into ice, and above 100°C (212°F), it becomes gaseous water vapour.

• Unlike most other substances, water is denser when it is liquid than when it is solid – that is why ice floats on the top of water instead of sinking.

• When water freezes into ice, it expands by nine per cent of its volume with a force that can burst pipes and split rock.

• Earth is the only place in the Solar System where conditions allow water to exist in liquid form at the surface. Some liquid water exists under the surface of the moons of Jupiter and Saturn.

• Water is essential for life, so astronomers look for it when searching for life on other planets.

• The body of an average adult man contains more than 40 litres (70 pints) of water.

• You need about 2 litres (4 pints) of water every day to keep healthy.

• About 30 per cent of the world's population do not have clean, safe running water at home.

• Water is not a resource that can be used up like oil. Water evaporates into the air, forms clouds, and falls back to Earth as rain. In areas of Earth that receive little rainfall, water can be a scarce resource.

WATER first incarnation is an art installation by British artist Sean Rogg. He collected water bottles from all over the world.

MATERIALS

Almost everything around us is made from some sort of material. Each has different properties, such as strength or flexibility, which makes it useful for making particular products. Some materials, such as wool or stone, grow or occur naturally. Synthetic materials are manufactured. Composite materials combine the properties of two or more materials to achieve the best possible product.

Kevlar is used to reinforce helmets, so that they are light but very strong

❸ **KEVLAR**

A light, flexible, synthetic material, Kevlar is used for protective clothing, such as bulletproof vests. Kevlar molecules are arranged in long chains with strong bonds between them, which makes Kevlar five times stronger than steel.

Concrete is the main material used for modern buildings

❶ **SILK**

This natural fibre is made from the cocoon of the silkworm. Each cocoon may produce 3 km (2 miles) of silk. Silk can be woven into an extremely fine fabric, and is prized for its texture and its shiny appearance.

❷ **CONCRETE**

Concrete is made by mixing sand, gravel, cement, and water. It is a liquid when freshly made, so it can be poured into a mould, where it sets to form an extremely hard and durable material.

Plastics can be moulded into almost any shape or size

Most metals are malleable and can be bent without breaking

❹ **WOOL**

This natural material comes from the fleece of sheep. The structure of its fibres means wool has a tendency to shrink, so it is often mixed with synthetic fibres to make easy-care fabrics.

❺ CARBON COMPOSITES

These materials are strong and light and can be turned into complex shapes, such as sports equipment. They are made from the carbon byproducts of coal, oil, and natural gas.

❾ LYCRA

Synthetic fabrics are designed to have better properties than natural materials, such as cotton. Lycra is a stretchy fabric that keeps its original shape, making it perfect for sports clothes.

⓬ CERAMIC

Ceramic materials are made by heating different types of clay to a high temperature. China, bricks, tiles, cement, and glass are all ceramics. These materials are hard, brittle, and resistant to heat.

❿ RUBBER

Natural rubber is an elastic material made from latex, a milky fluid from the rubber tree. Synthetic rubber is made from petrochemicals. Rubber is used in tyres and for waterproofing fabrics.

⓭ WOOD

Wood is a strong material compared to its weight, and is a good building material. It is also used for furniture and art objects because of its attractive texture. It is referred to as hardwood or softwood, depending on the type of tree it comes from.

⓫ NYLON

Developed in 1938, nylon was the first synthetic fabric. It can be produced in extremely fine threads, is cheap to manufacture, and was first used as a replacement for silk in stockings and parachutes.

⓮ COTTON

Cotton is a natural material produced from the long, flexible fibres in the fluffy seedpods of the cotton plant. The fabric is soft, comfortable to wear, and there is no static build-up as there is with some synthetic fabrics.

Wood can be cut, carved, and sanded into shape

Cotton fibres are spun into threads and then woven into fabric

Nylon rope lasts longer than one made of natural fibres

❼ PLASTIC

This group of synthetic materials is made from petrochemicals (derived from crude oil). They are strong, light, cheap to make, and can be shaped into flexible sheets, films, or fibres.

❻ METAL

When heated, metals can be shaped into anything from a paperclip to an aircraft. They are also good conductors of heat and suitable for carrying electricity.

❽ GLASS

This transparent ceramic is made by fusing sand, limestone, and soda at high temperatures, or by recycling old glass. Molten glass can be shaped in many ways, such as into windows, lenses, and threads for optical fibres.

⓯ STONE

Stone is a natural material quarried from the earth. It is hard and heavy and can withstand great pressure. Stone may be cut using diamond saws or extremely high-pressure jets of water.

Hand-carved granite makes a durable kitchen tool

GRAVITY

The force of gravity is a force of attraction that exists between all objects with mass, from microscopic atoms to stars and planets. On Earth, gravity can be seen when objects fall to the ground, pulled by an invisible force. In space, the force of gravity keeps the Moon in its orbit around Earth, keeps planets in orbit round the stars, and holds huge clusters of stars together as galaxies.

NEWTON'S DISCOVERY

An apple falling from a tree is said to have inspired English scientist Isaac Newton (1642–1727) to explore the force of gravity. He developed a theory stating that every mass attracts every other mass by a force between both masses. The more massive an object is and the nearer it is, the greater its gravitational attraction.

BIRTH OF A STAR

A star is born inside a cloud of dust and gas in space called a nebula. The dust and gas begin to clump together, forming a core. The clump's gravitational attraction increases as its mass increases, dragging in more and more matter. The centre, or core, becomes so massive and dense that nuclear fusion begins, and the star begins to shine.

MOON AND TIDES

As the Moon orbits Earth, its gravity tugs at the water in the oceans, making a mass of water bulge towards the Moon. The force of Earth's spin creates a matching bulge on the other side of Earth. These bulges cause the regular rise and fall of the water level at the sea's edge that we know as tides.

MASS AND WEIGHT

These are not the same. An object's mass is the amount of matter it contains. An object's weight is the force exerted on its mass by gravity. This means that on the Moon, where gravity is just one-sixth of Earth's gravity, an astronaut will weigh one-sixth as much as he weighs on Earth, although his mass is the same.

ZERO GRAVITY

In orbit around Earth, astronauts become weightless and float about their spacecraft as if gravity did not exist. In fact, gravity is still pulling the astronauts and their spacecraft towards Earth, but as the spacecraft travels forwards, it is also continually "falling" as it follows the curve of Earth. The craft and astronauts are in a state of free-fall, but falling without ever reaching the ground.

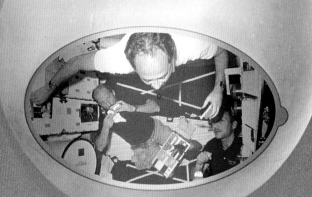

CENTRE OF GRAVITY

An object's centre of gravity is the point at which it balances. An object with a low centre of gravity is more stable – so a sports car is more stable than a double-decker bus. The secret to driving a car on two wheels is to ensure that the centre of gravity remains above the wheels – any further over and the car will tip over.

EINSTEIN'S THEORY

German-born scientist Albert Einstein (1879–1955) developed a theory of relativity to explain how gravity works in space. He compared space and time to a sheet of stretchy rubber, which everything in the Universe rests on. Massive objects like stars make a big dip in the rubber. Less massive objects like planets fall into these large dips and so are trapped orbiting stars. The dips create the effect we call gravity.

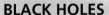

AIR RESISTANCE

In a vacuum, gravity causes everything to fall at the same speed. However, if an apple and a feather are dropped from the same height in Earth's atmosphere, the apple will fall faster. As they fall, objects are slowed down by air resistance, created by friction between the air and the object. The speed an object falls depends on the balance between gravity's pull and the air's resistance.

BLACK HOLES

When a massive star dies, its core may collapse. As it shrinks, the core becomes ever denser and forms a region of space called a black hole. The force of gravity in a black hole is so strong that anything entering it is swallowed up, including light. Although invisible, black holes can be identified by the effect their gravity has on everything around them. Material being sucked into the hole heats up, emitting X-rays that can be detected by X-ray telescopes.

DYNAMICS

Every object tends to resist any change in its speed or direction. This property is called inertia. An object's motion is only changed when a force, such as a push or pull, is applied. A heavy, fast-moving object is described as having lots of momentum. The more momentum something has, the more difficult it is to stop. A moving object also possesses kinetic (movement) energy. The principles of dynamics, or how forces make things move, were explained by scientist Isaac Newton (1642–1727) in his three laws of motion.

NEWTON'S FIRST LAW

The first law states that an object will stay still or continue to move at the same speed and in the same direction unless a force acts upon it. When cars approach each other in a crash-test laboratory, they move forward steadily. The dummies inside each car are carried along at the same speed as the car.

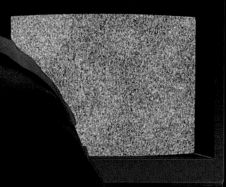

❶ Inertia If the dummy has no seatbelt, inertia will keep it moving forward at the same speed until it is stopped by a part of the car that has been slowed down by the impact – such as the windscreen.

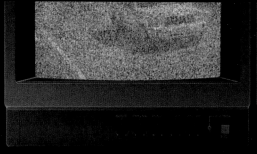

NEWTON'S SECOND LAW

This states that when a force acts on an object, it makes the object change speed or direction. As the two cars collide, the front of each car exerts a force on the other car, slowing it down. The dummies inside are slowed down as they experience the force of the seatbelt.

NEWTON'S THIRD LAW

The third law of motion says that when a force acts on an object, the object reacts by pulling or pushing back with equal force, but in the opposite direction. So, it is impossible for one car to push on the other without experiencing a push back with equal force.

❷ Collision When two cars collide, kinetic energy is converted to other forms of energy, such as heat and sound, as the fronts of the cars crumple. This is called an inelastic collision.

❸ Momentum If a heavy lorry collides with a car, the lorry's greater momentum pushes the car along for some distance, but cars of equal weight and speed are halted, as their equal but opposite momenta cancel out.

MAGNETISM

Magnetism is an invisible force that attracts (draws towards itself) or repels (pushes away) certain materials. Any object that can attract or repel magnetic materials is classed as a magnet. The area around a magnet that is influenced by its magnetism is referred to as its magnetic field. It is strongest at the "poles" (usually the ends) of the magnet. Opposite magnetic poles will attract each other, while like magnetic poles repel each other. Planet Earth has its own magnetic field, driven by the molten material that circulates beneath the surface.

Near this magnet the scissors are temporarily magnetic so there is attraction

The two silver ends of a horseshoe magnet are the north and south pole

The magnetic north pole is in northern Canada, about 1,600 km (1,000 miles) from the geographic North Pole

❶ MAGNETIC MATERIALS

When an unmagnetized magnetic material is placed in a magnetic field it becomes a magnet itself, either temporarily or permanently. Materials such as nickel and iron are easily magnetized and demagnetized and are known as soft magnets. Alloys (mixtures) of iron, nickel, and aluminium are difficult to demagnetize and are referred to as hard, or permanent magnets.

❷ ATTRACTION

Iron filings sprinkled around a magnet will reveal the magnetic force field in action. If you bring two magnets together so that a north pole is facing a south pole, then the filings will bridge the gap, showing attraction.

❸ REPULSION

If you bring two magnets together with their two north poles or two south poles facing, you can feel the pushing force between them as their magnetic fields come into contact and the like poles repel each other.

❹ MAGNETIC STRENGTH

The strength of the attraction that holds all these objects together can also be used in industry. Large cranes with a lifting magnet are used to move tonnes of scrap metals and old cars, as well as to load heavy machine parts.

North pole

South pole

Iron filings join because opposite poles attract

North pole

Iron filings push away because like poles repel

North pole

North pole

The red needle on this compass points to the magnetic north pole

This MRI scan shows soft tissues as well as bones

Steel pins are attracted by the magnetic force of the lodestone

● LODESTONE

Nearly 3,000 years ago, people discovered that a strange type of rock could attract iron objects. This rock, called lodestone or magnetite, is a form of iron oxide with strong natural magnetism. The first compasses were made from lodestone.

● MAGNETIC SCAN

In a magnetic resonance imaging (MRI) scan, a patient is placed in a magnetic field and radio waves are passed through the body, causing molecules within body tissues to vibrate. Different tissues vibrate in different ways, allowing each part to be seen clearly.

● MAGNETIC EARTH

Electric currents circulating inside Earth as the planet rotates cause it to act like a giant magnet, with a magnetic field that extends thousands of kilometres into space. Earth has magnetic poles, which are near, but not the same as, the geographic North and South Poles.

● COMPASS

In use from around the 12th century, a compass contains a magnetic needle, which is free to rotate on a pivot. The compass needle will always align itself with Earth's magnetic field, so that its needle points towards the magnetic north pole.

• Electricity is generated when coils of wire are rotated in a magnetic field. This forces electrons along the wire to form an electric current.

• In power stations, the force to rotate the coils is provided by water power (hydroelectricity), or by steam heated by oil, coal, gas, or the process of nuclear fission.

• A current only flows if it has a circuit to travel around. A current needs a conductor to flow through, something to power, and, usually, an energy source to drive the current.

• All conductors have a certain resistance to the flow of an electric current. When a conductor resists the current, the electrical energy is turned into heat.

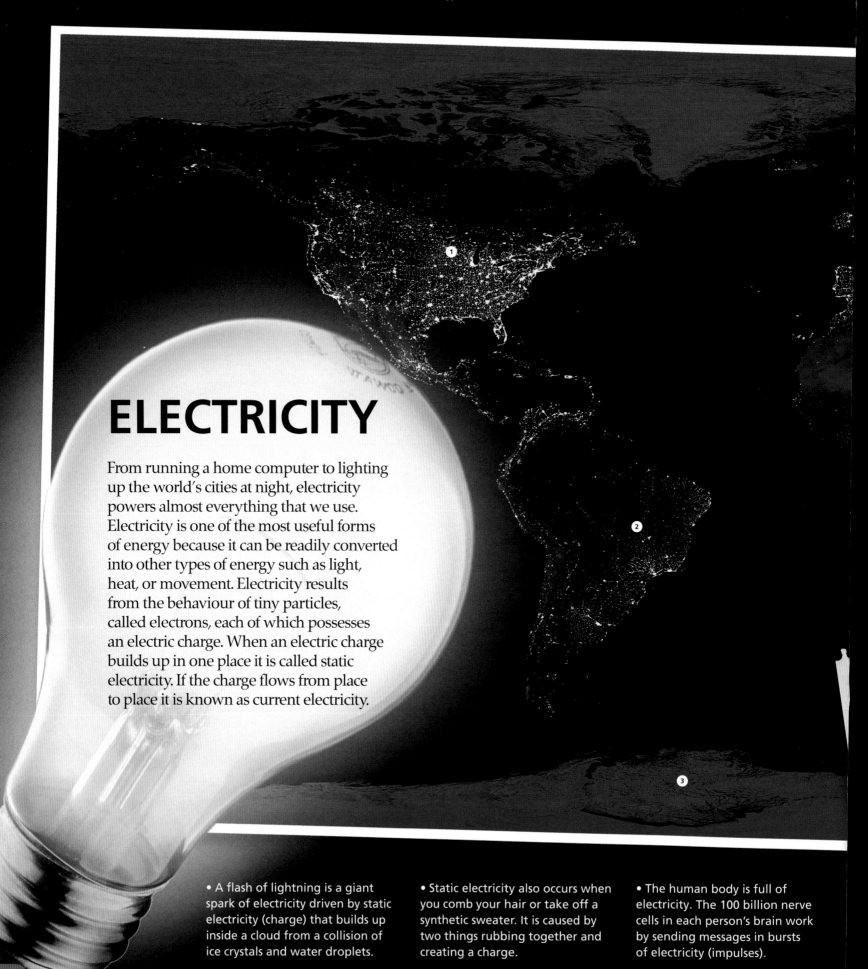

ELECTRICITY

From running a home computer to lighting up the world's cities at night, electricity powers almost everything that we use. Electricity is one of the most useful forms of energy because it can be readily converted into other types of energy such as light, heat, or movement. Electricity results from the behaviour of tiny particles, called electrons, each of which possesses an electric charge. When an electric charge builds up in one place it is called static electricity. If the charge flows from place to place it is known as current electricity.

• A flash of lightning is a giant spark of electricity driven by static electricity (charge) that builds up inside a cloud from a collision of ice crystals and water droplets.

• Static electricity also occurs when you comb your hair or take off a synthetic sweater. It is caused by two things rubbing together and creating a charge.

• The human body is full of electricity. The 100 billion nerve cells in each person's brain work by sending messages in bursts of electricity (impulses).

- Materials with electrons that cannot move are unable to conduct electricity and are known as insulators. Electric wire is insulated with plastic or rubber.

- Electricity leaves power stations through metal cables on tall pylons. The power is sent out at a much higher voltage than is used in most homes.

- Before arriving in a city, the voltage is reduced by a transformer at a sub-station. It then travels across the city in cables under the streets.

- In some earthquake-prone cities, such as Tokyo, Japan, electricity is carried in overhead cables. Underground cables would be too prone to earthquake damage.

1 North America The USA has less than 5 per cent of the world's population, but uses more than 15 per cent of the world's electricity, most of it generated in coal-fired power stations. In Canada, hydroelectric generation accounts for more than half of all electricity generated.

2 South America Some countries in this continent produce electricity using ethanol, a renewable "green" fuel made from the byproducts of sugar cane.

3 Antarctica The only people who live here are scientific researchers. Their electricity is mostly provided by diesel-powered generators, but also increasingly from wind and solar power.

4 Europe A variety of different sources are used to generate electricity in Europe, including nuclear power. France relies on nuclear power stations for more than three-quarters of its electricity.

5 Africa Less than half of the 1.3 billion people living in Africa have access to electricity, and in many countries people suffer from frequent power outages. Solar and geothermal generation holds great promise for the future.

6 Asia In recent years, China, Japan, and India have accounted for much of the increase in electricity generation and use. China relies on coal-fired power stations, but is rapidly increasing its use of solar power.

7 Australia Australia relies on coal-fired power stations for about half of its electricity, but in New Zealand 97% is generated by hydroelectric power.

NIGHT LIGHT
This image was compiled from pictures taken by a military weather satellite. It shows how light from the world's cities is visible from space.

ELECTROMAGNETIC SPECTRUM

Energy spreads in waves of electromagnetic radiation, like the ripples on a pond. It travels through space at the speed of light, around 300,000 km/sec (186,000 miles/sec). Although energy always travels through space at the same speed, its wavelength (the distance between any two peaks or troughs of the waves) can vary. Short waves, such as X-rays, carry high amounts of energy that can penetrate the human body, while longer, lower energy waves, such as light, cannot. Apart from visible light, all electromagnetic waves are invisible. Together these waves make up a continuous band of energy known as the electromagnetic spectrum.

VISIBLE LIGHT
The Sun emits most of its energy as visible light, which can be split into the colours of the rainbow. Earth's atmosphere allows visible light through, while blocking more harmful wavelengths. Visible light is vital for life. Without it, plants could not grow.

ULTRAVIOLET RAYS
With a slightly shorter wavelength than visible violet light, ultraviolet rays also carry more energy than visible light. Ultraviolet rays emitted by the Sun and tanning beds can damage skin not protected by sunblock, causing sunburn.

X-RAYS
These high-energy waves can pass through materials such as flesh and suitcase plastic, but not through bone or metal objects. This makes them a valuable tool for examining bones in hospitals and searching for weapons in airports.

GAMMA RAYS
Gamma rays are produced by radioactivity, such as a nuclear explosion. They have a short wavelength and carry large amounts of energy. They are very harmful to humans, but are used to treat cancer by killing damaged cells.

WAVELENGTHS
The difference between wavelengths at either end of the electromagnetic spectrum is immense. The wavelength of gamma rays is only a fraction of the size of an atom, while radio waves at the opposite end of the spectrum can be thousands of kilometres long.

INFRARED RAYS

Just beyond the visible red in the spectrum is infrared, which can be felt as heat. Often, when heat energy moves it is transported by infrared waves. Infrared satellite images of Earth's surface are used by weather forecasters to determine temperatures.

MICROWAVES

These have much longer wavelengths than visible light. Longer wavelength microwaves are used in a microwave oven. Shorter wavelength microwaves are used in radar systems that help ships and planes navigate by locating traffic and obstacles.

RADIO WAVES

These are the longest in the spectrum. Many forms of communication, such as TV, mobile phones, and radio, use radio waves, with different wavelengths carrying different signals. Radio waves from outer space are picked up by radio telescopes and used in studies of the Universe.

VIOLET

Light at the violet end of the visible spectrum has a shorter wavelength and higher frequency than light at the red end of the spectrum.

SYMBOLISM

We use colours as symbols to represent different ideas in culture and religion. However, the meaning of colours may vary. For example, in some cultures brides wear red, whereas in others they wear white.

Gifts of money are given in red packets at Chinese New Year, because red is the colour of luck

COLOUR

Light is the visible part of the electromagnetic spectrum. We see different wavelengths of light as different colours. The surfaces of objects absorb some wavelengths and reflect others. A white object looks white because it reflects all the wavelengths that fall on it. A black object absorbs all the wavelengths, so it appears dark.

Red food packaging is believed to cause feelings of hunger

COMPLEMENTARY COLOURS

If the colours of the spectrum are arranged in order on a colour wheel, colours located opposite each other, such as orange and blue, are called complementary colours. When complementary colours are presented side by side, they appear at their brightest.

Yellow New York taxis are easy to spot in the distance

REAL COLOURS

The light reflected from an object is made up of a range of wavelengths. An object that looks yellow might reflect 80 per cent of the light at the yellow wavelength, but also smaller amounts of other colour wavelengths.

COLOUR BLINDNESS

Our ability to detect colours depends on cells on the eye's retina, which are sensitive to specific wavelengths of light. The cells that detect certain parts of the spectrum are missing or inactive in a colour-blind person.

A yellow object absorbs all the wavelengths except yellow, which it reflects back to our eyes. The band of visible colours that make up light is known as the spectrum. Each shade blends into the next, but we usually divide the spectrum into seven colours: red, orange, yellow, green, blue, indigo, and violet.

INTENSITY

On a sunny day, things appear colourful because our eyes can see differences in the wavelengths of light. On a dark day, less light enters the eyes, so we cannot distinguish wavelengths as easily and colours look dull.

SPLITTING WHITE LIGHT

When white light passes through a block of glass called a prism, different wavelengths refract (bend) different amounts, so the light splits showing the colours of the spectrum. When light passes through raindrops this effect creates a rainbow.

Green plants contain a green pigment called chlorophyll

MACHINES

Simple machines make it easier for people to perform tasks, such as lifting or pulling, which would be difficult to do with muscle strength alone. There are six types of simple machines: the wheel, the screw, the lever, the pulley, the inclined plane, and the wedge. These machines change a force into a bigger or smaller force, or alter the direction in which a force acts. The most basic tools, such as crowbars or spades, are simple machines.

❶ WHEEL (GEAR)

Gears are toothed wheels that mesh and turn together, changing the strength, speed, or direction of a force. A force on the axle of a small gear driving a large gear will lead to a bigger turning force on the axle of the large gear.

❷ SCREW

The spiral thread on a screw changes a turning force into a much stronger up or down force. The screw has to be turned many times to create just a small up or down movement.

❸ LEVER

Most levers magnify the force applied to them, making it easier to move a load. A lever turns around a fixed point called a pivot. The further from the pivot the force is applied, the easier it is to move the load.

The second lever falls, bringing the wedge down onto the tomato

The downward motion of the wedge splits the tomato in two

❻

The turning motion of the wheels is converted into linear motion, moving the cart up the slope

❺

❼

❹ PULLEY

A pulley is a rope looped around a wheel to make a load easier to lift or move. The more ropes and wheels are used, the less force is needed to lift the load, but the further the rope has to be pulled.

❺ INCLINED PLANE

This is a flat surface with ends at different heights. Moving an object up an inclined plane reduces the amount of force needed to lift it up, but increases the distance it has to travel.

❻ WEDGE

This triangular object is used as a blade to split something or inserted under an object to lift it. As a downward force is exerted on the wedge, its widening shape produces a sideways force on the object.

❼ CART WHEELS

These wheels allow the cart to move smoothly up the ramp. Unlike gear wheels (1), these are not classed as a machine, because they do not change the size of the force applied to them to help do something.

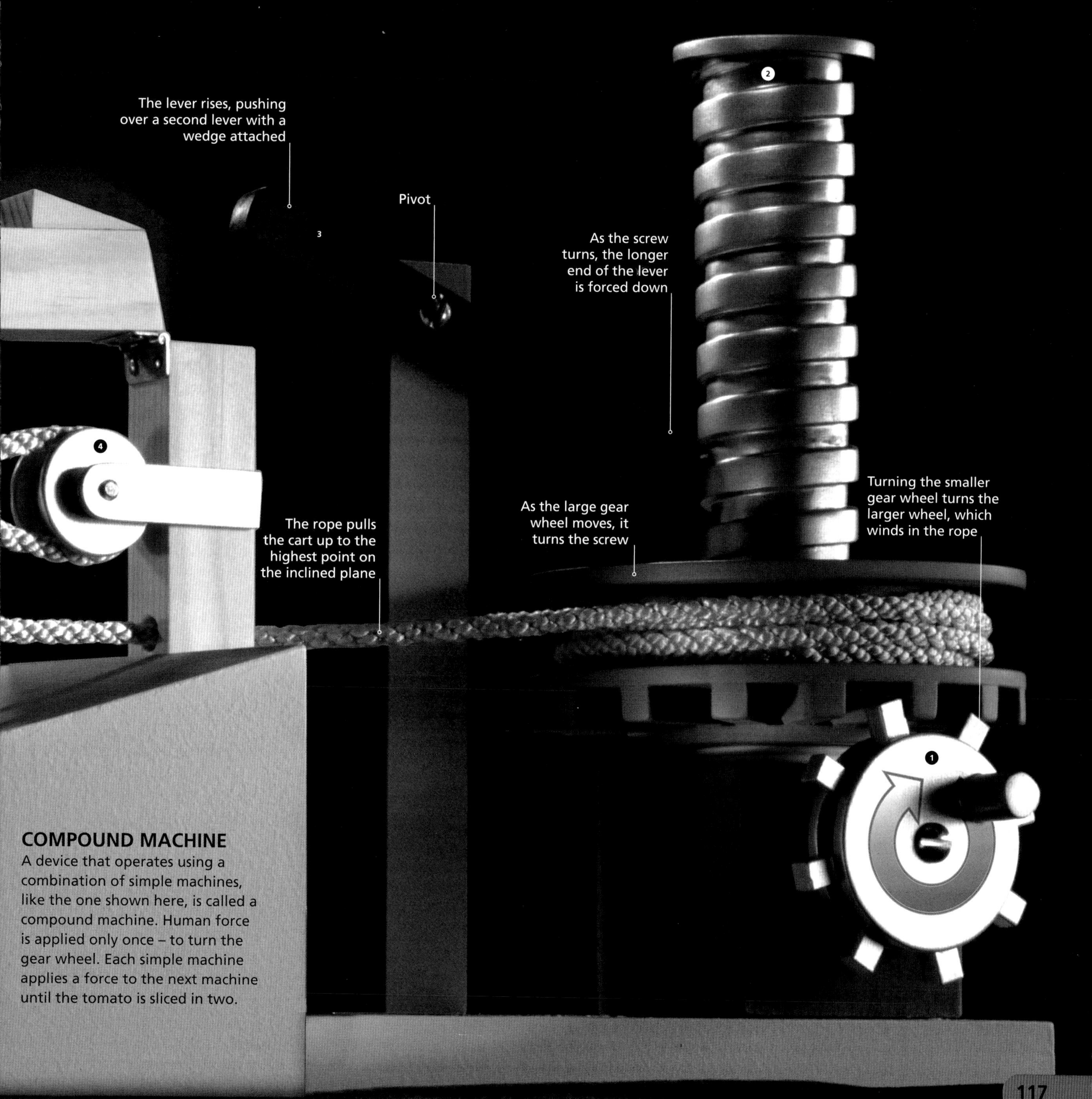

The lever rises, pushing over a second lever with a wedge attached

Pivot

3

As the screw turns, the longer end of the lever is forced down

Turning the smaller gear wheel turns the larger wheel, which winds in the rope

The rope pulls the cart up to the highest point on the inclined plane

As the large gear wheel moves, it turns the screw

COMPOUND MACHINE

A device that operates using a combination of simple machines, like the one shown here, is called a compound machine. Human force is applied only once – to turn the gear wheel. Each simple machine applies a force to the next machine until the tomato is sliced in two.

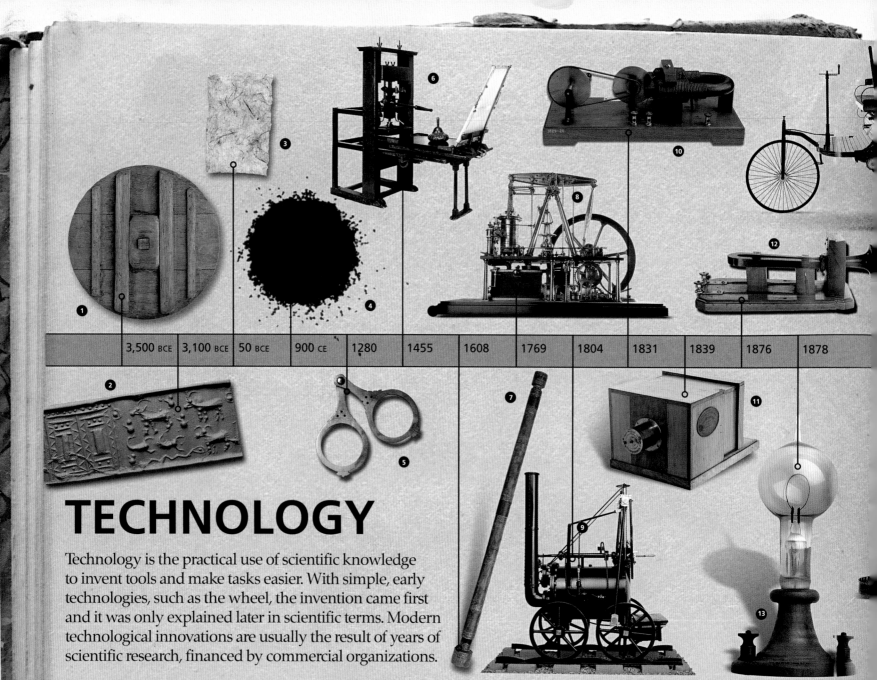

	3,500 BCE	3,100 BCE	50 BCE	900 CE	1280	1455	1608	1769	1804	1831	1839	1876	1878

TECHNOLOGY

Technology is the practical use of scientific knowledge to invent tools and make tasks easier. With simple, early technologies, such as the wheel, the invention came first and it was only explained later in scientific terms. Modern technological innovations are usually the result of years of scientific research, financed by commercial organizations.

❶ Wheel The first wheels were used in Mesopotamia (now Iraq).They were made from planks nailed together to form a circle.

❷ Writing In Mesopotamia, records of accounts and lists of goods were scratched on clay tablets, and people used seals with raised images to mark personal property.

❸ Paper The process of paper-making was also invented in China. Rags and plant fibres were mixed with water, beaten to a pulp, then spread out to dry into a sheet.

❹ Gunpowder The explosive properties of gunpowder were first used by the Chinese to produce fireworks and dramatic bangs to frighten enemies rather than kill them.

❺ Spectacles In the 11th century, the Chinese found that curved pieces of glass (lenses) could bend light. Spectacles were not produced until almost 300 years later.

❻ Printing The printing press developed by Johannes Gutenberg used a system of movable type – individual metal letters made quickly and cheaply – allowing books to be mass-produced for the first time.

❼ Telescope The first telescope was a refracting telescope that used two lenses to focus light from distant objects.

❽ Steam engine James Watt's rotary steam engine provided the power for the factories and mines of the Industrial Revolution by converting the energy in steam into motion.

❾ Railway locomotive The first railway locomotive used a high-pressure steam engine to move a train along rails.

❿ Electric generator Michael Faraday invented the first electric motor, which used electricity to produce motion. He then reversed this process, using motion to produce electricity, thus inventing the electric generator.

⓫ Photography The first practical photographic process was invented by Louis Daguerre. Known as the Daguerreotype, it used a copper plate coated with silver and light-sensitive chemicals to capture the image.

⓬ Telephone Alexander Graham Bell invented the telephone after discovering that voice vibrations could be converted to electrical signals, sent along a wire, and converted back into sound vibrations at the other end.

⓭ Light bulb Joseph Swan and Thomas Edison simultaneously came up with the light bulb, which works by causing a metal filament to glow when an electric current passes through it.

⓮ Petrol-engine motor car The first motor car with an internal combustion engine powered by petrol had a U-shaped steel frame and three wheels.

⓯ Cinema Brothers Louis and Auguste Lumière invented a combined camera and projector they

1885	1895	1903	1906	1920	1926	1947	1958	1962	1977	1979	1982	2007	2011

called the *cinématographe*, which projected moving images onto a screen.

🔟 **Aeroplane** Wilbur and Orville Wright built the first successful heavier-than-air, powered aircraft. Their first flight lasted only 12 seconds.

🔢 **Triode valve** First designed to control electric current, the triode valve went on to be used as an amplifier for radio and TV signals, and as "switches" in computers.

🔢 **Radio broadcast** The first public radio broadcasts were heard in 1906. By the mid 1920s, people were buying radio sets for their homes.

🔢 **Television transmission** John Logie Baird produced the first television transmission using a series of spinning discs to produce the image. This mechanical device was soon overtaken by the electronic cathode ray tube.

🔢 **Transistor** The transistor did the same job as a triode valve, but it was smaller, more reliable, and used less power, paving the way for more compact electronic devices.

🔢 **Microchip** This invention integrated thousands of transistors into single miniature chips of silicon, replacing mechanical control devices in household goods and bulky circuits in computers.

🔢 **Communications satellite** The launch of the first communications satellite, Telstar, allowed live television programmes and telephone calls to be transmitted around the world by bouncing signals off the orbiting space satellite to receiver dishes on the ground.

🔢 **Personal computer** The first successful desktop computer, Apple II, had an integrated keyboard, which connected to a television.

🔢 **Mobile phone** Calls are transmitted via a network of short-range local transmitters using radio waves instead of cables.

🔢 **Compact disc** The CD uses a laser to read sound information recorded as a series of pits under the disc's smooth surface.

🔢 **iPhone** As technology advances, electronic devices become smaller and more intricate. Gadgets, such as Apple's iPhone, are designed to perform many different functions, including playing music and videos, storing photos, and accessing the Internet.

🔢 **3-D printer** Unlike ordinary printers, these printers can create three-dimensional (3-D) objects, which have width and height, as well as length, or depth. Regular printers use ink, but 3-D printers mostly use layers of melted plastic to create a model. Metal, chocolate, or even concrete can be used as material to create models.

ROBOTS

A robot is a machine that appears to think and act for itself. The simplest type of robot is a mechanical toy, or automaton, which has been programmed to perform a series of actions that usually have no real function. Some robots are remote-controlled devices, guided at a distance by a human operator. The most complex robots have artificial intelligence – an ability to make decisions for themselves, solve problems, and learn.

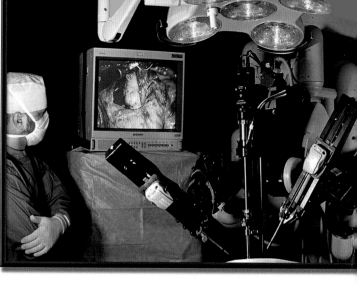

The lips and eyes move in a natural manner

This humanoid robot can hold basic conversations and make simple facial expressions

A team of engineers at the University of Science and Technology of China took three years to design Jia Jia

iCub uses its audio, visual, and tactile sensors to process information

◄ HUMANOIDS
Humanoid robots, such as Jia Jia, iCub, and NAO, are created to resemble human beings. They have a head and a face, and while some walk on two legs, others may roll on tracks or wheels.

NAO's flexibility allows it to play football and perform complex dance routines

▲ SURGEON ROBOT
Surgical robots, such as da Vinci, can insert minute instruments and a viewer called an endoscope into an incision just 1 cm (0.4 in) wide. The surgeon studies the operation site on a screen and moves the robot's instruments by remote control.

Mitsubishi's seabream fish mimics the energy-efficient motion of a real fish

▲ ANIMAL ROBOTS
Robots that imitate the way different types of animals move and behave are vital steps in the development of ranges of movement that may be needed in robots of the future.

Spinybot II has spiny feet to grip onto walls, imitating the actions of climbing insects

Sony's AIBO has complex software that makes it move and behave like a dog

INDUSTRIAL ARMS ▶
Most industrial robots are computer-controlled mechanical arms. They do jobs that would be difficult or dangerous for humans, or jobs that require constant repeated actions. A robot can do all these jobs more quickly or accurately than a human – and without needing to rest.

The task of welding in a car factory is carried out by robots

▲ SPACE TRAVELLERS
In space, robot spacecraft and surface vehicles called rovers, such as Mars 2020, are sent to explore places that are too dangerous to send human astronauts. The movements of these robots are pre-programmed or directed from Earth, though the rovers also use camera data to avoid obstacles.

HELP AT HOME ▶
Although no one yet has an android servant doing all the domestic chores, some robots are at work in homes, performing repetitive jobs such as vacuuming floors and mowing lawns. These robots are programmed to avoid hazards in their paths.

The Roomba Intelligent FloorVac has sensors to plot its vacuuming route

▼ HELPING AT WORK
Robots are increasingly equipped to help humans carry out tasks that may be boring, repetitive, or dangerous. They work independently, guided by sensors and cameras, and can sustain themselves in bad weather, tight spaces, and rugged terrain.

iRobot's CoWorker Office robot takes pictures with a camera on its rotating neck

MILITARY ROBOTS ▶
Robot vehicles are useful in warfare because they can enter dangerous situations without risking lives. Robot devices conduct surveillance over enemy land and can find and dispose of bombs and landmines while the operator remains at a safe distance.

HOBO (Hazardous Ordnance Bomb Operator) carries equipment to defuse an explosive device or explode it safely

Robug III's legs allow it to cross uneven surfaces to investigate hazardous situations with an onboard camera

TRANSPORT

The world today is constantly on the move. It is impossible to imagine life without the planes, trains, ships, and cars that transport people and goods, every day. Each of these incredible machines has been specifically designed to travel over land, through the air, and under or over the water.

BY ROAD ▼

Most road vehicles have an internal-combustion engine, which burns fuel to make the power that turns the wheels. In a car, the engine is usually in the front and drives either the front or the back wheels. In a motorbike, the engine is placed between the two wheels.

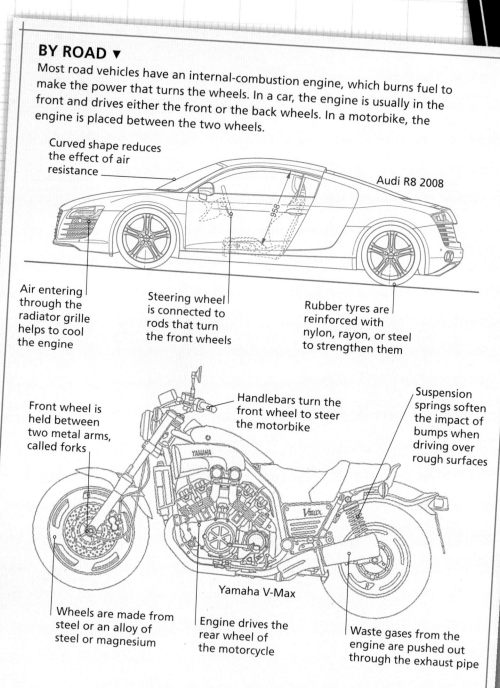

Curved shape reduces the effect of air resistance

Audi R8 2008

Air entering through the radiator grille helps to cool the engine

Steering wheel is connected to rods that turn the front wheels

Rubber tyres are reinforced with nylon, rayon, or steel to strengthen them

Front wheel is held between two metal arms, called forks

Handlebars turn the front wheel to steer the motorbike

Suspension springs soften the impact of bumps when driving over rough surfaces

Yamaha V-Max

Wheels are made from steel or an alloy of steel or magnesium

Engine drives the rear wheel of the motorcycle

Waste gases from the engine are pushed out through the exhaust pipe

BY AIR ▼

To travel through the air, aircraft must overcome the force of gravity, which pulls them towards the ground. They achieve this with the help of curved wings and rotors, which produce an upward force called lift as they pass through the air.

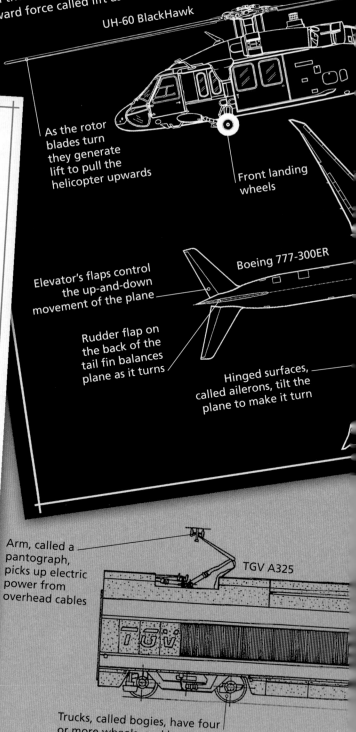

UH-60 BlackHawk

As the rotor blades turn they generate lift to pull the helicopter upwards

Front landing wheels

Boeing 777-300ER

Elevator's flaps control the up-and-down movement of the plane

Rudder flap on the back of the tail fin balances plane as it turns

Hinged surfaces, called ailerons, tilt the plane to make it turn

Arm, called a pantograph, picks up electric power from overhead cables

TGV A325

Trucks, called bogies, have four or more wheels, and large shock-absorbers to give a smooth ride

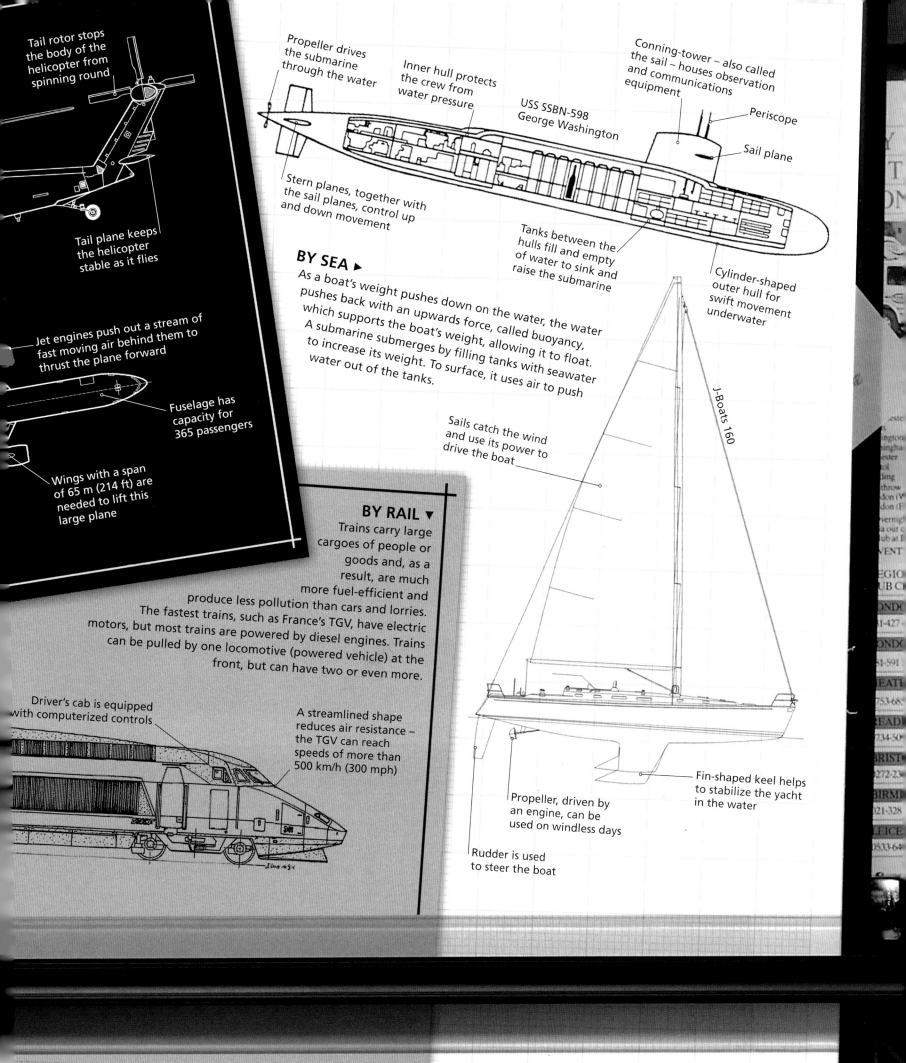

Tail rotor stops the body of the helicopter from spinning round

Tail plane keeps the helicopter stable as it flies

Jet engines push out a stream of fast moving air behind them to thrust the plane forward

Fuselage has capacity for 365 passengers

Wings with a span of 65 m (214 ft) are needed to lift this large plane

Propeller drives the submarine through the water

Inner hull protects the crew from water pressure

USS SSBN-598 George Washington

Conning-tower – also called the sail – houses observation and communications equipment

Periscope

Sail plane

Stern planes, together with the sail planes, control up and down movement

Tanks between the hulls fill and empty of water to sink and raise the submarine

Cylinder-shaped outer hull for swift movement underwater

BY SEA ▶

As a boat's weight pushes down on the water, the water pushes back with an upwards force, called buoyancy, which supports the boat's weight, allowing it to float. A submarine submerges by filling tanks with seawater to increase its weight. To surface, it uses air to push water out of the tanks.

Sails catch the wind and use its power to drive the boat

J-Boats 160

BY RAIL ▼

Trains carry large cargoes of people or goods and, as a result, are much more fuel-efficient and produce less pollution than cars and lorries. The fastest trains, such as France's TGV, have electric motors, but most trains are powered by diesel engines. Trains can be pulled by one locomotive (powered vehicle) at the front, but can have two or even more.

Driver's cab is equipped with computerized controls

A streamlined shape reduces air resistance – the TGV can reach speeds of more than 500 km/h (300 mph)

Fin-shaped keel helps to stabilize the yacht in the water

Propeller, driven by an engine, can be used on windless days

Rudder is used to steer the boat

123

SCIENTISTS

Scientists study the Universe in order to find out how and why things happen. There are many different branches of science, such as physics, chemistry, and astronomy. Scientists make careful observations of the phenomena they are studying. They construct possible explanations for their observations, known as theories or hypotheses. Then they experiment to test whether their theories are accurate.

❶ SIR ISAAC NEWTON

English physicist and mathematician Newton (1642–1727) proposed the laws of motion that explain how forces move objects, and went on to devise a theory of gravity. Newton also studied optics, the science of light, and explained how white light is made up of many colours.

❻ BLAISE PASCAL

Frenchman Pascal (1623–62) explored many practical applications of science and mathematics. He invented a mechanical calculator, a device made up of dials and gears, as well as a type of syringe. He also did experiments with air pressure.

❷ MARIE CURIE

Marie Curie (1867–1934) was born in Poland, but carried out her investigations into radioactivity in Paris with her French husband, Pierre. She discovered the elements (substances) polonium and radium in 1898, and won two Nobel Prizes. Marie Curie died of leukaemia, probably due to long exposure to radiation.

❼ GALILEO

Italian astronomer and mathematician, Galileo (1564–1642) was the first person to use a telescope for studying the sky. He discovered the four largest satellites of Jupiter, today known as the Galilean moons.

Pascal's mechanical calculator could only add up, and was not very accurate

The Bunsen burner, an adjustable gas burner used in science experiments, is named after German scientist Robert Bunsen (1811–99)

The unit of electric current known as ampère or amp is named after French scientist André-Marie Ampère (1775–1836)

❸ LUIGI GALVANI

Italian scientist Galvani (1737–98) studied the role of electrical impulses in animal tissue by experimenting on frogs. Although his theory that the electricity was coming from the animal tissue was wrong, his discoveries led to the invention of the battery by Alessandro Volta.

❽ COPERNICUS

Polish astronomer Copernicus (1473–1543) is considered to be the founder of modern astronomy. His studies of the orbits of the planets revealed that the Sun is at the centre of the Solar System. At the time, the predominant view was that Earth was the centre of the Universe.

❹ ALBERT EINSTEIN

Einstein (1879–1955) was born in Germany but after Hitler came to power, he fled to the United States. Einstein revolutionized physics with his studies of relativity, which show how matter, energy, space, and time are connected. Einstein was awarded the Nobel Prize for Physics in 1921.

❾ ALESSANDRO VOLTA

In 1800, research into electric currents led Italian physicist Volta (1745–1827) to invent the battery. Volta's battery, or "voltaic pile" was the first reliable means of producing an electric current, and so made it easier to perform further experiments with electricity.

❺ ALEC JEFFREYS

British geneticist Jeffreys (born 1950) discovered that each individual has certain distinctive patterns of DNA and worked out how to make images of these DNA sequences. He pioneered DNA fingerprinting, used by forensic scientists in criminal investigations to identify people from traces of DNA.

❿ BENJAMIN FRANKLIN

US statesman, writer, and scientist Franklin (1706–90) conducted research into electricity. He proved that lightning is an electrical current and suggested the use of lightning conductors to protect buildings from lightning strikes.

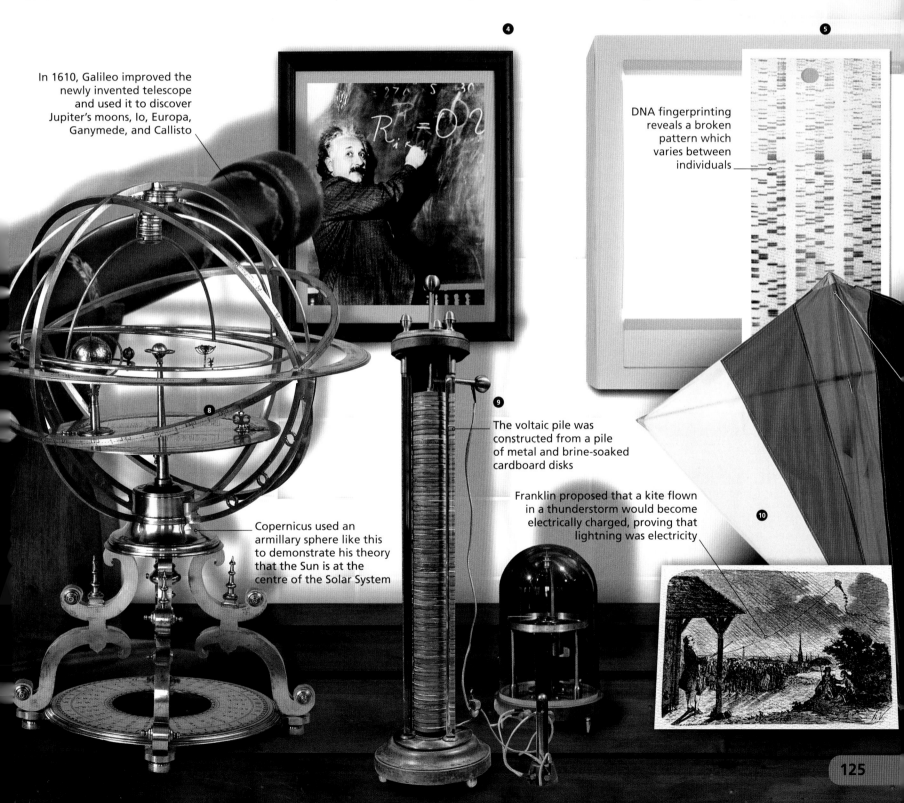

In 1610, Galileo improved the newly invented telescope and used it to discover Jupiter's moons, Io, Europa, Ganymede, and Callisto

DNA fingerprinting reveals a broken pattern which varies between individuals

The voltaic pile was constructed from a pile of metal and brine-soaked cardboard disks

Copernicus used an armillary sphere like this to demonstrate his theory that the Sun is at the centre of the Solar System

Franklin proposed that a kite flown in a thunderstorm would become electrically charged, proving that lightning was electricity

THE FIRST GALAXIES
This view is part of an image recorded by the Hubble Space Telescope that shows about 10,000 galaxies. It is the deepest view ever taken of the Universe, looking back through time to the very first galaxies.

Space

UNIVERSE

The Universe is everything that exists, from the smallest particle on Earth to the vast galaxies of deep space. Every part of it, including space and time, came into existence in the Big Bang – a huge explosion that occurred about 13.8 billion years ago. At that time, the Universe looked nothing like it does today, and it has been expanding, cooling, and changing ever since. The hydrogen and helium of the very young Universe formed stars, which in turn produced all the other elements in today's Universe, including those that make Earth and everything on it, including you.

THE BIG BANG

In the beginning, the Universe was unimaginably small, dense, and incredibly hot. Within a trillionth of a second it ballooned from being smaller than an atom to bigger than a galaxy. It was made of tiny particles of energy that turned to particles of matter. Within three minutes, the Universe was made almost entirely of the nuclei of hydrogen and helium atoms.

13.8
BILLION YEARS AGO

COSMIC BACKGROUND

By looking at the heat left over from the Big Bang, known as the cosmic microwave background radiation, scientists are able to build up a picture of the early Universe. This image is a heat map of the Universe 380,000 years after the Big Bang. It shows that matter was not evenly distributed – the hotter areas (red) are more densely packed regions, where galaxies will form.

380,000
YEARS LATER

Colours denote minute variations in the temperature of the matter – the red areas are the hottest

FORMATION OF GALAXIES

Over millions of years, hydrogen and helium clumped together to form vast clouds. These broke into fragments, which collapsed under gravity and became stars. About one billion years after the Big Bang, a Universe of dwarf galaxies had formed. These collided, merged, and changed shape to become spiral and elliptical galaxies.

12
BILLION YEARS AGO

10
BILLION YEARS AGO

The smallest, reddest galaxies date from about 800 million years after the Big Bang and are the oldest known

Galaxies and stars account for just 15 per cent of all matter in the Universe

BIRTH OF THE SOLAR SYSTEM

The Solar System formed from a cloud of gas and dust within the disc of the Milky Way galaxy. The spinning cloud, known as the solar nebula, collapsed in on itself under the force of gravity. It first formed a central sphere – the young Sun – and then the unused material surrounding the Sun formed the planets, moons, asteroids, and comets.

4.6
BILLION YEARS AGO

YOUNG MILKY WAY

The Milky Way galaxy, the galaxy we live in, formed at the same time as the other galaxies. Not all of today's Milky Way stars existed at that time. Since its beginning, the galaxy has produced stars that shine brightly for millions or billions of years, but that die eventually. Their remains produce a new generation of stars.

Water – in the oceans, lakes, atmosphere, and ice caps – has been a key factor in the developement of life on Earth

TODAY

HOME PLANET

Earth, the third rock planet from the Sun, is the only place in the Universe where life is known to exist. Life started in its oceans at least 3.7 billion years ago. Bacteria-like cells evolved into sea creatures, then land-based plants, and animals. Humans first walked on Earth about 1 million years ago.

Rock from Earth's mantle is thrown out as the asteroid hits the planet

4.5
BILLION YEARS AGO

FORMATION OF THE MOON

Earth formed as ever-larger lumps of unused material collided and joined together. Young Earth was hit by a Mars-sized asteroid. Molten rock from the collision splashed into space. This formed a ring of rubble around Earth which clumped to form a large sphere – Earth's Moon.

129

GALAXIES

A galaxy is a vast group of stars held together by gravity – it is thought that there could be some 2 trillion in our Universe. They are not scattered randomly but exist in clusters, vast distances apart. All the galaxies together take up just two millionths of space.

❶ SIZE
Galaxies are huge. The largest are more than a million light-years across (one light-year is the distance that light travels in a year). The smallest, called dwarf galaxies, are a few thousand light-years wide. Andromeda measures 220,000 light-years from side to side.

❷ SHAPE
A single galaxy is made of billions or trillions of stars arranged in one of four basic shapes: spiral, barred spiral, elliptical, or irregular. Spirals and barred spirals are disc-shaped with arms of stars. In a spiral, such as Andromeda, the arms wind out from a central bulge, while in a barred spiral, they flow from the ends of a central bar of stars. Elliptical galaxies are ball-shaped. Irregular galaxies have no clear shape.

❸ ORBITING STARS
Galaxies do not behave like solid objects. Each star follows its own orbit around the centre of the galaxy. Stars in a spiral galaxy typically take a few hundred million years to make an orbit. Those further away take longer than those closest to the core.

❹ SPIRAL ARMS
Stars exist throughout a spiral galaxy's disc. The arms simply stand out because they are full of very bright young stars.

❺ CORE
The core of a spiral galaxy typically consists of old red and yellow stars, with a supermassive black hole in its centre. Andromeda's black hole is as massive as 30 million Suns.

❻ DUST LANES
Dense clouds and lanes of dust within the galaxy's disc hide stars from view.

▲ **ANDROMEDA GALAXY**
Andromeda is one of the closest galaxies to our own, the Milky Way. It is a spiral galaxy 2.5 million light-years away from us – the most distant object that can be seen by the naked eye from Earth.

❼ DWARF GALAXY
M110 is one of the dwarf elliptical galaxies that orbit Andromeda. It is held in its orbit by Andromeda's gravity.

STAR BIRTH ▼

Stars are formed inside vast clouds of hydrogen gas, such as the Eagle Nebula. A small fragment of cloud collapses under gravity. It becomes increasingly squashed and eventually forms a spinning ball of gas termed a protostar – the first sign of a new star.

Eagle Nebula

Detail of the Eagle Nebula

Trapezium cluster

MID-LIFE STARS ▼

Most stars glow steadily for most of their lives. During this stage they are known as main sequence stars – the Sun is one. Planets orbit around some stars; others, such as Fomalhaut, have discs of dusty material that may form planets.

Fomalhaut

Sirius, the brightest star in Earth's night sky

Jewel Box cluster

Albireo, a double star system

◄ YOUNG STARS

A protostar gets denser and hotter as its gas becomes more squashed. When its core reaches about 10 billion°C (18 billion°F), nuclear reactions start. Hydrogen is converted to helium, energy is produced, and the star shines. Stars born at the same time and from the same region of cloud exist as a cluster. Some clusters, like the two shown here, remain together for millions of years, but eventually their stars drift apart.

STARS

Stars are huge spinning balls of hot, luminous gas. Each one is unique because stars differ in colour, temperature, size, brightness, and mass. Over time, characteristics change and the star evolves from one stage of star life to another. The key to a star's life is its mass – the amount of gas it is made from. Mass determines the star's life span, as well as its other characteristics and how these change.

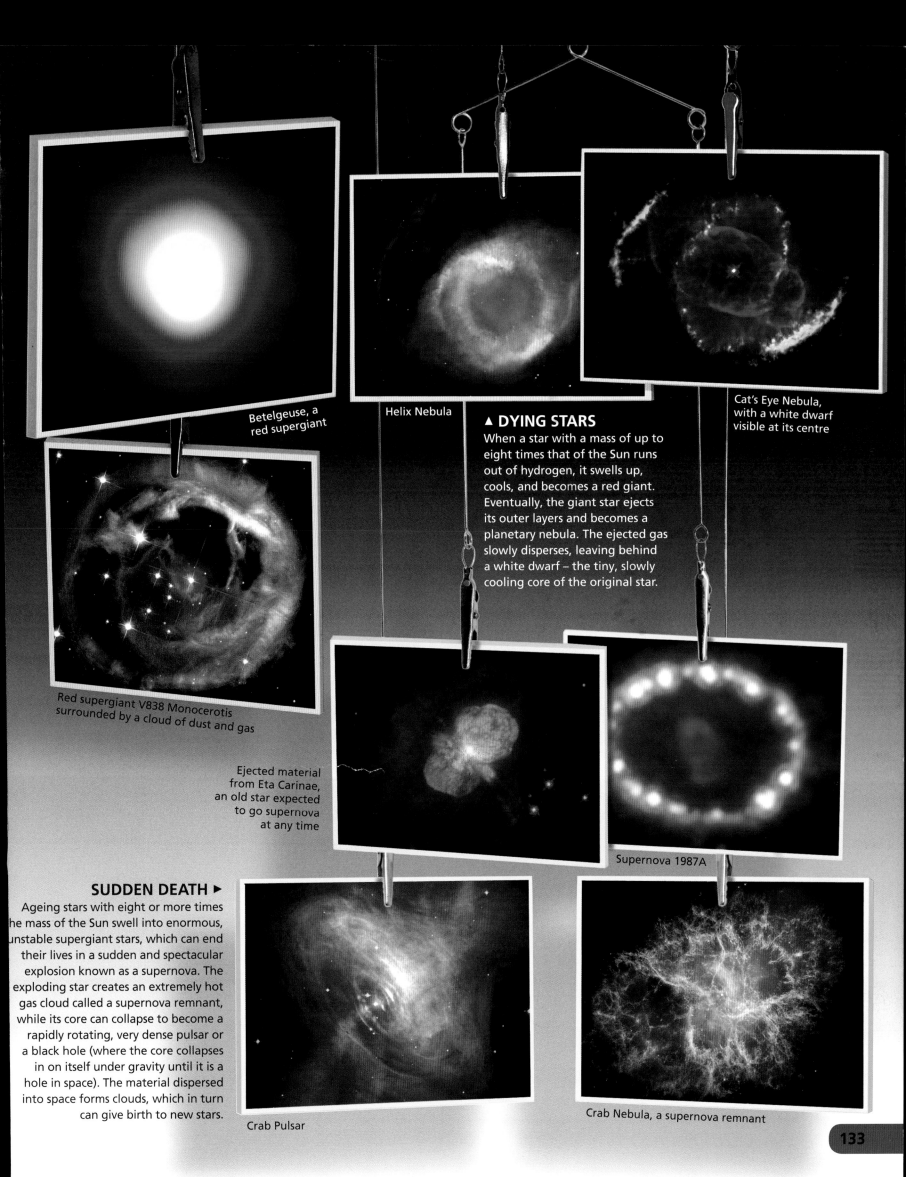

Betelgeuse, a
red supergiant

Helix Nebula

Cat's Eye Nebula,
with a white dwarf
visible at its centre

▲ DYING STARS

When a star with a mass of up to
eight times that of the Sun runs
out of hydrogen, it swells up,
cools, and becomes a red giant.
Eventually, the giant star ejects
its outer layers and becomes a
planetary nebula. The ejected gas
slowly disperses, leaving behind
a white dwarf – the tiny, slowly
cooling core of the original star.

Red supergiant V838 Monocerotis
surrounded by a cloud of dust and gas

Ejected material
from Eta Carinae,
an old star expected
to go supernova
at any time

Supernova 1987A

SUDDEN DEATH ▶

Ageing stars with eight or more times
the mass of the Sun swell into enormous,
unstable supergiant stars, which can end
their lives in a sudden and spectacular
explosion known as a supernova. The
exploding star creates an extremely hot
gas cloud called a supernova remnant,
while its core can collapse to become a
rapidly rotating, very dense pulsar or
a black hole (where the core collapses
in on itself under gravity until it is a
hole in space). The material dispersed
into space forms clouds, which in turn
can give birth to new stars.

Crab Pulsar

Crab Nebula, a supernova remnant

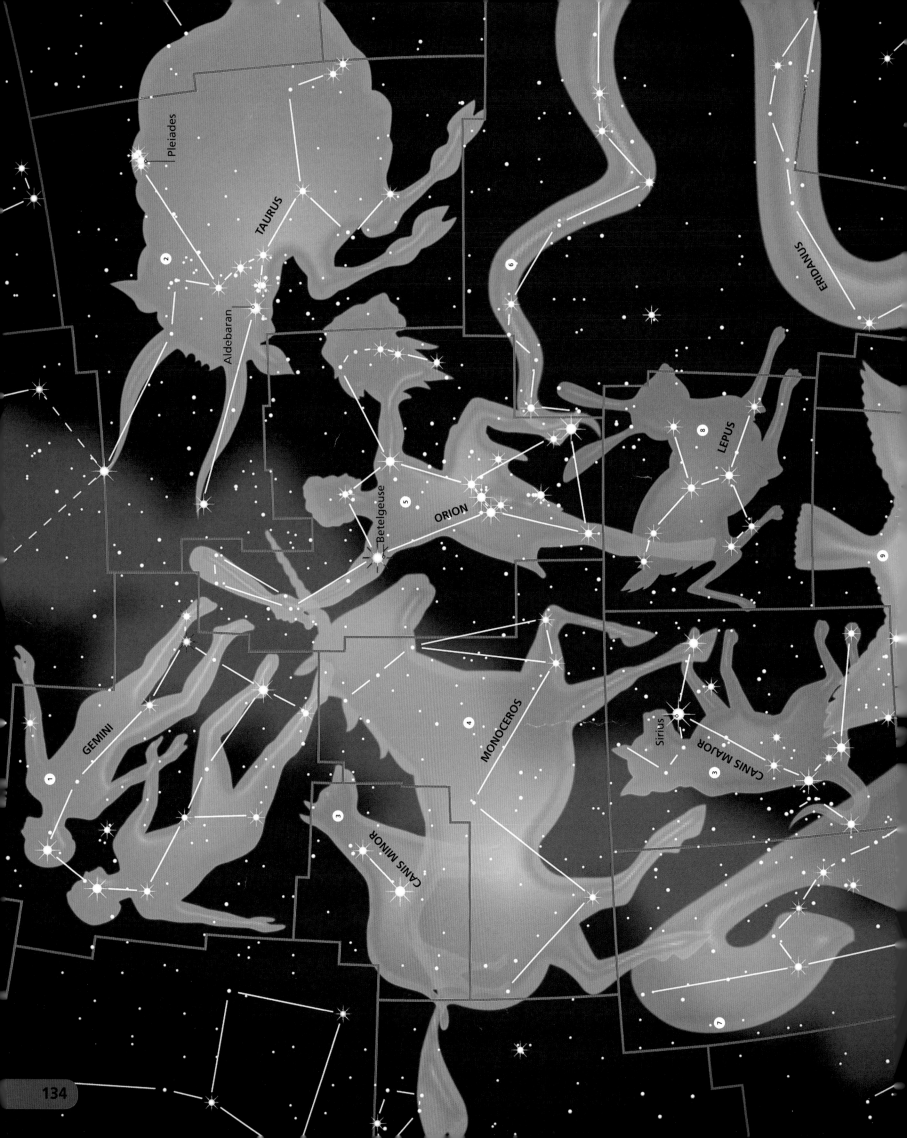

Pleiades

TAURUS

Aldebaran

ERIDANUS

②

⑥

LEPUS

⑧

Betelgeuse

ORION

⑤

GEMINI

①

MONOCEROS

CANIS MAJOR

Sirius

⑨

③

③

CANIS MINOR

④

⑦

134

CONSTELLATIONS

Stargazers have always looked for patterns in the night sky, using imaginary lines to link stars and form the shape of a creature or object. Known as constellations, these patterns help us navigate the sky. The first of them were used about 4,000 years ago. Today, Earth's sky is divided into 88 constellations. Just over half are characters from Ancient Greek mythology, such as Orion and Taurus.

NIGHT SKY

The region of sky above is centred on the constellation of Orion. Orange lines mark a constellation's boundary, white lines link its bright stars, and the imaginary pattern is shown in light blue.

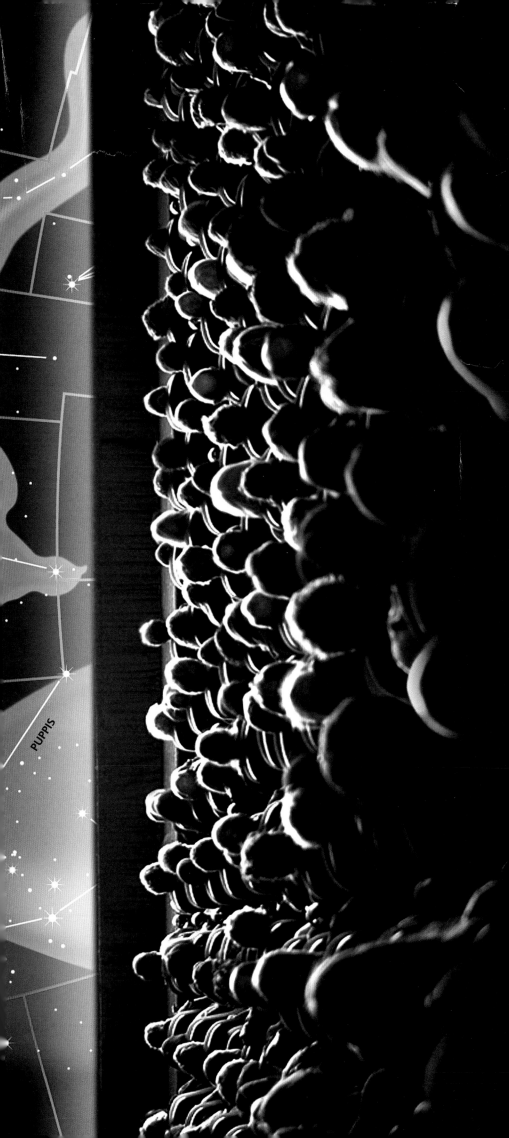

PUPPIS

① GEMINI

The two brightest stars in Gemini mark the heads of the mythological twins Castor (right) and Pollux (left). Castor's head is in fact six stars, and Pollux's is an orange-coloured giant star.

② TAURUS

The head of Taurus the bull is drawn around the Hyades, a V-shaped star cluster. Aldebaran, a red giant star, is the brightest of his eyes. The Pleiades star cluster marks his back.

③ CANIS MINOR AND MAJOR

Orion's dogs are known as Canis Major and Canis Minor. Canis Major, the larger dog, contains Sirius, sometimes called the Dog Star, the brightest star in the night sky.

④ MONOCEROS

The unicorn Monoceros was introduced in 1613. It lies in the path of the Milky Way – the glowing band of stars that stretches across the sky (here from bottom left to top centre).

⑤ ORION

The hunter Orion is visible from nearly everywhere on Earth. His raised arms hold a club and a lion's head. The red star in one of his shoulders is the red supergiant Betelgeuse.

⑥ ERIDANUS

This constellation is the sixth largest in the sky and represents the river into which Phaethon, the son of the Greek sun god Helios, plunged when he lost control of his father's golden chariot.

⑦ PUPPIS

According to Greek myth, Puppis is the stern of the ship sailed by legendary hero Jason. Other parts of the ship are represented by the constellations Carina (the keel) and Vela (the sails).

⑧ LEPUS

Orion's larger dog chases Lepus the hare across the sky. It is one of more than 40 creatures in the night sky. There are also 13 human figures and two centaurs (half-man, half-horse).

⑨ COLUMBA

It is thought that Columba, the dove, is the bird that was sent from Noah's ark to find dry land, as told in the Bible. It may also represent a dove sent out to guide Jason in Ancient Greek myth.

SUN

The Sun is the closest star to Earth and the centre of our Solar System. This vast ball consists of hot luminous gas kept together by gravity. About three quarters is hydrogen and almost all the rest is helium, with small amounts of about 90 other elements. More than half of the gas is squashed in the Sun's core where nuclear reactions convert hydrogen to helium and in the process produce huge amounts of energy. This energy is released through the Sun's surface, most familiarly as heat and light. The Sun has been producing energy in this way for about 4.6 billion years and will do so for another 5 billion or so. This image shows the Sun not as it appears to the human eye, but in ultraviolet light.

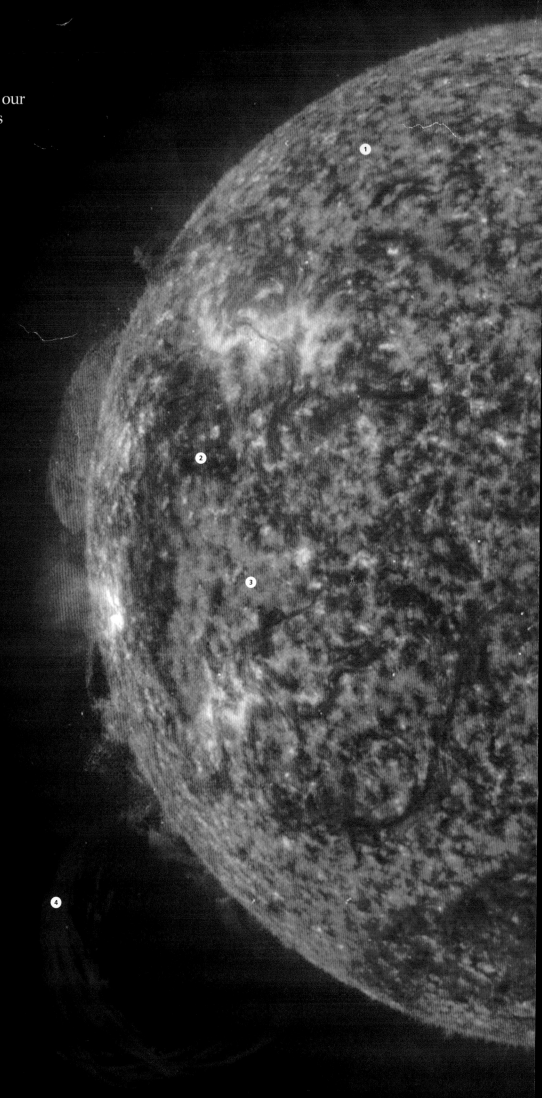

❶ SIZE
The Sun is the largest body in the Solar System. It measures 1.4 million km (870,000 miles) in diameter, which means that 109 Earths could fit across its face. The Sun is made of 330,000 times more material than Earth, and 1.3 million Earths would fit inside it.

❷ PHOTOSPHERE
Like other stars, the Sun is not solid but has a visible surface called the photosphere – a violent place where jets and flares of gas constantly shoot into space. It is made of 1,000-km (620-mile) wide short-lived granules of rising gas, which together resemble orange peel.

❸ TEMPERATURE
The temperature of the surface is 5,500°C (9,900°F), and it is this that gives the Sun its yellow colour. Cooler stars are red, hotter ones are white. Inside is much hotter. The core is 15 million°C (27 million°F) and nuclear reactions here convert 600 million tonnes of hydrogen to helium every second.

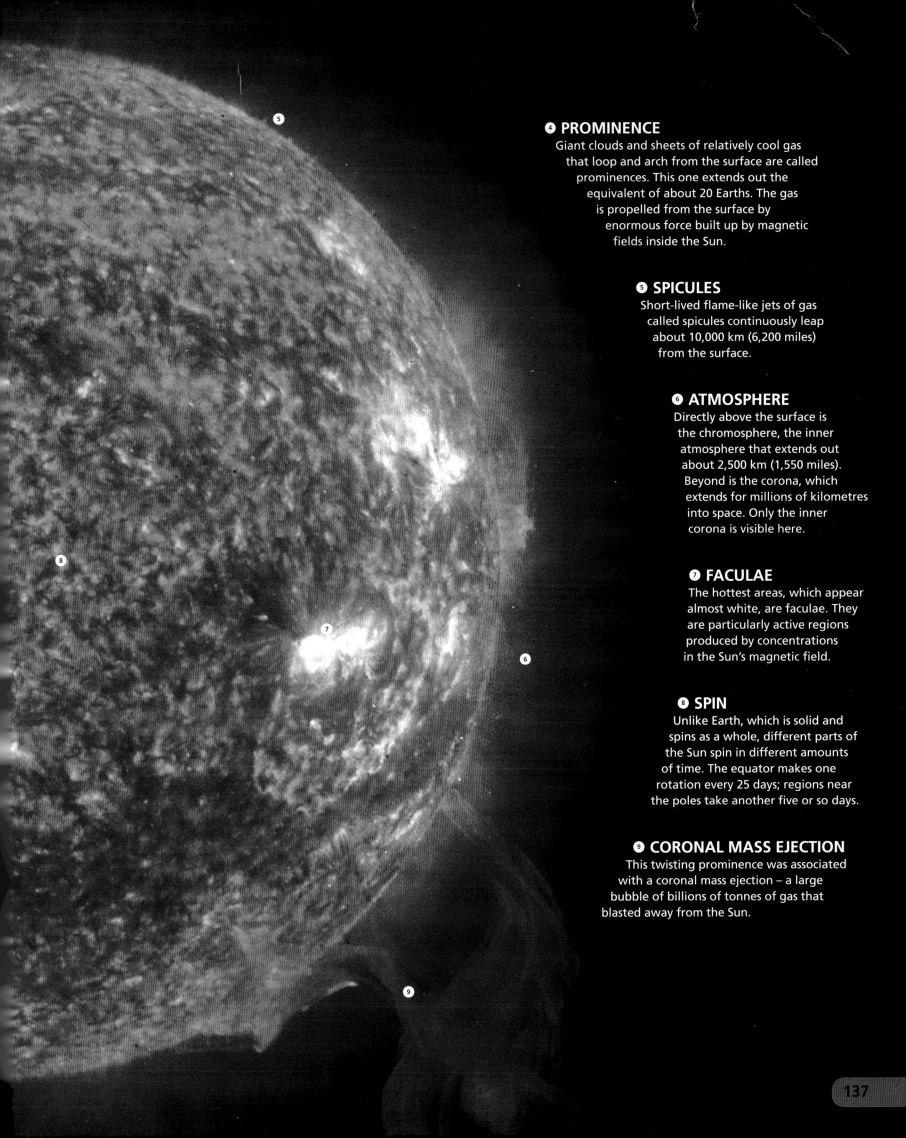

❹ PROMINENCE

Giant clouds and sheets of relatively cool gas that loop and arch from the surface are called prominences. This one extends out the equivalent of about 20 Earths. The gas is propelled from the surface by enormous force built up by magnetic fields inside the Sun.

❺ SPICULES

Short-lived flame-like jets of gas called spicules continuously leap about 10,000 km (6,200 miles) from the surface.

❻ ATMOSPHERE

Directly above the surface is the chromosphere, the inner atmosphere that extends out about 2,500 km (1,550 miles). Beyond is the corona, which extends for millions of kilometres into space. Only the inner corona is visible here.

❼ FACULAE

The hottest areas, which appear almost white, are faculae. They are particularly active regions produced by concentrations in the Sun's magnetic field.

❽ SPIN

Unlike Earth, which is solid and spins as a whole, different parts of the Sun spin in different amounts of time. The equator makes one rotation every 25 days; regions near the poles take another five or so days.

❾ CORONAL MASS EJECTION

This twisting prominence was associated with a coronal mass ejection – a large bubble of billions of tonnes of gas that blasted away from the Sun.

PLANETS

Hurtling around the Sun are eight planets. Those closest to the Sun – Mercury, Venus, our home planet Earth, and Mars – are made of rock. The vast outer planets – Jupiter, Saturn, Uranus, and Neptune – are called "gas planets" because all we see of them is their gas. All eight travel in the same direction around the Sun. The time taken to make one circuit, or orbit, increases with distance. Mercury takes just 88 Earth days to orbit, while Neptune's longer journey takes 164.8 Earth years.

❶ JUPITER

The largest and most massive planet, Jupiter is also the fastest spinner, rotating once on its own axis in less than 10 hours. This giant world is made mainly of hydrogen and helium, with a central rocky core. A thin faint ring encircles Jupiter, which also has a large family of moons.

Jupiter's visible surface is the top of a deep and thick atmosphere made from bands of swirling gas

❷ SATURN

Sixth from the Sun, and second largest, is pale yellow Saturn. Its distinctive feature is its ring system, which is made of billions of pieces of dirty water ice. Saturn is mainly hydrogen and helium with a rocky core. It has a large family of moons.

❸ URANUS

Nineteen times the distance of Earth from the Sun, Uranus is a cold, turquoise world bounded by a layer of haze. A sparse ring system encircles the planet's equator. Uranus is tilted on its side, so that its rings and moons seem to orbit it from top to bottom.

❹ MERCURY

Mercury is a dry ball of rock, covered by millions of impact craters. It is the smallest planet, the closest to the Sun, and has the widest temperature range of any planet. During the day it is baking hot, but at night it is freezing cold.

❺ VENUS

Second from the Sun, Venus is the hottest planet. This rock world is permanently covered by thick cloud that traps heat and makes it a gloomy planet.

❻ NEPTUNE

Neptune is the most distant, coldest, and windiest of all eight planets. Like Uranus, it is made mainly of water-, methane-, and ammonia ices with an atmosphere of hydrogen-rich gas. It is encircled by a thin ring system and has a family of moons.

❼ MARS

Sometimes called the "red planet", Mars is the outermost of the rocky planets and a cold, dry world. It has polar ice caps, giant volcanoes, frozen desert, and deep canyons, formed in the distant past. Mars has also two small moons.

❽ EARTH

The only place known to have life is Earth, the largest of the rocky planets and third from the Sun. It is also the only planet with liquid water. Movements in Earth's crust are constantly changing its surface. Earth has one moon.

❾ DWARF PLANETS

The Solar System has five known dwarf planets – small, roundish objects that orbit the Sun amongst other objects. Ceres orbits between Mars and Jupiter within a belt of rocky asteroids, while Pluto, Haumea, Makemake, and Eris are icy worlds that orbit beyond Neptune in a region called the Kuiper Belt.

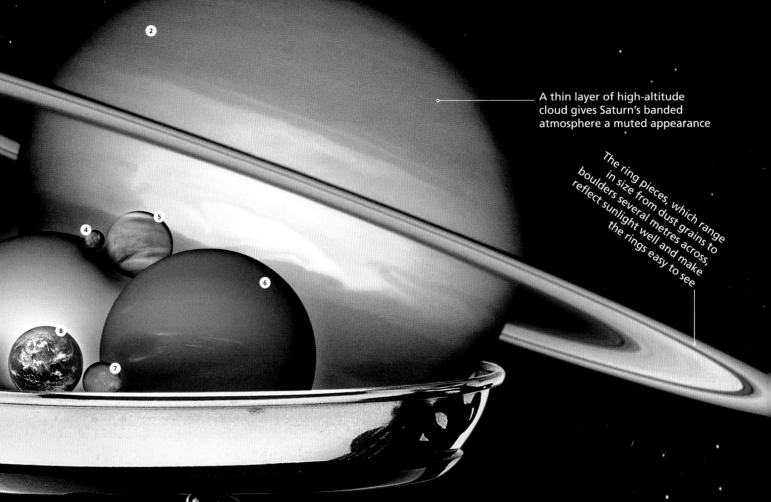

A thin layer of high-altitude cloud gives Saturn's banded atmosphere a muted appearance

The blue colouring of Uranus is due to methane in its atmosphere

The ring pieces, which range in size from dust grains to boulders several metres across, reflect sunlight well and make the rings easy to see

PLANET SCALES

Jupiter, fifth planet from the Sun, is much larger than all the other planets. It measures 142,984 km (88,846 miles) across and is made of about two and a half times as much material as all the other planets put together. The seven other planets and the five dwarf planets are shown here roughly to scale.

139

MOONS

The Solar System has more than 190 moons orbiting six of the planets – only Mercury and Venus are moonless. They range in size from Ganymede, a satellite of Jupiter, which is larger than Mercury, to S/2009 S1, a 300-metre moonlet orbiting within Saturn's rings. All are made of rock, or rock and ice, and many have surfaces littered with impact craters, formed when the moons were bombarded by asteroids in the past. Nineteen Solar-System moons are more than 400 km (250 miles) wide. These large moons are round but the more numerous smaller moons are irregular in shape.

Dark spots are major active volcanic centres – more than 80 have been identified

Io ②

Oceanus Procellarum (Ocean of Storms) is a vast lava-covered plain

The Moon ①

Callisto's icy surface is covered by impact craters

Callisto

Europa ③

Ganymede ④

Titan's hazy orange atmosphere conceals a deep-frozen surface with shifting icy continents and lakes of liquid methane

Titan ⑤

Tethys

Dione

Enceladus

Mimas

Rhea

Iapetus ⑦

Titania ⑥

Miranda

Uneven surface may be a result of the moon shattering then reassembling

Umbriel

Oberon

Long faults with icy floors formed when Ariel's crust expanded

Ariel

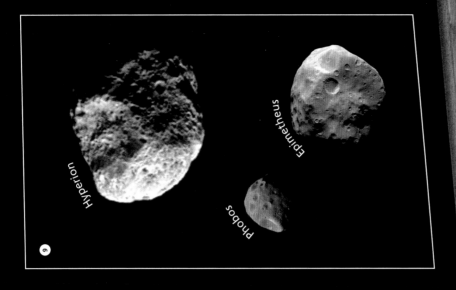

Hyperion

Epimetheus

Phobos

9

Proteus

Triton

8

Neptune's only large moon
probably began life as a
dwarf planet before being
captured by Neptune's gravity

① THE MOON

The Moon is Earth's only natural
satellite. It is about a quarter the size
of Earth and the fifth largest of all
moons. The surface of this dry ball
of rock is covered in impact craters.

② IO

Colourful Io is the most volcanic
moon in the Solar System. Its surface
is constantly being renewed as
molten rock erupts through its thin
silicate-rock crust, and fast-moving
columns of cold gas and frost grains
shoot up from surface cracks.

③ EUROPA

The smallest of Jupiter's four major
moons, Europa has an icy surface
criss-crossed with networks of
brownish grooves. The crust slowly
drifts around on top of a deep ocean
of liquid water that might be home
to alien life.

④ GANYMEDE

At 5,262 km (3,267 miles) across,
Ganymede is the largest moon in
the Solar System and belongs to the
largest family of moons – the moons
of Jupiter. Astronomers know of
79, but the number is likely to rise
as smaller moons are detected.
Ganymede is made of rock and
ice with an icy crust.

⑤ TITAN

Titan is the largest of Saturn's 62
moons. On its surface are bright
highlands, dark plains, and methane
lakes and seas. It is the only moon
with a substantial atmosphere,
which is rich in nitrogen and extends
out for hundreds of kilometres.

⑥ TITANIA

Titania is the largest of the 27 moons
orbiting Uranus. Titania and the
planet's other major moons, Oberon,
Umbriel, Ariel, and Miranda, are
named after characters in English
literature. Impact craters and large
cracks are seen on its grey, icy surface.

⑦ IAPETUS

Iapetus is a moon of contrasts. Most
of its crater-covered terrain is bright
and icy, but the rest appears to be
coated by a dark material. It is one
of Saturn's seven major moons, along
with Titan, Rhea, Dione, Tethys,
Enceladus, and Mimas.

⑧ TRITON

Triton is by far the largest of
Neptune's 14 moons, a rock-and-ice
ball with a young, icy surface. It
is nicknamed the cantaloupe as
its linear grooves, ridges, and
depressions resemble a melon's skin.

⑨ SMALL MOONS

Most moons are less than 400 km
(250 miles) across and irregular in
shape, like Saturn's Epimetheus and
Hyperion. Many of these smaller
moons, like Mars's two moons Phobos
and Deimos, may have started off
as asteroids or comets.

COMETS

More than a trillion comets surround the planetary region of the Solar System. They follow long orbits around the Sun and together make up a vast sphere called the Oort Cloud. Each comet is a lump of dirt and snow, called a nucleus, or "dirty snowball". Comets are so small that they are only visible when they travel close to the Sun and grow large and bright enough to be seen.

CHANGING COMET ▶

As a comet approaches the Sun it warms up. The snow turns to gas, which, along with loose dust, flows from the nucleus. When the comet passes closer to the Sun than the orbit of Mars, this material forms a head (called a coma) and two tails, one of gas and one of dust.

Coma A coma has formed around the nucleus of Comet Hale-Bopp as it travels towards the Sun.

Tails The comet's tails increase in length as it nears the Sun. They are pushed away from the Sun and always point away from it.

◀ COMET DISPLAY

More than 2,300 comets have been identified as they passed through the Sun's neighbourhood. About 200 make return visits, but most pass by just once. Three or four times a century, a spectacular one, such as Comet McNaught in January 2007, makes a stunning display.

This bright dot is the planet Mercury

The comet grows as it approaches the Sun

Comet McNaught

PASSING THE SUN ▶

These images from the SOHO spacecraft, track the progress of Comet McNaught as it rounds the Sun. Like most comets, it is named after its discoverer, Robert McNaught, who saw it first on 7 August 2006. It was at its biggest and brightest in January 2007, when closest to the Sun.

COMET STRUCTURE ▶

The nucleus of a comet is a city-sized lump, two-thirds snow and one-third rock dust. Halley's Comet orbits the Sun every 76 years. When it drew close to it in 1986, the Giotto spacecraft flew into the comet's coma and captured images of its nucleus.

Tail shapes The gas tail is blue and straight, and the dust tail is white and curved.

Closest to the Sun The tails are longest when closest to the Sun, then shrink as the comet moves away.

Sun's bright disc has to be masked so that the comet can be imaged

Several dozen mini-fragments trail behind the main one

One of more than 30 separate fragments of Comet Schwassmann Wachmann 3

Jets of dust and gas stream out of the nucleus

The nucleus of Halley's Comet is 15.3 km (9.5 miles) long

BREAKING UP ▶

As a comet passes a massive body, such as the Sun or Jupiter, it may be pulled apart by its gravity. Comet Schwassmann Wachmann 3 orbits the Sun every 5.4 years and astronomers have observed that it is disintegrating.

METEORITES

Thousands of tonnes of rocky material enter Earth's atmosphere each year. Most of it originates from asteroids, but some comes from comets, the Moon, and even Mars. As the rocky pieces close in on Earth they are termed meteoroids. Most burn up, but those that survive and land are known as meteorites. There are three main types: stony meteorites, iron meteorites, and stony-iron meteorites – the rarest kind.

▼ ESQUEL
This stony-iron meteorite was collected in Esquel, Argentina, in 1951. Golden-coloured crystals of the mineral olivine are embedded in the iron-nickel metal.

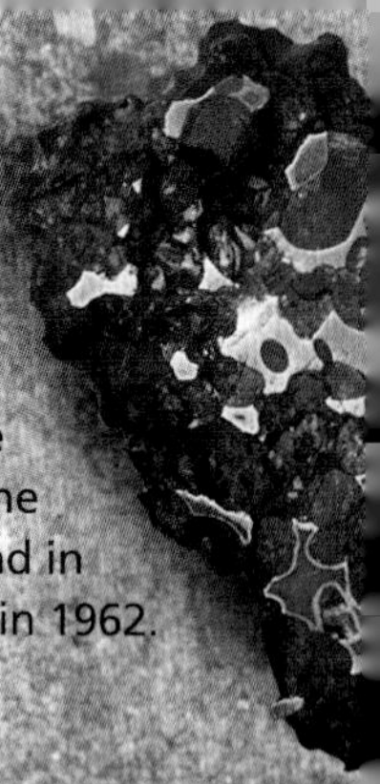

THIEL ▶
The Thiel Mountains stony-iron meteorite was one of the first found in Antarctica, in 1962.

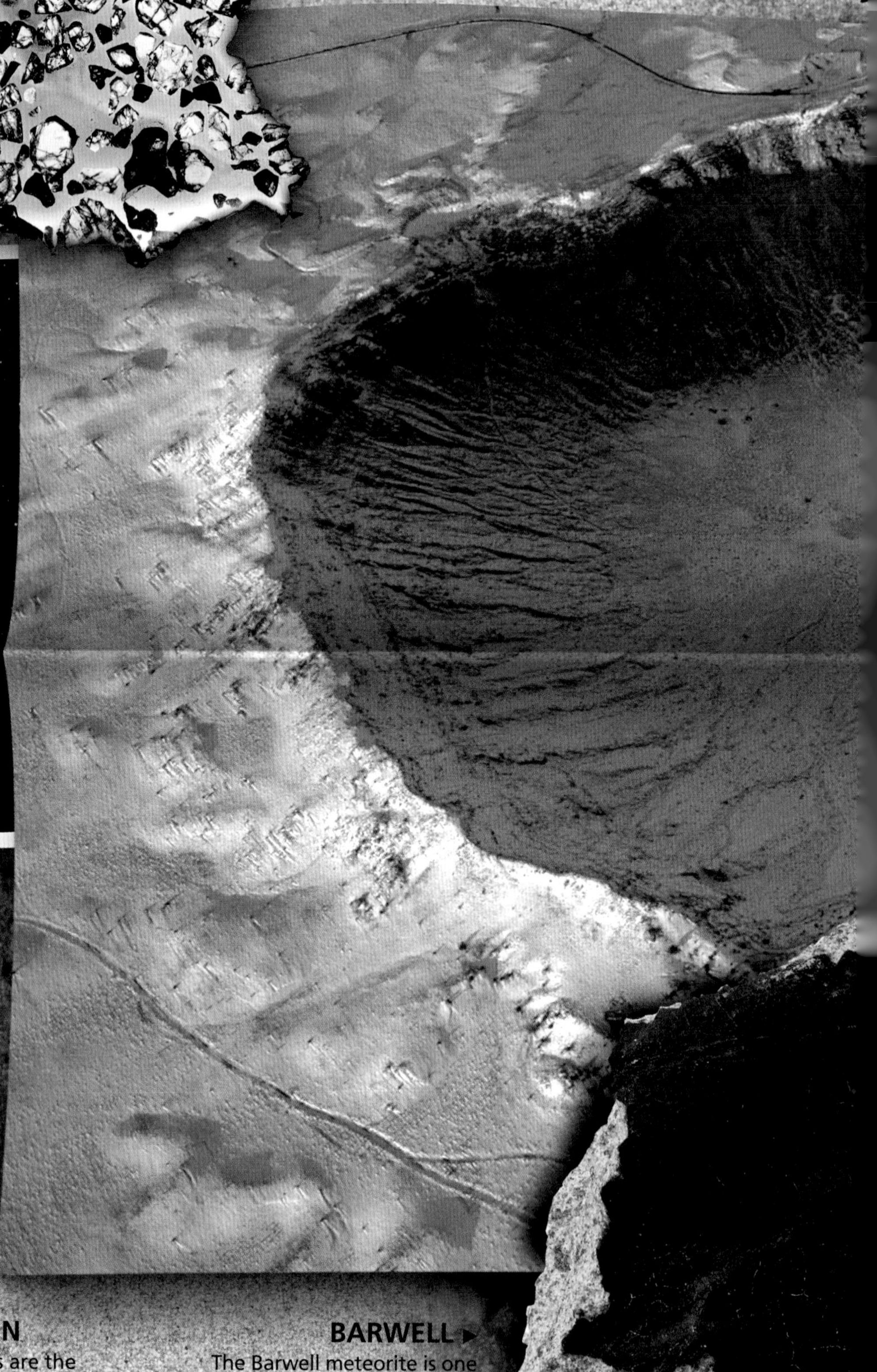

▲ METEOR
Meteoroids burning up in Earth's atmosphere produce bright trails. These short-lived streaks of light are termed meteors, or shooting stars. About a million occur every day.

◀ MURCHISON
Stony meteorites are the most common. This one, the Murchison, fell in Australia in 1969. It is one of the most studied meteorites and contains minerals, water, and complex organic molecules.

BARWELL ▶
The Barwell meteorite is one of a shower of stones that fell in England in 1965. As it plummeted through Earth's atmosphere, friction caused the outer surface to heat and melt. This later solidified into a black crust.

◄ CANON DIABLO
This sliced and polished iron meteorite is a piece of the asteroid that produced the Barringer Crater (below). The pieces found weigh 30 tonnes in total, yet they are only a small fraction of the original asteroid.

▼ IMPACT CRATER
Meteorites can produce craters when they crash into Earth. The Barringer Crater in the Arizona Desert, USA, shown here under a rare blanket of snow, measures 1.2 km (0.75 miles) across and was formed about 50,000 years ago.

▲ GIBEON
Iron meteorites are the second most common type, after stony meteorites. The Gibeon is mainly iron with a small amount of nickel. It is one of many found in Namibia since the 1830s.

▲ CALCALONG CREEK
More than 50 meteorites found on Earth originated on the Moon, blasted off by asteroid impact. The Calcalong Creek meteorite, found in Australia, is lunar surface soil that was turned to rock by such an impact.

▲ NAKHLA
This stony meteorite is one of more than 30 found on Earth that originated on Mars. It was blasted off the planet and spent many millions of years in space before landing in Egypt on 28 June 1911.

◄ TEKTITES
Small glassy bodies known as tektites can form when a large meteorite hits Earth. The impact shatters and melts surrounding Earth rock, flinging it upwards. It cools and hardens, falling back to Earth as glassy pieces.

THROUGH BINOCULARS ▲

The Orion Nebula is a massive star-forming cloud of gas and dust. The nebula becomes more obvious when looked at through binoculars – two low-powered telescopes working together. In standard binoculars the two main lenses are about 5 cm (2 in) wide and the image is magnified seven times.

IMPROVED VIEW ▶

A more powerful telescope improves the view of the nebula. Across the world there are about 50 telescopes with mirrors 2–5 m (6.5–16.5 ft) across and another 20 with mirrors up to 10 m (33 ft) across. These large telescopes are located on mountain-top sites where the air is clear and still. Computerized controls adjust their position, keeping them tracked on their target as Earth turns.

NAKED-EYE VIEW ▲

The constellation of Orion is easily visible to the naked eye. On a dark, moonless night, a faint, fuzzy patch of light may be visible below the three stars of Orion's belt. This is the Orion Nebula.

TELESCOPES

A telescope is the astronomer's basic tool. It makes distant objects appear bigger and reveals their detail. Telescopes work by using a lens or mirror to collect light and bring it to a focus, producing an image. Reflectors, which use a mirror, are the most widely used type of telescope – the bigger the mirror, the more powerful the telescope and the better the view.

Refracting telescope uses a lens, contained within the body of the telescope, to collect and focus light

Magnifying eyepiece is at 90° to the main tube for ease of use

◄ MEDIUM-SIZED TELESCOPE VIEW
The nebula's shape and form become visible through a telescope with a mirror about 20 cm (7.8 in) across. A camera attached to the telescope collects the light and records the image.

About 1,000 young stars are visible in this view because of the X-rays they emit

X-RAY AND INFRARED VIEWS ▲
X-rays collected by the Chandra space telescope were used to make this image on the left, which shows the heart of the Orion Nebula. The image on the right shows the same area taken by the Spitzer infrared telescope. Clouds of dust heated by starlight show up in red.

VIEW FROM SPACE ►
Some telescopes collect forms of energy other than light, such as radio waves, X-rays, and infrared energy. Earth's atmosphere prevents some of these from reaching Earth so they are collected by telescopes in space. This colour-enhanced image combines data from two space telescopes – Spitzer, which collects infrared waves, and Hubble, which collects both light and ultraviolet waves.

HEART OF THE NEBULA ►
Hubble's 2.4-m (7.9-ft) wide mirror collected the light for this detailed view of the Orion Nebula's bright central area. It includes the Trapezium, a cluster of ten young, brilliant stars that illuminate the nebula with their ultraviolet energy.

147

SPACE EXPLORATION

Humans have only been able to send spacecraft to explore space for about 50 years. In that time, more than 100 robotic craft have travelled into the Solar System to reveal what its planets, moons, asteroids, and comets are like. They fly by, orbit, or land on these other worlds. Humans have only been to the Moon, but aim to set foot on Mars in the future.

Apollo 18 with three US astronauts

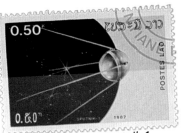

Russian satellite *Sputnik 1*

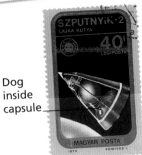

Dog inside capsule

Sputnik 2 takes Laika the dog into space

Mercury Atlas 5, with chimpanzee Enos on board

Yuri Gagarin, first human in space

Valentina Tereshkova, first woman in space

Alexei Leonov makes the first spacewalk

Apollo 8 orbits the Moon

Apollo 11 lifts off

In orbit over the Moon

Man walks on the Moon

Re-entering Earth's atmosphere

Apollo 11 crew return to Earth in command module *Columbia*

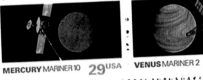

MERCURY MARINER 10   29 USA

VENUS MARINER 2   29 USA

EARTH LANDSAT   29 USA

MOON LUNAR ORBITER   29 USA   MARS VIKING ORBITER   29 USA

Spacecraft explore the major bodies of the Solar System

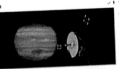

JUPITER PIONEER 11   29 USA

SATURN VOYAGER 2   29 USA

URANUS VOYAGER 2   29 USA

NEPTUNE VOYAGER 2   29 USA

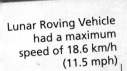

Lunar Roving Vehicle had a maximum speed of 18.6 km/h (11.5 mph)

Pioneer 10 flies by Jupiter in 1973, followed by its twin, *Pioneer 11*, in 1974

Pioneer craft investigate Jupiter

Apollo 15 mission

Soyuz 19 with two Russian cosmonauts

First international space rendezvous

Viking craft land on Mars

Columbia, the first space shuttle, takes off

Giotto craft flies into Halley's Comet

Hubble Space Telescope launched

P A T H F I N D E R

J U L Y 4, 1 9 9 7

Mars Rover *Sojourner*

$3.00 usa

Mars Pathfinder and its rover, *Sojourner*, touch down on Mars

TIMELINE OF SPACE EXPLORATION

14 October 1957
Sputnik 1, the world's first artificial satellite, is launched into Earth's orbit by Russia.

3 November 1957
Laika, a Russian dog aboard *Sputnik 2*, becomes the first creature to orbit Earth.

2 January 1959
Russian spacecraft *Luna 1* is the first to escape Earth's gravity.

13 September 1959
Luna 2 is the first craft to land on the Moon when it crashes onto its surface.

12 April 1961
Russian Yuri Gagarin is the first person into space. His flight lasts 108 minutes.

16 June 1963
Russian Valentina Tereshkova is the first woman in space.

18 March 1965
Russian Alexei Leonov makes the first EVA (extra vehicular activity), or spacewalk.

3 February 1966
Luna 9 lands successfully on the Moon.

24 December 1968
US spacecraft *Apollo 8* is the first manned mission to leave Earth's gravity and orbit the Moon.

20 July 1969
Neil Armstrong and Buzz Aldrin of *Apollo 11* are the first humans to walk on the Moon.

19 April 1971
The first space station, *Salyut 1*, is launched by the Russians.

3 December 1973
US craft *Pioneer 10* is the first to fly by Jupiter.

29 March 1974
US craft *Mariner 10* is the first to fly by Mercury.

17 July 1975
US craft *Apollo 18* and Russian *Soyuz 19* make the first international space rendezvous.

22 October 1975
Russian craft *Venera 9* transmits the first images from the surface of Venus.

20 July 1976
US craft *Viking 1* is the first to land successfully on Mars.

1 September 1979
Pioneer 11 is the first to fly by Saturn.

12 April 1981
Columbia, the first US space shuttle, is launched.

24 January 1986
US craft *Voyager 2* is the first to fly by Uranus.

13 March 1986
European craft *Giotto* takes the first close-up look at a comet.

24 August 1989
Voyager 2 is the first craft to fly by Neptune.

24 April 1990
The Hubble Space Telescope is launched.

15 September 1990
US craft *Magellan* starts a three-year mapping programme of Venus.

29 October 1991
US craft *Galileo* makes the first flyby of an asteroid as it passes Gaspra.

13 July 1995
Galileo arrives at Jupiter and releases a probe to enter its atmosphere.

4 July 1997
US craft *Mars Pathfinder* and its *Sojourner* rover touch down on Mars.

20 November 1998
Zarya, the first module of the International Space Station (ISS), is launched.

2 November 2000
The first crew arrives to stay aboard the ISS.

12 February 2001
The *NEAR* craft lands on asteroid Eros.

25 December 2003
Europe's first interplanetary craft, *Mars Express*, orbits Mars.

30 June 2004
US craft *Cassini* arrives at Saturn to study the planet and its moons. It releases *Huygens* to land on the moon Titan.

20 November 2005
Japanese craft *Hayabusa* lands on asteroid Itokawa.

4 August 2007
US craft *Phoenix* sets off for Mars, arriving in 2008.

18 March 2011
US *Messenger* spacecraft becomes the first vehicle to orbit around Mercury.

6 August 2012
US *Curiosity* rover lands in the Gale Crater on Mars.

6 August 2014
European spacecraft *Rosetta*, carrying the lander *Philae*, enters orbit around Comet Churyumov-Gerasimenko.

14 July 2015
US craft *New Horizons* makes the first flyby of the dwarf planet Pluto.

5 July 2016
US *Juno* spacecraft enters orbit around Jupiter to survey the planet's polar regions.

15 September 2017
Cassini ends its mission with a deliberate plunge into Saturn's atmosphere.

SPACE TRAVELLERS

Since the first manned space mission in 1961, more than 560 people have journeyed into space – 27 on missions to the Moon and the rest in orbit around Earth. To date, only Russia, China, and the United States have launched humans into space. However, humans are not the only space travellers. Animals such as dogs, monkeys, and spiders have all been sent into space to help with research.

❶ Alan Shepard was the second person, and first American, to journey into space.

❷ Ulf Merbold, from Germany, became the first European to fly aboard a space shuttle.

❸ Jim Voss set the record for longest spacewalk (8 hours 56 minutes) with Susan Helms.

❹ Susan Helms (see above).

❺ Laika was the first animal to orbit Earth. The Russian dog travelled in *Sputnik 2* in 1957.

❻ Alexei Leonov made the first spacewalk in March 1965. He spent 10 minutes in space secured to his *Voskhod 2* craft.

❼ Eileen Collins became the first female shuttle pilot in February 1995, and the first female shuttle commander in July 1999.

❽ Yang Liwei was the first Chinese astronaut (taikonaut). China's first manned space flight was launched in October 2003.

❾ Svetlana Savitskaya was the second woman in space and the first woman to spacewalk.

❿ Michael Collins was the third member of the *Apollo 11* mission in 1969. He orbited the Moon, as Armstrong and Aldrin explored its surface.

⓫ Dennis Tito was the first space tourist. He paid £14 million ($20 million) for a six-day trip in 2001.

⓬ Baker, a squirrel monkey, was launched into space on 28 May 1959. She travelled with a rhesus monkey called Able.

⓭ Eugene Cernan was part of the *Apollo 17* mission in December 1972. He was the last person to walk on the Moon.

⓮ Neil Armstrong was the first person to set foot on the Moon. He spent 2 hours 35 minutes exploring the lunar surface.

⓯ Yuri Gagarin was the first person to fly into space. His trip in April 1961 took him once round Earth and lasted 108 minutes.

⓰ Peggy Whitson holds the record for the longest female spaceflight (289.2 days).

17 Mike Melvill was the first commercial astronaut. He piloted *SpaceShipOne* in June 2004.

18 Valentina Tereshkova was the first woman to fly into space. She made a three-day journey aboard *Vostok 6* in June 1963.

19 Gennady Padalka holds the record for the total time spent in space. In his five trips, he has clocked up 878.5 days in space.

20 Sam was a rhesus monkey who was sent into space in 1960 to test equipment that would be used in future manned flights.

21 Valeri Polyakov holds the record for the longest time spent in space during one trip. His record stands at 437.7 days.

22 Bruce McCandless made the first untethered spacewalk in February 1984.

23 John Glenn was the first American to orbit Earth, in 1962. He became the oldest space voyager in 1998, aged 77.

24 Green tree frogs were taken to the Mir space station in 1990.

25 Buzz Aldrin was the second person to set foot on the Moon.

26 Swordtail fish travelled on board the space shuttle *Columbia* in 1998.

27 Squirrel monkeys and 24 albino rats were taken to Spacelab-3 in 1985.

28 Arabella, a spider, was sent to the Skylab space station in 1973. Once space-adapted, she spun perfect webs.

29 Albino rats (see above).

30 Quail chicks hatched from eggs on the Mir space station in March 1990.

31 Belka and Strelka became the first dogs to go into orbit and survive the journey in 1960.

32 Ham was the first chimpanzee to travel in space. In 1961, he was sent to test equipment that would be used in the first US manned space mission.

ANTARCTICA
The Transantarctic Mountains extend across Antarctica, dividing the continent into east and west. This region bordering the Ross Sea is known as Terra Nova and is famous for its spectacular ice caves.

Earth

PLANET EARTH

Earth was created some 4.5 billion years ago from a mass of iron-rich, rocky debris orbiting the Sun. The rocks smashed into the young planet as meteorites, and were welded together by heat generated from the energy of impact. The bombardment eventually generated so much heat that the whole planet melted. The heavy iron then sank towards the centre to become Earth's core, while the lighter rocks formed the mantle and crust.

EARTH'S STRUCTURE
The planet is layered like a peach. Earth's rocky crust forms its thin skin, while the hot, mobile rock of the mantle is like the peach's juicy flesh. At the heart of the planet lies its metallic core, like the hard stone at the centre of a peach.

❶ INNER CORE
The inner core is a heavy ball of solid iron and nickel. It is heated by nuclear reactions within Earth to 4,700°C (8,500°F), but the intense pressure at the core prevents it from melting.

The cool, rocky crust forms only a tiny fraction of Earth's vast mass

❷ OUTER CORE
The solid inner core is surrounded by a fluid mass of molten iron, nickel, and sulfur. Swirling currents in the molten metal of the outer core generate Earth's magnetic field.

The crust is fused to the top of the upper mantle, which is in constant motion

❸ LOWER MANTLE
The rocky mantle is 2,900 km (1,800 miles) deep, and is heated to 3,500°C (6,300°F) at its base. Intense pressure stops it melting, but rising heat keeps the hot rock moving slowly.

Plumes of heat rise through the mantle, pushing the plates of the crust apart

❹ UPPER MANTLE
The upper mantle is heated to almost 1,000°C (1,800°F). Where movement in the mantle cracks the cool, brittle crust, reduced pressure makes the hot mantle rock melt and erupt from volcanoes.

Mountains are pushed up where oceanic crust is dragged beneath continents

❺ OCEANIC CRUST
The crust between the continents is less than 11 km (7 miles) thick. It is made of heavy rock that erupts from the hot mantle at mid-ocean ridges to form the bedrock of the ocean floors.

❻ CONTINENTAL CRUST
The lightest of Earth's rocks form vast slabs that "float" on the heavy mantle like huge rocky rafts. Up to 70 km (45 miles) thick, they rise above sea level to form the continents we live on.

Huge impact craters have filled with dark lava erupted from ancient volcanoes

THE MOON
Soon after Earth formed, it was hit by a planet-sized asteroid that completely disintegrated. Most of its heavy metallic core melted into Earth, but the lighter rocky fragments drifted into orbit and eventually fused to form the Moon.

The Red Sea is a spreading rift in Earth's crust that will widen into an ocean

❼ LAND SURFACE
Exposed to frost, wind, rain, and hot sunlight, the rocks at the land surface are broken down by weathering and erosion. This releases minerals that are vital to plants and other life.

❽ OCEANS
The low-lying basins between the continents are filled with water, to an average depth of 3.7 km (2.3 miles). Most of the water erupted from volcanoes as water vapour early in Earth's history.

❾ WEATHER SYSTEMS
The heat of the Sun makes water evaporate from the oceans and rise into the lower atmosphere. The water forms swirling masses of cloud that spill rain onto the continents, allowing life to exist on land.

❿ ATMOSPHERE
Earth's mass gives it enough gravity to retain an atmosphere of nitrogen, oxygen, and other gases including carbon dioxide. This keeps Earth warm at night, and shields it from dangerous radiation.

More than 70 per cent of Earth's surface is covered by ocean water

ON THE SURFACE
Movement in the thick, hot mantle has made the thin, cool crust crack into several huge plates. The boundaries of these plates are marked by earthquake zones dotted with volcanoes, and mountain ridges pushed up where moving plates collide.

PLATE TECTONICS

Earth's crust is the brittle shell of a deep layer of hot rock called the mantle. This is moving very slowly, driven by heat generated deep within the planet. The movement has made the crust crack into separate plates, which are being pulled apart in some places and pushed together in others. As they move, the plates make oceans larger or smaller, and carry continents around the globe.

1

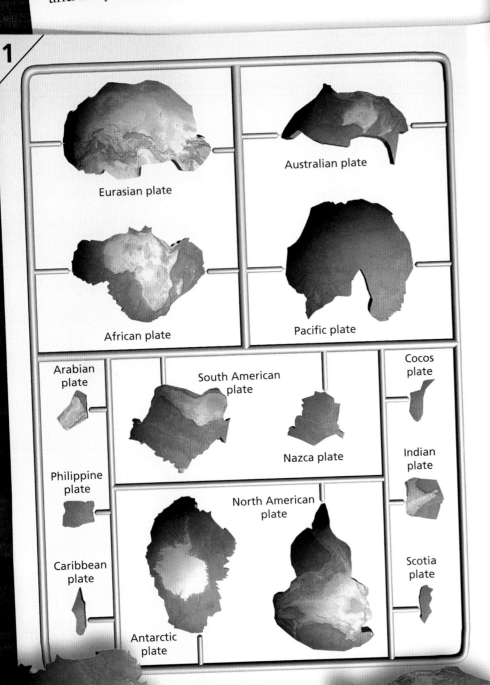

Eurasian plate

Australian plate

African plate

Pacific plate

Arabian plate

South American plate

Cocos plate

Philippine plate

Nazca plate

Indian plate

Caribbean plate

North American plate

Scotia plate

Antarctic plate

2 / PLATE BOUNDARIES

At some plate boundaries the plates are pulling apart, while at others they are pushing together. There are also places where one plate is sliding against another. All these movements cause earthquakes, and many boundaries are dotted with volcanoes.

Edge of continent rucked up to form mountains

Friction melts rock, making it erupt as volcanoes

Plate slides on mobile layer at top of mantle

Convergent boundaries
These are found where one plate grinds beneath another. Ocean floors always slide under continents, pushing up mountain ranges.

Erupting lava forms ridges of solid rock

Rift zone dotted with underwater volcanoes

Divergent boundaries
These occur where plates are pulling apart, usually on ocean floors. This allows hot mantle rock to erupt in the rift zone and solidify as new ocean floor.

◄ KIT OF PARTS

There are 15 large tectonic plates, and almost 40 smaller ones. They form the ocean floors, and some of the largest carry continents. Continental plates are made of thicker, but lighter, rock than the ocean floors. The oceanic parts of the plates are always changing size and shape, but the continents, although moving, do not change so much.

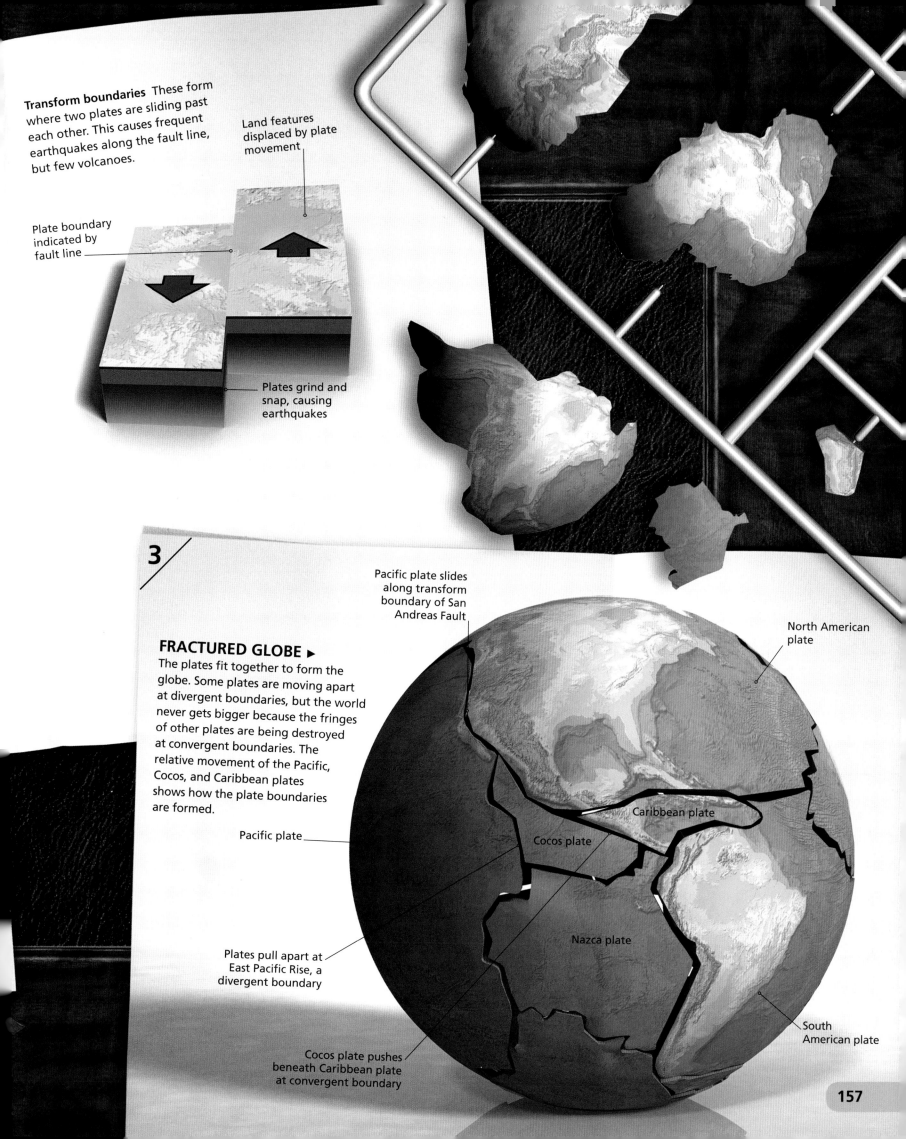

Transform boundaries These form where two plates are sliding past each other. This causes frequent earthquakes along the fault line, but few volcanoes.

Land features displaced by plate movement

Plate boundary indicated by fault line

Plates grind and snap, causing earthquakes

3

Pacific plate slides along transform boundary of San Andreas Fault

North American plate

FRACTURED GLOBE ▶
The plates fit together to form the globe. Some plates are moving apart at divergent boundaries, but the world never gets bigger because the fringes of other plates are being destroyed at convergent boundaries. The relative movement of the Pacific, Cocos, and Caribbean plates shows how the plate boundaries are formed.

Caribbean plate

Pacific plate

Cocos plate

Nazca plate

Plates pull apart at East Pacific Rise, a divergent boundary

South American plate

Cocos plate pushes beneath Caribbean plate at convergent boundary

157

VOLCANOES

Volcanoes are the most spectacular and destructive of Earth's geological features. Most volcanoes lie along plate boundaries, where the slabs of rock (plates) that form Earth's crust meet. Opening rifts and the friction of plates grinding against each other make the hot rock beneath the crust melt and burst up through fissures (cracks). Volcanoes also occur over "hotspots" away from plate boundaries, caused by rising plumes of heat in the mantle beneath Earth's crust.

KILAUEA

The Hawaiian islands are a chain of volcanoes that have erupted from the Pacific Ocean floor as it slips over a hotspot in Earth's mantle. The oldest volcanoes in the north are now extinct, but Kilauea in the south is the most active volcano on Earth.

Eruptions produce clouds of gas, made mainly of water vapour, carbon dioxide, and sulfur dioxide

Some of the molten rock hurled into the air cools and hits the ground as streamlined "lava bombs"

Lava, cinders, and volcanic ash build up a rocky but fragile ridge around the crater

The erupting lava has a temperature of about 1,000°C (1,830°F), making it glow bright orange

A small cinder cone surrounds Kilauea's most active crater

① ERUPTION

When Kilauea erupts, basalt lava and gas are forced up from deep within the volcano. Basalt lava is very fluid, so a lot of it just spills over the rim of the crater. Erupting gas can also cause explosive "fire fountains" of gas and red-hot lava, like this one.

② CRATER

Lava boils up through a vent to build up a cone of rocky debris. More eruptions make the inside of the cone collapse or even explode upwards to create a roughly circular crater. Its almost sheer walls reveal layers of cinders, ash, and solidified lava.

③ CONE

This small volcanic cone is just the summit of a huge, dome-shaped shield volcano, which rises all the way from the ocean floor 7,277 m (23,875 ft) below. The dome is built up by the fluid lava that erupts on Hawaii. Volcanoes that erupt stickier, less fluid lava have steeper sides.

④ LAVA FLOW

The lava that erupts from Kilauea is extremely hot, and is so fluid that it flows downhill away from the crater like a river of fire. Since 1983 the volcano has been erupting almost constantly, spilling lava over more than 100 sq km (40 sq miles).

⑤ TYPES OF LAVA

Hawaiian lava is molten basalt rock pushed up from beneath the ocean floor. It is fluid because it contains very little silica (the mineral used to make glass). Other volcanoes erupt lava that is high in silica, which is much stickier and does not flow far.

⑥ LAVA TUBE

As the lava streams away from the active crater of Kilauea, the surface of the flow cools and hardens. Underneath, however, the hot lava keeps flowing. This creates "lava tubes" that extend to the coast, where the lava spills into the sea in clouds of steam.

Lava flows downhill at speeds of up to 100 km/h (60 mph)

The surface of the lava cools to form a wrinkled or rough, fractured skin of solid black rock

The lava that erupts on Hawaii solidifies into black basalt – a heavy, iron-rich rock

EARTHQUAKES

The vast rocky plates of Earth's crust are always moving. Where the plates meet, the movement causes earthquakes. Frequent slight movement just causes tremors (shaking), but often the rocks on each side of a plate boundary lock together. The strain builds up, distorting the rocks until the locked section gives way. The rock springs back, often shifting several metres, and the shock of this can cause a catastrophic earthquake.

CHILE 1960

The biggest earthquake ever recorded struck Chile in 1960. It reached 9.5 on the Richter Scale, which was devised in 1935 by American scientist Charles Richter as a way of measuring earthquakes using instruments called seismographs.

ALASKA 1964

On 27 March 1964, the Pacific Ocean floor slid 20 m (66 ft) beneath Alaska in a few minutes, causing a colossal earthquake. So few people live in this remote region, however, that only 125 lost their lives.

MEXICO CITY 1985

Mexico's capital city is built on the dried-out clay bed of an ancient lake. The earthquake that hit the city in 1985 made the clay shake like jelly, making the shock waves six times as destructive. More than 400 multistorey buildings in the city were shaken to the ground, and at least 9,000 people died.

SAN FRANCISCO 1906

The San Andreas Fault in California, USA, marks where the Pacific plate is sliding past North America. San Francisco is built on the fault line, and in 1906 the city was almost destroyed when the fault slipped 6 m (20 ft) and triggered disastrous fires.

KOBE 1995

Japan was created by intense earth movements in the western Pacific, and it has more earthquakes than almost anywhere else. In 1995, an earthquake wrecked the city of Kobe, destroying this elevated highway and killing 6,433 people.

TSUNAMI 2004

The Asian tsunami that killed more than 283,000 in 2004 was caused by an earthquake on the ocean floor off Sumatra. The shock sent huge waves racing across the Indian Ocean, devastating communities all around its shores.

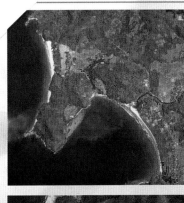

Above left: the city of Banda Aceh, Sumatra, Indonesia, as it was in April 2004

Left: the same area pictured in January 2006, after the tsunami had struck

INDONESIA 2006

In 2006, a serious earthquake struck the Indonesian island of Java, wrecking up to 135,000 houses and killing at least 5,780 people. It also damaged the ancient Hindu temple of Prambanan, a World Heritage Site, but did not destroy it.

MOUNTAINS

The world's mountains were raised by the titanic forces that keep the plates of Earth's crust moving. Where the plates grind together, the edges of continents are forced up into high, folded ridges, like the Andes mountains in South America. Hot rock deep beneath the surface may erupt through cracks in the folded rock to form volcanoes. These also erupt where the crust is being torn apart, and over "hotspots" deep within Earth. The landscape below has been created from images of the highest peaks on each continent, and one that rises from the depths of the Pacific Ocean.

❶ MOUNT EVEREST
The world's highest peak, Everest lies 8,850 m (29,035 ft) above sea level. It is part of the Himalayas, a range of fold mountains created by the collision of India with Asia 50 million years ago. India is still moving north, so the Himalayas are still rising.

❷ MOUNT ACONCAGUA
The Pacific Ocean floor is plunging beneath South America, rucking up its western edge to form the rugged, earthquake-prone mountains of the Andes. Mount Aconcagua is the highest peak, at 6,959 m (22,834 ft).

Hundreds of people attempt to climb Everest every year ❶

The snowy summit of Aconcagua is part of Earth's longest mountain range ❷

The Alaskan peak of Mount McKinley is covered with snow throughout the year ❸

❸ MOUNT MCKINLEY

Rising 6,194 m (20,321 ft) above sea level, Mount McKinley in Alaska is the highest peak of the North American Western Cordillera. Its isolation and bulk make it one of the world's most spectacular mountains.

❺ MAUNA KEA

The highest point on Hawaii is the top of a huge volcano that rises 10,000 m (33,000 ft) from the Pacific Ocean floor. So although its peak is only 4,205 m (13,796 feet) above sea level, it is the biggest mountain on Earth.

❼ MONT BLANC

The folded ridges of the European Alps have been raised by the northward movement of Africa. Mont Blanc is the highest peak at 4,808 m (15,774 ft), but since its summit is a dome of ice its height varies from year to year.

❹ MOUNT KILIMANJARO

The highest mountain in Africa, Kilimanjaro is actually a colossal volcano with three volcanic cones. The highest peak on the tallest cone, Kibo, rises 5,895 m (19,340 ft) above sea level. The other volcanic cones are Mawenzi and Shira.

❻ VINSON MASSIF

The most remote mountains on Earth lie on the frozen continent of Antarctica. Overlooking the vast mass of the Ronne Ice Shelf, Vinson Massif in the Ellsworth range is the highest point at 4,897 m (16,067 ft).

❽ AORAKI (MOUNT COOK)

The highest peak in New Zealand, Aoraki's name means "cloud piercer" in the native Maori language. The mountain is also known as Mount Cook. Now 2,744 m (12,284 ft) high, Aoraki was 10 m (33 ft) higher before a landslide in 1991.

Mount Kilimanjaro's cone, Kibo, has a 2.4-km (1.5-mile) wide crater on its summit

The vast bulk of Mauna Kea is slowly sinking as the ocean floor sags beneath its weight

The frosty crags of Vinson Massif pierce the thick snow and ice shrouding its slopes

The icy summit of Mont Blanc can rise 16 m (52 ft) above its highest rocky peak

Heavy snowfall feeds two glaciers that flow down Aoraki's flanks

OCEANS

The oceans cover more than two-thirds of the surface of Earth, with an average depth of 3.8 km (2.4 miles), but they are not just huge pools of salt water. The ocean floors are where the great plates of Earth's crust are splitting apart or grinding together, creating long, high ridges and deep trenches dotted with volcanoes. As a result of this, the oceans are changing their size and shape all the time.

Iceland

Hudson Bay

Aleutian Trench

Sargasso Sea

Atlantic Ocean

Gulf of Mexico

Hawaii is just one of many volcanic islands and seamounts

Caribbean Sea

Pacific Ocean

East Pacific Rise

Mid-Atlantic Ridge has been built up by a spreading rift in the ocean floor

Peru-Chile Trench has been created by the Pacific floor sliding under South America

Atlantic Ocean

PACIFIC OCEAN

As big as all other oceans put together, the Pacific is shrinking as the edges of its floor slip into deep ocean trenches like the Mariana Trench. The East Pacific Rise, however, is the most active mid-ocean ridge, spreading at up to 22 cm (8.5 in) a year.

ATLANTIC OCEAN

The Atlantic formed when North and South America split from Europe and Africa and gradually moved west. The ocean is still growing as new ocean floor is created at the Mid-Atlantic Ridge. The ridge breaks the surface in the north to form Iceland, with its volcanoes and geysers.

Arctic Ocean

Baltic Sea

Black Sea

North Sea

Caspian Sea

Mediterranean is an enclosed, almost tideless sea that was once a great ocean

The 2004 Asian tsunami was caused by an earthquake in the Java Trench off Sumatra

Red Sea

Maldives

Pacific Ocean

Indian Ocean

Great Barrier Reef is the world's biggest coral reef

Southern Ocean

ARCTIC OCEAN

Most of the Arctic Ocean is covered by thick floating ice in winter. A lot of this melts in spring, allowing sunlight to reach the cold waters and fuel the growth of ocean life. The sea near the North Pole stays frozen in summer, but the area covered by ice is shrinking every year because of global warming.

Ocean trench marks where the Pacific floor is grinding beneath Japan, causing earthquakes

Mariana Trench is the lowest point on Earth, 11 km (6.8 miles) below the waves

INDIAN OCEAN

This mainly tropical ocean is notorious for the tsunami that swept across it from Sumatra in 2004. It had a serious impact on nearby coasts and low-lying coral islands like the Maldives, which crown the peaks of an underwater mountain ridge extending south from India.

SOUTHERN OCEAN

With no obvious northern boundaries, the Southern Ocean forms a ring of cold, stormy water around Antarctica. Ice covers a vast area in winter, and the giant icebergs that break off Antarctic glaciers and ice shelves sometimes drift well north.

ROCKS AND MINERALS

Rocks are mixtures of natural chemical compounds called minerals, which form crystals with distinctive shapes. There are three main types of rock. Igneous rock is formed when molten rock cools and hardens, a metamorphic rock is one that has been changed by heat or pressure, and sedimentary rock is generally made from fragments of rock cemented together.

1 Slate This dark rock is created when sedimentary shale is put under intense pressure. It forms thin sheets that can be cut into squares and used for roofing.

2 Cockscomb barite This whitish mineral is often found in veins running through rocks. Its crystals form clusters that can resemble cockscombs (roosters' head crests).

3 Schist Like slate, schist is created by pressure and heat, which transforms a soft sedimentary rock into a very much harder metamorphic rock.

4 Chalk A type of limestone, chalk is built up from the remains of tiny marine organisms, which sank to the bottom of a tropical sea during the age of dinosaurs.

5 Marble Hard and usually pale, marble is a metamorphic form of limestone. It can be carved and polished into statues, and decorative slabs are used in architecture.

6 Calcite The main mineral in limestone and marble, calcite forms the stalactites and stalagmites seen in limestone caves.

7 Limestone All limestones are made of chalky minerals, particularly calcite. They are easily dissolved by rainwater, creating extensive cave systems.

8 Halite Formed by the evaporation of salt lakes, halite is rock salt – the mineral that we use to flavour our food.

9 Biotite Dark brown biotite is a type of mica, a mineral found in most granites and schists. Its plate-like crystals resemble thin, flaky sheets of hard plastic.

10 Eclogite A dense, heavy metamorphic rock formed deep beneath Earth's surface, eclogite contains bright green pyroxene and glittering red garnet minerals.

11 Tremolite Thin, transparent, fibrous-looking crystals of tremolite form from limestones that have been subjected to intense heat deep underground.

12 Beryl This very hard mineral forms transparent, often greenish crystals that can be cut to create emeralds and aquamarines.

13 Granite One of the main rocks that form continents, granite results from molten rock cooling slowly deep underground to form big quartz, feldspar, and mica crystals.

14 Breccia This sedimentary rock is made of broken, sharp-edged rock fragments cemented together by finer particles.

15 Obsidian Also known as volcanic glass, this shiny black or dark green rock is formed when molten lava cools too quickly to form crystals.

16 Gabbro This is a coarse, dark, iron-rich, crystalline rock that makes up much of the deep ocean floor.

17 Pumice Gas erupting from volcanoes often forms bubbles inside cooling lava. This can then form pumice, which has so many gas bubbles that it floats on water.

18 Corundum This dull-looking stone is a type of corundum, the hardest mineral after diamond. Its crystals are used to make rubies and sapphires.

19 Albite A pale, sodium-rich form of feldspar, albite is a common ingredient of granite, visible as big, blocky crystals that glint in the sunshine.

20 Graphite Made of pure carbon – like diamond – graphite is a soft, metallic mineral that leaves a dark streak. It is used to make the "lead" in pencils.

21 Basalt Heavy, dark basalt is the fine-grained form of gabbro, created when iron-rich lava from oceanic volcanoes cools quickly, often underwater.

22 Sandstone Sand cemented together by other minerals forms sandstone. This red sandstone was once a desert dune.

23 Pyrite Known as "fool's gold", this yellow metallic mineral is actually made of iron and sulfur. It often forms big cubic crystals like the ones seen here.

24 Conglomerate Very like breccia, this rock is a solid, cemented mass of rounded pebbles, like those found on riverbeds and lake shores.

Amethystine spinel is named for its amethyst colour.

Golden sapphire is a golden form of blue sapphire.

Brown tourmaline is one of hundreds of the gem's colours.

Chrysoberyl can be honey yellow to mint green.

Green beryl is a pale variety of emerald.

Danburite is colourless, yellow, green, or brown.

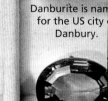
Danburite is named for the US city of Danbury.

Mauve spinel is mined in Myanmar (Burma), like most spinels.

Amethystine sapphire is made of hard corundum.

Pied tourmaline has two colours in one crystal.

Yellow beryl is tinted with iron and uranium.

Citrine is a warm yellow type of quartz.

Garnet was a favourite with ancient civilizations.

Andalusite glints with green and orange.

Red spinel is often used in place of rubies.

Ruby is the same mineral as sapphire, but red.

Red tourmaline that looks like ruby is called rubelite.

Chrysoberyl is valued as a good luck charm.

Amethyst is always violet or purple.

Topaz is said to dispel sadness, fear, and anger.

Opal has changing colours caused by scattered light.

Opal matrix is polished rock with veins of opal.

Blue zircon is the most desirable form of zircon.

Tanzanite is named after Tanzania where it is found.

Green tourmaline can resemble a fine emerald.

Iolite looks different colours from different angles.

Green tourmaline is sometimes called verdelite.

Emerald catseye a pale stripe

Green beryl is a paler form of emerald.

Chrysoprase is prized for its apple colour.

Catseye quartz has a pale, glowing streak or "cat's eye".

Carbuncle is a polished, domed form of garnet.

Tiger eye is striped with yellow and brown.

Albite is always white.

Moonstone is a magical gem in India.

Zircon is one of the heaviest gemstones.

Star sapphire has a star pattern on its surface.

Amethyst is a violet form of common quartz.

Tourmaline has more colours than any other gem.

Green zircon is more rare than the blue form.

Brown zircon is one of many colour varieties.

Colourless topaz can be mistaken for a diamond.

Blue spinel, also called cobalt spinel, is rare.

Pink sapphire is the same gem as a pale ruby.

Green tourmaline is tinted with traces of chromium.

Chrysoberyl is often a honey-coloured brown.

Morganite is a pink beryl with manganese.

Iolite can look black from some angles.

Sphalerite is a soft stone that sparkles like a diamond.

ophire containing iron oxide is tinted yellow.

Indicolite is a blue variety of tourmaline.

Chrysoberyl is thought to promote harmony.

Aquamarine is a light blue variety of beryl.

Topaz is meant to protect against sudden death.

Peridot is made from vivid green olivine crystals.

Almandine garnet is bigger than a typical garnet.

reen zircon can glitter like a reen diamond.

Yellow sapphire is rarer than blue but less valuable.

Sapphire frequently shows a starry pattern.

Yellow tourmaline comes from Malawi.

Kunzite often flashes various shades of violet.

Fire opal is a clear opal with red in it.

Topaz is usually yellow but can be colourless.

ink tourmaline catseye has a right highlight.

Jade has been known for at least 7,000 years.

Jade is usually green but can be mauve.

Haematite is a lustrous form of iron ore.

Lapis lazuli was one of the first gems to be worn.

Star garnet glints with a starry pattern.

Opal is often mounted on onyx as a "doublet".

Jade is often carved, and was once used for tools.

Sinhalite is a rare stone from Sri Lanka.

Rhodolite is a velvety red form of garnet.

Kunzite was unknown until 100 years ago.

Garnet is usually a warm, brownish red.

Turquoise gets its sky blue from copper.

Moonstone is named for its shimmering glow.

GEMS

The natural minerals that make up rocks can form glassy crystals, which can be cut into glittering gems. Many are extremely hard, and contain different impurities that tint gems such as sapphire, tourmaline, and topaz a sparkling array of colours. They can be extremely valuable. The gem collection shown here is worth almost a million dollars.

METALS

Metals are minerals with a closely packed atomic structure, which makes them excellent conductors of electricity and heat. Most are also strong, workable materials, ideal for making a huge range of artefacts. Pure metals are elements, with only one type of atom in their chemical structure. In nature, many are mixed with rocks, or combined with other elements to form chemical compounds. These ores must be mined and processed to extract the pure metals.

Lead scuba weights

Galena (lead ore)

◄ LEAD
Very dense and heavy, lead is a dark, soft metal with a low melting point, which makes it easy to shape. It is widely used in lead-acid car batteries, but also for heavy weights and roofing. The main lead ore is galena, a compound of lead and sulfur that forms big crystals.

The nickel in the stainless steel makes this hip joint corrosion-proof

Native silver

SILVER ▲
One of the most prized metals, silver occurs in pure "native" form in volcanic rocks. It is very shiny when polished, but soon tarnishes. Since it is quite soft, it is often mixed with other metals to make harder alloys such as sterling silver.

Sterling silver flute

Platinum ring

Platinum

Garnierite (nickel ore)

◄ PLATINUM
A beautiful, very heavy metal, platinum is often used in jewellery because, like gold, it never tarnishes. It is tougher than gold, and rarer, so it is more precious. It is sometimes found as nuggets of pure metal.

▼ COPPER
Copper is a soft metal, often alloyed with zinc to make brass, or with tin to form bronze – both much harder. A good conductor, it is widely used for electric wire. Its main ore is chalcopyrite, a compound of copper, iron, and sulfur.

▼ GOLD
Easily worked, always shiny, and the only metal that is always found in pure form, gold has been used to make precious objects for thousands of years. It is also used to make electrical contacts that do not degrade by tarnishing.

Chalcopyrite (copper ore)

Gold audio connectors

Copper pipes and wires

Gold nugget

deep-sea
submersible

nautile

Ifremer

Ifremer
nautile

ALUMINIUM ▶
Abundant and
resistant to corrosion,
lightweight aluminium is
widely used for foil, cans, and in
aircraft. Its ore, bauxite, is a rock that
contains many aluminium compounds.

Aluminium baking foil

Bauxite
(aluminium ore)

TITANIUM ▶
Light yet very strong, titanium is
often combined with other metals
to make lightweight alloys used in
aircraft, spacecraft, and the pressure-
proof capsules of deep-sea submersibles.
One of its main ores is rutile, a
compound of titanium and oxygen.

Rutile (titanium ore)

Hematite
(iron ore)

Mercury thermometer

MERCURY ▼
The only metal that is liquid at room
temperature, mercury is most familiar
as the silvery contents of a medical
thermometer. Its ore, cinnabar,
is a colourful compound
of mercury and
sulfur found
near volcanoes.

Steel nuts and bolts

▲ IRON
The most useful of all
metals, iron is strong,
abundant, and easy to work
with, especially when refined
into various types of steel. Its
main ore is hematite, an iron
oxide – the same thing as rust.

Stainless steel hip replacement

◀ NICKEL
Rarely used on its own,
nickel is often alloyed with iron
to make stainless steel. This is used
for all kinds of applications, from
knives and forks to replacement hip
joints. Nickel is also alloyed
with silver to make coins.

Cinnabar (mercury ore)

Sphalerite
(zinc ore)

ZINC ▶
Zinc is a white metal that is
alloyed with copper to make
brass. Its main use, however,
is plating or "galvanizing"
steel to make it rust-
proof. Its main ore is
sphalerite, a sparkling
mineral that is a
compound of zinc,
iron, and sulfur.

Tin can

Cassiterite
(tin ore)

TIN ▲
Well known for its use in tin cans – which
are actually tin-plated steel – tin is widely
used in electronic components because of
its high electrical conductivity. It is also
alloyed with lead to make the solder used
to assemble electronic circuits.

Galvanized
chain

PALAEOZOIC ERA (ANCIENT LIFE)

Life began in the Precambrian era, more than 3.5 billion years ago, but for most of that time life was restricted to single-celled organisms like bacteria. The start of the Palaeozoic era 540 million years ago saw an explosion of multicellular life, such as marine arthropods, molluscs, and primitive relatives of fish.

Sea lilies were plant-shaped relatives of starfish, attached to the seabed by stalks

FOSSILS

The remains, impressions, or traces of organisms (such as plants and animals) that have been preserved in the rocks are known as fossils. The process of fossilization generally takes millions of years, and as special circumstances are needed for fossils to form, only a tiny proportion of Earth's organisms have been fossilized. It is not always easy to date fossils absolutely, so the palaeontologists who find, analyze, and identify fossils usually assign them to named eras and periods. These cover the major phases in the long history of life on Earth.

Resembling woodlice, trilobites lived on seabeds throughout the Palaeozoic era

Lobe-finned fish are the cousins of all modern animals with four legs

Finely detailed fossils show the feathers of *Archaeopteryx*, one of the first known birds

Whole animals such as insects are preserved in amber, or fossilized tree resin

This model of a *Deinonychus* skull helps palaeontologists understand the biology of this predator

Fossil ammonites (prehistoric sea creatures) were recorded in this book more than 100 years ago

Familiar animals, like this dragonfly, were already common 150 million years ago

MESOZOIC ERA (MIDDLE LIFE)

Beginning 252 million years ago, this was the age of the dinosaurs, when giant reptiles stalked the land, pterosaurs swooped through the skies, and marine reptiles such as ichthyosaurs swam alongside squid-like ammonites. Flowering plants and small mammals also appeared on land. The era ended with a mass extinction 66 million years ago.

Fossils from about 10 million years ago reveal details of ancient corals

CENOZOIC ERA (RECENT LIFE)

Non-bird dinosaur fossils do not appear in rock formed less than 66 million years ago in the Cenozoic era, showing that they had died out by that time. Yet mammal fossils become more varied, and include early relatives of humans, which date back to 6–7 million years ago. The first true humans appeared about a million years later.

Large collections of specimens help with the identification and dating of fossils

Mammoth tooth found on the bed of the North Sea shows the sea was once dry land

Reconstructed fossil fragments form this skull of *Homo habilis*, an extinct cousin of modern humans

Hammer and chisel used to remove rock from around fossil

Magnifying glass

Geological hammer

Chisels

PALAEONTOLOGY

The word "palaeontology" means the study of ancient life, preserved as fossils. But palaeontologists also study non-bony life forms such as molluscs, plants, and even bacteria. Their work involves carefully removing, cleaning, and preserving the fossils, as well as identifying them and recording their features. Special tools ranging from hammers to medical scanners help them prepare and interpret their finds.

Split rock reveals the mineralized fossil of an ammonite, and a cast of its shell

FOSSILIZATION

Normally only the hard parts of living things, such as shells and bones, survive as fossils. Over millions of years these become impregnated with minerals, so they become stony. Often the original shell or bone disappear, leaving a mould later filled by another mineral. Rarely, soft body parts such as feathers may leave detailed impressions in fine-grained rock.

Opalized marine snail

This footprint of a three-toed predatory dinosaur is known as a "trace fossil"

This late Mesozoic clam left a mould that has become filled with opal to create a cast fossil

DINOSAURS

Long ago, life on Earth was dominated by the dinosaurs, a group of reptiles that included huge, lumbering plant-eaters and fearsome, agile hunters. Except for the birds, dinosaurs became extinct 66 million years ago (MYA), but their fossilized remains survive in the rocks of ancient continents, allowing scientists to reconstruct what they looked like and how they lived.

❶ STRUTHIOMIMUS

Standing taller than a man, this agile, fast-running dinosaur was more like an ostrich than a typical reptile. It had no teeth in its long jaws but had a beak made from keratin, like birds. It was probably a herbivore.

❷ ALLOSAURUS

Although it probably looked very like *Tyrannosaurus*, the fossils of this massive meat-eater have been found in rocks that are at least 70 million years older. This timespan is longer than the period that separates the last dinosaurs from our own time.

STRUTHIOMIMUS
(78–77 MYA)

ALLOSAURUS
(155–150 MYA)

SAUROLOPHUS
(70–68 MYA)

TYRANNOSAURUS
(68–66 MYA)

VELOCIRAPTOR
(75–71 MYA)

❸ TYRANNOSAURUS

The biggest of the tyrannosaurs, *Tyrannosaurus rex* grew to 12 m (39 ft) and had thick, banana-shaped teeth up to 15 cm (6 in) long. Its fossilized remains have been found in rocks in North America, notably in Montana and South Dakota.

❹ VELOCIRAPTOR

Found in Mongolia, the fossil bones of this smallish dinosaur are similar to those of the first birds, and recent research shows that it may have had feathers. It was an agile, high-speed hunter that probably jumped on its prey and gripped with its hooked claws.

❺ SAUROLOPHUS

This plant-eater had a bony crest on its skull that may have supported an ornamental crest. Fossils from Asia have longer crests than fossils found in America, showing that there were at least two different species.

❻ IGUANODON

Iguanodon was a large, bulky herbivore with a strange spike on its thumb. Scientists are still unsure how this spike was used.

IGUANODON
(129–125 MYA)

6

DIPLODOCUS
(154–152 MYA)

9

7

STEGOSAURUS
(155–150 MYA)

TRICERATOPS
(68–66 MYA)

8

OVIRAPTOR
(75–73 MYA)

10

❽ **TRICERATOPS**

The bony neck shield and three sharp horns of *Triceratops* were used in combat with other *Triceratops*. Judging from fossilized bones found in North America, the animal grew to at least 9 m (30 ft) long.

❼ **STEGOSAURUS**

Stegosaurus fed on plants in what is now North America and Europe, 155–150 million years ago. Scientists still puzzle over the function of the huge bony plates on its back, which are not attached to the backbone. Two pairs of spikes on the tail were likely to be used to ward off predators.

❾ **DIPLODOCUS**

This giant dinosaur lived in what is now North America at the same time as *Allosaurus*, but used its long neck to browse over a large area. It was up to 27 m (89 ft) long, with a small head and whip-like tail.

❿ **OVIRAPTOR**

Similar to the larger *Struthiomimus*, this bird-like dinosaur had short powerful jaws and possibly a beak. It was earlier thought to have been an "egg-thief" because the first fossil specimen was found on a nest of dinosaur eggs, and scientists believed that it may have died trying to steal them. However, further research suggests it is likely that that the *Oviraptor* was just incubating its own nest, not stealing the eggs.

▲ THUNDERSTORMS

Hot sunshine causes water to evaporate and rise into the air, where it cools and forms clouds. Some clouds build up to immense heights of 15 km (9 miles) or more. They contain a huge weight of water that is eventually released in dramatic thunderstorms of torrential rain.

TORNADOES ▲

Thunderclouds are built up by rising warm, moist air that spirals up into the cloud. Sometimes this can develop into a tight, swirling vortex of rising air, called a tornado. Wind speeds inside the vortex can exceed 500 km/h (310 mph), and the powerful updraft can easily rip the roof off a house.

▲ LIGHTNING

Ice crystals tossed around inside a thundercloud can charge the cloud with electricity like a giant battery. Eventually the charge is released as a colossal spark of lightning, which heats the air along its path to about 30,000°C (50,000°F) in a split second.

HAILSTONES ▲

Big thunderclouds contain updrafts that carry raindrops to heights where they freeze. The pellets of ice fall through the cloud, but are carried up again so more ice freezes onto them. This can happen many times, building up hailstones that can be bigger than golf balls.

FLOODS ▲

Heavy rain can swell rivers until they overflow their banks, flooding nearby low-lying land. The water may rise slowly, but it can also surge down valleys in sudden "flash floods" that sweep everything before them. Either way the flood water can wreck homes and even swamp cities.

WEATHER

Driven by the heat of the Sun, circulating currents of air swirl through the lower atmosphere, creating the winds that carry clouds, rain, and snow from the oceans over the land. Without these weather systems the continents would be barren deserts, where life would be impossible. Sometimes, however, the weather can be so violent that it causes destruction on a terrifying scale.

▼ HURRICANES

The most devastating weather occurs over tropical oceans, where intense heat creates huge storm clouds that revolve around zones of very low air pressure. Winds spiral into the centre at 300 km/h (185 mph) or more, heaping ocean water into "storm surges" that can drown coastal cities. Hurricanes that form over the Pacific Ocean are called typhoons.

ICE STORMS ▶

Freezing winter weather is normal in many regions, but freak conditions can sometimes cause unusually destructive ice storms. If moist air is swept over a very cold region, falling rain may freeze where it lands to form thick ice. This can bring down power lines, paralyze rail networks, and turn roads into death traps.

PREDICTING WEATHER ▶

Satellite images like this view of a hurricane in the Gulf of Mexico can help meteorologists predict the weather. Forecasters also gather data on wind, temperature, air pressure, and other variables, and feed them into computers that are programmed with mathematical models of the atmosphere. The computers use the new data to predict how the atmosphere may react, and so produce a weather forecast.

In deserts, the wind picks up grains of sand and hurls them against bare rock, scouring the surface and widening any cracks. Deep beds of sandstone, like these in North America, may be worn into spectacular wave-like shapes, revealing layers of rock laid down over millions of years.

Wind erosion has turned the Coyote Buttes in Arizona, USA, into a natural work of art

WEATHERED GRANITE ▶
Granite is an extremely hard, crystalline rock, but it can still be broken down by erosion. It is formed deep underground, and when exposed to the air the change of pressure makes the outside layers flake away in a process called exfoliation. It can also be attacked by the acids in rainwater, and scoured by ice.

The granite walls of El Capitan in California, USA, have survived millions of years of erosion

Horseshoe Bend on the Colorado River, USA, formed as the river cut down through uplifted rock

◀ CLIFFS AND STACKS
Waves crashing against coastal cliffs can cut them away at a dramatic rate. The softer rock gives way first, often leaving headlands and isolated stacks of harder rock. These stacks off the southern coast of Australia near Melbourne are known as the Twelve Apostles.

Rock is undercut by the waves so the rock above collapses, leaving a sheer cliff

Moving ice loaded with rock fragments would have once filled this Alpine valley

◄ MESAS AND BUTTES

In arid terrain, occasional flash floods cut down through weak points in the rock to form valleys. These get wider and wider, carrying away the softer rock so the harder layers collapse. Eventually all that remains are sheer-sided mesas and smaller buttes, each protected by a cap of hard rock.

Rock debris forms steep scree (rubble) slopes below the towering buttes of Monument Valley, USA

KARST TERRAIN ►

Rainwater is slightly acid, and this enables it to dissolve limestone. The result can be a landscape called karst, with heavily weathered bare rock riddled with caves. In tropical areas the rock is often eroded into spectacular pinnacles.

◄ RIVER EROSION

Rivers cut V-shaped valleys and steep-sided gorges, especially where fast-flowing water carries a lot of rocky debris. The most dramatic gorges form where the land has been slowly uplifted by titanic earth movements, forcing the river to cut deeper and deeper into the landscape.

EROSION

Landscapes are under constant attack from wind, rain, ice, searing heat, oceanic waves, and flowing water loaded with rock fragments. These forces gnaw away at even the hardest rocks, in the processes known as erosion and weathering. Over time they can flatten the highest mountain ranges, carrying the rocky debris away as gravel, sand, and silt. This is deposited in the lowlands or in the sea – where, eventually, it may form new rocks.

Sharp pinnacles of limestone form the Stone Forest near Kunming, China

SLOT CANYON ►

Sandy water pours off high mesas during rare, but torrential desert rainstorms. It funnels through cracks in the rock at the edges of the mesas, eroding them into deep, winding slot canyons. Unlike valleys, these are often broader at the bottom than at the top.

A beam of sunlight gleams through the narrow top of Antelope Canyon, USA

▲ VANISHED GLACIERS

In mountains, and in uplands affected by the last ice age, huge glaciers grinding along the courses of former rivers scoured them out to form deep U-shaped valleys. Where the glaciers have melted, the valleys remain, often with small rivers flowing down them.

RIVERS

Most rivers flow downhill from hills or mountains to the sea. They start as fast-flowing streams, which join together to create small rivers. These often cascade down steep slopes, cutting deep valleys, until they reach flatter ground. Here, regular seasonal flooding creates broad, fertile floodplains. Each river wanders across its floodplain, growing in size but flowing more slowly, until it reaches the estuary or delta where it spills into the sea.

SOURCE ▼

All rivers have a source. It may be a lake, a swamp, or a spring bubbling out of the ground, which feeds the main stream of the young river. In high mountains, the source may be a stream of meltwater pouring from the end of a glacier.

▼ UPPER COURSE

The upland part of a river is known as its upper course. It is usually fast-flowing, with a rocky bed, rapids, and even waterfalls. Here the Churun River cascades over the rim of the flat-topped Auyantepui mountain in Venezuela, South America, at Angel Falls – the highest waterfall on Earth, at 979 m (3,212 ft).

The main stream of a river is joined by other streams, called tributaries. They all add to the flow, especially after heavy rain and during the spring thaw when mountain snow melts. At such times, they turn into torrents, carrying masses of gravel downhill and flowing in "braided" (plaited) patterns. These braided streams flow down from Aoraki (Mount Cook), New Zealand, to join the Hopkins River.

LOWER COURSE ▼

When rivers reach the lowlands they flow more slowly, but carry more water. If they are not controlled they tend to flood each year, spilling over their banks and swamping the landscape. The floodwater leaves layers of fine silt, which build up to form a floodplain of deep, fertile soil. This makes excellent farmland. Here the Willamette River flows across its floodplain in Oregon, USA.

▼ESTUARIES AND DELTAS

At the coast, fresh river water meets the salt water that pushes upriver at high tide. As a result, the river drops mud particles, building up the mudflats of an estuary. If the river flow is more powerful than the flow of the tide, the flats extend out from the shore to form a wide flat area with many outlet channels, known as a delta. This view from space shows the delta of the River Niger as it meets the sea in Nigeria.

VALLEYS AND GORGES ▼

As a river flows down from its upper course, the water usually erodes a winding V-shaped valley through the land. Some rivers pass through steep-sided gorges, like Tiger Leaping Gorge on the River Yangtze in China. Gorges are often created by the collapse of limestone cave systems that once concealed underground rivers.

MEANDERS ▼

As it flows around a bend, river water cuts away the bank on the outside of the bend and drops sand and mud on the inside. This makes the bend more pronounced, so over time its winding course may become a series of exaggerated loops, or meanders. Sometimes a loop is cut off to become an "ox-bow lake", seen here (centre left) as the River Amazon flows through rainforest in Peru, South America.

CAVES

When rock is worn away by coastal erosion or rainwater, weak areas tend to collapse while the surrounding stronger rock survives. This creates cave systems, which may extend for many kilometres in limestone country, and contain huge caverns and underground rivers. Flowing water beneath glaciers can also erode caves in the ice. In places like Hawaii, erupting volcanoes may create lava tubes – tunnels that once contained rivers of red-hot molten rock.

LIMESTONE CAVES

Rainwater dissolves carbon dioxide from the air, turning it into weak carbonic acid. In limestone country, the acidified rainwater drains into the rock and dissolves it, creating chains of potholes and caverns. Where water containing dissolved rock drips from cave ceilings, it leaves stony deposits that build up into hanging stalactites, and stalagmites that grow up from the cave floor.

This big stalagmite is made of stony calcite deposited by centuries of dripping water ___

UNDERGROUND WATER

The water that creates limestone caves flows through the cave systems as underground streams and even rivers. In wet weather these can fill the caves, eroding them into fantastic shapes that are revealed as the water level drops. In some limestone regions, such as the Yucatan in Mexico, there is no surface water at all because all the rivers flow underground. In places they are open to the sky, forming beautiful natural wells called cenotes.

Crystal clear water reveals the banded rock structure of this cave

CRYSTALS

Water dripping through cave systems contains dissolved minerals, such as calcite and gypsum. If the water evaporates or changes its chemical nature slightly, the minerals may become solid again, forming crystals with glittering, faceted, jewel-like shapes.

Delicate calcite crystals have grown on the end of this stalactite where it enters a pool

COASTAL CAVE

On exposed rocky coasts, pounding waves force water into cracks in the rock at such high pressure that they blow the rock apart. This cuts away the rock at water level. Often the rock above collapses to form a sheer cliff, but if the waves cut into a weaker seam they can create deep caves and even rock arches.

GLACIER CAVE

Near the end of a glacier, melting ice creates streams of meltwater that often drain down through crevasses to form vertical sinkholes. When the water reaches the bottom of the glacier, it flows between the ice and rock to erode tunnels and caves in the ancient glacier ice. At times when the melting rate is high these can fill with water, which pours through the ice in a torrent before finally emerging at the glacier tip or snout. In midwinter, however, these glacier caves may be safe to explore.

Ice covers the floor of this glacier cave during a period of reduced melting

ICE CAVE

In some mountain regions, the air inside limestone caves can be so cold that water seeping into the cave immediately freezes. This creates glassy icicles and frozen cascades. The temperature is critical to the formation of these ice caves, so they are quite rare. If the rock around the cave is too cold, water freezes solid before it can enter the cave. If the cave is too warm, all the ice melts and the water drains away through the cave floor.

Water dripping into the Grotte Casteret, in the Spanish Pyrenees mountains, forms a frozen cascade

LAVA TUBE

Now cold and empty, this cave was once filled with a torrent of red-hot lava erupting from a Hawaiian volcano. The lava from such volcanoes is so hot and liquid that it flows like water. As it pours downhill, the top of the flow cools and may become solid, forming the roof of a lava tube. This keeps the heat in and allows the lava inside to keep flowing. When the eruption stops, the lava may flow out to leave a long cave.

Solidified lava forms the roof of the lava tube

CALCITE BARRIERS

Water flowing through the limestone cave of Akiyoshi-do in Japan is saturated with dissolved calcium carbonate, or calcite. Where the water flows over the sloping cave floor, calcite has crystallized to form a series of barriers. The water overflows these in a gentle cascade that falls from one pool to the next.

Water is beautifully clear, despite being full of calcite

CLIMATE ZONES

Variations in the intensity of sunlight striking different parts of Earth drive global air movements and weather systems. Between them, these influences create a variety of climate zones, ranging from steamy tropical rainforests to the icy deserts of Antarctica. Most of these climate zones have a distinctive type of vegetation, which is the basis of a whole wildlife community, or biome.

TROPICAL RAINFOREST ▶
Intense sunshine near the Equator makes moisture evaporate and rise into the air to form huge storm clouds. These spill heavy, warm rain on the land below, fuelling the growth of dense rainforests.

MOUNTAIN ▲
High mountain peaks are very cold, like Arctic tundra, and they have similar tough, low-growing vegetation. Lower mountain slopes are warmer, allowing trees to grow. The upper edge of this zone is called the tree line.

TEMPERATE FOREST ▶
Temperate climates are neither very hot nor very cold. Near oceans, the mild, damp weather allows trees to grow well in summer, but many lose their leaves and stop growing in winter.

DESERT ▶
Some regions get so little rain that they are deserts. Many lie in a zone of hot, dry air near the tropics, but others are just too far from oceans. Some plants live in deserts, so they are not quite barren.

POLAR AND TUNDRA ▲
The polar regions get only weak sunlight in summer, and are dark all winter. They stay frozen all year, but in the north this icy region is surrounded by tundra, which thaws in summer allowing some plants to grow.

MEDITERRANEAN ▲
The dry shrublands that lie between the temperate zones and the main desert regions are named after the Mediterranean area where they are most common. The tough-leaved plants that live there can survive drying out in the hot summers.

CLIMATE ZONES ▼

The climate zones of the world form bands, with tropical rainforest near the Equator, most deserts in the subtropics, and boreal forest in the far north. Grasslands develop where it is too dry for trees.

POLAR AND TUNDRA

BOREAL FOREST

MOUNTAIN

TEMPERATE FOREST

MEDITERRANEAN

DESERT

TEMPERATE GRASSLAND

TROPICAL GRASSLAND

TROPICAL RAINFOREST

TROPICAL GRASSLAND ▲

Tropical regions that are not within the zone of heavy rainfall are too hot and dry to support dense forest. They are seas of grass, often known as savannas, sometimes dotted with trees that can withstand long droughts.

TEMPERATE GRASSLAND ▲

Some temperate areas get little rainfall, usually because they lie at the hearts of great continents. Too dry for trees, they are naturally grassy steppes and prairies – although many are now farmland.

BOREAL FOREST ▲

To the south of the Arctic tundra, the northern continents support a band of dense forest. Most of the trees are conifers with stiff needle-like leaves that can survive the long, freezing winters.

Maize kernels on the cob

Soya bean pods

Dried soya beans

Soya flour

Rice seeds

Rice cakes

Rice

SOYA BEANS ▲
High in protein and rich in oil, soya beans were once known only in the Far East. Now popular with vegetarians, they are grown in warm climates worldwide.

RICE ▼
One of the world's three staple foods – along with maize and wheat – rice is a type of grass that grows in warm climates. It is usually cultivated in flooded "paddy" fields, which cover large areas of the tropics.

MAIZE ▶
The "corn" grown in the Americas is actually maize, a giant grass that grows well in sunny climates. Its big kernels can be cooked and eaten as they are, or ground into flour to make tortillas and corn chips.

Soy sauce

Soya milk

Cooked rice

Corn tortillas

Corn chips

Tofu is a food made from soya

Dried cocoa pod

Grains of rice

Cocoa beans

Fresh cocoa pod

◄ COCOA
The main ingredient of chocolate, cocoa beans come from the pods of the cocoa tree, grown mainly in West Africa and tropical America. The beans are first left to ferment in the sun, then dried, roasted, and either ground into powder or made into cocoa butter.

Bar of chocolate

FARM CROPS

All our plant foods are grown on farms of some kind – from the huge wheat and maize fields of North America, to the banana plantations and coconut groves of the tropics. The crops we harvest today are descended from plants that once grew wild, but which have been bred to give high yields of juicy fruit, edible seeds, or rich vegetable oils.

POTATOES ▶
The potato is the tuber (storage root) of a plant related to tomatoes. It was brought to Europe from South America in the 16th century, and since then it has become one of the world's main foods.

White potatoes

Red potatoes

WHEAT ▼
Wheat is the most important grain crop in mild northern climates, where it is cultivated on a vast scale. A member of the grass family, wheat has been bred to have large seeds for grinding into flour.

Fresh tea leaves

Tea bags

◄ TEA
The leaves used to make tea come from an evergreen bush that grows in tropical and sub-tropical climates. It is cultivated mainly in China and India, where the leaves are hand-picked and quickly dried. Leaf tea can be used as it is, or in paper tea bags.

Bread made from wheat flour

Vine of red tomatoes

Inside a yellow tomato

TOMATOES ▲
Closely related to potatoes, and introduced from the same region of South America in the late 1500s, the tomato is now grown almost worldwide.

Bunch of wheat seedheads

Dried tea leaves

GRAPES ▲

One of the oldest cultivated plants, the grape was grown by Ancient Egyptians 6,000 years ago. Planted in permanent vineyards in warm climates, grapes are harvested for winemaking, eating fresh, and drying as raisins, sultanas, and currants.

Grapes on the vine

Currants and raisins

Sunflower oil

Black grapes

White grapes

SUNFLOWERS ►

The spectacular blooms of sunflowers are made up of hundreds of big seeds. These can be eaten as snacks, but most are processed to produce oil, which is used in cooking. Bees love sunflowers, and turn the nectar into honey.

Sunflower seeds

Stalk of sugar cane

◄ SUGAR CANE

Grown on plantations in tropical and sub-tropical regions of the world, sugar cane is the thick stalk of a large grass. More than half the world's sugar comes from sugar cane. It is also made into alcohol used in biofuels (fuels made from renewable organic material, such as plants).

Brown sugar

Dried sunflower seedhead

Sunflower in bloom

Molasses, or treacle, is a sticky juice produced when sugar cane is boiled

The coconut grows inside a thick, fibrous husk

Ripe banana

◄ BANANAS

Bananas grow in bunches of up to 200, sprouting from clusters of huge leaves that shoot up from fleshy roots. They are a valuable crop throughout the tropics, and are usually cut while green so they are perfectly yellow and ripe when sold.

Green bananas

Desiccated coconut

Fresh coconut

Creamed coconut

COFFEE ▼

Coffee is one of the most valuable crops produced in the tropics. It is made from the seeds of a small tree. Each red berry contains two seeds, or beans, which are dried in the sun before being roasted and ground.

Red coffee berries

COCONUTS ►

The big nuts of the coconut palm are an important crop on many Pacific islands. The fibrous husk is used for matting and rope making. The white "meat" of the nuts is used for food, either fresh, desiccated (dried), as creamed coconut, or as coconut oil.

Inside the coconut is a layer of white "meat"

Roasted coffee beans

of coffee

ENVIRONMENT

As the human population grows and we exploit more of the world's resources, we inflict a lot of damage on our environment. We are doing this partly by destruction of natural habitats, such as forests and wetlands, and partly by pollution of the land, oceans, and atmosphere. Many plants and animals are endangered, and entire ecosystems such as coral reefs and rainforests are under threat.

▼ LAND AND SEA POLLUTION

A lot of the things that we throw away end up scattered over the landscape, or dumped in the sea. Most plastic never rots down and is dangerous to wildlife. Raw sewage and other waste is also poisoning enclosed seas such as the Mediterranean.

▼ GLOBAL WARMING

The most serious threat to the environment is global warming. This is caused by pollution of the air by gases that absorb heat and warm up the atmosphere. This may lead to changes in rainfall patterns and rise in sea levels as polar ice caps melt.

Smog shrouding the Los Angeles skyline, USA

Rubbish in Guanabara Bay, Brazil

▲ AIR POLLUTION

Smoke and gases released by industry, power plants, homes, and vehicles have caused visible air pollution, known as "smog", in many cities. Badly polluted air can be dangerous to breathe, but the main threat from this kind of pollution is global warming.

Plastic waste floating in the sea can trap and kill marine animals, as well as pollute beaches

Coral reefs are dying as oceans become warmer, and many types of coral may soon be extinct

▼ ACID RAIN

Smoke and fumes from industry and power plants combine with moisture in the air to form weak sulfuric and nitric acids. When this acid rain falls it can kill trees and turn lakes too acidic to support life. This is a serious problem in Canada, Russia, and China.

The worst effects of acid rain are suffered in areas that are close to industrial regions

▼ DEFORESTATION

All over the world, vast areas of forest are being destroyed each year. Tropical forests in particular are being felled for timber, and to clear land for farming. This is wrecking some of the richest natural habitats on Earth, and is one of the main causes of climate change.

Coral reef, Fiji

Forest destroyed by acid rain near the Appalachian Mountains, USA

Rainforest clearance in Chiapas, Mexico

◄ LOSS OF BIODIVERSITY

As wild habitats are destroyed, plants and animals have fewer places to live. This makes survival harder for many species. As endangered species die out, it reduces the rich variety of life that is vital to the health of the planet.

Giant panda in Wolong Nature Reserve, Chengdu, China

Cycling to work in San Francisco, USA

PROTECTING EARTH ►

Protecting the environment is not just the job of governments. We can all help by altering the way we live. By cycling to work instead of driving, these city workers are reducing the amount of pollution they produce.

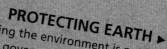

PAINTED BRIDE
At a traditional wedding in the Balkan village of Donje Ljubinje, the bride's face is painted to ward off bad luck. The custom is unique, as is the villagers' language – a mixture of Serbian, Macedonian, and Turkish.

People and places

AFRICA

The discovery of fossilized remains in Africa has led experts to agree that the world's first humans originated from this continent millions of years ago. Today, the population stands at about 1.3 billion, with many people living in rural regions of the 54 countries. Africa's diversity is seen in its varied cultures, long-standing customs, striking scenery, and wildlife. This captivating mix attracts a steady stream of visitors.

INDUSTRY

Nigeria, Algeria, and Libya are major sources of oil and prosperous. Minerals and gas, while South Africa have natural diamonds. Minerals and are mined in the exported from Zambia. Gold and copper and tin are made in are prospered from Namibia.

MUSIC

Celebrations in Africa are usually accompanied by music, with percussion instruments the most popular. Many types of drums are used to create traditional beats, with animal horns and shells blown to make different sounds. Stringed instruments, such as the kora, and double bells, such as the kuge, are also played.

FOOD

Africa's staple foods are crops such as maize, yams, cassava, and plantains. Fish and meat are rarely eaten as a main dish but are added to other ingredients, including beans and lentils. In towns all over Morocco and Tunisia, people sell their home-grown produce at local markets.

Drum

Kuge

Kora

Sahara desert

Mount Kilimanjaro lies on the Tanzania/Kenya border and rises 5,895 m (19,340 ft)

Mediterranean sea

Gulf of Sirte

TUNISIA

MOROCCO

ALGERIA   LIBYA

The Masai "jump-dance" to music, as a show of strength

Nigeria is one of the world's main oil producers

Injera is an African flat bread, served here with beef stew and vegetables

One-third of the world's gold is produced in Johannesburg

Moroccan spices

Stunning views over Cape Town and Table Mountain in South Africa

LANDSCAPE

North Africa boasts the world's largest desert, the Sahara, where temperatures can top 50°C (122°F). Africa's centre is mainly rainforest and rivers, a contrast to the grassy plains down south. Natural landmarks include Kilimanjaro (Africa's highest mountain), the Nile (the longest river), and Lake Victoria (the largest lake).

WILDLIFE

Kenya and Tanzania have Game reserves to protect Africa's wildlife. Game reserves established, giraffes, and big human been zebras, freely without fear of elephants, is Today, zebras roam nowhere else. Three-quarters of cats roam the continent. Three-quarters of hunters. The wildlife are found nowhere else. also rich with animals are found nowhere else. Madagascar's animals.

Ring-tailed lemurs are native to the island of Madagascar

Endangered mountain gorillas live in Rwanda's Volcanoes National Park

Dates

Cocoa pod

TOURISM

Visitors to Africa go on safari to see the wildlife at close range. The economy is also boosted by tourists soaking up the sun on the beaches of Tunisia, Morocco, and South Africa, as well as the islands of the Seychelles. One of Africa's most visited historic sites is the ancient pyramids of Giza in Egypt, built some 4,500 years ago.

FARMING

Many Africans in rural villages grow root vegetables and maize (corn) to sell at markets. Northern Africa has the best climate for cultivating dates, olives, and citrus fruits. Kenya's rainfall yields high tea production, while the Ivory Coast and Ghana put together produce more than half the world's cocoa. Cotton is grown for export.

Fibres from the cotton boll plant are used to weave cloth

Head of corn

ERITREA DJIBOUTI SOMALILAND (not internationally recognized) Gulf of Aden ETHIOPIA SOMALIA Equator SEYCHELLES COMOROS MAURITIUS MADAGASCAR INDIAN OCEAN Mozambique Channel CHAD SOUTH SUDAN UGANDA KENYA RWANDA BURUNDI DEM. REP. CONGO TANZANIA MALAWI MOZAMBIQUE CENTRAL AFRICAN REPUBLIC CONGO ZAMBIA ZIMBABWE ESWATINI (formerly SWAZILAND) LESOTHO CAMEROON GABON ANGOLA NAMIBIA BOTSWANA SOUTH AFRICA Tropic of Capricorn NIGERIA EQUATORIAL GUINEA SAO TOME & PRINCIPE BENIN TOGO BURKINA GHANA IVORY COAST LIBERIA SIERRA LEONE GUINEA GUINEA-BISSAU THE GAMBIA SENEGAL

Freshwater Crocodile

Tiger

The *Sasakia charonda* butterfly, nicknamed Japanese emperor, is Japan's national butterfly

The stock exchange in Tokyo is the third largest in the world

South Korea is the fifth-largest car manufacturing nation in the world

WILDLIFE

Some of the world's most endangered mammals are found in Asia, including the snow leopard, red panda, and Asiatic black bear. The forests of Malaysia, Indonesia, and Borneo shelter elephants, tigers, and orang-utans from the heat. Sharks, turtles, and manta rays live among the reefs off the coast of southeast Asia.

INDUSTRY

By exporting resources of oil and natural gas, Asian nations such as Saudi Arabia, Iraq, and Kuwait have become wealthy. Japan, too, has seen rapid economic growth from its cutting-edge technology. India, China, and other Asian countries have benefitted from mass-producing cars, clothes, and electronics for export.

SPORT

There is a long tradition of martial arts in Asia, which includes judo, karate, and sumo wrestling in Japan and kung fu in China. Tibetans were once expert horse-riders and racing remains a common pursuit. India, Pakistan, and Sri Lanka excel at cricket, while table tennis is also popular. Table tennis, along with football, is China's most popular sport

Judo

Rice is Asia's staple food and has been cultivated for more than 9,500 years

194

ASIA

The largest continent is a land of extremes. From the ice of the Arctic to the heat of the Indian Ocean islands, Asia takes in treacherous mountains, desolate dunes, treeless steppes, fertile plains, and tropical rainforests. The continent's 48 countries show many contrasts, with businesses booming in the expanding cities, while rural communities farm the fields. Today, more than 60 per cent of the world's population call Asia their home.

CULTURE

India's successful "Bollywood" film industry produces more than 1,000 films a year from its base in Mumbai. Art, music, and dance are also deep-rooted in Asian culture, with Bhutan's masked temple dancers, Cambodia's classical dances, and Indonesia's masked puppets.

Dragon masks make a colourful sight at dragon boat festivals and Chinese New Year

Petronas Towers in Kuala Lumpur, Malaysia

Pho Bac, beef noodle soup

Sushi

FOOD

Asia's dishes are derived from the rich mix of cultures. Culinary delights from India (unique blends of spices for curries), China (fried rice, meat, and vegetables), Thailand (curries with coconut milk and rice or noodles), and Japan (raw or cooked fish dishes called sushi) have made Asian cuisine a hit with locals and tourists alike.

China grows the most tea in the world, followed by India. In India, the plants are grown in the cooler hill regions of the north

CITIES

The economic boom in Asia has produced super-cities: Dubai, Kuala Lumpur, and Hong Kong are now centres where ancient people and tourism. Many in a The economic boom in Asia has produced super-cities. Dubai, Kuala Lumpur, and Hong Kong are now where offices, resulting in a next to high-rise cities for luxury living, leave rural areas of slums and home to combination

The bright lights of Hong Kong, home to 7.4 million people

A traffic jam in Delhi, India's second largest city

At the Western Wall in Jerusalem, Jewish people gather to offer prayers

Bathing on the banks of the River Ganges at Varanasi is a holy act for Hindus

Golden Buddha

RELIGION

All the main religions started in Asia: Although the three faiths differ from country to country, Hinduism, and Islam, the most followed in Asia are Buddhism, Hinduism, and Islam, today, people worship by chanting or praying, at home, in temples, or in mosques. Buddhism and Hinduism focus is on spiritual enlightenment.

FOOD
The USA is famous for its fast food, especially hamburgers, hot dogs, and soft drinks. These foods can be prepared and served quickly. A wealth of fresh fruit and vegetables grown in California and Florida provide a healthy option. Down Mexico way the preference is for spicy foods with chillies.

Most of the peanuts grown in the USA are made into peanut butter

CULTURE
American movies and TV shows are popular around the world. Many famous music styles, such as rock-and-roll, jazz, blues, country, and soul, have their roots in the USA. Canada's annual Calgary Stampede celebrates its cattle-trading roots, while Mexico has parades and feasts on saints' days.

Elvis Presley became the ultimate icon of US rock-and-roll music

Canada's maple trees produce 71 per cent of all maple syrup worldwide – a favourite on pancakes

The USA grows 10 per cent of the world's oranges

Baseball glove and ball

SPORT
The highlight of the American football calendar is a championship game called the Super Bowl. This is the most watched television event in the USA. Baseball and basketball are also longstanding favourites. The colder climate of Canada has made skiing, ice skating, and ice hockey the main winter pursuits.

501

Statue of Liberty

LANDMARKS
New York's Statue of Liberty welcomed immigrants arriving by boat, while the One World Trade Center is the city's tallest building. Another feature is Mount Rushmore, where the faces of four US presidents are carved into the rock. Far older landmarks can be found in Central America with the ruins of Aztec and Mayan civilizations.

Mount Rushmore

Ice hockey boot has a blade to enable hockey players to glide across the ice

PACIFIC OCEAN

Alaska (USA)
Gulf of Alaska
C A
UNITED STA OF AMERIC
MEXICO
Gulf of Mexico
THE BA
GUATEMALA
BELIZE
EL SALVADOR
JAMA
Carib
COSTA RICA
HONDURAS
NICARAG
PANAMA

Mexico's guitar groups play and sing their traditional mariachi music

The Rocky Mountains stretch from Alaska in the north to the US border in the south

LANDSCAPE
One-third of Canada lies inside the Arctic Circle and stays frozen most of the year. Heading down through North America's snowy Rocky Mountains and forested Appalachians, the scenery turns into grassy plains, known as prairies. The USA is a mix of plains, deserts, and national parks such as Yellowstone and Yosemite. Further south are the beaches of Mexico and the Caribbean.

Oscars are statues given to film industry winners at Hollywood's Academy Awards

NORTH AMERICA

Before the arrival of Europeans in the 16th century, tribes of native peoples were the only inhabitants of North America. Since then, waves of immigration to both Canada and the USA have made these countries pioneers of financial growth and contemporary culture. The mainly Spanish-speaking countries of Central America have lush, mountainous landscapes and are rich in tradition and culture.

The Grand Canyon was formed by water and ice over millions of years

Bison

Grey-banded kingsnake

Canada's harp seal pups are born with fluffy white fur for extra warmth

American football helmet

INDUSTRY
The USA grew wealthy by producing vast quantities of wheat, iron, steel, electronics, cars, and aircraft. Fishing is an important industry along the Pacific Coast, with salmon canned for export. Canada is the largest exporter of forest products, mainly softwood used in construction, while Mexico sells its natural gas and oil reserves.

Computer chips from California, the centre for microelectronics

WILDLIFE
Northern parts of Canada host more animals than people, including bears, elk, and moose in the Rocky Mountains. Across the USA, national parks protect bison, antelope, and deer. Florida's Everglades is a unique wetland area, with many rare animals such as the Florida panther and manatee. Snakes and scorpions can survive the heat of Mexico's Sonoran desert.

Combine harvesters farm wheat on the American prairies

Cadillac car

DRM CARS

The tango dance evolved in Argentina's slums during the late 19th century

In 2002 Brazil won football's World Cup for a record-breaking fifth time

Coffee beans

CROPS
Brazil produces one-third of the world's coffee, while Ecuador's climate is ideal for growing tomatoes and bananas. Steep hillsides are terraced for farming in Chile and Peru, where potatoes are planted on the higher slopes of the Andes, and corn is sown lower down.

Sap is collected from rubber trees in the Amazon rainforest to produce rubber

Banana

Brazil nuts

CULTURE
Music and dance form the heart of South American culture. The rhythmic dance of the samba is a notable highlight of Rio de Janeiro's famous five-day carnival, which features spectacular parades and parties in Brazil's capital. Another common sight is football games on the streets and beaches.

In the rainy season, the River Amazon floods, covering large parts of the rainforest in water

WILDLIFE
The Amazon is the world's largest rainforest and could contain 10 per cent of all animal species. The tree canopy teems with jaguars, sloths, and the forest floor teems with snakes, lizards, and insects. Colourful toucans, macaws, and kingfishers swoop over the River Amazon, where dolphins and turtles swim.

Red-eyed tree frogs are active at night, searching for insects to eat

The toucan's large beak enables it to pick fruit from trees

PHYSICAL FEATURES
Three contrasting landscapes dominate South America. From the west, leading down to the Pacific Ocean, are vast, grassy plains called the pampas (which means "flat" in Spanish). To the south Amazon rainforest is the dense Andes Mountains. In the northeast spreads half of Brazil. From the mountains, towering peaks rise the heart of South

Angel Falls in Venezuela drops 979 m (3,212 ft) and is the highest uninterrupted waterfall in the world

The Patagonia region at the southern tip of the continent is known for its dramatic glaciers

Sharp-teethed, meat-eating piranhas swim in South American rivers

ATLANTIC OCEAN

French Guiana (to France)

SURINAME

GUYANA

VENEZUELA

COLOMBIA

ECUADOR

PERU

BRAZIL

Caribbean Sea

Equator

SOUTH AMERICA

Rich in history, language, and culture, South America is a vibrant place. Nature has made its mark in the trees of the Amazon rainforest, while ancient civilizations have left theirs in the city of Machu Picchu in the Andes Mountains. The influence of Spanish and Portugese colonization remains in the languages, while samba sounds and traditional tangos resonate at the festivals.

INCAS
The Incas were the last great civilization to emerge in South America. During the 12th century, expert architects created their capital at Cusco. By the 15th century, their empire had spread from Equador through Peru to Chile. Hearing of great riches, the Spanish arrived in 1532 to set up colonies and ended the Inca reign.

This ear ornament was made by the Chimu, a people who were eventuallly conquered by the Incas

Yerba mate leaves are used to make a popular tea, drunk from a hollow gourd (shell)

Peruvian dolls were hand made from llama or alpaca wool

Hippeastrum is a colourful plant that thrives in Peru and Chile, and produces flowers up to 25 cm (10 in) across

Beef is a key component of Argentine cuisine

FOOD
Maize is a staple food used in bread and cakes stuffed with meat or cheese. Potatoes, squash, rice, and different types of beans are also meal-time favourites. Peruvians love spicy foods, so hot chilli peppers are often on the menu.

TREES AND PLANTS
A large part of the continent is pampas (grassy plain), which is one of the richest grazing areas in the world. Variety comes from the Amazon rainforest, where about 40,000 species of plants flourish. Unique plants grow in Venezuela's sandstone hills and Chile's Atacama desert, where species have adapted to survive the lack of water.

Cardon cactus

Tropic of Capricorn

ATLANTIC OCEAN

PACIFIC OCEAN

PARAGUAY

URUGUAY

ARGENTINA

CHILE

Falkland Islands (to UK)

Roger Federer celebrates winning a Wimbledon title at the famous tennis competition in London

SPORT

The British, Spanish, and Italian football leagues are considered the best in the world. Football and rugby are played throughout the year, tennis and cricket are summer sports, and mountain ski resorts have busy winter seasons.

The Tour de France was first held in 1903 and is now the world's biggest cycling race

This famous clock tower is part of Britain's Houses of Parliament

Formula 1 motor racing is a popular sport in Europe

Portugal has some of the best deep-sea fishing in Europe

Germany is one of the world's leading car producers

The steel industry is thriving in eastern Europe

Flower farming, especially tulips, is an important industry in Holland

INDUSTRY

Germany is the continent's industrial leader, with its car production and high-tech goods industries. Forestry flourishes in Finland and Sweden, while cod-fishing is big business in Norway and Iceland.

About 60 per cent of farmland in Greece is used to grow olives

Map labels

ICELAND
NORWAY
SWEDEN
FINLAND
Shetland Islands
Orkney Islands
Outer Hebrides
Scotland
ESTONIA
North Sea
LATVIA
Northern Ireland
LITHUANIA
IRELAND
UNITED KINGDOM
DENMARK
RUSSIA (Kaliningrad)
Wales
England
BELARU
NETHERLANDS
POLAND
BELGIUM
GERMANY
LUXEMBOURG
CZECH REPUBLIC (CZECHIA)
Bay of Biscay
FRANCE
SLOVAKIA
LIECHTENSTEIN
AUSTRIA
SWITZERLAND
HUNGARY
SLOVENIA
ROMANIA
CROATIA
MONACO
PORTUGAL
ANDORRA
SAN MARINO
BOSNIA & HERZEGOVINA
SERBIA
SPAIN
Corsica
ITALY
Mallorca
Menorca
MONTENEGRO
KOSOVO (disputed)
BULGARIA
Ibiza
Sardinia
ALBANIA
MACEDONIA
Gibraltar (to UK)
Balearic Islands
Tyrrhenian Sea
Mediterranean Sea
Aegean Sea
Sicily
Ionian Sea
GREECE
MALTA

CITIES
Many European cities feature castles and cathedrals. The centre of the Czech capital Prague is a World Heritage Site. Paris and Milan are fashion leaders, while the financial centres of London and Geneva are amongst the world's richest cities.

Norway's spectacular fjords are one of Europe's most photographed landscapes

LANDSCAPES
Across the continent, landscapes differ dramatically. Iceland's glaciers and Norway's fjords contrast with the mountain ranges of the Alps and Pyrenees. Around the Mediterranean are fertile fields and sandy beaches.

The active volcano of Mount Vesuvius in Italy stands 1,280 m (4,200 ft) tall

EUROPE

For a small continent, Europe has a made a big impact. In centuries past, its inhabitants spread across the globe, building empires. Those days are gone, but the continent's influence remains clear in the European languages, architecture, and entertainment still evident around the world. Thanks to industrial growth and big business, many of the 44 countries are wealthy, with people enjoying a high standard of living.

RUSSIA

Russia is famous for its ballet companies, such as the Bolshoi Ballet of Moscow and the Kirov Ballet of St Petersburg

Bronze statue crafted by celebrated 20th-century British sculptor Henry Moore

CULTURE
Europe has a rich heritage of literature, art, music, opera, and ballet, with many pioneering writers, artists, composers, and dancers capturing the public imagination. Museums, theatres, opera houses, and art exhibitions draw crowds in the major cities.

KAZAKHSTAN

Painted in 1888, *Sunflowers* by the Dutch painter Vincent Van Gogh is one of the world's best-known works of art

RAINE

Paella is a rice-based dish containing meat and seafood

Sea of Azov

Caspian Sea

Black Sea

GEORGIA

AZERBAIJAN

TURKEY

FOOD
Pizza and pasta are Italian favourites, while France is synonymous with strong cheese, crêpes, and mussels. Germans serve smoked sausages, Spaniards prepare their speciality paella, and sweet-toothed Belgians are known for their luxurious chocolates.

Crêpe is a type of thin pancake

Mussels are a popular dish in Belgium and France

CULTURE

The beliefs, culture, and art of the continent's original inhabitants form a rich heritage. Aboriginal Australians have a deep-rooted respect for the natural world. The Maoris of New Zealand practise a traditional dance called the haka. The Polynesians of the Pacific Islands enjoy a family-centred culture.

Aboriginal art depicts patterns or scenes from the natural world

Religious and mythical symbols were carved into the wood of Polynesian dolls

Maori tools were blessed by their creators to ensure they worked well

SPORT

The climate allows Australasians to make the most of the great outdoors. Cricket, rugby, and golf are popular pastimes, while sailing and surfing are coastal favourites. Preferred spectator sports are tennis, cricket, and rugby. Australia's cricket side and New Zealand's rugby union team enjoy huge success.

Funnel-web spiders live in eastern Australia, and can kill a person with a single venomous bite

WILDLIFE

Australasia's best-known native creatures are marsupials (mammals that hold their young in a pouch), such as kangaroos, koalas, and wombats. Many birds are also unique to the continent, including kookaburras and emus. Some of the world's deadliest snakes and spiders live there as well.

Koalas

MICRONESI

PALAU

Equator

New Guinea

Australia's thorny devil is a spiny lizard that blends in with its desert surroundings

Kangaroos

The trunk of the baobab tree stores water to survive periods of drought

TREES AND PLANTS

Australasia has many trees and plants that don't grow anywhere else. About 80 per cent of New Zealand's plants are unique, while nearly all the world's eucalyptus trees originated in Australia. The country's centre is hot and barren, but trees, plants, and fungi thrive in the humid rainforests.

Tropic of Capricorn

AUST

A U S T

INDUSTRY

Sheep and cattle farming has made lush New Zealand a major exporter of wool, meat, and dairy products. Rich in natural resources such as iron ore, gold, nickel, silver, and diamonds, Australia is the leading exporter of coal. Minerals such as copper and gold are Papua New Guinea's main exports.

Gabiny fruit

Eucalyptus leaves provide the main source of food for koalas

Australia's cricket team

New Zealand's
All Blacks rugby team

The huge sandstone rock of
Uluru is an ancient site
sacred to Aboriginal people

PHYSICAL FEATURES
From New Zealand's geysers and glaciers
to Australia's coral reefs and coastlines
and the many volcanic islands of the Pacific,
the region is a kaleidoscope of dramatic
panoramas. The ancient rock of Uluru and
the steaming vents of New Zealand are two
of the region's most famous features.

MARSHALL
ISLANDS

PACIFIC OCEAN

NAURU

KIRIBATI

KIRIBATI

TUVALU

Tokelau
(to NZ)

Cook
Islands
(to NZ)

Gushing springs of hot
water, called geysers,
erupt regularly on New
Zealand's North Island

GUINEA

SOLOMON
ISLANDS

SAMOA

TONGA

Niue
(to NZ)

French
Polynesia
(to France)

VANUATU

FIJI

PACIFIC OCEAN

Australia's Sunshine
Coast is a popular stretch
of beaches and bays

Coral
Sea

New Caledonia
(to France)

Diamonds

LIA

NEW
ZEALAND

AUSTRALASIA
AND OCEANIA

This southern-hemisphere region includes Australia, New
Zealand, Papua New Guinea, and neighbouring
Pacific islands. As all 14 countries are islands, much
of the wildlife is unique and the landscapes are largely
unspoilt. Settlers from southeast Asia first arrived in
Australia thousands of years ago. By the 18th century,
European immigrants had reached the region, which is
now home to more than 30 million people.

Tasmania

Gold nugget

There are about
27.6 million sheep in
New Zealand. Some are
sheared for their wool

The Three Sisters
is a distinctive rock
formation in the Blue
Mountains, Australia

TOURISM
Australia and New Zealand are popular
tourist destinations all year round thanks
to the stunning scenery. Bustling harbour
cities, such as Sydney and Auckland, offer
a mix of beach life and culture. Famous
buildings include the Sydney Opera House
and Sydney Harbour Bridge.

Sydney Opera House

ANTARCTICA

In the coldest continent on Earth, the temperature can drop to -80°C (-112°F) and human skin can freeze in seconds. Yet thanks to scientists who are specially equipped to brave this harsh habitat, research on some of the world's most remote landscapes and wildlife is underway. Only discovered in 1820, Antarctica covers 14 million sq km (5.5 million sq miles) and, incredibly, 98 per cent of it is covered with ice.

RESEARCH
About 70 permanent and more than 100 temporary research stations have been set up in Antarctica. Scientists analyze Antarctica's weather, climate, wildlife, and geology. Projects include monitoring ice samples to detect changes in the atmosphere, and tracking penguins.

The Amundsen-Scott research base is named after the two famous expedition leaders who raced to reach the South Pole in 1911

Telescopes at Concordia research base provide astronomers with exceptional views of the clear skies above Antarctica

TOURISM
Since the 1950s, cruise ships have brought tourists to Antarctica, and today about 50,000 people visit each year. They arrive either by ship or take sightseeing trips by plane over the South Pole, the southernmost point on the planet. Insulated clothing and goggles are essential at all times.

Tourists stay on board the cruise ships overnight as there are no resorts

The largest penguin of all, the emperor penguin huddles in groups to keep warm during blizzards

Despite their name, crabeater seals eat krill (tiny marine creatures)

Humpback whales are sociable mammals, preferring to eat and travel in groups, which are called pods

WILDLIFE
Animals face a struggle for survival in Antarctica, but fish, seals, and whales can thrive in the sea. The Antarctic Peninsula has the mildest climate of the continent, making it a hub for wildlife. In summer, millions of seals and birds breed on the peninsula and nearby islands.

205

LANDSCAPE

Dramatic seas, steep glaciers, and giant icebergs up to 295 km (183 miles) long are the main features of this unique landscape. The continent is separated into east and west Antarctica by the Transantarctic Mountains, which stretch for 3,500 km (2,175 miles).

Mount Erebus on Ross Island is the southernmost active volcano in the world

Ice shelves form where the land ice meets the sea, with Ross Ice Shelf the continent's largest

SOUTHERN OCEAN

SOUTHERN OCEAN

Scotia Sea

Riiser-Larsen Sea

Fimbul Ice Shelf

Dronning Maud Land

Enderby Land

Brunt Ice Shelf

Weddell Sea

Coats Land

Kemp Land

Larsen Ice Shelf

Antarctic Peninsula

Filchner Ice Shelf

Mac Robertson Land

Amery Ice Shelf

Wilkins Ice Shelf

Ronne Ice Shelf

Princess Elizabeth Land

West Ice Shelf

Bellinghausen Sea

ANTARCTICA

South Pole

Transantarctic Mountains

Shackleton Ice Shelf

Wilkes Land

Vincennes Bay

Ross Ice Shelf

Terre Adélie

Porpoise Bay

George V Land

Dumont d'Urville Sea

Ice cores are samples taken by scientists for use in the study of global warming

CLIMATE

In winter, the Southern Ocean freezes, and the ice cap of Antarctica almost doubles in size. In summer, the temperature rarely rises above freezing. Less than 5 cm (2 in) of snow falls a year, making the area drier than the Sahara Desert. With gales blowing at more than 300 km/h (186 mph), it is the windiest continent, too.

FLAGS

Historically, army leaders carried flags into battle as a rallying point for the soldiers. Today, flags are used to decorate buildings, mark public events, start races, honour the dead, or to spell out messages or warnings from one ship to another. But by far the most recognizable ones are national flags – vibrant in colour and unique in symbolism. Organizations and citizens fly the flag for their countries, building up a strong sense of identity, pride, and unity.

Saudi Arabia

Canada

Norway

Bhutan

Australia
①

Denmark

Philippines

PHILIPPINES

Iceland

Chile

India
③

KAZAKHSTAN

Kazakhstan

South Korea
②

USA
④

Japan

Kenya
⑤

Somalia

Mexico
⑥

Germany

PERU

PERU

Peru

⑦

PHILIPPINES PHILI

⑧ Ireland

Spain ⑨

New Zealand

NEW ZEALAND

Jamaica ⑩

Antigua and Barbuda

South Africa

Guyana

St Lucia

COLOMBIA

BELIZE

Belize

Colombia

China

URUGUAY

Russia

Uruguay

Sweden

IRELAND
⑧ This has been the flag of Ireland since 1919. The orange stands for Protestants, the green for Catholics, and the white for the peace between them.

INDIA
③ At the centre of the tricolour (three colours) is the *ashoka chakra*, meaning "wheel of law". This symbolizes the hope that the country will continue to move forward peacefully.

MEXICO
⑥ Traditionally, these colours had religious and military connotations, but the new meanings are defined as hope (green), unity (white), and the blood of heroes (red). The central image is a symbol from an earlier Aztec heritage.

SPAIN
⑨ This young flag was established in 1981. On the left-hand side, where the flag gets hoisted, is the Spanish coat-of-arms, which includes the royal seal.

AUSTRALIA
① The flag features a combination of the United Kingdom's flag, the Commonwealth Star (with its points symbolizing the original states of Australia), and the Southern Cross constellation (only visible in the Southern Hemisphere).

USA
④ This flag is nicknamed the "Stars and Stripes". The 50 stars represent the states of the Union, while the red and white stripes are the 13 original colonies to join the Union.

GERMANY
⑦ During the Napoleonic wars of the 19th century, German soldiers wore black uniforms with red braid and gold buttons. These became the country's official colours, appearing on the national flag. Public buildings often fly the flag vertically.

JAMAICA
⑩ The flag of this Caribbean country shows a gold diagonal cross, which embodies the shining sun, green, for the fertile land, and black, which represents strength and creativity.

SOUTH KOREA
② A red and blue Yin Yang symbol on the South Korean flag represents the Chinese philosophy that everything in the Universe has an opposite. The four surrounding trigrams (groups of three lines) represent the ideals of balance, circulation, harmony, and symmetry.

KENYA
⑤ Since 1963, Kenya's flag has been dominated by a shield and spears, used by the country's Masai people. This symbol shows how the nation is determined to defend its freedom.

Netherlands

Brazil

France

United Kingdom

MAPS

Maps provide visual representations of the world, revealing the layout of our planet in a variety of ways. Some depict Earth's geographical features, or the borders and boundaries between nations. Other maps detail road routes and street names, or aid navigation on urban transport networks. Scales on maps can be used to work out real distances, and keys explain map symbols.

SATELLITE IMAGE

Space satellites are used to photograph Earth, capturing its surface in great detail. Orbiting thousands of kilometres above the planet, satellites track changes in the land, the ocean, and the atmosphere.

BUILDING PLAN

When planning a new structure, engineers first map out the building. Details such as layout, walls, and entrances are marked to assist workers during the construction. Precise measurements are added to give the true size of the project.

STREET MAP

Useful tools for navigating cities and towns, street maps include road names and notable landmarks such as railway stations, hospitals, churches, and parks. Street maps are available online and via some mobile phones.

GEOLOGICAL MAP

Different rock types are coded by colour on geological maps. Geologists study these maps to determine the location of minerals and oils, while structural engineers ensure rock types suit their construction plans before laying foundations.

SAILING CHART

Nautical maps of coastal or ocean areas are called charts. They include information about tides, currents, depths, potential hazards, and features of the seabed. Sailors carry these charts on board their ships to help with marine navigation.

POLITICAL MAP

National and state borders are shown on political maps. Contrasting colours highlight different countries, so the legal boundaries stand out more clearly. To aid understanding, major cities, rivers, seas, and oceans are also labelled.

ROAD MAP

This visual aid for road-users is the most commonly used map of all. Covering a much larger area than a street map, road maps use different colours and lines to represent motorways, main roads, and country routes.

PHYSICAL MAP

Permanent natural features are depicted on physical maps. Deserts, mountains, lakes, rivers, and oceans are identified, as well as the contrast between high and low land. Some physical maps go into more detail, pointing out land use and soil type.

ALLIANCES

All over the world, groups of people or nations come together for common causes. The unions they form are called alliances. With financial backing and international influence, these alliances pursue shared goals.

UN ▲
After World War II ended in 1945, the United Nations (UN) was set up to promote peace. Today, the UN also plays a part in human rights, economic development, and fighting disease.

INTERPOL ▶
Established in 1923, Interpol helps national police forces co-operate on criminal cases across countries.

WORLD BANK ▲
The World Bank was founded in 1944 to help rebuild postwar Europe. Today, it gives poorer nations financial and technical assistance.

NATO ▶
The North Atlantic Treaty Organization (NATO) was established in 1949. The alliance protects the safety of its American and European members.

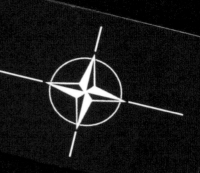

▲ WORLD TRADE ORGANIZATION
Created in 1995, this is the only international organization managing the laws of trade between countries.

OIC ▶
In 1969, Islamic leaders formed an alliance to protect Muslim interests. Today, the Organization of Islamic Cooperation (OIC) has 57 member nations.

OPEC ▶
The Organization of Petroleum Exporting Countries (OPEC) consists of 15 of the largest oil-producing nations. Its goal is to ensure there is a regular and constant supply of oil.

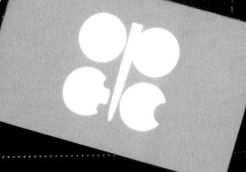

LA FRANCOPHONIE ▲

About 220 million people speak French worldwide. To celebrate this, a group of French-speaking nations set up La Francophonie in 1970 to promote French language and culture.

EU ▲

The European Union (EU) was created in 1993 to ensure that goods, services, finance, and labour could move freely between member nations.

CIS ►

After the communist Soviet Union collapsed in 1991, leaders of the new republics formed the Commonwealth of Independent States (CIS). Its 12 states coordinate foreign and economic policy.

LATIN UNION ▼

Languages such as Italian, Spanish, and French are derived from the Latin of Ancient Rome. The Latin Union was founded in 1954 to preserve and promote the common heritage of countries with Latin-based languages, until 2012 when it was dissolved.

◄ AFRICAN UNION

In 2001, the African Union was established to reduce conflict and poverty across Africa. With its headquarters in Ethiopia, the organization has 55 member nations.

ASEAN ►

In 1967, Thailand, Indonesia, Malaysia, Singapore, and the Philippines founded the Association of Southeast Asian Nations (ASEAN). Today, ten member nations share the goals of peace and economic growth.

ECONOMY

Since ancient times, farmers have taken goods to markets, where customers bartered over prices and sales were agreed. Today the range of goods is massive, but the principles remain the same. Societies function by people working together to grow, build, manufacture, or distribute products for consumers who want them. Such a system, for the production, distribution, and consumption of goods, is called an economy.

These umbrellas for toes might seem useless, but if there is a demand, then a supply will follow

SUPPLY AND DEMAND
An economy works because there are people supplying goods and services to people who will pay for them. When there is a big demand, the price of these goods and services goes up, but if there is a huge supply, the prices drop to encourage the demand.

PRODUCTION
Every country uses its raw materials and its people to make all kinds of products to sell. The best ways to maximize profit are to reduce production costs, pay the workforce less, and use the speediest manufacturing tools. As production increases, so the economy grows.

TRADITIONAL ECONOMY
In less wealthy countries, a traditional economy is more common. People produce a few goods for themselves and sell what is left. Rural farmers may grow produce such as fruit and vegetables to feed their families, and then sell the rest at local markets.

DOMESTIC WORK
Any unpaid work done at home is not counted as part of the economy. Housework, for example, only contributes to the market economy if a cleaner is paid for the job.

COMMAND VERSUS MIXED

The government takes control in a command economy, and is in charge of the country's economic activity. However, in a mixed economy, some industries, such as health and transport, are publicly owned and run by the government, but the rest are privately owned.

RAW MATERIALS

Some goods are used to create a different product. These are usually raw materials or partly finished items, such as steel, coal, wood, and paper. These goods are often unrecognizable in the final product.

CONSUMER GOODS

Producers must recognize what people want in order to create consumer goods that will prove popular, sell well, and increase profit. A wide range of goods, such as cars, clothing, toys, and food, are offered by many different producers to ensure that individual consumer needs are satisfied.

German flag

In times of war, governments can call upon citizens to fight for their country

CITIZENSHIP ▲

People born into a country or state are called its citizens. This gives them the right to protection by the government as well as the right to vote. Along with rights come responsibilities, and citizens are expected to abide by the laws of the land. Immigrants and refugees can sometimes become citizens of another country. Each country or state is identified by its national flag.

THE STATE

Throughout history, countries have been run by a variety of leaders and governments. At one time, heads of state were royalty, ruling with absolute authority. In many countries, power has now passed to the people, as democratic elections have replaced royal rule. Many citizens have the right to vote for their political leaders and to protest against them when necessary. Having won a place at the forefront of government, prime ministers and presidents run many world states.

A passport is an official government document that allows each citizen to travel abroad

PROTEST ▼

If the citizens of a state or nation do not agree with the actions or policies of the ruling government, they sometimes rally together to stage a public protest. Often marching to the government's headquarters, people voice their concerns in an attempt to bring about change.

Protesters demonstrate outside the Philippine presidential palace in 2007

Megaphones are often used by protesters to make their voices heard

LEGISLATURE ▶

States have elected representatives who are responsible for making laws, known as legislating. Government members debate new policies or changes to existing laws. Once the laws have been agreed, they are officially drafted by the legislatures. These laws must then be followed by all citizens.

Ceremonial mace is kept in the UK's House of Commons

United States Congress where new laws are passed

In the House of Commons, ministers debate changes to law and government policy

A ballot box is a locked container into which citizens place their confidential votes

Wigs are worn by judges in some countries as part of legal tradition

◄ LAW AND ORDER

A country's judges, collectively called the judiciary, make rulings on criminal allegations or civil disputes in courts of law. They interpret and uphold laws passed by the government before delivering their verdicts to the citizens involved. The law in most countries is upheld by a police force.

German police cap

DEMOCRACY ▲

In democratic societies, citizens have the opportunity to vote for their preferred candidate from a range of political parties. On election day, people cast their vote and the party with the majority is established as the new government.

Coloured rosettes are sometimes worn by members of political parties to show their allegiance in the run-up to an election

A gavel and block used by a judge to maintain silence in court

United States presidential seal

◄ MONARCHY

In the past, most countries were ruled by a king or a queen and, as head of state, the monarch's word was considered law. Although some countries still maintain a monarchy, their role is mainly ceremonial. It is the elected government that generally takes responsibility for how the country is run.

Presidents in South America, such as Chile's former leader Michelle Bachelet, wear sashes as symbols of office

Crafted with priceless gems in 1838, the State Crown was first worn by British queen, Victoria

REPUBLICS ▲

Countries that have a president as their head of state instead of a king or queen are called republics. Presidents can be elected by the citizens or appointed by the legislature, and usually act as head of the nation's government.

This imperial seal of China shows a dragon guarding a pearl, which represents wisdom

215

ABRAHAM LINCOLN ▶

A passionate opponent of slavery, Lincoln led the Union States to victory in the Civil War of 1860–65. His speech at Gettysburg, on the principles of human equality, is one of the greatest in American history.

JAMES GARFIELD ▼

The twentieth US president was James Garfield, an army general. In 1881, he was assassinated after less than four months in office.

BENJAMIN HARRISON ▼

Electricity was first installed in the White House during the Harrison presidency (1889–93) – his wife would not touch the switches, fearing electrocution.

US PRESIDENTS

The United States is a superpower, dominating global affairs. The nation's head of state, the president, is regarded as one of the most powerful people in the world. Presidential elections are followed closely by other countries, as political decisions made by the US president can impact the rest of the world. The president serves a term of four years, and today can hold office for a maximum of two terms.

▲ GROVER CLEVELAND

Grover Cleveland is the only president to have served two non-consecutive terms in office, 1885–89 and 1893–97. His second term was plagued by industrial strikes.

◀ HERBERT HOOVER

The Hoover presidency saw the Great Depression of 1929, and public opposition to prohibition (the banning of alcohol). He did not win a second term.

▲ FRANKLIN D ROOSEVELT

"FDR" served a record four terms in office from 1933–1945. He brought an end to the Depression with a "New Deal" to bring relief to the unemployed, and took the USA into World War II.

HARRY TRUMAN ▲

Truman saw the USA through a difficult postwar period. The Cold War (period of tension with communist Russia) began and the country went to war with Korea (1950–53).

▲ GERALD FORD

Called to office after Nixon's resignation in 1974, Gerald Ford is the only president not to have been elected either president or vice-president.

▲ JIMMY CARTER

During Carter's term of office, the USA was beset by crises. At home, there was recession. Abroad, US citizens were taken hostage in Iran.

◀ RONALD REAGAN

Shortly after taking office in 1981, former Hollywood actor Ronald Reagan survived an assassination attempt. He went on to cut taxes, increase national defence, and improve relations with Russia.

OUR COUNTRY'S CHOICE

GROVER CLEVELAND

THOMAS A HENDRICKS

DEMOCRATIC NOMINEES

THEODORE ROOSEVELT ▶
A reformer, Roosevelt promised a "Square Deal" for all. The teddy bear is named after Roosevelt, who refused to shoot a bear on a hunting trip.

DO YOU SMOKE? SINCE 1896

THAT'S WHAT McKINLEY PROMISED

◀ CALVIN COOLIDGE
Coolidge believed the government should not control too many aspects of people's lives. A man of few words, he was nicknamed "Silent Cal".

WILLIAM McKINLEY ▶
The first to campaign using advertising techniques, McKinley won the 1896 election promising to tax foreign goods.

McKINLEY AND ROOSEVELT FOUR YEARS MORE OF THE FULL DINNER PAIL

OUR PRESIDENT

DEEDS - NOT WORDS

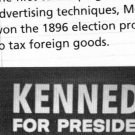

FOR '56

KENNEDY FOR PRESIDENT

LEADERSHIP FOR THE 60's

JOHN F KENNEDY ▲
In 1961, "JFK" became the youngest elected US president, aged 44. Kennedy's leadership inspired hope. His assassination in 1963 left the country shattered.

THINK

Don't let this happen to YOU!

VOTE FOR IKE

DWIGHT EISENHOWER ▲
Known as "Ike", Eisenhower launched the race between the USA and Russia to explore outer space.

NIXON   AGNEW

RICHARD NIXON ▲
In 1974, Nixon became the only president to resign, because of his involvement in the Watergate scandal (illegal spying in the opposition party's headquarters).

BARACK OBAMA

PRESIDENT 2008

BARACK OBAMA ▲
The 44th president of the USA, Obama was the first African-American to hold the office and served for two continuous terms.

BUSH QUAYLE

1988

GEORGE BUSH ▲
George Bush became president in 1989. From 1990–91, he led an alliance of troops in the Gulf War, in response to Iraq's invasion of Kuwait.

CLINTON

A CURE FOR THE BLUES

BILL CLINTON ▲
A long period of economic growth meant that, despite allegations of scandals, Bill Clinton always remained popular.

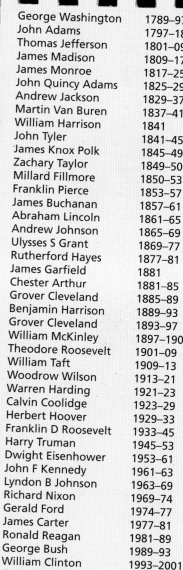

George Washington	1789–97
John Adams	1797–1801
Thomas Jefferson	1801–09
James Madison	1809–17
James Monroe	1817–25
John Quincy Adams	1825–29
Andrew Jackson	1829–37
Martin Van Buren	1837–41
William Harrison	1841
John Tyler	1841–45
James Knox Polk	1845–49
Zachary Taylor	1849–50
Millard Fillmore	1850–53
Franklin Pierce	1853–57
James Buchanan	1857–61
Abraham Lincoln	1861–65
Andrew Johnson	1865–69
Ulysses S Grant	1869–77
Rutherford Hayes	1877–81
James Garfield	1881
Chester Arthur	1881–85
Grover Cleveland	1885–89
Benjamin Harrison	1889–93
Grover Cleveland	1893–97
William McKinley	1897–1901
Theodore Roosevelt	1901–09
William Taft	1909–13
Woodrow Wilson	1913–21
Warren Harding	1921–23
Calvin Coolidge	1923–29
Herbert Hoover	1929–33
Franklin D Roosevelt	1933–45
Harry Truman	1945–53
Dwight Eisenhower	1953–61
John F Kennedy	1961–63
Lyndon B Johnson	1963–69
Richard Nixon	1969–74
Gerald Ford	1974–77
James Carter	1977–81
Ronald Reagan	1981–89
George Bush	1989–93
William Clinton	1993–2001
George W Bush	2001–09
Barack Obama	2009–17
Donald Trump	2017–present

Bishop's mitre This mitre (hat) is worn by a bishop in the Roman Catholic Church, the largest Christian body.

Saint Antony People who have led especially holy lives are named as saints by the Church.

Cross Because Jesus died on a cross, it is a powerful symbol of the Christian faith.

CHRISTIANITY

Christianity is based on the belief that Jesus Christ is God's son. The Bible, Christianity's sacred book, contains the story of Jesus's life and how he was put to death. Christians believe his sacrifice means that followers will have an eternal life with God.

Chalice In the ritual of Holy Communion, bread and wine represent the body and blood of Jesus. The wine is often served in a chalice.

Icon of Christ Paintings remind Christians that God lived as a human through Jesus.

Buddha The founder of Buddhism, Siddhartha Gautama, was born in what is now Nepal in 563 BCE.

Statues of Buddha are often made of gold to show his importance

Merit sharing Buddhists believe that if they live caring lives, they will build up merit (good will) and have a better next life. They can pass on merit to others in a merit-sharing ceremony.

In the temple, water is poured from one vessel to pass along merit to others

BUDDHISM

Unlike most religions, Buddhism is not based on worshipping a god or gods. Instead, it is based on the teachings of the Buddha, who showed his followers how to live a good life and avoid sufffering by controlling their desires. Buddhists hope to achieve true wisdom, known as enlightenment.

Chanukiah This nine-branched candlestick is used to celebrate Hanukkah, the Jewish festival of light. The central branch holds the candle used to light the others.

Prayer wheel and prayer As this Buddhist prayer wheel turns, a mantra (a blessing or prayer) written on a scroll inside "repeats" itself over and over again.

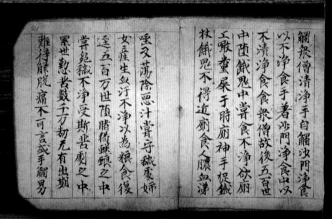

JUDAISM

This is the religion of the Jews, also called Hebrews. Judaism was the first successful religion based on the idea that there is only one God, and it formed the basis for both Christianity and Islam. Central to Jewish belief is that God chose the Jews as a special holy nation, and gave them a set of laws to follow. The story of the first Jewish people is told in the Hebrew Bible (the Christian Old Testament).

Kippas Some Jewish men wear skullcaps, known as kippas, when they pray as a sign of respect to God.

Water shaker In one Hindu ritual, priests sprinkle water over the worshippers.

HINDUISM

One of the oldest religions, Hinduism began 5,000 years ago in India. Hindus believe in a supreme spirit, Brahman, who reveals himself through hundreds of gods and goddesses. Hindus practise their faith in different ways, but share a belief in reincarnation – the idea that a person's soul has lived before and will live on after death in another form.

Ganesh Hindus pray to Ganesh, the elephant god of wisdom and help, when facing a new challenge.

Om This is an image of the sacred sound, Om, spoken after Hindu prayer.

Krishna This popular Hindu god is thought to bring great happiness to believers.

Krishna is usually shown as a smiling youth with sky-blue skin

Islamic scribe Because the Qur'an is believed to contain God's exact words, great care is taken when Muslim scribes recreate them.

Islamic tile The sacred words of the Qur'an appear on many decorative objects, such as this tile.

Prayer beads God, or Allah, is thought to have 99 names. This string of 99 prayer beads can be used to remind Muslims of the many names of the one God.

Qibla Muslims must face the holy city of Mecca when they pray, five times a day. This instrument helps them to find its location.

ISLAM

Muslims believe that God revealed his words through an angel to the prophet Muhammad, who collected them in the Qur'an, the holy book. The faithful try to live by the rules in this book. The most important duties are the Five Pillars: prayer, helping the needy, fasting for one month a year, making a pilgrimage to Mecca, and showing faith in God.

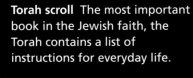

Torah scroll The most important book in the Jewish faith, the Torah contains a list of instructions for everyday life.

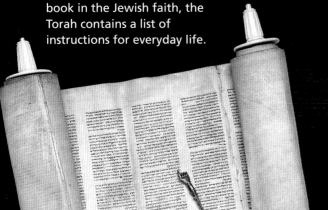

RELIGION

A religion is a set of beliefs that helps explain life's mysteries. People seek guidance from their religion on how they should live their lives. Most people with religious faith believe in either one God or many gods. They express their faith through rituals, such as gathering together with others to worship, and by studying sacred books. There are many different religions, but those included here have the most followers around the world.

FESTIVALS

Across the world, people celebrate festivals for a range of reasons. Though many form part of religious worship, others were created to mark a change in seasons, to focus on cultural traditions, or to celebrate an important milestone in history. Some festivals take place on the same day every year, others are based on ancient calendars or a new moon, so the dates change. Special food is almost always a part of each festival.

❶ CHRISTMAS
This Christian festival celebrates the birth of Jesus Christ, and is celebrated in most countries on 25 December. Traditions include decorating fir trees, exchanging gifts, attending church, and waiting for a visit from Santa Claus.

❷ DAY OF THE DEAD
During this Mexican festival, held on 1 November, families believe that the souls of dead relatives are able to return to the land of the living for one night. They decorate altars in homes and cemeteries with candles and flowers.

❸ THANKSGIVING
This North American festival is held on the fourth Thursday of November in the USA and the second Monday in October in Canada. Families get together to give thanks for the first good harvest of the European settlers more than 400 years ago.

❹ DRAGON BOAT FESTIVAL
This festival is celebrated in east Asia. According to legend, when a Chinese official named Qu Yuan drowned in a river, people rowed out on boats with dragon-head prows and dropped parcels of rice wrapped in bamboo (*zongzi*) into the water to divert the hungry fish away from his body.

Pumpkin is an autumn vegetable, made into a pie at Thanksgiving

Family and friends gather for a Christmas meal, with treats such as this *stollen*, a spicy fruit cake

Skulls made from sugar and water may be decorated with the names of the dead

Sticky rice, with sweet or savoury filling, is wrapped in triangular parcels

A mooncake is cut into wedges and served with tea

❺ MID-AUTUMN FESTIVAL

This east Asian celebration, which dates back more than 3,000 years, falls near the traditional harvest, when the Moon is at its lightest and brightest. Family and friends gather in the evening to eat mooncakes, rich rounds of pastry with lotus-seed fillings.

❻ FEAST OF ST LUCIA

Each year, on 13 December, people in Sweden and Norway celebrate the feast of Saint Lucia (a Christian girl who died for her faith). Early in the morning, a young girl dressed in white (often the youngest daughter in the house) takes a tray of hot saffron buns to her family.

❼ EID AL-FITR

This Muslim festival marks the end of Ramadan, a month-long fast. The celebration lasts for three days, starting with the sighting of the new moon. People dress in their best clothes and go to the mosque.

❽ DIWALI

Also known as the Festival of Lights, Diwali celebrates the victory of good over evil. Hindu families light oil lamps and put them on ledges and balconies. They also send cards with wishes for a good year.

❾ PASSOVER

In March or April, Jews celebrate Passover to remember when Moses led the Israelites from slavery in Egypt. Passover lasts for seven or eight days and includes a special meal called a *seder*. Each part of the meal has a symbolic meaning.

❿ EASTER

The Christian festival of Easter recognizes the resurrection of Jesus on the third day after his death. It falls between late March and April each year. People attend church and exchange Easter eggs.

During Eid, children enjoy sweets made with pastry, nuts, and honey

Matzoh, a flat, cracker-like bread, is eaten to remember how Jews left Egypt in haste, not waiting for their bread dough to rise

Horseradish represents the bitterness of slavery

A roasted egg reminds Jews of sacrifices made in the temple in Jerusalem in Biblical times

Shank bone is a reminder of the lamb sacrificed at the first Passover

Parsley is dipped in salt water to remember the tears of the slaves

Apple and nut mix represents the mortar that held Egyptian buildings together

Green vegetable, often lettuce, represents new life

During Diwali, people take gifts of sweets to the houses of their friends

Chocolate or painted eggs are given as Easter gifts

CITIES

Cities have existed since ancient times, when they functioned as trading hubs, often at the heart of sprawling empires. By the early 20th century, one in 10 people lived in a city. Industrialization has led to massive urbanization, and more than half the world's population are now city-dwellers. Modern cities are centres of commerce, culture, and government.

▼ CITY-STATE

In Ancient Greece, it was common for cities to establish themselves as independent states, with their own political systems. By the 5th century BCE, there were hundreds of city-states, and Athens was one of the most important. Today, Athens is the Greek capital.

HIGH-RISE ▶

The first high-rise buildings, now known as "skyscrapers", were constructed in the 1880s. With limited space in city centres, building upwards became the solution. Today, more than 7,000 skyscrapers tower above the city of Hong Kong.

Modern Athens was built around the ruins of the ancient city-state

RIVER LIVING ▶

Towns and cities were often built next to rivers, to take advantage of the trading opportunities and transport links they offered. Founded by the Romans, the city of London now spreads far and wide on both sides of the River Thames.

▲ RELIGIOUS CENTRE

Some cities are important religious sites. Mecca, in Saudi Arabia, is sacred to Muslims as the birthplace of the prophet Muhammad. All Muslims should make a pilgrimage to Mecca once in their lifetime.

CONURBATION ▶

When a city expands to merge with neighbouring towns, it becomes one huge urban area called a conurbation. The world's largest conurbation is Tokyo, Japan, with currently 37 million inhabitants.

The Palace of Westminster is home to the British parliament

◄ POPULATION GROWTH

Until recently, the majority of the world's population lived in rural areas. Today, most people live in cities, where they have migrated in search of work and opportunity. In many cities, such as Mumbai in India, this has led to overcrowding as temporary shelters spring up on the outskirts.

WORLD HERITAGE ►

The United Nations Educational, Scientific, and Cultural Organization (UNESCO) has listed sites of outstanding cultural or natural importance in order to preserve them. Called World Heritage Sites, these include cities such as Djenné in Mali, with its large mud brick mosque.

◄ DESERT CITY

At night, the lights of Las Vegas shine out across the Nevada Desert, USA. *Las vegas* means "the meadows" because the vast city was once just a place where travellers stopped for water as they crossed America.

▲ PURPOSE-BUILT

Until 1960, the capital of Brazil was Rio de Janeiro on the east coast. However, the government wanted to encourage growth and development in the centre of the country, and so a brand new capital was purpose-built in the interior – the modern capital of Brasília.

CITY WITHIN A CITY ►

Few city-states remain today, but one exception is the Vatican City in Rome, Italy, home of the Pope and the centre of the Roman Catholic Church. The Vatican remains a city-state with its own flag, coins, national anthem, and postage stamps.

EXTREME LIVING

Humans have found a way of living in some of the most inhospitable environments on Earth – including the scorching deserts, the icy Arctic, and the steamy rainforests. Desert dwellers have to cope with the daily problem of finding water. In the Arctic, the challenges are keeping warm and finding food to eat. The rainforests are full of life, but many of the animals are dangerous, and some of the plants are poisonous.

Tuareg headscarf Wound around the head and neck, this headscarf protects the Tuareg people from the blistering sun and sandstorms.

Sun hat Worn by the Fulani of west Africa, this hat shades the face.

Boomerang This throwing stick, was used by Australian aboriginals for hunting wild animals.

ARCTIC

The frozen Arctic is one of the toughest places on Earth to survive. There are no plant foods, so Arctic people came to rely on hunting seals, walruses, whales, birds, and fish. Without timber, they used skins and bones to build shelters, sleds, and boats. Modern inventions, such as the snowmobile, have made life in this frozen wilderness easier.

Snowmobile This motorized sled has skis for gliding over the snow.

Icebreaker A sharp pick is used to break thick, solid ice.

Fishing rod Arctic dwellers fish through holes in the ice.

Lapp stick This stick with a spade-like blade is used by the Arctic Lapp people for probing and digging.

RAINFOREST

Unlike the Arctic and the desert, the South American rainforest has a wide variety of animals and plants. The problem is that many of the animals and birds suitable for eating live high up in the canopy. Hunters scan the trees above for prey, such as monkeys, and then shoot them down using blowpipes firing poison darts.

Mosquito net Protection from insect bites is crucial when sleeping, as diseases like malaria are spread in this way.

Poison dart frog This frog produces deadly poison, used to tip blowpipe darts.

Hammock The hammock allows people in the rainforest to sleep in mid-air, away from snakes and insects.

DESERT

The extremes of temperature faced in the desert – extremely hot during the day, and very cold at night – is the main problem desert dwellers face. They are constantly on the move, searching for fresh water supplies, sometimes using the flight of birds and insects as their guide. Having found water, they must make sure that not a drop is wasted.

Goatskin bag The Arabian Bedouin draw water from deep wells and transport it in goatskin bags.

Ostrich egg The San people of the Kalahari desert, in southern Africa, fill ostrich eggs with water and bury them for using later.

Camels Bedouins travel using camels, which can go without water for long periods thanks to the fat stored on their backs.

Skin shoes The Sami of Northern Scandinavia wear shoes made of reindeer skin.

Traditional parka The Inuit of the Canadian Arctic wear thick, warm clothing made from caribou skins.

Modern Arctic clothes These are just as warm as the traditional wear, but are lighter and more flexible.

House on stilts Rainforest people build these as protection from flooding and creepy-crawlies.

Blowpipe Crafted from wood, blowpipes are used to hunt birds and monkeys.

History

PREHISTORY

Our distant past, before writing was invented, is called prehistory. Without written records, we rely on the objects that prehistoric people left behind them, such as tools, to find out how they lived. The first tools, made around 2.5 million years ago, were of stone, bone, and wood. Later, prehistoric people learned to use metals – first copper, then bronze, and finally iron.

Sickle A long flint, mounted in a wooden handle, forms a farmer's sickle, used to harvest grain.

Polished axe This axe, with its polished flint blade, was used by farmers to clear land to create fields.

Chopper This chopper was made 2.5 million years ago, by chipping a pebble to make a cutting edge. It would have been used to smash bones to get to the marrow inside.

Handaxe Invented 1.5 million years ago, the handaxe was the first stone tool made to a design. The pointed end was used for cutting meat or digging up edible roots.

Flint   Iron pyrite

Scraper The best stone tools were made from flint, which forms sharp edges. This tool would have been used for scraping animal skins clean.

Flint blade

Adze This adze, with its flint blade set in a wooden sleeve, was used to shape wood.

Antler hammer A toolmaker used an antler hammer to strike flakes from a flint to shape it.

Making fire Prehistoric people learned to make fire by striking flints against lumps of iron pyrite.

Mammoth-shaped hook held the spear in a long, straight handle, which launched the spear with great force and speed

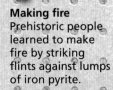

Spear thrower From 30,000 BCE, people made carvings of the animals they hunted. This spear thrower is in the shape of a mammoth.

THE AGE OF FARMING ▲

Between 10,000–9,000 BCE, people in the Middle East invented a new way of life – farming. They learned to store and sow the seeds of plants, and to breed animals, such as sheep and goats. By controlling their food supplies, farming people were able to settle down in permanent villages. As the supply of food became more regular, populations rose and the farming way of life spread.

HUNTER-GATHERERS ▲

For most of prehistory, people lived by hunting animals and gathering wild plant foods. Hunter-gatherers lived in small bands, which were often on the move, following herds of animals and looking for fresh sources of food. The first humans lived in Africa, but gradually spread across the globe, settling first in Asia and then Europe. Humans reached Australia by 50,000 BCE, and the Americas between 30,000–14,000 BCE.

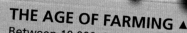

Antler pick European farming people mined for flints, digging with picks made from deer antlers.

Arrowheads Farming people continued to hunt wild animals, using bows and arrows with skilfully shaped flint heads.

COPPER AND BRONZE ▼

The next discovery was how to make tools from metals. Around 5,000 BCE, people in Europe and Asia learned how to extract copper by heating certain rocks. They used the bright metal to make tools and jewellery. Around 3,500 BCE, they discovered that adding a small amount of tin to copper made a harder metal, called bronze.

Bronze sword The discovery of tougher bronze led to the invention of a new weapon – the sword. This one has been cleaned to show its golden colour.

Belt boss This decoration, which would have hung from a belt, was made by flattening a piece of bronze and hammering patterns into it.

Bronze pin Bronze, with its gleaming golden colour, was popular for jewellery among the rich. These pins were used to fasten clothes.

Axe head Bronze tools, such as this axe head, were made by pouring the molten metal into moulds.

Short sword This Ancient Egyptian weapon has a smooth handle so that it could be gripped tightly. The blade is ridged for extra strength.

Sickle Iron was used for everyday tools, such as the blade of this sickle, set in an antler handle. A sickle was used for cutting hay or crops.

Royal dagger This bronze dagger, decorated with sea creatures in gold and silver, belonged to a ruler of Mycenae in Greece.

Spearhead This is the head of a huge spear, which would have been thrust rather than thrown. Together with its wooden shaft, it measured more than 2 m (6.5 ft).

Neck ring This bronze neck ring was worn by a British Iron Age warrior as a protective charm.

Iron dagger The scabbard of this iron dagger is decorated with bronze strips. It was found in the River Thames, England, and dates from c. 550–450 BCE.

Iron Age sword Iron made stronger swords than bronze. This fine iron sword, which is 70 cm (2.3 ft) long, was discovered in 1987 in an Iron Age grave. It is a rare find because iron objects are usually destroyed by rust.

Mirror This is the back of an intricately decorated bronze mirror. The other side was highly polished to give a reflection.

THE IRON AGE ▲

Although iron is the commonest metal on Earth, it was the last to be used to make tools. Unlike copper and tin, iron does not melt when heated in a fire. People did not learn how to shape iron, by heating and beating it with a hammer, until around 1,550 BCE. While bronze was a metal for the rich, everyone could afford iron.

FIRST CIVILIZATIONS

More than 5,000 years ago, farming peoples in the river valleys of Mesopotamia (modern-day Iraq), Egypt, and India, created the world's first civilizations. In Sumer, southern Mesopotamia, people known as Sumerians built the first cities. Each city was ruled by a king, who governed on behalf of the local god. This scene shows the king of the city of Ur receiving goods from his people.

❶ King Sumerians believed that kingship was handed down from the gods. This king wears no crown, but his importance is shown by his kilt and the fact that he is larger than everyone else.

❷ Servants Two men move between the king and his guests, bringing food and drink. Their low status is shown by their smaller size. They would have lived in the palace or in mud-brick homes.

❸ Nobles These men may have been priests, relatives of the king, or wealthy landowners. They are shown sitting on chairs with delicately carved legs, evidence of luxury at the palace.

❹ Musicians This man is shown playing a lyre, which has a wooden sound box decorated with the head of a bull. Other instruments from the time included harps, lutes, reed pipes, and drums.

5 Singer The only woman in the scene is singing with the lyre player to entertain the guests. Music and dancing played a key role in religious rituals, such as giving thanks for a good harvest.

6 Farmers Although the area was hot and dry, silt from the rivers kept the soil fertile. Farmers also dug canals to divert water to their crops, which included barley, turnips, onions, and dates.

7 Fishermen Rivers offered a plentiful supply of fish for all early civilizations. From the Indus in India, the Nile in Egypt, and the Euphrates and Tigris in Sumer, fish were caught with nets or spears.

8 Animals Sheep, goats, cattle, and pigs were vital to the first civilizations. They provided meat, milk, leather, and wool. Oxen were used to pull ploughs and donkeys were used for transport.

9 Workers This man carries a bundle on his back, the heavy load strapped to his head. It was thanks to the toil of workers like this that massive temples for the gods could be built.

10 Clothing Made from either wool or flax, both men and women wore tufted kilts, designed to resemble sheepskins. Wealthy men and women also owned elaborate gold jewellery.

▲ THE STANDARD OF UR
This mosaic of blue lapis lazuli, red sandstone, and white shell, was made in the city of Ur in about 2,500 BCE. It decorates one side of a small wooden box found in a royal grave. The purpose of the box is not known. This side shows a peaceful banquet, while the other side depicts scenes of war.

231

CLASSICAL WORLD

The civilizations of Ancient Greece and Rome are collectively known as the "classical world". The word "classical", in this instance, refers to culture of the highest quality. The Greeks were pioneers in science and the arts. They influenced the Romans, who spread this style of art, architecture, and literature across their own empire. Men in both societies were eager to find fame, often through military might.

Although little is known about Homer's life, it is generally thought that he was blind

Socrates was described as having a round face and a snub nose

Lionskin headdress of legendary hero Heracles, renowned for his superhuman strength

HOMER

During the 8th century BCE, Homer wrote two great epic poems about the legendary Greek war against the city of Troy. The *Iliad* recounts the story of the Greek warrior Achilles. The *Odyssey* describes the adventures of another hero, Odysseus, as he journeys home after the war. Homer's writing is so powerful that it is said to have influenced writers through the ages. He was so important to the Greeks that they simply called him "the poet". Homer's poems were originally sung or chanted, to the accompaniment of a lyre.

PYTHAGORAS

A philosopher, astronomer, and mathematician, Pythagoras lived in the 6th century BCE. He is remembered today for his work in geometry – particularly his theorem about triangles – but he was also a religious teacher. Pythagoras wanted to unlock the secrets of the Universe, and saw mathematics as the key to everything. He believed that numbers were the ultimate reality.

SOCRATES

Socrates (469–399 BCE) was an Athenian thinker whose influence on philosophy was so great that all earlier philosophers are referred to as "pre-Socratic" (before Socrates). However, unlike previous thinkers, such as Pythagoras, Socrates did not try to understand the Universe. He believed that it was more important to find the best way to live. Accused by his enemies of being a bad influence, he was put on trial and sentenced to death by drinking poison.

ALEXANDER THE GREAT

One of the world's greatest generals, and bravest of soldiers, Alexander (356–323 BCE) was king of Macedon, to the north of Greece. After forcing the Greeks to unite under his leadership, he conquered a vast empire, stretching from Egypt to northwest India. By the time of his death, aged just 32, he had won lasting fame and was forever known as Alexander the Great.

PERICLES

A statesman and general, Pericles (c. 495–429 BCE) was a leading figure in Athens when the state was a democracy (meaning "power by the people"). He filled Athens with temples, such as the Parthenon, which was dedicated to Athena, goddess of the city. Pericles also promoted the arts, and made Athens the cultural centre of Greece.

Julius Caesar was known to be balding, and combed his hair forward to try and disguise the fact

Like Augustus, Trajan wears the oak wreath, called the civic crown

Oak wreath was an award given to Augustus for saving Roman lives

Trajan's goatskin cloak is worn for godly protection, and displays the image of the snake-headed Medusa

Although Augustus lived to be 76, his statues always showed him as a handsome young man

JULIUS CAESAR

Politician, general, and writer, Julius Caesar (c. 100–44 BCE) is famous for his conquest of Gaul (modern-day France), which he described in his book *The Gallic Wars*. He also fought and won a civil war against a rival Roman general, Pompey. Caesar marched on Rome and was declared dictator for life. He was later murdered for acting like a king, which went against the principles of the Roman republic.

EMPEROR AUGUSTUS

Augustus (the revered one) was the title given to Julius Caesar's adopted heir, Octavian, when he became Rome's first emperor. Augustus (ruled 27 BCE–14 CE) took power after defeating his rival, Mark Antony, in battle. He ruled Rome for more than 40 years, and brought peace and stability to the empire after years of civil war.

TRAJAN

A Spaniard by birth, Emperor Trajan (ruled 98–117 ce) was the first Roman ruler to be born outside Italy. He was a successful general, and his conquests in the Balkans and what is now Iraq brought the Roman Empire to its largest size. In Rome, a famous column was built in his honour decorated with scenes of his campaigns.

AGRIPPINA

The wife of Emperor Claudius, Agrippina (15–59 CE) was a powerful and ambitious woman. She persuaded her husband to adopt Nero, her son from a previous marriage. She is thought to have then poisoned Claudius so that the 16-year-old Nero could come to the throne. At first, Nero was dominated by his mother, but he eventually grew tired of her interference and had her murdered.

SULLA

As a Roman general, Sulla (138–78 BCE) was a ruthless and ambitious man. His quarrels with a rival general, Marius, led to the first in a series of bloody civil wars – in which Romans fought against each other. Sulla was the first general to march on Rome as the head of an army and seize power. Julius Caesar later followed his example.

Castles were the stately homes of France's richest nobles

Wheat was cut using a curved blade called a sickle

Women covered their hair with a linen headdress called a wimple

The falconer was a well-paid professional huntsman

HUNTING

The Duke of Berry was a very powerful man and had many castles and lands. This painting shows his castle at Etampes, where a group of richly dressed nobles take birds of prey to hunt partridges, swans, ducks, pigeons, and other birds. Throughout the Middle Ages, hunting was the favourite sport of the rich.

The castle was a fortress and a garrison for soldiers

Vineyards surrounded by walls

A peasant sows seeds – like most farm work this had to be done by hand

Peasants had few rights – they could not marry or leave the village without the lord's permission

FEUDAL SOCIETY

Medieval society was organized into a "feudal system", based on giving land in exchange for service. At the top was the king who granted land to his nobles. In return, the nobles supplied the king with soldiers. At the bottom were the peasants who worked the land in exchange for a piece of land to farm for themselves.

MEDIEVAL LIFE

Medieval means "middle age", and is the name given to the period of European history between the fall of the Roman empire, in the 5th century, and the beginning of modern history around 1500. During the Middle Ages, 90 per cent of the population lived in the countryside as peasants – poor labourers who worked for wealthy nobles.

CASTLE BUILDING
In September, the grapes were harvested, as seen here in the grounds of the castle of Saumur. Many magnificent castles and cathedrals were constructed during the Middle Ages, using only simple tools and the great skill of the masons who cut and carved the stone.

The castle was designed both to show off the lord's power and wealth and to repel enemy armies

Drawbridge

The low wall at the tournament ground separated the knights as they charged each other on horseback armed with lances

Peasant life was harsh and many children did not live beyond the age of 10

FARMHOUSE
This painting shows life on a farm in winter. Farmhouses were usually simple buildings with just one or two rooms where everyone would eat, sleep, and live together. The windows were small and did not have glass, which was very expensive.

The church was the centre of village life

Doves and pigeons were kept for meat in a "dovecote" tower

Haystack

Beehives provided honey to sweeten food and make medicines

The farmer had to give one tenth, or tithe, of all he produced to the local priest

BOOK OF HOURS
These paintings are taken from a prayer book called a "Book of Hours". It was made for the French Duke of Berry around 1410 and details prayers to say at different times of the day and year. In the Middle Ages books were rare and precious objects, handwritten and illustrated by monks, and most were religious texts.

AMERICAN CIVILIZATIONS

Until the arrival of European invaders in the 16th century, complex and powerful civilizations flourished in the Americas. From 250 to 900 CE, the Mayan kingdoms of Central America built cities with huge stone temples, and developed systems of mathematics and astronomy. From the 14th century, the mighty Aztec empire built pyramid temples and made sacrifices to their sun god. In the 15th century, the Inca empire stretched for more than 3,200 km (2,000 miles) along the Pacific coast of South America, with a network of roads and fortress cities high in the Andes mountains.

❶ EVERYDAY LIFE

The Aztec, Inca, and Mayan civilizations were all based on farming. The most important food crop was maize (or corn), used to make pancakes, called tortillas, and beer. As well as farming the land, people had to serve their rulers as soldiers, builders, or labourers.

❷ POTTERY

American people made pots by rolling clay into long strips, which they coiled to make the walls of their vessels. Pottery served both a practical purpose, such as carrying liquids and boiling food, and a decorative one.

Rain god Chac, the Mayan rain god, had a long nose and fangs.

An Inca walks behind a Spanish invader

Pipes of different lengths make different notes

Flint blade with serrated edge

Knife There were no metal tools, so knives were made of stone.

Music The Incas made music by blowing across the top of cane pipes.

Drink The Incas drank "chicha" (maize beer) from painted wooden beakers.

Conical base for standing the pot in a hollow on the ground

Inca designs were influenced by basketry weaving patterns

The hunters, disguised as deer, creep on all fours

Jaguar skin decorated with feathers

Inca pots The Incas used these pots to carry and store maize beer. People carried them on their backs, using a rope passed between the handles.

Plate Paintings on pots often reveal details of daily life. This Mayan plate shows how people hunted deer using blowpipes.

Mixtec cup This cup was made by the Mixtecs, the Aztecs' southern neighbours.

A blue hummingbird perches on the rim, ready to take a sip

Gold was the "sweat of the sun" to the Incas

❸ GODS

The Aztecs and Mayans worshipped many gods and goddesses, whose statues they kept in pyramid temples. They believed that the gods made the sun rise in the morning, the rain fall, and the crops grow. For the Incas, the Sun, Moon, and Earth were themselves gods. Inti, the sun god, was the most important of them.

❹ KEEPING RECORDS

These civilizations had various ways of keeping records. The Aztecs used a picture writing system, with pictures standing for words and ideas. The Maya had a more complex system, with signs standing for sounds. The Incas did not write, but kept records using lengths of knotted string, called quipus.

❺ RITUALS

People believed that the gods needed to be given offerings to ensure their continued goodwill. The most precious offering was human life, and the Aztecs, Maya, and Incas all practised human sacrifice. The Aztecs and Maya went to war to capture prisoners, whose hearts were offered to the gods.

Offering Gold figurines were left by the Incas as offerings to the Sun and Earth.

Aztec signs for different days

Chac carries a ball of incense, which was burned at religious ceremonies

Calendar This book is a calendar, used by Aztec priests to predict the future.

Quipu The colour, size, number, and position of the knots all had a significance to the Incas.

Mayan records Mayan books were painted on paper made from fig tree bark, which folded up like a concertina.

Knots were used for counting

Shield Aztec warriors wore colourful costumes and carried shields decorated with feathers.

Tezcatlipoca, an Aztec god of war and strife

This mask is from Teotihuacán – an earlier civilization than the Aztecs

Eye shapes were often part of the knife's decoration

Funerary urn Burned bones of Aztec warriors who died in battle were buried in urns.

Stone mask Carved stone masks were placed as offerings in Mexican temples.

Sacrificial knife Aztec priests used stone knives to cut out the hearts of prisoners of war.

SEAFARERS

Sea-going craft have been built for at least 50,000 years. The first boats were probably log rafts or hollowed out tree trunks. At some point, people came up with the idea of catching the wind by raising a piece of cloth – the first sail. As ship building methods improved, sailors set off on longer voyages, using their ships to explore, to trade, and to raid.

Taut rope running from each end of the ship prevents it from sagging

EGYPTIAN SHIP ▲
This Egyptian sea-going merchant ship is constructed from planks tied together with rope, and dates from 2,450 BCE. Its collapsible mast carried a single square sail. Travelling against the wind, the crew lowered the mast and used oars.

Oars were used to power the ship when the wind dropped

The size of the sail could be adjusted with ropes

◄ VIKING LONGSHIP
From the 8th to 11th centuries, Vikings built ships strong enough to sail the stormy Atlantic Ocean, and light and slim enough to travel up shallow rivers.

CARAVEL ►
The caravel was a ship for exploration, invented by the Portuguese in the 15th century. It had lateen (triangular) sails, which are much better at sailing into the wind than square sails. In ships like this, explorers found the sea route to India.

Sails are painted with Christian crosses

A look-out sat in the crow's nest on the mast

◄ GALLEON
This 16th-century English galleon warship was also used in trading and exploration. It had several decks, with many openings in the sides of the hull from which guns were fired. European navies used the galleon until the 18th century.

ROMAN MERCHANT SHIP ▶

The Romans built merchant ships with big, round bellies that could store large amounts of cargo. This shape made them stable but very slow. They were usually safe from attack, because the Romans had rid the Mediterranean Sea of pirates.

The stern post was carved into the shape of a swan's neck for luck

◀ ARAB DHOW

From the 8th century, Arab merchants and fishermen crossed the Indian Ocean in dhows. They sailed with the monsoon winds, trading goods between India and North Africa.

A pair of lateen (triangular) sails could catch side winds

Sail made from fibre matting

CHINESE JUNK ▶

The stern-mounted rudder, easier to control than a steering oar, was invented by the Chinese, 2,000 years ago. Chinese ships, called junks, could have up to nine masts, and were the largest wooden sailing ships in history.

Clippers had dozens of sails, making them very fast

CLIPPER ▶

The clipper was a 19th-century trading ship with a long, slim hull and multiple sails. The name "clipper" was originally a nickname for a fast horse. British and US clippers sailed all around the world on trading journeys.

239

WAR

Throughout history, wars have broken out between tribes or nations over land, resources, and status. Methods of fighting changed over time, as people invented new, deadly weapons to fight with and improved ways of protecting soldiers from injury in battle.

❶ BOW AND ARROW

The bow and arrow, invented more than 12,000 years ago, is one of the oldest weapons used in war. There are various types. The longbow was often used by foot soldiers, while this short Mongol bow is designed to be used from horseback.

❷ ARMOUR

The earliest soldiers wore armour made from wood, leather, and bone. After people discovered how to work metals, soldiers could wear armour made of mail (interlocking metal rings) or metal plates.

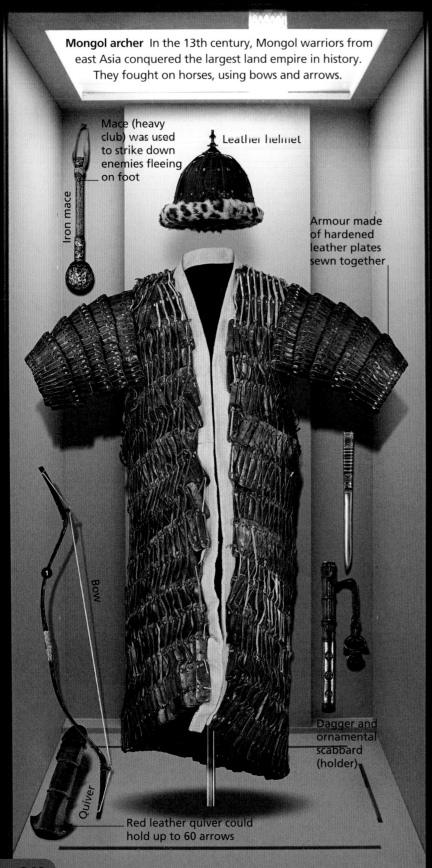

Mongol archer In the 13th century, Mongol warriors from east Asia conquered the largest land empire in history. They fought on horses, using bows and arrows.

Mace (heavy club) was used to strike down enemies fleeing on foot

Leather helmet

Iron mace

Armour made of hardened leather plates sewn together

Bow

Quiver

Dagger and ornamental scabbard (holder)

Red leather quiver could hold up to 60 arrows

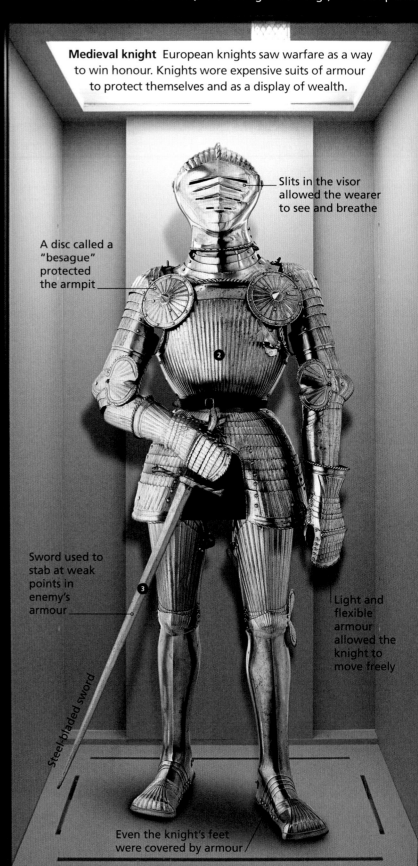

Medieval knight European knights saw warfare as a way to win honour. Knights wore expensive suits of armour to protect themselves and as a display of wealth.

Slits in the visor allowed the wearer to see and breathe

A disc called a "besague" protected the armpit

Sword used to stab at weak points in enemy's armour

Steel-bladed sword

Light and flexible armour allowed the knight to move freely

Even the knight's feet were covered by armour

❸ SWORD

Swords are weapons for close combat (hand-to-hand fighting). They have a point for stabbing, and one or two sharp edges for slashing. A crossguard above the hilt (handle) prevents the user's hand from sliding down onto the blade, and protects it from an enemy's sword.

❹ UNIFORM

In the confusion of battle, soldiers need to be able to tell friend from foe. Uniforms mark out which side a soldier belongs to and encourage discipline – soldiers wearing identical uniforms are more likely to act together as a group.

❺ FIREARMS

Invented in China in the 14th century, firearms (portable guns) increased a soldier's ability to kill his enemy from a distance. These weapons ended the age of the knight, whose expensive armour could offer little protection.

❻ CAMOUFLAGE

In the 20th century, brightly coloured uniforms were replaced by clothes that helped soldiers blend in with their surroundings. Colours and patterns like the green and black stripes on this uniform are known as camouflage, from the French *camoufler* (to disguise).

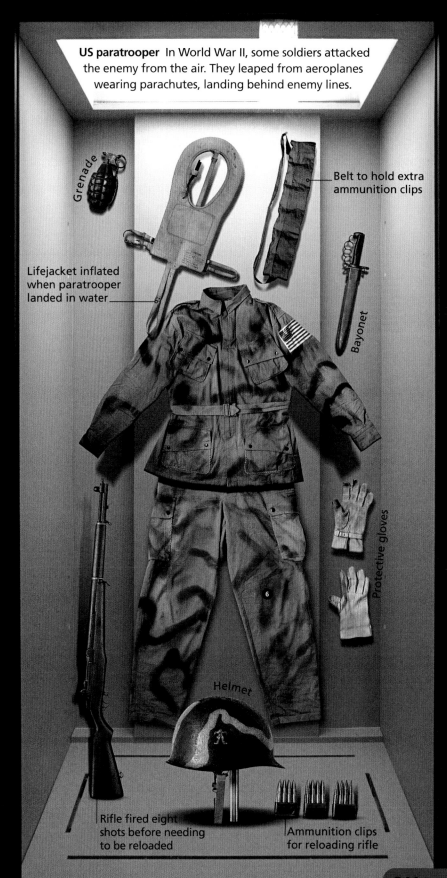

French infantryman In the Napoleonic wars (1803–15), soldiers marched in ranks to the beat of a drum. At a signal, one line all fired their muskets.

Sewing kit for repairing uniform

Ammunition pouch with fitting for carrying bayonet

Shoes had metal studs to make them sturdier

Short sword was of limited use in battle, but useful for chopping wood in camp

Bayonet (knife that attaches to the end of a gun)

Musket able to fire just three times per minute

The shako (hat) gave little protection, but made the soldier look taller

US paratrooper In World War II, some soldiers attacked the enemy from the air. They leaped from aeroplanes wearing parachutes, landing behind enemy lines.

Grenade

Belt to hold extra ammunition clips

Lifejacket inflated when paratrooper landed in water

Bayonet

Protective gloves

Helmet

Rifle fired eight shots before needing to be reloaded

Ammunition clips for reloading rifle

REVOLUTIONS

A revolution is a sweeping social change that takes place in a short period of time. This is often violent, as unpopular governments are overthrown, either by mass uprisings or small groups of organized revolutionaries. The aim of revolutionaries is to create a better society – to make people more equal, or more free. Yet it is often easier to destroy a bad government than it is to create a better one.

▼ AMERICAN REVOLUTION
Between 1775–81, Britain's 13 colonies in North America fought a war of independence, in which they successfully threw off the rule of King George III. In their 1776 Declaration of Independence (below), the American leaders declared that "all men are created equal" with the right to "life, liberty, and the pursuit of happiness".

▲ FRENCH REVOLUTION
In 1789, rioting against the government of King Louis XVI spread across France. Using the slogan of "liberty, equality, fraternity", revolutionaries overthrew the king. In 1793, the French leaders launched a reign of terror, during which they executed all opponents, including the king, by guillotine.

◄ RUSSIAN REVOLUTION

The Bolshevik Party, led by Vladimir Lenin, seized power in Russia in October 1917 and founded the first communist state. The communists set about creating a new kind of society, a "workers' state" based on common ownership of industry and land.

◄ CUBAN REVOLUTION

In 1956–59, Cuban rebels, led by Fidel Castro and Che Guevara (left), overthrew the corrupt government of the dictator, Fulgencio Batista. Although Castro went on to rule as another dictator, he improved conditions for the Cuban poor, and provided them with greater access to hospitals and schools.

▼ CULTURAL REVOLUTION

In 1949, communists, led by Mao Zedong, took power in China. In 1966, Mao, who feared that China was sliding away from communist principles, launched a "cultural revolution" to root out old ways of thinking. Opponents and intellectuals were persecuted, and the country came close to chaos.

▲ VELVET REVOLUTION

Mass protests in November 1989, and a general strike in Czechoslovakia, proved enough to bring down the unpopular communist government. The lack of violence led to this being called the "velvet", or soft, revolution. Here marchers carry the flag of the new Czech Republic (Czechia).

INDUSTRIAL REVOLUTION

From the late 18th century, the invention of machines that could do things faster than ever before brought dramatic changes in the way people lived and worked. Known as the Industrial Revolution, these changes took root in Britain and quickly spread to Europe and the USA. It began in the textile industry, with new machines powered first by water and later by steam. This led to a huge demand for coal, to fuel the engines, and iron, to make the machines. New towns sprang up as farm labourers moved from the countryside to work in the factories.

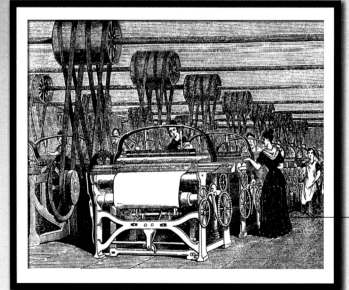

◄ FACTORIES

Huge buildings, called factories, were constructed to house the new machines, row upon row. Machines, such as these looms for weaving cotton into cloth, were powered by a steam engine and the noise they made would have been deafening.

Factory workers endured hot, humid conditions and air thick with cotton dust

Woollen shirt

Woollen shawl

FACTORY WEAR ►

Factory owners preferred to hire women and children to men, because they were cheaper and easier to discipline. Women in the factories wore heavy, durable clothes, which were products themselves of the Industrial Revolution's textile boom.

RAILWAYS ►

In 1804, British inventor Richard Trevithick built the first steam-powered locomotive. Early locomotives carried coal from mines. From 1825, passenger trains were built, and armies of workers lay down railway lines.

"Puffing Billy", built in 1813–14, is the world's oldest surviving steam locomotive

Leather boots studded with hobnails for durability

▲ NEW TOWNS

In the factory areas, villages grew into huge towns almost overnight. Workers' houses were built as cheaply as possible, and often crammed closely together. The industrial towns were dark places, where the air was filled with smoke from the factory chimneys.

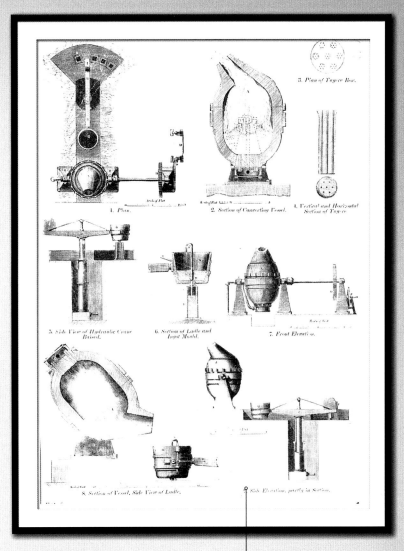

▲ INVENTIONS

The driving force of the Industrial Revolution was the rapid development of new ideas, methods, and machinery. Newly invented steam engines were used to power innovative new machines that transformed the mining, textiles, and metalworking industries.

Plans for a new method of converting iron into steel, invented by Henry Bessemer in 1855

▼ DISEASE

People lived crowded together in the new factory towns. They had no proper sewers, rubbish collection, or clean drinking water. Diseases like cholera, typhus, and typhoid often swept through the towns, killing thousands.

Medicine box used to treat cholera

DISEASE

Wherever people have lived together in large numbers, diseases have spread. As ships travelled around the world, diseases like bubonic plague, flu, and cholera spread from country to country. In the past, treatment was often ineffective as people did not understand the true causes of these diseases. We now know that they are caused by microscopic bacteria and viruses.

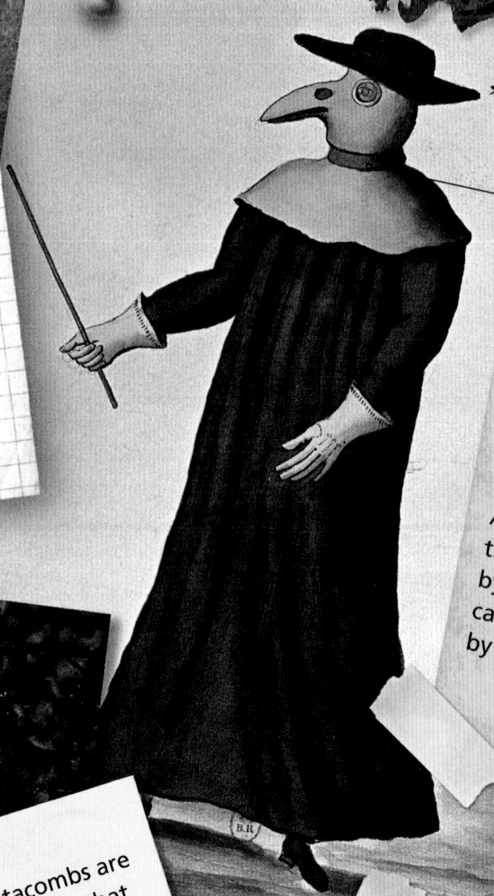

Some doctors wore bird-like masks stuffed with herbs believed to ward off the plague

◄ BUBONIC PLAGUE

In the 1340s, bubonic plague killed around half the population of Europe, and millions more in Asia and Africa. People believed that they could catch the plague by breathing bad air. The true cause was bacteria, passed on by flea bites.

CHOLERA ▲

These bones in the Paris catacombs are from victims of cholera, a disease that originated in India and was brought to Europe by merchant ships in 1829. It is caused by drinking water polluted with sewage, which carries the cholera bacteria. Victims die a painful death, after hours of vomiting and diarrhoea.

Smallpox caused painful raised blisters, which left scars behind after they healed

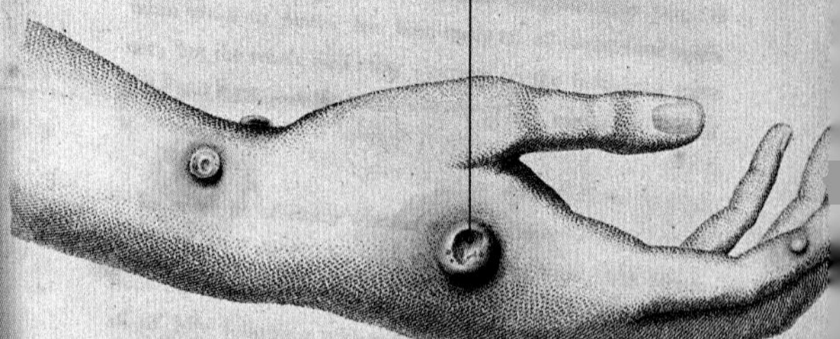

FLU PANDEMIC ►

A widespread outbreak of disease is called a pandemic. The worst case in history took place in 1918–20, when a deadly strain of flu spread around the globe, killing 50–100 million people. Face masks were widely worn, for it was correctly understood that flu is spread by coughs and sneezes.

SMALLPOX ▲

Smallpox was a disease that could scar, blind, and even kill its victims. Like flu or the common cold, it was caused by a virus, a minute agent that can only grow or reproduce inside the cells of living things. Smallpox is one disease that has been wiped out by modern medicine.

JEYES' DISINFECTANTS

Fluid"
Powder.
ehold
oap.

Toilet Soap
Soft Soap
40 Prize Medals
Awarded

IN CASE OF SICKNESS. ALWAYS USE
JEYES' DISINFECTANTS

◀ HYGIENE

Until the 1860s, people did not understand the importance of hygiene in preventing infections. Surgeons did not even wash their hands before operating. In 1865, an English surgeon called Joseph Lister began to clean the wounds of his patients with carbolic acid. This killed the bacteria that infected the wounds.

A nurse washes her hands in disinfectant in a 19th-century advertisement

BACTERIA ▶

Bacteria are microscopic single-celled organisms that infect wounds and cause diseases. In 1928, Scottish scientist Alexander Fleming discovered that a mould growing in his laboratory killed harmful bacteria. He used this discovery to create a new type of anti-bacterial medicine, called an antibiotic.

Fleming grew bacteria in a petri dish

A new sewer is built in London in 1845

SANITATION ▲

The 19th century saw several cholera pandemics in Europe. These were eventually ended by building proper sewers, which stopped bacteria polluting drinking water. The last European pandemic took place in Russia in 1923. Cholera is still a problem in Asia and Africa, with an outbreak in Yemen in 2016.

◀ VACCINATION

A vaccine is a weak form of a disease that helps the body fight a more serious disease. English doctor Edward Jenner realized that people who caught cowpox (a mild form of smallpox), did not get the deadlier disease. In 1796, he injected eight-year old James Phipps with pus from a cowpox blister. When he later tried to infect the boy with smallpox, James did not catch the disease and the first vaccine had been created.

MONEY

Before money existed, people traded by bartering, or swapping, different goods. The problem with bartering was that each trader had to want what the other trader was selling. Money was invented as a medium of exchange – something with a recognized value that could be used to buy other goods. Money is usually made of rare materials, such as precious metals or colourful feathers. The first written records of money date back to Mesopotamia (now in southern Iraq) where weighed silver was used about 4,500 years ago.

Tobacco leaves were the currency for the British settlers in North America in the 17th and 18th centuries

At different times in history, cowrie shells have been used as payment in China, India, and Africa

Gold doubloons made by the Spanish invaders of Central America

❶ EGYPTIAN HOARD

In Ancient Egypt, payments were made with various metals and their value was based on weight not shape. This resulted in a wide array of bars, rings, and pieces of gold, silver, and copper.

❷ BURMESE WEIGHTS

During the 18th century, silver weights called "flower silvers" were used as money in Burma (now Myanmar). Liquid silver was poured into a mould, and a floral pattern added.

❸ TRADER'S MANUAL

Coins were regularly shipped overseas in the 16th century. To identify the different coins and their value, Dutch merchants used handbooks detailing foreign currency.

❹ FEATHER MONEY

The Pacific Islanders of Santa Cruz used long coils made of feathers to buy canoes. The brightest and boldest feathers had the highest value.

❺ CHINESE COINS

In 500 BCE, bronze coins in China were made to resemble tools or the cowrie shells of an earlier currency. The shapes were so awkward they were replaced by circular coins with square holes.

❻ BANK NOTE

Paper money has its origins in 10th-century China. Handwritten receipts provided by merchants gained such importance that the government started printing paper receipts for specific sums.

❼ WAMPUM

Native Americans created belts, known as wampum, from white and purple clam shells. These belts represented money and were used to seal deals.

❽ STONE MONEY

Heavy currency was used by the islanders of Yap in the Pacific Ocean. The huge stone discs they used to pay for items were often too weighty to lift, some measuring 4 m (13 ft) across.

❾ CHEQUE

An alternative to cash is a cheque – a form that details how much money should be transferred from one bank account to another. In medieval times, the Knights Templar issued cheques to pilgrims so they could travel across Europe without carrying money.

❿ CREDIT CARDS

First used in 1920s America to buy petrol, many people now rely on plastic credit cards. Issued by banks and businesses, cards are a convenient alternative to cash.

Up until the 17th century, silver rings were the method of payment in Thailand

Shells stored in
wicker container

Red feathers were
woven into rolls

BANCO DI S. SPIRITO DI ROMA
La presente Cedola vaglia Scudi Trentuno
Moneta Romana da julj X per Scudo da
pagarsi all' Esibitore.
VAGLIA PER LO STATO ECCLESIASTICO R8°. N°. 189

This bank note
from Rome was
issued in 1786

Japanese ingot
coins in the
17th century were
hammered gold
or silver bars

Embedded
microchip acts
as a computer

CREDIT CARD

4275 3156 0372 5493

AMERICAN EXPRESS

4444 8888 5555 0000

DEBIT CARD

249

20TH CENTURY

The 20th century saw more changes in the way people lived their lives than any other century. Among the century's many new inventions were television, computers, the Internet, and nuclear power. The century began with the first aeroplane flight, lasting just 12 seconds, in 1903. By 1969, US astronauts had flown to the Moon and walked on its surface.

CONFLICTS

World War I (1914–18) left 20 million dead, mostly young soldiers. Military air power during World War II (1939–45) made cities vulnerable to attack. Around 60 million people died, many of them civilians. This was followed by the Cold War, a long stand-off between the USA and communist Russia.

Protests The 1960s saw many people march in anti-war protests.

UN The United Nations (UN) is an international organization, which was set up in 1945 to help prevent wars.

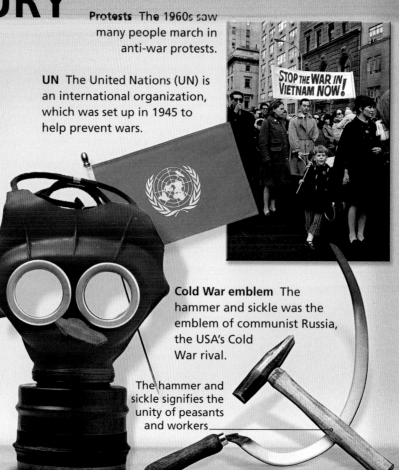

Gas masks These were issued to soldiers in World War I, and to both soldiers and civilians in World War II.

Cold War emblem The hammer and sickle was the emblem of communist Russia, the USA's Cold War rival.

The hammer and sickle signifies the unity of peasants and workers

Refrigerator Mass production of home refrigerators began after World War II.

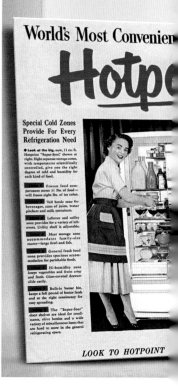

World's Most Convenien

Hotp

Special Cold Zones Provide For Every Refrigeration Need

LOOK TO HOTPOINT

ENTERTAINMENT

Radios were invented at the beginning of the century, and the 1920s saw the arrival of radio broadcasts. In the 1930s and 1940s, going to the cinema was the most popular leisure activity. In the 1950s and 1960s, the popularity of cinemas waned, as people stayed at home to watch the new invention, television.

Walkman In the 1980s, the personal cassette player let people listen to music on the move.

Gramophone The first record players were powered by turning a handle at the side.

Television Early televisions were small, and showed only grainy black and white pictures.

Radio In the early part of the century, the whole family would sit around listening to the radio.

AIDS From the 1980s onwards, a terrible new disease called AIDS claimed the lives of millions of people around the world.

Cinema People flocked to the cinema to watch their Hollywood idols.

Famine Many countries faced humanitarian crises.

DOMESTIC LIFE

Many new labour-saving devices were invented for the home, including refrigerators, freezers, washing machines, dishwashers, and vacuum cleaners. The ability to stop food decaying by freezing it enabled food to be transported greater distances and allowed people to buy and store it in bulk. Shortly after, pre-cooked frozen meals emerged, changing mealtimes for ever.

TV dinner Prepackaged meals could be heated, then eaten while watching television.

TRAVEL

The developments in transport in this century allowed people greater freedom to travel. Millions of families bought cars, and new motorways were built to make journeys faster. The air travel industry really took off from the 1930s. Journeys, which before the aeroplane would have taken days by rail or sea, could now be completed in a matter of hours.

Bikini A week in the sun on a foreign beach became a regular holiday event for many.

Globe Faster transport opened up the world to more people.

Air travel Cheaper air travel allowed many families to travel overseas for foreign holidays.

Souvenirs As overseas travel increased, many countries came to rely on tourism for income.

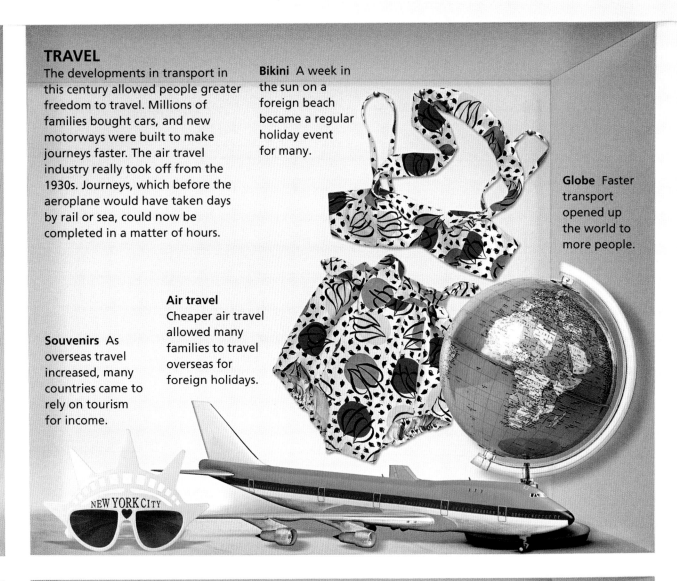

ISSUES

The world's population rose from 1.65 to 6 billion people during the century, with a widening gap between rich and poor nations. There was inequality between men and women and people of different races.

Apartheid Nelson Mandela led the successful struggle to win equal rights for black South Africans.

Votes This medal was given to a female hunger striker campaigning for the vote for women.

WORK

The role of women in the workplace greatly changed during the century. Women had limited career options in the early decades, but gained more employment rights and opportunities as the century progressed. The workplace was also transformed by new methods of communication, including the computer and Internet. New technologies led to automated factories, reducing the need for manual labour.

Women in the workplace In the 1970s, women fought for the right to the same work opportunities and pay as men.

Computer technology From the late 1970s, personal computers began to revolutionize the workplace.

Telephone Improved communication technology enabled businesses to go global.

Typewriter For much of the century, office workers used typewriters to write documents.

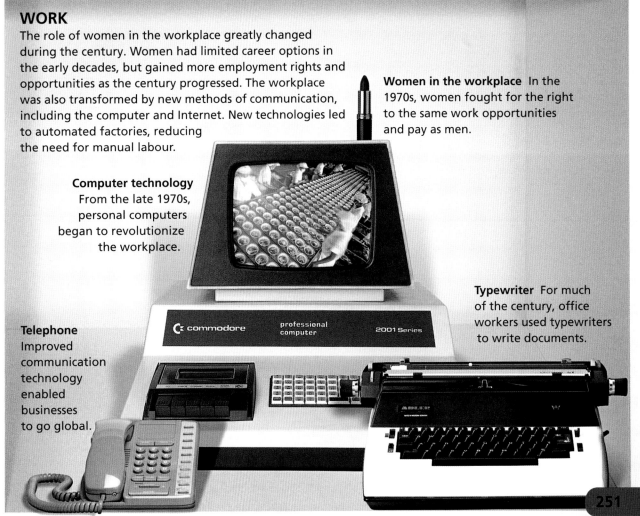

PICTURE GALLERY
David Teniers' 1651 painting
*Archduke Leopold Wilhelm in
his Picture Gallery* features one
of the greatest art collections of
the age, which numbered 1,300
works. The archduke governed
Southern Netherlands (Belgium).

252

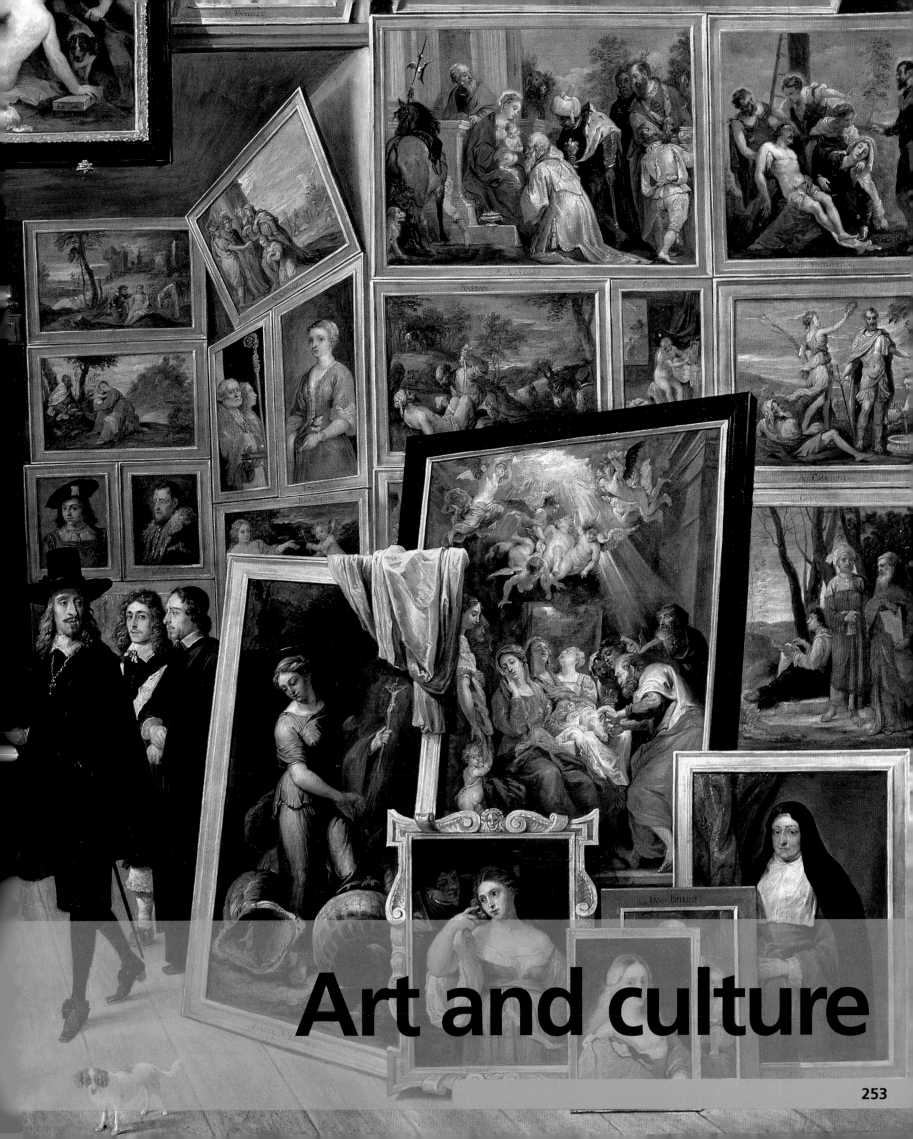

Art and culture

ART

Some artists seek to create a beautiful object, others use art to reveal something about the world. In the past, art also served a religious, or magical, or mystical purpose. Styles of art vary widely, and artists from different cultures have shown the human form in many different ways.

The first art This carving of a pregnant woman, found in Austria, was made 25,000 years ago. Her hair is shown in detail, yet she has no facial features.

Tomb art Egyptian painters showed each part of the body from its most distinctive angle. Heads and limbs were viewed from the sides, with eyes and torsos shown from the front.

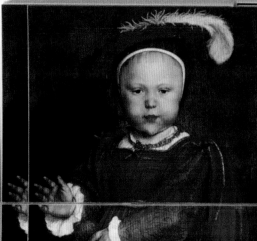

Mona Lisa With her mysterious half-smile, this is the world's most famous work of art. It was painted in 1503–7 by Italian artist Leonardo da Vinci.

Royal portrait German artist, Hans Holbein, was court painter to Henry VIII of England. His 1539 portrait of Henry's son, Edward, shows the clothing in great detail.

Self-portrait Dutch artist Rembrandt van Rijn (1606–69) painted 60 self-portraits to experiment with techniques and to document his life.

Indian art This painting, made in 1770, is not a realistic image, but follows set rules. The athletes' heads are shown in profile while their chests face out.

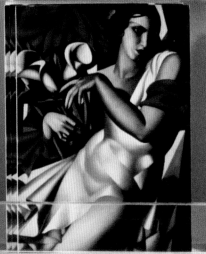

Emotion art In *The Scream* (1893), Norwegian Edvard Munch aimed to express emotion rather than depict a real scene.

New forms Spanish artist Pablo Picasso (1881–1973) took the human form apart and reassembled it in startling ways.

Art Deco Polish artist Tamara de Lempicka (1898–1980) belonged to the Art Deco movement, which saw art as purely decorative.

Self-image Mexican artist, Frida Kahlo (1907–54) painted self-portraits using scenes drawn from fantasy.

Terracotta Army In 209 BCE, more than 8,000 life-sized pottery figures of soldiers were buried to guard the tomb of China's first emperor. Every soldier has different features.

Prayer book Medieval European art often served a religious purpose. This illustrated book depicts the Virgin Mary holding the baby Jesus.

African mask These elaborate works of art were worn for ritual dances, when the wearer communicated with spirits.

Japanese print In 1794, artist Toshusai Sharaku made this woodcut print of an actor called Otani Oniji. He is shown performing the role of a villain, grimacing threateningly.

Brush strokes Like Rembrandt, Dutch artist, Vincent Van Gogh (1853–90), painted many self-portraits, 30 of them in the last five years of his life. He had a loose style, with each brush stroke visible.

Impressionism French artist Edgar Degas (1834–1917) founded an artistic movement called Impressionism. Its aim, shown in this painting of ballerinas, was to capture changing light and movement.

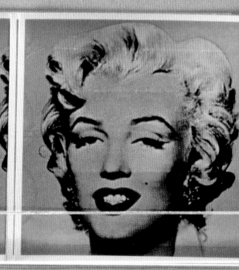

Sculptural curves Reducing human figures to simple curving shapes was a speciality of British sculptor Henry Moore (1898–1986).

Pop art Andy Warhol (1928–87) used subjects drawn from popular culture. In 1962, Warhol used a photo of movie star Marilyn Monroe to make this screenprint.

Cartoon art US artist Keith Haring (1958–90) started his career as a graffiti artist, drawing cartoon-like figures.

ARCHITECTURE

The art and science of designing buildings and other structures is known as architecture. From early times, people designed buildings both for practical reasons, such as shelters to live in, and religious reasons, such as stone tombs and places to worship the gods. Over the centuries, architecture has evolved to become an art form using high-quality materials to create ever more daring designs.

❶ THE COLOSSEUM

The first permanent amphitheatre in Rome, the Colosseum was completed in 80 CE. It is amazing not only for its size but also for its design. Up to 50,000 spectators poured safely in and out of 80 doors to watch all-day gladiator battles and other public spectacles.

❷ HEDDAL STAVKIRKE

As 12th-century Norwegians turned away from Viking beliefs to follow Christianity, they built a thousand beautiful wooden stave churches along trade routes in Norway. Carvings of animals often decorated the door frames.

❸ KUNSTHAUS GRAZ

Nicknamed "the friendly alien" by locals, this Austrian art museum, completed in 2003, has a blue outer skin of acrylic glass that can display images and animations. Inside, two large spaces can be adapted to display different exhibitions.

❹ DISNEY CONCERT HALL

This striking home for the Los Angeles Philharmonic Orchestra took 16 years to complete from design to opening night in 2003. Its striking exterior is made of stainless steel curves. The wood-panelled main auditorium features state-of-the-art acoustics.

❺ CHRYSLER BUILDING

This 1920s skyscraper in New York City remains the tallest brick building in the world at 319 m (1,047 ft). It was designed to house the Chrysler automobile company, and the gargoyles that jut from the building were designed like car mascots.

❻ REICHSTAG

This building housed the German Republic parliament from 1894 until it burned down in 1933. When Germany reunited in 1990, the Bundestag (the new parliament) returned to Berlin. The original building was gutted and a new home built inside the old walls.

❼ DJENNÉ MOSQUE

The largest mud-brick building in the world, the present mosque in Mali dates from 1909. The thick walls are coated with a smooth layer of plaster-like mud to even out the surface. Palm-wood supports help people scale the walls to repair them each spring.

The lower classes sat in the top levels, while the nobles sat close to the action on the lower level

Nozzles on top of the building let natural light flood the museum galleries

The church is coated with a mix of tar and oil to preserve the wood

Pointed gables were often decorated with carved crosses and dragon heads, like those on Viking ships

In 2005, some panels were sanded down after nearby residents complained about the glare and heat of reflected light

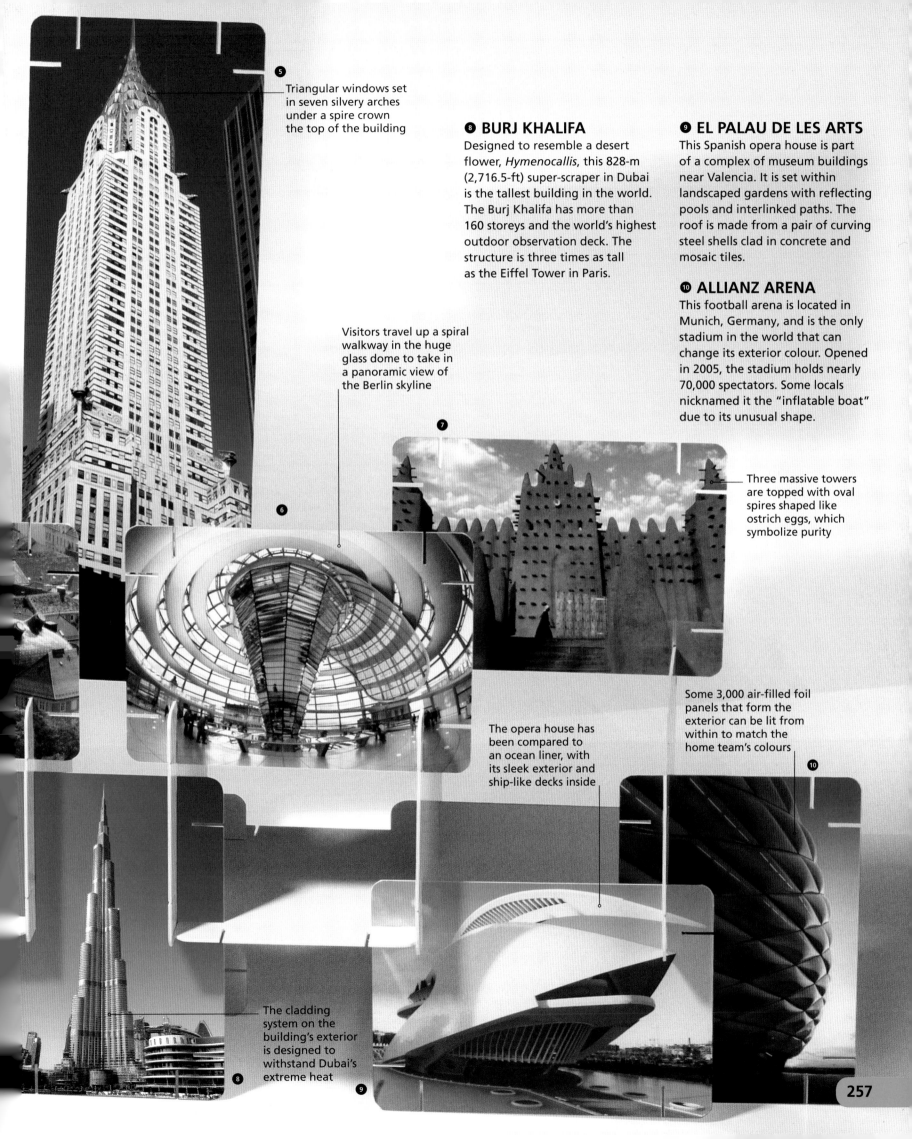

⑤ Triangular windows set in seven silvery arches under a spire crown the top of the building

❽ BURJ KHALIFA

Designed to resemble a desert flower, *Hymenocallis*, this 828-m (2,716.5-ft) super-scraper in Dubai is the tallest building in the world. The Burj Khalifa has more than 160 storeys and the world's highest outdoor observation deck. The structure is three times as tall as the Eiffel Tower in Paris.

❾ EL PALAU DE LES ARTS

This Spanish opera house is part of a complex of museum buildings near Valencia. It is set within landscaped gardens with reflecting pools and interlinked paths. The roof is made from a pair of curving steel shells clad in concrete and mosaic tiles.

❿ ALLIANZ ARENA

This football arena is located in Munich, Germany, and is the only stadium in the world that can change its exterior colour. Opened in 2005, the stadium holds nearly 70,000 spectators. Some locals nicknamed it the "inflatable boat" due to its unusual shape.

Visitors travel up a spiral walkway in the huge glass dome to take in a panoramic view of the Berlin skyline

⑦

Three massive towers are topped with oval spires shaped like ostrich eggs, which symbolize purity

Some 3,000 air-filled foil panels that form the exterior can be lit from within to match the home team's colours

⑩

The opera house has been compared to an ocean liner, with its sleek exterior and ship-like decks inside

⑥

The cladding system on the building's exterior is designed to withstand Dubai's extreme heat

❽

❾

SYMBOLS

From a fire-breathing dragon to a four-leaf clover, people use symbols – images, objects, and figures – to represent abstract ideas or concepts. Symbols can best be described as something visible that represents something invisible. We use them everyday without thinking about it. For example, our written language and numbers are made up of symbols.

RELIGION

Followers of different faiths can express religious concepts, such as their idea of God, through symbols. Religious symbols have many meanings and uses, and may be used in places of worship or as part of other religious practices.

Apsaras This supernatural being represents the female spirit in Hindu mythology.

Star and Crescent These are linked with the Islamic faith, and appear on the flags of many Muslim nations.

Yin Yang This symbol of the Taoist belief represents harmony and unity in the Universe.

Wheel of Law The eight spokes of this Buddhist symbol represent the eight paths to enlightenment.

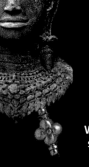

Star of David Named for King David of Israel, this has been a symbol of the Jewish faith since medieval times.

Crucifix This shows Jesus Christ's death on the cross – a reminder to Christian worshippers of his sacrfice.

Anubis The Ancient Egyptian god of the dead, Anubis led the mummification process and protected the dead.

GOOD LUCK

People hoping to protect themselves from misfortune or evil may carry a good-luck symbol. It could be a trinket, a piece of jewellery, or something from nature. Many symbols are lucky only to a particular culture and the superstition can stretch back centuries.

Saint Christoper Some Christians wear pendants showing the patron saint of long journeys to protect them when they travel.

Fu Thought to bring good fortune, this Chinese symbol decorates envelopes given to children for Lunar New Year.

White heather Regarded as a symbol of good luck in Scotland, some say heather grew on battlefields where no blood had been shed.

Four-leaf clover Most have three leaves, so superstition has it tha finding one by accide brings good luck.

Horse shoe In Europe and the USA, hanging a horsehoe by the front door will bring good fortune.

Evil eye This symbol is meant to block a curse sent by the nasty stare of an envious person.

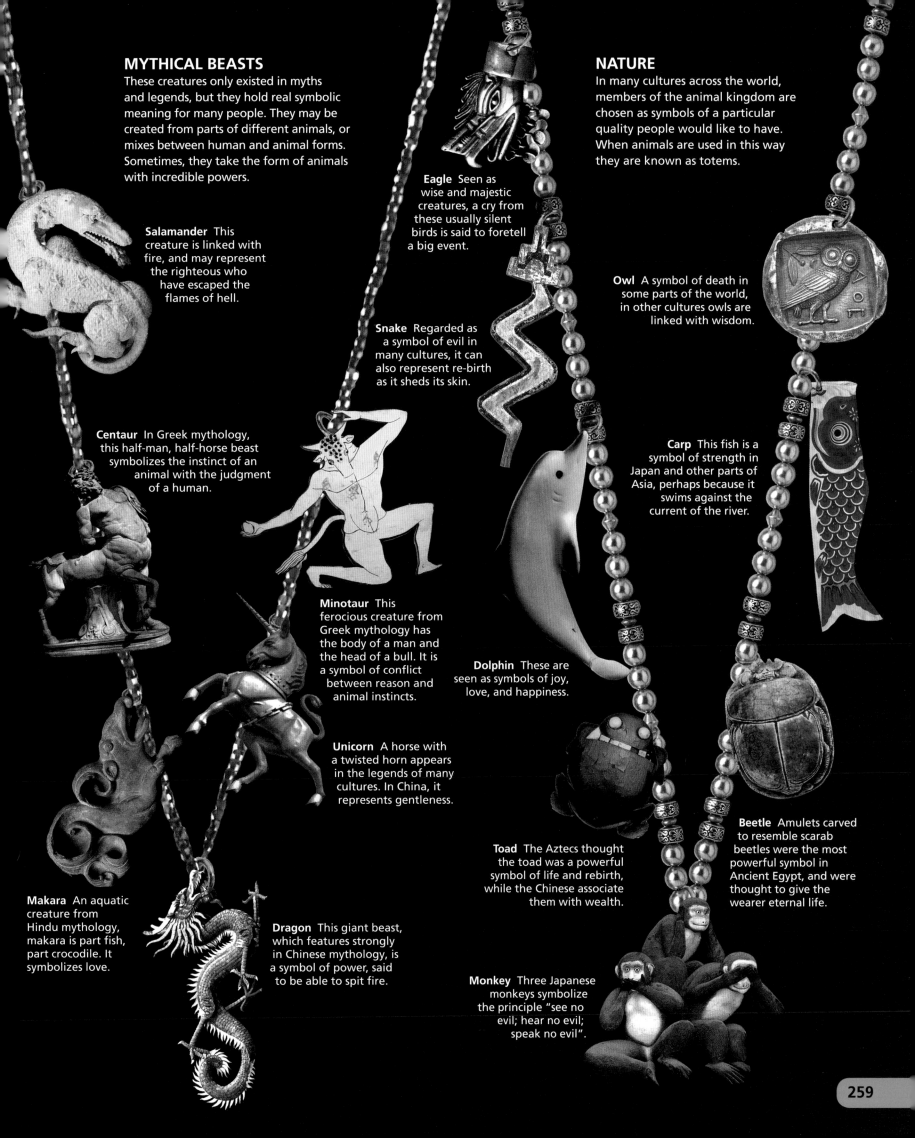

MYTHICAL BEASTS

These creatures only existed in myths and legends, but they hold real symbolic meaning for many people. They may be created from parts of different animals, or mixes between human and animal forms. Sometimes, they take the form of animals with incredible powers.

Salamander This creature is linked with fire, and may represent the righteous who have escaped the flames of hell.

Centaur In Greek mythology, this half-man, half-horse beast symbolizes the instinct of an animal with the judgment of a human.

Minotaur This ferocious creature from Greek mythology has the body of a man and the head of a bull. It is a symbol of conflict between reason and animal instincts.

Unicorn A horse with a twisted horn appears in the legends of many cultures. In China, it represents gentleness.

Makara An aquatic creature from Hindu mythology, makara is part fish, part crocodile. It symbolizes love.

Dragon This giant beast, which features strongly in Chinese mythology, is a symbol of power, said to be able to spit fire.

NATURE

In many cultures across the world, members of the animal kingdom are chosen as symbols of a particular quality people would like to have. When animals are used in this way they are known as totems.

Eagle Seen as wise and majestic creatures, a cry from these usually silent birds is said to foretell a big event.

Snake Regarded as a symbol of evil in many cultures, it can also represent re-birth as it sheds its skin.

Owl A symbol of death in some parts of the world, in other cultures owls are linked with wisdom.

Carp This fish is a symbol of strength in Japan and other parts of Asia, perhaps because it swims against the current of the river.

Dolphin These are seen as symbols of joy, love, and happiness.

Toad The Aztecs thought the toad was a powerful symbol of life and rebirth, while the Chinese associate them with wealth.

Beetle Amulets carved to resemble scarab beetles were the most powerful symbol in Ancient Egypt, and were thought to give the wearer eternal life.

Monkey Three Japanese monkeys symbolize the principle "see no evil; hear no evil; speak no evil".

LANGUAGE

People communicate through language, whether the words are spoken or written down. Today, there are some 7,000 different languages spoken around the globe. Many more languages were spoken in the past, which have now been forgotten. The languages of the most powerful economic and political nations are spoken by millions of people.

① Chinese 1.3 billion people are native speakers of one of the family of Chinese languages. Some 880 million people communicate in Mandarin Chinese, a group of dialects (language variations) from northern and southwestern China.

② French Spoken by 220 million people worldwide, French is an official language of the United Nations. It is one of the family of Romance languages, which developed from Latin.

③ Hebrew The holy language of the Jewish faith, Hebrew is spoken by 9 million people around the world. Many religious texts are written in an ancient form of Hebrew, in use from the 12th to the 6th century BCE.

④ Arabic Some 300 million people communicate with a dialect of Arabic, a family of very old languages closely related to Hebrew. The Qu'ran, the holy book of the Islamic faith, is written in Arabic.

Written French has five accent marks to indicate pronunciation

The Hebrew alphabet uses 22 characters, written from right to left

Portuguese writing has 26 letters and five accent signs

Artists may use calligraphy (decorative writing) to write Arabic text in Islamic manuscripts

Japanese writing is often printed vertically

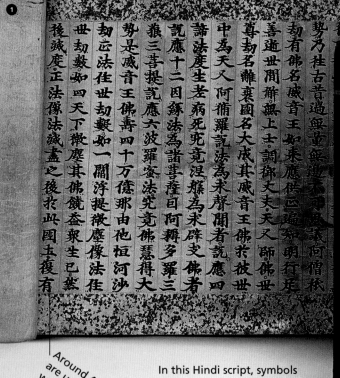

Around 4,000 characters are used in everyday written Chinese

In this Hindi script, symbols are joined together by a horizontal bar

In traditional written Spanish, 28 letters are used

5 Hindi The family of languages spoken in northern and central India is known as Hindi. As well as 425 million native speakers, there are many Indians who use Hindi as a second language.

6 Portuguese This Romance language originated in Portugal, but spread to parts of South America in the 16th and 17th centuries. Today, it has 230 million speakers worldwide.

7 Japanese Used by 130 million people, the Japanese language can be adapted by the speaker to show respect to someone, according to their age and social status.

8 Spanish Originating in northern Spain, this romance language has 577 million speakers. It is widely spoken in Central and Southern America. Today, Mexico has the most Spanish speakers.

9 Bengali Also known as Bangla, this language is India's second most spoken language. Bengali is also used in other parts of southern Asia, with 230 million native speakers.

10 Greek This ancient language has used the same alphabet since the 9th century BCE. Today, about 13 million speakers in Greece and Greek communities worldwide keep this language alive.

11 Latin The language of the Roman empire, Latin developed into the family of Romance languages, as well as lending its vocabulary to a number of other languages.

12 Russian With 160 million native speakers and many more using it as a second language, Russian is an important language in Europe and one of six official languages of the United Nations.

13 English This widely spoken language went global through British colonization. Today, there are 400 million native speakers, and it is the most used language on the Internet.

In early Greek writing, there are no gaps between individual words

Many Bengali characters stand for a combined consonant and vowel sound

Latin is rarely spoken today, but its alphabet is the most widely used across the globe

Written Russian uses the Cyrillic alphabet, a medieval system named after its inventor, St Cyril

The global use of English means that the language is constantly growing, with thousands of new words entering the language each year

LITERATURE

Any form of creative writing is called literature. It includes fiction, such as novels, poems, and plays, and non-fiction, including reference books, diaries, letters, and autobiographies. In all these literary forms, writers use their imagination to shape their material. They set out to convey information, ideas, or feelings in a clear and informed way that will interest and engage the reader.

ФЕДОР ДОСТОЕВСКИЙ
Преступление и наказание

АЗБУКА-КЛАССИКА

THE BODLEY HEAD

Crime and Punishment is a novel by Russian writer Fyodor Dostoevsky

▲ NON-FICTION

Writing that is based on fact is called non-fiction. Authors need to thoroughly research and understand their subject so they can bring to life actual events – historical, political, and personal. Non-fiction titles also include biographies (accounts of people's lives) and autobiographies (authors' accounts of their own lives).

Anne Frank wrote about her experiences as a Jewish girl hiding from the Nazis in World War II

Romance This popular fiction focuses on a love story between two people, usually with a happy ending. It may take place against a modern or historical setting.

Crime This type of fiction covers the exploits of criminals and their crimes, and follows the detectives who crack cases and foil their plans.

▲ FICTION

Authors who write fiction create events, settings, and characters from their imaginations. Although writers may base their stories on true events, there are always some elements that are made up. Works of fiction can include short stories, novels (long stories containing at least 60,000 words), poems, and plays.

Science fiction Authors may use scientific fact and modern technology to explore and imagine an alternative world, set now or in the future.

DRAMA ▶

Stories written for an audience fall into the category of drama, which may be performed in a theatre or in the movies, or on the radio or television. The audience expects something to happen, so writers use language to create characters and situations that will hold their interest.

English playwright William Shakespeare is considered the world's most successful dramatist

J. K. Rowling

Harry Potter
ET LA COUPE DE FEU

When a book is a success, the author may follow it up with one or more sequels to create a series

ALD DAHL
he BFG

▲ CHILDREN'S BOOKS

Today, young readers enjoy a huge range of literature, both fiction and non-fiction. Writing for children is a specialized area, and authors often work alongside illustrators to get the story across effectively. In general, children's books follow the adventures of a main character who is a similar age to the reader. The storyline may also introduce the reader to challenges in their own lives, such as bullying or a bereavement.

llustrations by Quentin Blake

BESTSELLERS

Hugely popular books that sell to vast numbers of readers are referred to as bestsellers. The biggest seller of all time is the Bible, with approximately 6 billion copies sold. Former Chinese leader Mao Zedong's Quotations from Chairman Mao sold some 1 billion copies. The holy book of Islam, the Qur'an, is close behind with 800 million copies. One of the most important works of Western literature, the Spanish novel Don Quixote by Miguel de Cervantes Saavedra, has to date sold about 500 million copies.

- More than 2 billion copies of Agatha Christie's crime novels have been sold worldwide.

- The bestselling playwright is William Shakespeare, with an estimated 4 billion copies sold.

- The seven books in J K Rowling's Harry Potter series have sold more than 500 million copies.

- The Lord of the Rings by J R R Tolkein has sold more than 150 million copies.

- The Bible has been translated into more than 2,000 languages.

Basho (1644–94) was Japan's most famous haiku poet

◀ FOLK TALES

These magical stories usually feature fantastic characters facing near impossible challenges, set in an unspecific time in the past. The original tales, found in every culture, have no known authors. They were first intended for a general audience, but now folk tales are often thought of as children's books. They are usually beautifully illustrated with images of the people and places.

Exquisitely illustrated Russian folk tale

◀ POETRY

In contrast to prose, poetry is often written in lines rather than paragraphs. Poets choose words that will best express an image, an idea, or a feeling. Some poetry rhymes, but not all. An ancient form of poem is the Japanese haiku, which requires the poet to use words made up from 17 syllables (single units of speech) to convey an idea or image.

263

MEDIA

The many ways people seek to communicate information to a large audience are known as the media. This communication can be in written, spoken, printed, or digital form. Throughout history, leaps in technology from the invention of printing to growth of the Internet have led to better, faster ways of reaching people. Today, information can be relayed around the globe in seconds.

❶ DIGITAL MEDIA

The word "digital" refers to the way that information is turned into number-based codes before being sent or stored via electronics. The Internet is the key form of digital media, and has opened up mass media to the individual. Anyone with a blog or website can express opinions to a huge audience.

❷ CONVERGENCE

In this digital age, media content is available on many different platforms. News, films, and television programmes can be viewed on smartphones, tablets, computers, and smart televisions. In addition, these digital devices also enable people to create as well as consume media content, via social media platforms such as Facebook and Twitter.

❸ TELEVISION AND FILM

Since the early broadcasts of the 1930s, television has brought news and entertainment to a wide audience. Today, television and films can be watched from home. DVDs, smart televisions, and online streaming services, such as Netflix, allow viewers to choose between thousands of shows, as well as record, pause, and rewind them.

❹ RADIO

In 1938, a radio dramatization of *The War of the Worlds* in the United States convinced many listeners that an actual Martian invasion was in progress. Today, radio stations still fill the airwaves with music, talk, news, and drama.

This book is a media product and was created using digital technology

Laptop computer

Newspapers are usually printed on inexpensive paper called "newsprint"

Smartphone

Powerful microprocessors enable modern phones to perform multiple functions at the same time

High-definition flat-screen TV

Satellite dish

A satellite dish attached to a building receives signals from an orbiting satellite

⑤

⑤ GLOBAL NETWORKS

Media is a global business. The majority of the world's media outlets are controlled by just a handful of international companies. Satellites orbiting Earth transmit television broadcasts around the world.

⑥ NEWSPAPERS

Published daily or weekly, newspapers contain news, information, feature stories, and advertising. China leads the world with more than 100 million copies circulating daily. Today, many papers are available to read online.

⑦ MAGAZINES

The content of a magazine does not usually date as quickly as that of a newspaper. Magazines may cover current events or they may be aimed at a specific audience, for example, movie or music fans.

PURE

④

Digital radios deliver high-quality sound through a digital signal

ONE

Magazines are usually printed on glossier paper than newspapers

⑦ LE FIGARO MAGAZINE

CAR OF THE Y

WHO WINS THE SHOWDOWN OF

SCIENCES ET AVENIR
Novembre 2007

NOBEL FRANÇAIS DE PHYSIQUE 2007
Albert Fert, le magnétique

60 GRANDES QUESTIONS

Le temps existe-t-il
La fin des civilisations
Le réchauffement climatique
9 milliards d'hommes sur la planète
Décrypter le cerveau
Avant le Big Bang
La vie extraterrestre...

DER SPIEGEL

Geboren am 9. November '89
Die Kinder des Mauerfalls werden volljähr

AVANTS

265

PHOTOGRAPHY

Photography is a method of making pictures of the real world by capturing light from objects. Light can be captured on film – a sheet of plastic coated with light-sensitive chemicals – or by an electronic sensor. Since cameras were invented, in the early 19th century, photographers have changed the way we see the world. They have shown us the wonders of nature, microscopic bacteria, the horrors of war, distant galaxies, sporting triumphs, and family portraits.

The speed of the shutter catches individual drops of water

❶ ACTION

Modern cameras are very sensitive, and can open and close their shutters in a fraction of a second. This allows them to freeze a moment in time, showing a footballer scoring a goal, or a swimmer powering through the water.

❷ PORTRAITS

Before photography was invented, only the very rich could afford to have portraits painted by artists. In the early days of photography, people wore their best clothes to strike a pose in a photographer's studio. Today, family photo albums chronicle birthdays, holidays, weddings, and everyday life.

❸ EARLY CAMERAS

The first cameras, developed in 1839, were large boxes, which had long exposure times (the time needed for photographic film or an image sensor to be subjected to light). Early sitters look stiff and uncomfortable, for they often had to hold a pose for up to 20 minutes. Over time, cameras became smaller and more sensitive to the light.

Sepia, a brown pigment derived from cuttlefish, made printed photos more durable

❹ ADVERTISING ART

The photos we see most often are adverts, blown up on street hoardings and in glossy magazines. These photos are often "retouched" so that the models look more perfect. In a lipstick advert, teeth can be whitened, and lips made to shine.

Collapsible bellows allow the lens to be folded back into the camera

❺ LENSES

Cameras work by focusing light from objects using curved pieces of glass called lenses. A zoom lens (above) uses an assembly of several lenses. By adjusting their distance from each other, the photographer can zoom in on distant objects.

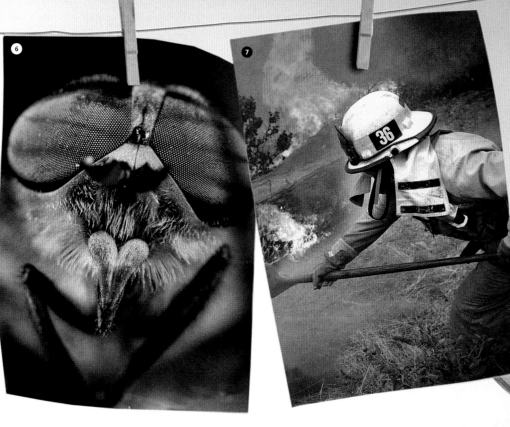

❻ MACRO

This type of photography uses a special lens to take close-up pictures of tiny objects, such as flies. A macro lens can only focus on a limited area of an object. While this fly's eyes are in sharp focus, its body is blurred.

❼ REPORTAGE

Photojournalists are reporters who use pictures, rather than words, to tell news stories. Armed with their cameras, they visit war zones and scenes of natural disasters, such as floods and fires, often risking their lives to bring back photographs that will tell an accurate story.

In a studio, a photographer can control how a shot is lit

This "portrait" view is unusual for landscape photography, which gave its name to horizontally oriented photos

❾ LANDSCAPES

Like painting, photography is used to record beautiful and often dramatic scenery. Some of the best landscape photographs are taken either in the hour after sunrise or before sunset. The Sun, low in the sky, bathes the world in a warm golden glow.

❿ DIGITAL CAMERAS

Modern cameras contain computers, which record images electronically rather than on film. Photographers with digital cameras can take as many pictures as they want without wasting film. Images can also be sent easily over the Internet from one computer to another.

Lights on stands can be raised and set at different angles

❽ FILM CAMERAS

Early cameras used heavy metal or glass plates. The roll of film, invented in 1888, made cameras both smaller and cheaper. The image was captured on the film in reverse, as a negative, which was used to print positive copies on paper.

THEATRE

Theatre has its origins in Ancient Greece, where performances included singing and dancing as well as acting. In medieval times, plays were based on religious stories and were staged on large wagons in public places. It was not until the 17th century that theatres were built with a raised, framed platform, separating the audience from the stage by a curtain. Today, modern theatres provide the setting for performances of all kinds, from plays and pantomimes to opera and ballet.

❶ PROSCENIUM

The decorated arch that divides the stage from the audience is known as the proscenium. It acts as a picture frame for the performance on stage. This type of arch was invented in Italy in 1618, although many modern theatres now have an open stage without a curtain.

❷ CURTAIN

Made from heavy cloth, such as velvet, the curtain screens the stage from the audience while the stagehands are changing the scenery. The flameproof safety curtain prevents fire from spreading from the stage to the rest of the theatre.

❸ BOX

The auditorium, where the audience sits, is made up of private boxes, tiered seats called the stalls, the dress circle, and the upper circle. Private boxes contain the most expensive seats and usually have the closest view of the stage.

❹ WINGS

The offstage areas on each side of the curtain are called the wings. Concealed by the proscenium, the actors wait in the wings before they make their entrance on stage.

❼ ACTORS

The success of a theatrical performance often depends on the skills of the actors, who use facial expressions, tone of voice, and gestures to make the audience believe what is happening on stage. The first recorded actor was a Greek poet called Thespis who was writing and acting out his own plays in the 6th century BCE.

❽ SCENERY

Set designers use scenery to create atmosphere, set the location of the story, and give the illusion of distance and space on stage. Above the stage is a "fly" space in which scenery and equipment hang. A complex system of pulleys hoists heavy pieces of scenery to and from the stage.

❾ STAGE

In the theatre, the stage is the platform where the performance takes place. Traditionally, the stage is made from wooden boards and often contains a trap-door through which performers and scenery can be raised and lowered.

⑤ COSTUMES

The actors' costumes are the responsibility of the wardrobe department. The wardrobe manager researches, designs, and looks after the costumes and helps the actors change outfits between scenes.

⑥ ORCHESTRA

Beneath the front of the stage is the orchestra pit, where the musicians and sound technicians sit. The conductor stands facing the stage to coordinate the music in time with the actions of the singers, dancers, and actors.

MOVIES

From 1895, when the Lumière brothers first delighted French audiences with their "moving pictures" to today's multi-billion-dollar film industry, movies have become a popular type of entertainment, an important art form, and a way to shape people's opinions. The "magic" of movies is that they are created from a series of individual images shown in rapid sequence.

▼ SILENT
Until the late 1920s, the technology to add recorded sound to movies did not exist. Instead, bits of dialogue or key story points appeared as words on screen, and actors relied on body language. Live piano music helped to set the mood.

▼ WESTERN
Set in the tough American West, these movies captivated huge audiences in the 1950s and '60s. Westerns tell of cowboys, outlaws, gunslingers, and good guys as they faced the challenges of frontier life.

▼ HORROR
These movies are created to terrify and shock the audience. In a typical horror film, characters must overpower evil – be it a monster, a ghost, or a serial killer. Horror films are often quite violent and gory.

▲ SCI-FI AND FANTASY
Imaginative and visually stunning, science fiction and fantasy allow filmmakers to explore future worlds, use special effects, and speculate about our relationship with technology.

▲ ACTION-ADVENTURE
These movies often follow the exploits of a hero, with plenty of fast-paced stunt work, chases, fistfights, and shoot-outs. From intrepid crime-fighters to special agents, these daring heroes always save the day.

▲ ANIMATION
These movies are created when a rapid sequence of drawings (or models) is run together to give the illusion of movement. Animation also uses computer-generated images (CGI).

▼ BOLLYWOOD

From the early 1900s, Hollywood has been the centre of movie-making. Today, more than 1,000 films a year are made in India. Many are lavish, colourful Bollywood musicals (the name is from the "B" in Bombay, the old name for Mumbai).

▼ COMEDY

From slapstick to spoofs, audiences have always loved comedy films. Some rely on the dialogue for the laughs, others on physical quirks of the actors – or a combination of both. These films often have happy endings, even if they explore the darker side of life.

▼ DISASTER

Asteroids hurtling to Earth, shipwrecks, and earthquakes have all been subjects of disaster movies. Since the 1990s, the introduction of CGI special effects has made it easier to create visually spectacular disasters.

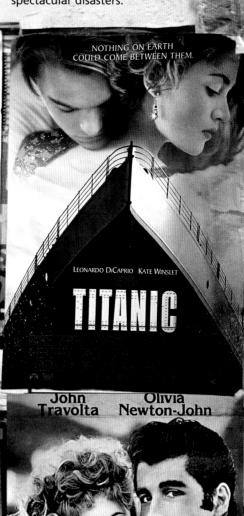

▲ THRILLER

Action-packed and fast-paced, thriller movies create audience tension as the hero tries to outwit an evil adversary. Some thrillers feature plenty of action, while others rely on creating an atmosphere of suspense.

▲ MARTIAL ARTS

These Asian-based action films feature spectacular fight sequences using one or more of the martial arts. Among the martial artists who became stars due to their skills are Bruce Lee and Jackie Chan.

▲ MUSICAL

Featuring singing and dancing as part of the storytelling, musicals are often adapted from stage productions. Recently, Hollywood musicals have played to wide audiences in a revival of the genre.

271

DANCE

Energetic or graceful, dancers use athletic skill and flexibility to perform a series of movements, often in time to music. Dancing is a form of expression that may be a type of performing art, part of a special ritual, or a fun social activity. The earliest dancers used movement to worship gods and spirits and to act out stories. In performances, dancers often follow a pre-planned series of steps and movements devised by a choreographer.

Arm movements are coordinated with the legs for balance and effect

BALLET ▶
Ballet is a theatrical dance with graceful moves. Dancers undergo rigorous training and wear special hard-toed ballet shoes in order to dance *en pointe* – on the tip of their toes.

◀ DISCO
In the 1970s, pop songs with strong dance beats ruled the airwaves and people gathered in clubs to disco dance. Some dances had set steps; others were created by the dancers themselves, perhaps inspired by the film *Saturday Night Fever*.

Bamboo poles help the dancers to move the dragon in a realistic way

The dragon is a symbol of power and strength. The longer the dragon, the more luck it will bring

CHINESE DRAGON DANCE ▶
In this ceremonial dance, dating back to the Han Dynasty (206 BCE–220 CE), a team of performers carries a colourful dragon, held up with poles. They lift and lower the poles to make the dragon dance. This dance is a key part of Chinese New Year celebrations.

BHARATANATYAM ▶
In ancient times, Hindu temple dancers in south India performed a set of moves and postures to tell the stories of the gods. These evolved into the Bharatanatyam dance style. In this dance, certain poses – especially hand gestures – are held to represent different meanings.

◄ TANGO

This dramatic dance for couples began as a street dance in Argentina and Uruguay during the mid-1800s. With hands tightly clasped, dancers either face each other, or look in the same direction, as they move to the beat. Tango is also the name for the music associated with the dance.

CAN-CAN ►

This high-kicking, cartwheeling dance began in Paris in the 1830s, and was originally for couples. French dance troupes soon took up the can-can in music halls, where chorus lines of girls performed the energetic dance.

Dancers swirl their skirts and petticoats as part of the performance

Castanets were not originally part of "true" flamenco, but were introduced to add drama

◄ TRIBAL DANCE

These traditional African dances, often performed to the beat of a drum, are important parts of many ceremonies, both joyful (weddings and coming-of-age celebrations) and sad (funerals). Tribal dances help to unite and uplift the community.

Touching the limbo pole means the dancer is out of the competition

Flamenco dress features a tight-fitting bodice with a layered skirt for easy movement

LIMBO ►

The limbo was created in the Caribbean Islands. Performers have to dance under a horizontal pole without touching it or losing their balance. The pole is lowered after each round until one limbo champion dancer remains.

▲ FLAMENCO

With its roots in small villages of the Andalusian region in Spain, flamenco is a passionate style of music and dance with a strong, powerful rhythm. Dancers click their fingers and stamp their feet to match the drama of the guitar music.

MUSIC

Music is a performance art created by the sounds of singers and instruments, and covers an incredible range of styles. It can be enjoyed live or through various media forms from television and radio to the Internet. Music has always been written and performed, but it was not until the 20th century, when new technology to record and share music developed, that musicians could become global stars.

A disco ball hung over the dancefloor was a regular feature of discotheques

① DISCO
In the 1970s, pop music with a dance beat known as disco (from *discothèque*, a French word for nightclub) filled dance floors across the globe. Disco music topped the charts and created major stars, but faded from popularity in the 1980s.

② CLASSICAL
Classical music is a general name for the various types of music written to be performed in a concert hall. It may be composed for the instruments of an orchestra (either a full symphony or a small group of players), or written for a choir or opera company. The music of composers like Bach and Beethoven is still popular, centuries after it was written.

A score (manuscript of musical notes) is used by classical musicians so they can keep track of which parts they play

③ MUSIC AND VISUALS
From the late 1970s, bands made short music videos to accompany and promote their songs. The arrival of music video networks and the Internet has created a huge boom in this area. The virtual band Gorillaz, who previously only existed as cartoon animations in music videos, turned the form on its head in 2005 when they performed live as a normal band.

A relatively modern instrument, saxophones became key to the emerging jazz sound

④ DANCE
The popularity of electronic instruments like synthesizers, and the ability to use computers to make music, led to a new generation of music written to fill the dance floors. DJs became stars, using turntables to mix live music.

Turntables and vinyl records are used by DJs to create and mix live music

GORILLAZ

Rapping evolved when DJs used microphones to talk – or "rap" – over music

Touring provides a major income stream for today's global pop stars, such as Justin Timberlake

❺ JAZZ

Jazz was born in early 20th-century America, when elements of European music were blended with the rhythmic music brought by African slaves to the south.

❻ ROCK

In the 1940s and 50s, rock-and-roll music sprang up in the United States. It was played on electric guitars, bass guitars, and drums, and featured exciting vocals, catchy tunes, and a strong beat. This evolved into rock music, a group of many diverse styles that remains popular worldwide.

❼ POP

This type of rock music is aimed mostly at a young audience. Pop songs can be fairly simple in their structure, with lots of repetition in the lyrics, so it's easy to sing along. Today's major pop stars reach an international audience with their hit songs.

❽ R&B

Rhythm and blues, or R&B, music started in the United States in the 1940s, originally performed by and for a mainly African-American audience. Today's version of the style is closely related to disco and dance music, but is smoother and features softer vocals.

❾ REGGAE

This style of music originated in Jamaica in the 1960s. It has a characteristic rhythm style and a slow and steady tempo (speed). The bass guitar keeps the rhythm and is the most prominent instrument. Reggae is associated with the Rastafarian religion.

❿ COUNTRY

Mixing the traditional music of the southern states of America with rock-and-roll and other musical styles, country music is one of the largest-selling music genres today, with major stars, huge record sales, and enormously successful tours.

Rock band The Killers's first album, Hot Fuss, is estimated to have sold over 7 million copies worldwide

Women singers, such as Beyoncé, are among the world's top-earning pop stars

Jamaican music legend Bob Marley is the most famous reggae star

Wireless speakers can be paired wirelessly with many devices, such as smartphones, to play music anywhere

Smartphones are now used to store and listen to music

The electric guitar is the main instrument in many musical styles, especially rock

Many country music stars have adopted the cowboy image

ORCHESTRA

An orchestra is a large group of instrumental musicians playing together under the direction of a conductor. Orchestras usually include four sections: percussion, brass, woodwinds, and strings. Players of similar instruments sit together, with the conductor keeping time up front.

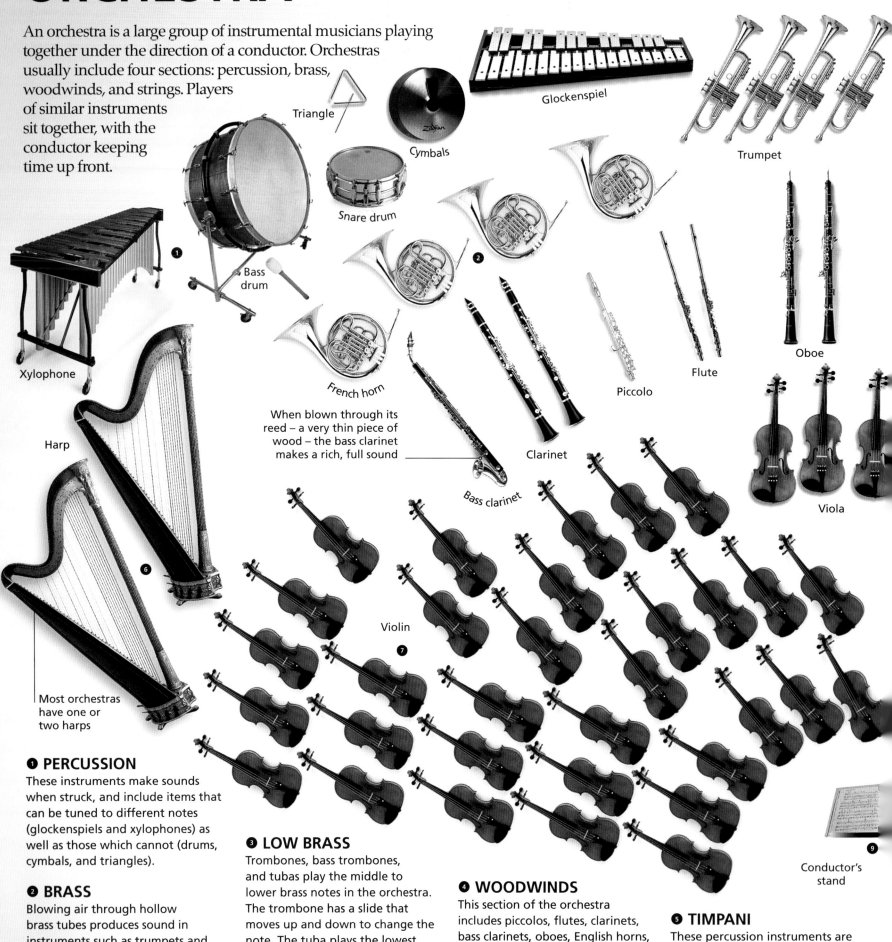

Triangle

Cymbals

Glockenspiel

Trumpet

Bass drum

Snare drum

Xylophone

French horn

When blown through its reed – a very thin piece of wood – the bass clarinet makes a rich, full sound

Bass clarinet

Clarinet

Piccolo

Flute

Oboe

Viola

Harp

Violin

Most orchestras have one or two harps

Conductor's stand

❶ PERCUSSION
These instruments make sounds when struck, and include items that can be tuned to different notes (glockenspiels and xylophones) as well as those which cannot (drums, cymbals, and triangles).

❷ BRASS
Blowing air through hollow brass tubes produces sound in instruments such as trumpets and French horns. The note is changed by pressing down valves.

❸ LOW BRASS
Trombones, bass trombones, and tubas play the middle to lower brass notes in the orchestra. The trombone has a slide that moves up and down to change the note. The tuba plays the lowest notes, which boom out from its bell-shaped end.

❹ WOODWINDS
This section of the orchestra includes piccolos, flutes, clarinets, bass clarinets, oboes, English horns, bassoons, and contrabassoons. Players blow air over a hole or through a reed to make notes.

❺ TIMPANI
These percussion instruments are giant copper bowls with skin-like heads struck by wool-topped sticks. They are also called kettledrums.

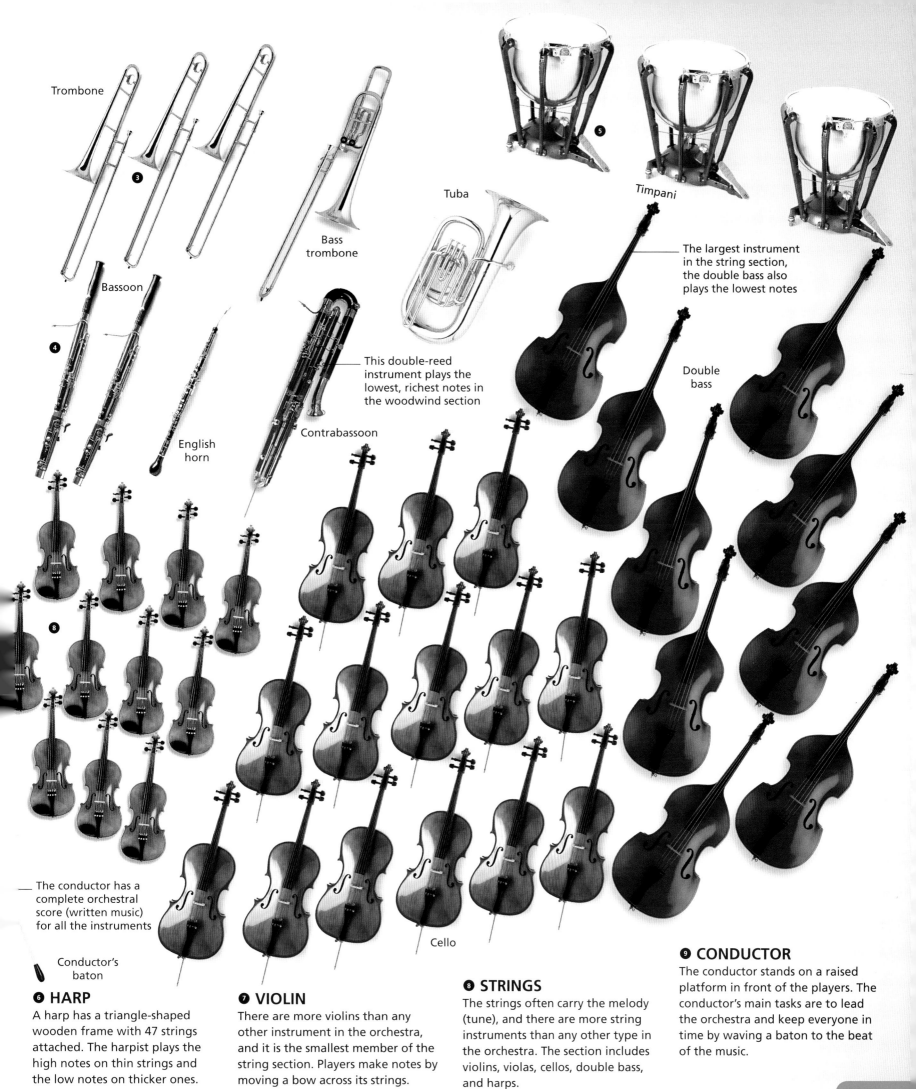

Trombone

③

Bass
trombone

Bassoon

④

English
horn

Contrabassoon

Tuba

This double-reed
instrument plays the
lowest, richest notes in
the woodwind section

⑤

Timpani

The largest instrument
in the string section,
the double bass also
plays the lowest notes

Double
bass

⑧

The conductor has a
complete orchestral
score (written music)
for all the instruments

Conductor's
baton

Cello

❻ HARP

A harp has a triangle-shaped
wooden frame with 47 strings
attached. The harpist plays the
high notes on thin strings and
the low notes on thicker ones.

❼ VIOLIN

There are more violins than any
other instrument in the orchestra,
and it is the smallest member of the
string section. Players make notes by
moving a bow across its strings.

❽ STRINGS

The strings often carry the melody
(tune), and there are more string
instruments than any other type in
the orchestra. The section includes
violins, violas, cellos, double bass,
and harps.

❾ CONDUCTOR

The conductor stands on a raised
platform in front of the players. The
conductor's main tasks are to lead
the orchestra and keep everyone in
time by waving a baton to the beat
of the music.

SPORT

Many sports developed from ancient times, when running and throwing skills were essential to survival. Any activity governed by rules and requiring physical ability is considered a sport – and at the heart of many sports is a ball.

1 Hurling This fast-paced Irish game involves teams of 15 "hurlers" with axe-shaped sticks, two goals, and a small ball.

2 American football Points are scored by players carrying or throwing an oval ball into the opposition's area.

3 Polo This ball game is played on horseback. Riders use long-handled mallets to drive a ball into the goal.

4 Football The world's most popular sport involves two teams of 11 players trying to score goals in the opposition's net, with each game lasting 90 minutes.

5 Hockey In this game, two teams armed with hockey sticks try to score by smashing a ball into the opponent's net.

6 Shotput Players compete to throw a 7 kg (16 lb) metal shot as far as possible.

7 Gaelic football With its roots in an ancient Irish game called caid, players score by kicking or hitting the ball through H-shaped goals.

8 Aussie Rules football Players pass the oval-shaped ball to team-mates by kicking or throwing it. To score, they must kick the ball between four posts at each end of the field.

9 Juggling balls Jugglers keep several balls in the air at once. Experienced jugglers can swap balls for knives and fire torches.

10 Lacrosse Invented by Native Americans, players catch and throw a rubber ball with netted sticks. They must throw it into the opposition team's goal to score.

11 Softball In this team sport, players use a bat to whack a ball as far as possible to give them time to run around four ground markers.

12 Rugby Players attempt to gain points by landing the oval ball beyond the other team's goal line or kicking it over a high H-shaped goal.

13 Medicine ball Athletes put these weighty balls on their bodies to increase their muscle strength while exercising.

14 Baseball This sport is very similar to softball, but played with a smaller, harder ball.

15 Cricket A bowler throws the ball at a wicket (set of wooden poles), which is defended by a batsman.

16 Golf A club is used to hit a small ball a long distance to get it into, or as near as possible to, each hole on a course.

Rugby balls are oval shaped to make them easier to hold against the upper body while running

Modern footballs have 32 stitched panels

Medicine balls can weigh from 2.5 to 7 kg (5 to 15 lbs)

17 Boules Very popular in France, players compete to throw heavy balls at a much smaller ball, called a jack.

18 Bowls On well-maintained lawns, players try to roll balls closer to a small target ball than their opponents.

19 Snooker Using sticks called cues, two players attempt to pot 15 red balls and six different coloured balls into six pockets on a special wool-covered table.

20 Rounders Two teams take turns at batting and fielding. A rounder is scored when a player hits the ball far enough to run around four posts before the ball is returned by a fielder.

21 Basketball The game was first played using peach baskets on poles for hoops. If a team scored, the referee climbed a ladder to get the ball.

22 Netball Based on basketball, this team sport is played on courts and is most popular with women in Australasia.

23 Volleyball Two teams of six players compete to pass a ball over a high net using only their hands. If the ball touches the ground, the other team gains points.

24 Croquet French peasants in the 14th century used wooden mallets to whack a wooden ball through hoops crafted from bent branches, inventing the game of croquet.

25 Tennis Played on grass or clay courts, two players (singles) or four players (doubles) use racquets to hit a felt-covered ball over a net.

26 Pool Similar to snooker, two players use cues to sink either red or yellow balls into pockets. The winner is the player who pots the final black ball.

27 Squash Inside a walled court, players take turns to smash a rubber ball against the wall with a racquet.

28 Beach volleyball First played on California's sandy beaches in the 1920s, this sport can now be played on artificial sand courts.

29 Table tennis This sport began in Victorian England, when dinner guests turned their table into a mini tennis court. Champagne corks were used as balls.

30 Water polo Players swim to catch the ball to stop the opposing team from reaching their goal.

31 Tenpin bowling Players hurl a heavy ball down a wooden lane to knock down the 10 pins.

32 Marbles Players compete to throw glass marbles inside a designated circle or at another target marble.

The ball used in netball is smaller than the one used to play basketball

A water polo ball has a special non-slip surface

Hollow table tennis balls are hit with bats called "paddles"

A beach volleyball is softer and larger than a regular volleyball

Three finger holes are drilled into a bowling ball so it can be gripped

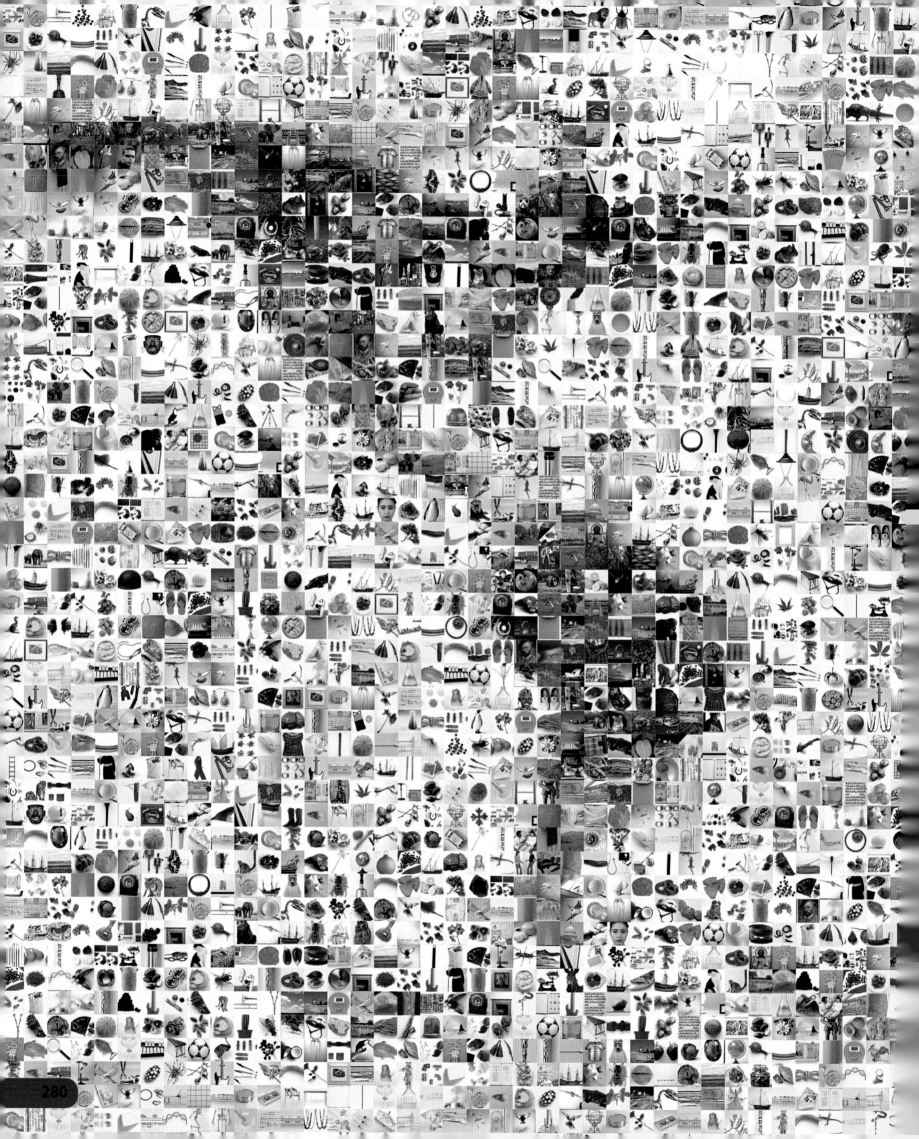

Reference

Nature

Lichen are only a few centimetres tall, but they **live for a very long time** in the coldest places on Earth. Some lichens in **Antarctica** are more than

4,000 years old.

After a **tree dies**, all the carbon dioxide it absorbed when alive is eventually released back into the **atmosphere**. The same amount of **carbon dioxide** is released whether the tree burns or rots.

The **largest water plant** is the Amazonian giant lily. Its leaves are **so big** that a child could sit on it **without sinking**.

Magnolias are amongst the most ancient flowering plants. **Fossils** of magnolias have been found that are *20* million *years old*.

The *nepenthes* is the world's largest *carnivorous* (meat-eating) plant. It catches insects in its huge *vase-shaped* pitcher leaves. It is sometimes called the "monkey cup" because monkeys like to drink out of its *pitchers*.

Fungi live by **feeding** on dead organisms or their waste. **Pilobolus** fungi feed on cow dung.

*The **largest fungus** ever found is an Armillaria ostoyae in Oregon, USA, which covers nearly 10 sq km (4 sq miles) of forest floor and is estimated to be up to **8,500** years old.*

The **streaks of colour** in cheeses such as **Stilton** and **Danish Blue** are made by **mould**, which is a microscopic fungus.

A typical bed is home to about *2 million* dust mites.

Many desert plants have **very long roots** to **find water** deep underground. The tropical American mesquite tree's roots grow up to *50 m* (150 ft) long.

The smallest flowering plant is the duckweed *Wolffia*, which is just 0.6 mm long.

Tiny nanoplankton, less than 20 thousandths of a millimetre in diameter, are the **most plentiful organisms** in Earth's oceans.

Aphids are born pregnant and can **give birth** just **10 days** after they are born themselves.

European eels lay their eggs in the oceans. The baby elvers then make their way to freshwater rivers. A female eel can lay up to

4 million

eggs in one year.

The seeds of the **coco de mer** are the largest of any plant. They can weigh up to 20 kg (45 lb).

*One type of **lungfish can breathe** underwater **using gills** and in the air **using lungs**.*

The **smallest mammal by weight**, the **Etruscan shrew**, weighs just 1.8 g (0.06 oz) – **lighter** than a penny coin.

A domestic rabbit can give birth to up to **20** babies a month.

The hummingbird is the only bird that can fly straight up, down, and backwards.

Bamboo is the tallest grass. It can grow up to *50 m* (150 ft) tall.

A male walrus's tusks can grow up to *1m* (3 ft) long.

A **male howler** monkey's **howls** can be **heard** up to 5 km (3 miles) away.

Freshwater and saltwater **crocodiles cry**. They do it to lubricate the eyes and get rid of excess salt in their bodies, not because they are sad.

Sharks have a very good sense of smell. They can detect *one* part of blood in *100 million* parts of water.

Prairie dogs live in huge burrows called towns. One town in Texas was home to

400,000,000 individuals.

A woodpecker can peck up to **20** times per second.

The digestive juices of a hyena are strong enough to break down bones.

Octopuses have three hearts – two to pump blood to their gills and one to pump blood around their bodies.

Ants *never* sleep

There is enough poison in a single *poison dart frog's* skin to kill **10,000** mice.

The **pregnancy** of an Indian **elephant** lasts for about 22 months.

The biggest living cat is the Siberian tiger, which weighs up to 300 kg (660 lb).

A mole can tunnel through **100 m** *(330 ft) of earth in a day.*

Some species of **springtails**, a kind of **insect**, can survive in temperatures as low as -38ºC (-36ºF) because their bodies contain **antifreeze**.

A red **kangaroo** can cover **8 m** (25 ft) in a single **hop**.

The world's **largest** living **rodent**, the capybara, can weigh up to **65 kg** (140 lb).

A **termite** queen lays **30,000 eggs** a day.

Whale milk is nearly **50%fat**.

The blue whale is the largest animal that has ever lived. Its heart alone can weigh **180 kg** (400 lb).

China's earthquake **early warning** system involves the close monitoring of **snakes**, which leave their nests shortly before an **earthquake**.

A pile of **elephant dung** may contain **7,000** beetles.

Male humpback whales sing songs that last **20 minutes** or longer. They may be doing this to **serenade** females.

Camels can go up to **two weeks** without drinking, but when there is **water** around, they can down 200 litres (40 gallons) in 10 minutes.

Monarch butterflies migrate **4,000 km** (2,500 miles) from North America to Mexico or Butterfly Grove in San Francisco to **spend** the winter, even though they have **never been there** before.

A **bee's buzz** is made by its wings, which flap **250 times a second**.

A blue **whale's whistle** can be heard more than 100 km (62 miles) away **underwater**.

Whales and dolphins put **half their brains** to sleep at a time so that they **don't drown**.

There are more than **370,000** known species of **beetle**.

A dog can make about 100 different **facial expressions**, most of them involving its **ears**.

*The part of a **dog's brain** involved in **sensing smell** is **40 times** bigger than that of **humans**.*

Cows have four stomachs, which they use to **process** hard-to-digest grass and **vegetation**.

Beaver dams can be **300 m** (1,000 ft) long and may be *hundreds* of years old.

Spiders usually prefer to live alone, but very occasionally team up to build **huge webs**. A web found in 2007 in Lake Tawakoni State Park in Texas, USA, measured 180 m (590 ft) across. It was built by **lots** of different **species** of spider.

A flea can cover 30 cm (12 in) in one jump – that's 200 times the length of its own body.

With a wingspan of up to **3.5 m** (11 ft), the *wandering albatross* has the longest wingspan of all flying birds, which means that each of its wings is *almost as long* as an **adult human** is tall.

LEARN MORE ABOUT THE NATURAL WORLD ON PAGES 8–59

Human body

Your body sheds tens of thousands of **skin flakes** every minute. Over a lifetime, a body loses **20 kg (44 lb)** of skin flakes.

Your brain weighs about 2 per cent of your total body weight, but uses 20 per cent of your blood supply.

The brain of an adult is **three times heavier** *than that of a newborn baby. From the age of 20, the brain loses* **1 g** *(0.03 oz) a year as* **brain cells die** *and are not replaced.*

Your **eyes** stop growing when you reach puberty and stay the same size for the rest of your life.

Nose hairs act like a net to trap and remove nasty particles from the air.

The bones in the hands and feet account for more than half the bones in the human body.

The liver handles more than **500** *different jobs, including the disposal of dead blood cells, making proteins, and storing sugars.*

There are **100 trillion cells** in your body. A billion of them die every 20 seconds.

The largest human cell is the female ovum.

The smallest is the male sperm.

There are more muscles in a caterpillar than there are in a human body.

You spend *half an hour* every day blinking.

The left lung is smaller than the right lung to make room for the heart.

It takes about 40 hours for food to pass through the large intestine.

Everyone has a unique tongue print.

At rest, you **breathe** about once **every four seconds**. This rises to once every second during exercise.

We make 1 litre (2 pints) of saliva in our mouths every day.

Tiny bacteria make up 3 per cent of your body weight.

Women's hearts are smaller than men's, but they beat on average 75 times per minute compared to 70 times for men.

About **a third** of adults snore.

Stretched out straight, the small intestine is about 6 m (19 ft) long.

Food spends up to six hours in your stomach being digested.

The smallest muscle in the human body is the stapedius. It is inside the ear and is less than 2 mm (0.8 in) long.

There are more than

600

muscles in the human body. Muscles are 40 per cent of the body's total weight.

Blood travels 19,000 km (12,000 miles) every day. That's half way around the world.

After the age of **60**, you will lose about half your taste buds.

The **stomach** continually produces new layers of mucus to protect the lining and stop the stomach from digesting itself.

The average person eats **30 tonnes** of food in a lifetime – that's the weight of **80 horses**.

There are around 1,000 trillion bacteria in your body – 10 times more than the number of body cells.

The loudest snore ever recorded was more than 80 decibels, as loud as a pneumatic drill.

The average human head has 100,000 hairs growing on it, but redheads have only 90,000.

An **adult man** normally needs to **eat** about **10,000 kilojoules** (2,500 calories) a day. *Arctic explorers* need about *three times* that much to keep them going in the **cold**.

A fingernail would grow 28 m (90 ft) long if never cut. The middle nail grows fastest, the thumb slowest.

There are the same number of hairs on the body of a human being as on a chimpanzee.

The longest beard ever measured was more than

5 m (16 ft) long and belonged to Norwegian *Hans Langseth.*

Babies start dreaming before they are born.

The average human blinks 23 times a minute. That's 12 million times a year.

A body releases 2 litres (3.5 pints) of gas per day as burps or farts.

The largest organ is the skin, which has a surface area of about 2 sq m (20 sq ft) and weighs about 10 kg (22 lb).

Babies don't have bony kneecaps. Their soft kneecaps begin to become bony between the ages of three and six.

73 per cent of babies' bodies are water. This drops to 60 per cent in adult men and 55 per cent in adult women.

The most common time of birth is between 3 am and 4 am.

There are 250,000 sweat glands in a pair of feet. They can produce a quarter of a litre (half a pint) of sweat in one day.

When you sleep, you lose up to 42 g (1.4 oz) in weight every hour.

Common colds can be caused by one of more than 200 types of virus.

A cough releases air at speeds up to *100 km/h* (60 mph).

A single sneeze might contain up to 100,000 viruses.

More people died during the flu pandemic at the end of World War I than were killed during the war.

19th-century British surgeon Robert Liston could cut off a leg in ***28 seconds***.

Life expectancy at birth in Japan is 84.2 years – the highest in the world.

The **oldest** person ever documented was French woman **Jeanne Calment**, who died in 1997 aged 122 years and 164 days.

One in **2,000 babies** is born with a **tooth.**

In an average lifetime, you will walk the equivalent of five times around the Equator.

The first successful heart transplant took place in 1967. There are now eight heart transplants in the USA alone every day.

The largest artery, the **aorta**, is about **2 cm** (0.78 in) in diameter. That's as wide as a **hose pipe**.

During puberty, boys can grow 9 cm (3.5 in) in a year.

Children grow faster in spring.

In a whole lifetime, a human passes **45,000 litres** (10,000 gallons) of urine. That's enough to fill a **swimming pool**.

In your lifetime, you will drink about 70,000 litres (16,000 gallons) of water.

Standing upright burns up 600 kilojoules (140 calories) of energy in an hour.

You cannot *sneeze* with your eyes open.

SEE AND EXPLORE THE HUMAN BODY ON PAGES 60–87

Science and technology

The **smallest particle** scientists have found is the **quark**. It is **so small** that nobody has seen one, and we only know it is there because of its **effect** on things **around it**.

The number **zero** **was first used in India around 875** BCE.

The **smallest** Standard International (SI) **unit of weight** is the **yoctogram**, which was added to weigh **sub-atomic particles**. The **largest unit**, the **yottagram**, is used to **weigh stars** and planets – Earth weighs in at 6,000 yottagrams.

A *jiffy* is a *unit of time* equal to one hundredth of a second.

In June 2018, Summit became the world's fastest *supercomputer*. It can operate at a speed of *200 petaflops* – that is 200 million billion calculations per second.

The study of large numbers is called googology.

There are **six** kinds of **quarks**, which scientists have named up, *down*, top, *bottom*, **charm**, and **strange**.

One byte in a computer's **memory** is made up of eight **bits**. A group of four bits is called a *nibble*.

With the help of **computers**, more recorded data has been produced in the last **10 years** than in all of previous **recorded history**.

Hydrogen is the lightest, simplest, and by far the most **common element** in the Universe – *93 per cent* of all atoms are hydrogen atoms.

Atoms are mostly made of empty space. If the nucleus were a fly in the middle of a football pitch, the electrons would be like dust particles flying around in the stands.

A proton is **1,835** times **heavier** than an electron.

The **densest naturally-occurring element**, osmium, **weighs** 23 g/cm³ (13 oz/in³).

Scientists in Europe are developing a laser that will produce light ten trillion times as bright as sunlight.

Thomas Babbage came up with his idea for a computer when he was just 19 years old.

Tungsten has the **highest melting point** of any metal. It remains a **solid** until the **temperature** reaches **3,422°C** (6,192°F), when it finally melts.

Acid rain caused by industrial **pollution** was first noticed in the Midlands, UK, in the 19th century.

The Internet domain name *business.com* was bought by Marc Ostrofsky in 1999 for *$7.5 million*.

Airships **float** because they are filled with **helium**, a gas that is many times **lighter** than air.

At atmospheric pressure, **carbon dioxide** turns from a **solid** into a **gas**, without melting, at -78°C (-108°F).

When a **gas condenses** into a liquid, it takes up, on average,

1,300

times less space.

The metal lithium is so light that it floats on water.

Diamonds are formed from **carbon** that is **compressed** 150 km (90 miles) below Earth's surface.

Pure water has a **neutral pH of 7**, but **rainwater** is **acidic**, with a **pH of 6 or less**.

The *first ever email* was sent by American Ray Tomlinson in 1971. The *message* was sent from one *computer* to another right *next to it*.

There is the **same** amount of **water** on **Earth** now as there was **2 billion years ago**.

Mercury is the only metal that is **liquid** at room temperature.

Two-thirds of the water used in the home is used in the bathroom.

It is not safe to **skate** on **ice** until it is at least **13 cm** (5 in) **thick**.

Sound can damage **your hearing** at 90 decibels (dB), the volume of very **heavy traffic**. It starts to become painful when it exceeds 130 dB, a **plane taking off**.

Noise is a jumble of different frequencies of sound. Musical notes have one dominant frequency. Middle C has a frequency of 256 hertz.

The scale used to measure **light intensity** uses a unit called a **candela**. It was originally based on the amount of light given out by a candle. A **flash of lightning** gives off 80 million candelas per sq m (8.6 million per sq ft).

In a vacuum, light travels at a speed of

299,792,458 m

(983,571,056 ft) per second.

On a **sunny day**, 1,000 trillion **photons** (light particles) hit an area the size of a pinhead every second.

*A normal **light bulb** turns just five per cent of the electrical energy it is powered by **into light**.*

Red is the longest visible wavelength of light at about 0.7 micrometres

Blue light travels further through **water** than **colours** with a longer **wavelength**, such as red or green. This is why everything **looks blue** underwater.

The most powerful manmade laser is a **million times** brighter than **sunshine**.

The first telephone cable under the Atlantic Ocean was laid in 1956.

Ultrasound scans use high-frequency sound at around 10 million hertz to give **an image** of a baby in the womb.

X-ray

technology has shown that there are **three different versions** of Leonardo da Vinci's *Mona Lisa* under the visible one.

The *first ever robot* was probably built in *Ancient Greece* by Archytas of Tarentum *2,500* years ago. It was a *mechanical bird* powered by *steam*.

Maglev trains are powered by **strong magnets**. The fastest commercial maglev train is in **Shanghai**, China. It covers the 30.5 km (19 miles) from the airport to the city centre in just **7 minutes 20 seconds**, reaching a top speed of 431 km/h (268 mph).

There are **7,000 robots** in the US military. They carry out dangerous work such as **bomb disposal**.

The world's largest airliner, the Airbus **A380** "**Superjumbo**", can carry up to 853 passengers.

The maximum speed (terminal velocity) of a skydiver, if they pull their limbs in, is 320 km/h (200 mph).

The pocket calculator was invented in **1966** by Texas Instruments.

Wilhelm Conrad Röntgen won the first **Nobel Prize** for physics in **1901** for his discovery of **X-rays**.

More than two-thirds of the energy stored in **fossil fuels** is lost when those fuels are burned in **power stations** to make electricity. Most of the energy is **lost** as heat.

*A plane's flight data recorder, or **black box**, is actually bright **orange** so that it is easy to spot after a crash. It can withstand temperatures of more than 1,000°C (1823°F).*

The world's smallest guitar is just 10 millionths of a metre long. It was made by Cornell University, and produces notes 17 octaves higher than a normal guitar.

English scientist Sir Isaac Newton's dog **Diamond** knocked over a **candle** and started a fire that destroyed **20 years'** worth of his work.

The first instant camera was made by Polaroid in 1948.

Newton was one of the **greatest** scientists in history. He also invented the **cat flap**.

Any **Rubik's Cube** can be solved in **26** moves or fewer.

SEE WHAT ELSE SCIENTISTS HAVE DISCOVERED ON PAGES 88–125

Space

On a clear, **moonless night**, you can see about **2,500 stars** with the naked eye.

The Sun contains more than 99 per cent of all the material in the Solar System.

Uranus was discovered in 1781 and **Neptune** in 1846.

The gravity on the **Moon's** surface is just **17 per cent** of that of Earth. If you can jump 1 m (3 ft) high on Earth, you would be able to jump 6 m (19 ft) on the Moon.

*The **Moon** moves **3 cm** (1.25 in) away from **Earth** each year.*

*The **Moon** appears to be the same size as the **Sun** from Earth because, although the Sun is **400** times wider than the Moon, it is also **400** times further away.*

Space rockets need to reach a speed of **40,000 km/h** (25,000 mph) to escape the gravitational pull of Earth. This is called the **escape velocity**.

Earth is the densest planet in the Solar System, with a density of 5.5 g/cm³ (3.2 oz/in³).

The clouds on Venus are made of sulfuric acid. Its atmosphere is 96.5 per cent carbon dioxide.

Jupiter is **1,321** times the volume of Earth. **Mercury** is just **0.05 times** the volume of Earth.

The Sun viewed from Mars is two-thirds the size of the Sun viewed from Earth.

*In **winter** on **Uranus**, it is **dark** for **21 Earth years**.*

Saturn would **float** in a giant bath, as it is **less dense** than water.

Pluto was classified as a **planet** from its discovery in 1930 until 2006.

More than **22,500 meteorites** that landed on Earth have been **collected** and **catalogued**.

The **same side** of the **Moon** always faces **Earth**. This is because the Moon rotates in the same time as it takes to orbit – **27.3 days**.

The **dwarf** planet Ceres is the **largest** asteroid, at **960 km** (596 miles) across.

*The largest **volcano** in the **Solar System** is **Olympus Mons** on **Mars**. It is **648 km** (403 miles) **wide** and **24 km** (15 miles) **high**.*

*Jupiter is **rotating** so quickly that it **bulges** in the middle.*

The **Great Red Spot** visible on the surface of **Jupiter** is a **storm**, wider than two Earths, that has been observed *raging* for the past **340 years**.

The **black hole** at the centre of the Milky Way is as massive as **4.1 million Suns**.

*There is no wind or rain on the **Moon**, so **footprints** made by astronauts are likely to remain there for **millions of years**.*

Neptune is the *windiest* planet. Gusts there can reach **2,160 km/h** (1,340 mph).

At a speed of 95 km/h (60 mph), it would take you 177 years to **drive to the Sun**.

Astronauts are up to **5 cm** (2 in) **taller** in space because their **spines expand** in the **weightlessness**.

*It takes **84 Earth years** for **Uranus** to **orbit** the Sun.*

The **Sun** is **half-way through its life**. It has been *burning* for **4.6 billion years**, and will run out of fuel in **5 billion years'** time.

Our **Sun** is orbiting the **black hole** at the centre of the **Milky Way galaxy** at a speed of **900,000 km/h** (550,000 mph). It takes **225 million** years to complete one orbit.

The Universe is expand**ing** in all directions at the speed of light.

*As we look into space we see the **Universe** as it was in the **past** because of the **time** it takes for the **light** of distant stars and galaxies to reach us.*

The tail of the **Great Comet**, which passed by Earth in **1843**, was more than **800 million km** (500 million miles) long – about the distance from the Sun to Jupiter.

In 1971, US astronaut Alan Shepard stood on the **Moon** and hit a **golf ball**.

Saturn's rings were first seen by **Galileo** in **1610** using one of the *first ever telescopes*.

The *biggest stars* of all are *500 times larger* than the *Sun* and *100,000 times as bright*.

The **brightest** objects in the Universe are *quasars* – extremely distant galaxies that have incredibly bright centres. The quasars that we can see are so far away that their light has taken *billions* of years to reach Earth.

If you counted the stars in the **Milky Way** at a rate of one a second, it would take you about **5,000 years** to count them all.

*Robert Goddard first suggested flying to the **Moon** in a **rocket** in **1912**. People thought he was crazy.*

The planets of our **Solar System** occupy a disc-shaped region extending **4.5 billion km** (2.8 billion miles) from the Sun.

Comet Encke is the most frequent visitor to Earth, passing by once every **3.3 years**.

There are more than **1 million asteroids** larger than 1 km (0.6 miles) wide in the Main Belt of asteroids between the orbits of Mars and Jupiter.

About every 50 million years a meteorite more than 10 km (6 miles) in diameter hits Earth.
Two of the world's largest **optical telescopes** are found at the Mauna Kea Observatory in Hawaii. The twin **Keck telescopes** both have mirrors **10 m** (32.8 ft) in diameter.

*The **largest meteorite** on Earth is the **Hoba West**, which remains where it fell in **Namibia**, southwest Africa. It weighed **66 tonnes** when it was found in 1920.*

Astronauts on the **International Space Station** have been **growing plants** in space. The techniques they develop will be needed on any future mission to Mars, as the astronauts will need to grow their **own food**.

The *Voyager 1* spacecraft left Earth in 1977 and is now the most distant human-made object in space.

*Light from the Sun takes just over **eight minutes** to reach Earth. The light from the next nearest star, Proxima Centauri, takes **4.3 years** to reach Earth.*

There is *no sound* in space, as sound cannot travel through a *vacuum*.

Mars has **ice caps** at its **poles**, just like Earth.

*The largest canyon system in the Solar System is **Valles Marineris on Mars**, which is more than **4,000 km** (2,500 miles) long.*

Volcanoes last erupted on the Moon about 3.2 billion years ago.

The *Orion* vehicle is NASA's new spacecraft. From the early 2020s, it will carry astronauts to the **Moon** and, later, on the first stage of a mission to **Mars**.

Yuri Gagarin's **mother** first found out about his **flight into space** when news of the mission broke.

It takes the Space Shuttle *eight minutes* to reach its orbital speed of **27,000 km/h** (17,000 mph).

FOR MORE FACTS AND FIGURES ABOUT THE UNIVERSE, SEE PAGES 126–151

Earth

The rotation of Earth is slowing down, so days are becoming longer. In the age of the dinosaurs, **60 million years ago**, an **Earth day** was less than **23 hours long**.

At **midnight** on 21 June each year, it is **light** everywhere north of the **Arctic Circle**.

The pressure at the centre of Earth is *3 million* times greater than that at the surface.

In the 20th century, the surface temperature of Earth rose by 0.6⁰C (1⁰F).

Almost 20 per cent of Earth's **oxygen** is produced by the **Amazon rainforest**.

There are about **750** different species of **tree** in *one hectare* (2.47 acres) of the **Amazon rainforest**.

It would take a heavy object more than an hour to sink from the surface to the seabed at **Challenger Deep** in the Pacific Ocean, which is **11,034 m** (36,201 ft) deep.

Looking out to **sea** from the **beach**, the *horizon* is about **5 km** (3 miles) away.

*After it was measured using satellites in 1999, the official height of **Mount Everest** was raised from **8,848 m** (29,029 ft) to **8,850 m** (29,035 ft).*

*A large thunderstorm cloud, called a **cumulonimbus**, can hold enough water to fill **500,000 baths**.*

Over half the planet is covered by water more than 1.6 km (1 mile) deep.

Six million tonnes of **gold** are dissolved in the water of the world's oceans.

The **volume** of water in the **Pacific Ocean** is the same size as the **Moon**.

Lightning strikes Earth **100** times every second.

The **Great Barrier Reef**, at more than **2,000 km** (1,200 miles) long, is the largest living structure on Earth. It is even visible from space.

Nine out of ten volcanoes are under the sea. More than 1,000 of the 1,500 active volcanoes in the world are in the South Pacific Ocean.

Coal is made from the compressed remains of plants that died **300 million years ago**.

When the volcanic island of **Krakatoa**, in Indonesia, erupted in **1883**, it could be heard a quarter of the way around the world.

*In **1811**, an earthquake sent water in the **Mississippi River** flowing temporarily in the **wrong direction**.*

China's Yellow River is the world's *muddiest* river. Two billion tonnes of mud wash down it every year.

Fresh snow is more than *90 per cent* trapped air.

The biggest **desert** in the world, the **Sahara**, covers a **third** of the area of **Africa**.

*The **driest** place in the world is the **Atacama Desert** in **Chile**. When it rained there in **1971**, it ended a **drought** that had lasted for **400 years**.*

Sand dunes move like waves across deserts at a speed of about 1 m (3 ft) per year.

*The lowest temperature ever recorded is **-89.2⁰C** (-128.5⁰F) at **Vostok, Antarctica,** on 21 July 1983.*

The highest temperature ever recorded was **56.7⁰C** (134.1⁰F) at **Furnace Creek, California,** on 10 July 1913.

The **strongest** gust of wind ever recorded blew at **372 km/h** (231 mph) on **Mount Washington**, USA, in 1934.

The driest continent is *Antarctica* because it receives so little rain.

There is enough **electricity** in a single fork of **lightning** to **light** a town for a year.

Seawater freezes at -2°C (28°F) because the salt in it lowers its freezing point.

The surface of the **Dead Sea** in the Jordan Valley is 408 m (1,340 ft) below sea level. Its water is so **salty** that nothing can live in it except simple organisms, such as algae.

*The world's **shortest river** is the **North Fork Roe River**, in Montana, USA, which is just **18 m** (59 ft) long.*

In **1873**, *frogs* rained down from the sky in Kansas City, USA. In **1948**, a group of golfers in Bournemouth, England, was showered with *herring*. The animals had been swept up into the clouds by strong winds.

*The **hardness of rocks** is measured using the **Mohs scale**, with **soft talc** at **1** and **hard diamond** at **10**.*

The largest meteor crater is Vredefort in South Africa, which is 300 km (186 miles) wide. It was created when a meteor about 10 km (6 miles) wide collided with Earth 2 billion years ago.

As **deserts** grow larger, the amount of **land** available to grow **crops** is **shrinking** at a rate of **120,000 sq km** (46,000 sq miles) every year.

*Enough water to fill **2 million baths** flows out of the **River Amazon** into the Atlantic Ocean in one second. This is **five times** as much water as the second-largest flow, from the **River Ganges**.*

On average, there are just **five days** a year when it doesn't **rain** on Mt Waialeale in Hawaii.

On the afternoon of 31 May 1985, **41 tornadoes** were reported around the States of Pennsylvania and Ohio in the USA. **Seventy-five** people were killed.

The eruption of **Mount St Helens** in the USA on 18 May 1980 set off an **avalanche** travelling at 400 km/h (250 mph).

No two *snowflakes* have the same shape, but they all have *six sides*.

The Holderness coastline in east England is being eroded away by the North Sea at a rate of 1.5 m (5 ft) per year.

More than **30 per cent** of **New Zealand's greenhouse gas** comes from methane in the **burps** and **farts** of the country's 45 million **sheep** and 10 million **cows**.

Earth's atmosphere is **700 km** (430 miles) thick.

Greenland is the **largest island** in the world, with an area of **2,133,086 sq km** (836,109 sq miles). **Australia** is **larger**, but is considered to be a **continent** rather than an island.

*The **largest diamond mine** in the world is at Mirny in Siberia. The hole in the ground is **1,200 m** (4,000 ft) across – so big that **helicopters** are **sucked into it** if they fly too close.*

There are 14 mountains more than 8,000 m (26,000 ft) high, all of them in the Himalayas.

Clouds contain tiny droplets of water floating in air. A raindrop contains up to **2 million** cloud **droplets**.

A delay of **three seconds** between seeing **lightning** and hearing **thunder** means that the lightning is **1 km** (0.6 miles) away.

There are **15,000** bush fires in Australia every year, as trees and shrubs burst into flames in the extreme heat. Many plants rely on these fires to release their seeds.

The **oldest rocks** in the **Grand Canyon** were formed **2 billion** years ago.

Over the last 10,000 years, **80 per cent** of the world's **forests** have been **cut down** by humans.

Seven per cent of the world's **oceans** are covered in **ice**.

TO TAKE A CLOSER LOOK AT OUR PLANET, SEE PAGES 152–189

People and places

Vatican City isn't actually a city. It is a ***country***, although it is only the **size** of **50 football pitches** and its official **population** is just **840 people**.

Nigeria is the most densely populated country in Africa with more than **197 million people**, but **Algeria** is the largest country geographically with a total area of **2,381,741 sq km** (919,595 sq miles).

*Niger has the youngest population in the world. More than half its inhabitants are aged **18 or under**.*

Singapore is both a city and a state. It is the only member of the UN with a completely urban population.

China and India both have more than 1.3 billion inhabitants. The next biggest country by population, the USA, has fewer than 330 million.

*Istanbul in Turkey is the only city to straddle **two continents** – Europe and Asia.*

Damascus in Syria is the world's **oldest city**. People have lived there for more than 10,000 years.

There are 195 countries in the world.

*There is **enough stone** in the **Great Pyramid** in Egypt to build **a wall** 1 m (3 ft) high around France.*

The football **World Cup** has only ever been won by countries from ***Europe*** or ***South America***.

With **4 billion** viewers, **football** is the most- watched **sport** in the world.

Before humans arrived in **New Zealand** around 1,000 years ago, there were **no mammals** there except bats. **Flightless birds**, such as the **kiwi**, walked the land instead.

The bricks of the traditional **rondavel** houses of Rwanda are stuck together using **cow dung**.

The city of **Troy** was thought to be **mythical** until its ruins were found in Turkey in the 1870s.

The **tallest building** in the world is the **Burj Khalifa** in Dubai. It is **828 m** (2,700 ft) high, the tallest structure ever built by humans.

It is estimated that **3.6 billion** people watched the **2016 Rio de Janeiro Olympics** on TV.

The flag of **Nepal** is the only national flag that is not rectangular. It looks like one **triangle** on top of another.

Mongolia is the most ***sparsely populated*** country in the world. There are only **1.9** people per sq km (4.7 per sq mile).

WalMart, a US company with a chain of stores, is the largest company in the world with **2.3 million** employees.

France is the world's most **popular** holiday destination with more than **89 million** tourists each year.

Between 1800 and 2000, the population of the world grew from **1 billion** to **6 billion**.

In 27 CE **Rome** became the **first** city to have **1 million** inhabitants.

*In 2008, for the first time in history, more than **half** the people of **the world** lived in cities and towns rather than rural communities.*

There are **50 states** in the USA. The most recent to join was ***Hawaii***, on 20 August 1959.

Tokyo is the ***largest city*** in the world. If you include all its suburbs, its population is ***37 million***.

English is an official language in **67** countries.

There are about **110,000 Inuit people**, almost equally distributed between **Alaska**, **Canada**, and **Greenland**.

About 7,000 different languages are used around the world, of which half are spoken by fewer than 10,000 people.

The first map to name the newly discovered continent **America** was drawn by German cartographer Martin Waldseemüller in 1507.

Fewer than 100 people still speak **Votic**, a language of northern Russia.

Over 700 languages are spoken in Indonesia.

Australians eat more *meat* than anyone else.

Two million people converge on the holy city of **Mecca**, in Saudi Arabia, each year during the week of the Muslim pilgrimage called the **hajj**.

The **oldest known map** was drawn around **2,500** BCE on a clay tablet in **Babylonia**, in **modern-day Iraq**, showing the area around the **River Euphrates**.

Iceland's **Althing** is the oldest parliament in the world. Its first meeting was held in 930 CE.

*In 1978, Argentinian **Emilio Marcos Palma** became the first person to be born in **Antarctica**.*

About 4,000 people, mainly **scientists**, live in **Antarctica** in the **summer**. This number drops to 1,000 in the winter.

About *1 billion* people do *not* have enough to *eat*.

Absolute monarchies are states that are ruled directly by a hereditary leader. **Saudi Arabia**, Brunei, Oman, and Swaziland are the only absolute monarchies that survive today.

*The **Trans-Siberian railway** runs from **St Petersburg** in the west to **Vladivostok** in the east. It is **9,288 km** (5,772 miles) **long** and goes through **eight different time zones**, without ever leaving **Russia**.*

There are more than **30** megacities with more than **10 million** inhabitants in the world.

The widest avenue in the world is **Avenida 9 de Julio** in **Buenos Aires**, Argentina. It has **12 lanes of traffic**.

At any given time of day, there are more than a *million* people in the *air* somewhere in the world.

*There are **1 billion bicycles** in the world, **400 million** of them in **China**.*

The United Nations was formed by **51** countries in **1945**. It now has **193** members since **Montenegro** joined in **2006**.

There are **55** different **ethnic groups** in **China** besides the Chinese.

Experts predict that India will overtake China as the most populous nation on Earth by 2030.

The **first mobile phone network was launched in Sweden in 1956.**

The world's **busiest airport** is **Atlanta** in the USA. More than **88 million people** pass through its doors each year.

The first country to give women the vote was New Zealand in 1893.

Russia, the largest country by area, is almost twice the size of the second largest, Canada.

About *half* the world's people regularly eat *insects*. About *2,000* different species appear on the menu.

*The **Rio de Janeiro Carnival** in Brazil is the world's biggest street party, with more than 2 million people packing the streets. London's **Notting Hill Carnival** in England is the second largest.*

80 per cent of the world's **toys** are made in **China**.

FOR MORE AMAZING PEOPLE AND PLACES, SEE PAGES 190–225

History

An early **writing system called cuneiform** was developed in **Mesopotamia** (part of modern-day Iraq) around **3,100 BCE**. It was written by making wedge-shaped marks on clay tablets.

Modern humans settled in **Australia** at least **10,000** years before they reached Europe.

King Pepi II became **king of Egypt** in **2,275 BCE** aged just **six**. He ruled for **94 years** until his death aged **100**.

*The minimum period of **service** for legionaries in the **Roman army** was **25 years**.*

About **2,000 years ago**, traded goods from **China** began to reach **Europe** and **Africa** along a route that became known as the **Silk Road**, as silk was one of the goods traded.

In **1519**, the **Aztec capital *Tenochtitlán*** had a **quarter of a million** inhabitants. It was five times larger than London at the time.

*Of the **270** **crew members** who set out from Lisbon with **Ferdinand Magellan** in 1519 to sail around the world, just **18** completed the journey. Magellan himself died half-way round.*

The Inca thought of gold as the *sweat* of the Sun, and *silver* as the tears of the Moon.

The **Inca empire** covered **900,000 sq km** (350,000 sq miles). In 1532, it was conquered by Spaniard Francisco Pizarro and just 168 men.

The ***first*** ever female head of state was ***Queen Merneith***, who ruled ***Ancient Egypt*** around ***3,000 BCE***.

The **Roman empire** reached its greatest extent in **117 CE**, when it stretched from Britain in the northwest to the Persian Gulf in the southeast.

***The* Roman *legal system is the basis* for the laws of all countries *in* Europe *and* Latin America.**

The gladiator **Spartacus** led a revolt of more than **100,000 slaves** against the army of the **Roman empire** in **72 BCE**.

The Aztecs used cocoa beans as a form of money.

English explorer **Mary Kingsley** climbed ***Mount Cameroon*** in Africa on her own in 1895 when local guides refused to take her.

*The first English-speaking **colony** in **North America** was set up in **1585** in Roanoke in North Carolina. It only lasted one year.*

The *Islamic calendar* started in **622 CE**. It uses a year that is 11 days shorter than a full solar year.

Greenland was given its name by ***Viking chieftain Erik the Red*** around ***1000 CE*** in an attempt to attract settlers.

14th-century Arabian explorer **Ibn Battuta** travelled **117,000 km** (73,000 miles) and visited every **Islamic country** in the world.

In the census called the **Domesday Book** carried out in 1086, **10 per cent** of the population of **England** were listed as **slaves**.

***Polynesian sailors** crossed the Pacific Ocean **1,000 years** ago, using charts made of sticks to find their way.*

The **Ancient Chinese invented** many things. The so-called *"Four Great Inventions of Ancient China"* were **paper**, the **compass, printing,** and **gunpowder**.

*Between 1760 and 1840, **7,000 km (4,300 miles)** of **canals** were built in **Britain** to carry goods from the new factories around the country.*

Zimbabwe is named after the **ancient city** of Great Zimbabwe in southern Africa, **built of stone** between the 11th and 15th centuries, but then **mysteriously abandoned**.

People first settled **North America** around **20,000 years** ago. They walked across a land bridge that connected **northern Siberia** with **Alaska**.

The **Statue of Liberty** was a present given by France to the USA in 1877 to mark the **100**th **anniversary** of the *American Declaration of Independence*.

The earliest written **constitution** still in use in a republic today is that of the tiny European state **San Marino**. It dates back to **1600**.

In the first factories and mines of the Industrial Revolution in Britain, children as young as five worked 16-hour shifts.

Between **1848 and 1855**, about **300,000** people went to *California*, USA, to find their fortunes in the **Gold Rush**.

The longest **reigning** monarch is currently Elizabeth II of **United Kingdom**, who came to the throne in **1952**.

One century ago, **Ethiopia** was the only country in **Africa** that was not ruled by a European power. All African countries are now **independent** from Europe.

In the year 1900, **one quarter** of the population of the world lived under **British rule**.

*Approximately 13 million soldiers from **Russia** were killed in **World War II**, more than all other countries put together. More than **1 million** died in the siege of **Stalingrad** alone.*

King Richard II of England (1367–1400) threw extravagant **parties** for as many as **10,000 people** at a time.

In the 13th century, **Constantinople** and **Baghdad** were the largest cities in the world, with about **1 million** inhabitants each.

Japan's monarchy dates from **660** BCE to the present day, during which time there have been **125 emperors**.

The **Hundred Years' War** between **France** and **England** actually lasted **116** years, from 1337 to 1453.

In 1783, a **sheep**, a **duck**, and a **rooster** became the first aircraft passengers when they **flew** in the Montgolfier brothers' **hot-air balloon**.

The Viking law court was called the Thing.

*In medieval European courts, animals could be tried for crimes. A swarm of **locusts** were once **convicted**, in their absence, of illegally eating crops.*

Between 1793–94, at least **17,000** people were executed in the nine-month-long **"Reign of Terror"** during the **French Revolution**.

*The **Black Death**, an outbreak of the bubonic plague, reached **Sicily** in southern Europe in **1347**. Less than three years later it had spread to the **Arctic Circle**, 3,500 km (2,200 miles) to the north.*

The toilets of **16th-century English** homes were cleaned by a worker called a **gong farmer**.

Of the **seven wonders** of the ancient world, only the *Great Pyramid of Giza* still exists.

The *Great Plague of London* was ended in **1666** by the *Great Fire of London*, which burned down the affected areas.

Ghamdan Palace in Sana'a, Yemen, built in the **3**rd **century** CE, may be the world's first ever **castle**.

The **Great Wall of China**, built to protect China's northern border, is 6,500 km (4,000 miles) long.

Art and culture

The first blocks of **flats** were built in **Rome** in the 1st century BCE.

Eleven Christian **churches** were carved out of solid rock at Labilela in **Ethiopia** in the 12th century CE. They took 24 years to complete.

The **first** ever **skyscraper** was the **10-storey**-high Home Insurance Building, built in **Chicago**, USA, in **1885**.

The **Circus Maximus** stadium in Ancient Rome could hold **250,000** people – a quarter of the population of the city.

In 1923, **marathon dancing** competitions became popular in the USA after Alma Cummings danced for **27 hours** without stopping.

After a performance of the opera **Otello** in Vienna, Austria, in 1991, starring Spanish tenor **Placido Domingo**, the audience **applauded** for 1 hour 20 minutes.

Irish-born James Devine is the world's fastest **tap dancer**. He made **38 taps per second** in a performance in Sydney, Australia, in 1998.

Ancient Greek theatres were open-air. The biggest could hold 10,000 spectators.

Agatha Christie's whodunit play **The Mousetrap** has been playing in London's West End since 1952. There have been more than **27,500** performances so far.

The **"Whirling Dervishes"** of the Sufi order of Islam perform their **spinning dance** as an aid to religious meditation.

In the Mayan **ballgame court** at Chichen Itza, the acoustics are so good that a **whisper** at one end of the court can be heard at the other end **150 m** (500 ft) away.

The **marble** and precious stones used to build the **Taj Mahal** in Agra, India, were carried there by **1,000 elephants**.

In 2005, China had 39,425 **cinema screens** – more than any other country.

The first modern novel was called **The Tale of Genji**, written **1,000 years** ago by Japanese author Murasaki Shikibu.

Americans spend an average of **five hours** a day watching television.

The film **Gandhi** had **294,560 extras**.

The **Harry Potter** novels by JK Rowling have been translated into **80** different languages.

Playing cards date from 12th-century Persia and India, when a pack contained 48 cards.

The most **expensive film** ever made was the **Pirates of the Caribbean: On Stranger Tides**, with a budget of **$378.5 million**.

The world's biggest cinema screen is the **IMAX** in Sydney, Australia. It is as high as an **eight-storey** building.

On average, it takes **eight weeks** to shoot a **Hollywood feature film**. Editing and adding special effects takes many months more.

French author Marcel Proust's novel **In Search of Lost Time** contains just under 1.5 million words.

The epic ancient Indian poem **The Mahabharata** is four times longer than the Bible.

The **deputy electrician** on a film set is called the **"best boy"**, even when she's a girl.

The **biggest library** in the world is the Library of Congress in Washington DC, which has more than **32 million books**.

The **Asterix** books, by French duo **René Goscinny** and **Albert Uderzo**, have sold over 370 million copies worldwide.

English playwright **William Shakespeare** (1564–1616) is credited with inventing **1,700** new words.

The most prolific **novelist** in history was South African writer **Mary Faulkner**, who wrote **904 books**.

The **Codex Leicester**, one of **Leonardo da Vinci's** notebooks, was bought by US billionaire **Bill Gates** in 1994 for $29 million.

In May 1990, Dutch artist **Vincent van Gogh**'s painting *Portrait of Dr Gachet* sold for **£49 million**. In his lifetime, he was unable to make a living from his art.

Italian artist **Michelangelo** spent *five years*, between 1536 and 1541, painting Biblical scenes on the walls of the **Sistine Chapel** in Rome.

In 1872, Austrian composer **Johann Strauss** conducted an orchestra of **987 musicians** and a choir of **19,000 singers** in Boston, USA.

The slowest musical tempo is called **larghissimo**, Italian for as slow as possible. The fastest is **prestissimo**, meaning as fast as possible.

The first permanent **photograph** was taken by **French inventor** *Nicéphore Niépce* in **1826**. It needed eight hours of exposure time.

An estimated 1.5 billion people watched the 1985 charity concert Live Aid on television.

The drawings of animals on cave walls in Chauvet, France, are approximately 36,000 years old.

The world's **largest statue** is the statue of Sardar Vallabhbhai Patel, one of the heroes of India's independence movement. The statue stands 182 m (600 ft) tall in the state of Gujarat, India.

The first museum to open its doors to the public was the **Uffizi Gallery** in Florence, Italy, in 1591.

In the 1930s, German company Blütner made a **baby grand piano** out of **aluminium** and **pigskin**, so that it would be light enough to be carried in an **airship**. It weighed **180 kg** (397 lb).

The best-selling album of all time is **Thriller** by US pop star Michael Jackson, with an estimated 66 million copies.

In December 2006, the **Netherlands** *became the first country to* **switch off** *its analogue* **TV** *signal, forcing everyone to use digital receivers.*

The lowest voice in opera singing is called a *basso profundo*, Italian for "deep bass".

The term for actor, **thespian**, comes from the first actor known to history, Thespis from Ancient Greece.

The fastest ball game in the world is **pelota**, *played in the Basque region of northern Spain and southern France. The ball can move at up to* **300 km/h** *(185 mph).*

The first **compact disc** *went on sale in 1982.*

La Scala opera house in Milan, Italy, has 3,600 seats.

The practice of awarding **caps** *for international sports appearances started in England in* **1886**. *Footballers in their first international were presented with a white* **silk cap** *with a red rose on the front.*

The highest paid sportsman of the **21ˢᵗ century** is *Michael Jordan,* with earnings of around **$1.85 billion**.

Athletics was the first sport to hold organized competitions. The first such event probably took place in Ancient Greece **5,000 years ago**.

It is now possible to watch more than 2,000 different TV channels from around the world online.

On 31 December 1994, British pop singer **Rod Stewart** *played a concert on* **Copacabana Beach**, *Rio de Janeiro, Brazil, to an estimated* **3,500,000** *New Year's Eve revellers.*

Walt Disney was nominated for **64 Oscars** and won **26**, more than anyone in history.

The **marathon** is a race run over a distance of **42.195 km** (26.218 miles). This is the distance Greek soldier **Pheidippides** ran without stopping from the town of Marathon to Athens in 490 ʙᴄᴇ to announce victory in battle over the Persians.

Over its **21** separate stages, **12 million** people came out to watch the **Tour de France** bicycle race in 2017.

The English language has about **500,000** words, compared to **185,000** in German and **100,000** in French.

LEARN MORE ABOUT ART AND CULTURE ON PAGES 252–279

Index

Acknowledgements

DK would like to thank:
Sonakshi Singh for design assistance; Dharini Ganesh and Aishvarya Misra for editorial assistance; Rituraj Singh for picture research; Ben Hung for DTP assistance; Adam Shorrock for creative retouching assistance; Caroline Gates for loaning knitted body parts; David Donkin for the machine model; Nikid for digital artworks; Tall Tree for supplying the reference section; Jackie Brind for the index; Hazel Beynon and Jenny Finch for proofreading; Nigel Sapp and the Ocular Prosthetics Department, Moorfields Eye Hospital; Jamie Owen and the Natural History Museum; Dr Tony Irwin, curator of natural history, Norwich Castle Museum and Archaeology Service; William Edwards and the Gordon Museum, Guys Hospital; Sean Rogg for kind permission to photograph his bottled water exhibition; Hanh Thi Luc for assistance with props; Zygmunt Podhorodecki for supplying and handling wasps and bees; Pia-Henrike Böttger, Cladia Vasconcellos, and Riley's Snooker Club, Walthamstow, for supplying props.

The publisher would like to thank the following for their kind permission to reproduce their photographs:

Key:
a–above; b–below/bottom; c–centre; f–far; l–left; r–right; t–top

123RF.com Laurent Davoust / daboost 249fbr; jipen 249fbr; **The Advertising Archives:** 247tl, 250-251tc; **akg-images:** 262tr; Johann Brandste 104t; **Alamy Images:** AL 119ftr; AA World Travel Library 192cl; ArkReligion.com 258cr; Auscape International 202cl; Bill Bachmann 197tl; J.R. Bale 106-107c; David Barnes 182cl; Brett Baunton 184bl; Pat Behnke 194cl; blickwinkel 53c; Oote Boe Photography 240cl, 240cr (display cabinet), 241cl, 241cr; Tibor Bogna 163cr; Paul Chauncey 197bl; CW Motorsport Images 105tr; David Noton Photography 163cr; Kathy deWitt 215t; Dennis Frates 196-197; David Hosking 183bl; Interfoto 201tc; Sean Justice 224-225c; Kim Karpeles 112-113c; James Kubrick 242-243c; Iain Masterton 271bc; Eric Nathan 192-193c (background); Gavin Newman 182bc; Ron Niebrugge 162cr; Nordic Photos 44-45c; M. Timothy O'Keefe 37cr; Pictorial Press Ltd. 271br; Christopher Pillitz 212tr; Sue Walsham 217cb; Helene Rogers 202-203c; Alex Segre 270-271c; Jeff Smith 145r; vario images GmbH & Co.KG 120br; Visual Arts Library 226-227c; David Wall 180crb, 203cr; Andrew Woodley 223cr; World Religions Photo Library 258br; Krivosheev 265tl; **Andy Rouse Wildlife Photography:** Andy Rouse 8-9c; **The Art Archive:** Marco Polo Gallery, Paris / A. Dagli Orti 254fcr; Museo del Prado, Madrid / A. Dagli Orti 254cr; National Gallery of Art, Washington 254cl; São Paulo Art Museum / G. Dagli Orti 255cr; Tate Gallery, London / Eileen Tweedy / © DACS 2008 254bl; **the-blueprints.com:** Onno van Braam 122bl, 122tl, 122-123b, 122-123b, 122-123b, 123br, 123tr; **The Bridgeman Art Library:** Bibliotheque Nationale, Paris, France, Archives Charmet 246tr; British Library 255cl; The Chambers Gallery, London/Private Collection 243bl; City of Westminster Archive Centre, London 242br; Musee Conde, Chantilly, France / Giraudon 260cra (Hebrew); English School/ Private Collection 245tr; Guildhall Library, City of London/Shepherd, Fred 247bl; The Estate of Keith Haring / Deichtorhallen, Hamburg / Wolfgang Neeb 255bl; Louvre, Paris, France, Giraudon 233br; Moscow Museum of the Revolution 242-243tc; National Portrait Gallery, London, E.Seeman (after) 124cl; Peter Newark American Pictures/ Private Collection 216cl; Peter Newark American Pictures/Private Collection 216c,

217c, 217cr, 217tl; Skelton, William/ Bibliotheque de la Faculté de Médecine, Paris, France, Archives Charmet 246br; Vatican Museums and Galleries, Vatican City, Italy 233tl; Victoria and Albert Museum, London 234b, 234t, 235b, 235t; **British Library:** 262cl, 262-263bc; **The Trustees of the British Museum:** 229r; **Bryan and Cherry Alexander Photography:** articphoto/Troels Jacobson 204br; **Corbis:** 199br; Peter Adams/zefa 257cr; London Aerial Photo Library 222b; Albright-Knox Art Gallery / © DACS 2008 254fbr; Theo Allofs 198bl, 204-205c; Mario Anzuoni/Reuters 275c; Apple Handout/epa 119fbr; The Art Archive 125bc, 233c, 233tr; Yann Arthus-Bertrand/ 203tr; Asian Art & Archaeology, Inc. 263br; Simon Baker 202-203tc; Beateworks/David Papazian 213c; Nathan Benn 199tl; Bettmann 124c, 125c, 160t, 216tc, 216tl, 216cr/2 (Truman items), 216tr/3 (all Harrison items), 217cla, 217tr/2 (Roosevelt items), 217tc/3 (McKinley items), 247tr; Jonathan Blair 144-145c; Gene Blevins 151cla; Christophe Bolsvieux 182tr; Gary Braasch 181tl (l); Tom Brakefield 31tl, 55cl; Burstein Collection / The Munch Museum / The Munch-Ellingsen Group / © DACS 2008 254fbl; Christie's Images / © DACS 2008 254br; Tim Clayton 203tl; Ashley Cooper 166-167c (background); Richard Cummins 233cr; Tim Davis 39bl; Michael DeYoung 179br; DLILLC 192tr; Momatluk-Eastcott 204bc; epa 161cl; epa/Jon Hrusa 251clb; epa/Larry W. Smith 177bl; epa/Marcelo Sayao 188c; epa/Valdrin Xhemaj 190-191c; Eurasia Press/Steven Vidler 197tr; Macduff Everton 195tc; Warren Faidley 176cl; Michael & Patricia Fogden 34-35c; David J. & Janice L. Frent Collection 217cl/2 (Eisenhower items); Paulo Fridman 223cl; The Gallery Collection 252-253c; Lynn Goldsmith 275clb; Michael Goulding 267tr; Darrell Gulin 178cl; Robert Harding World Imagery/Occidor Ltd. 179tr; Rune Hellestad 201crb; Chris Hellier 246cl; Jon Hicks 223tl, 257tl; Fritz Hoffman 251cb; Robbie Jack 201cr; Peter Johnson 205tr; Wolfgang Kaehler 225bl; Ed Kashi 192tl; Karen Kasmauski 223bl; Brooks Kraft 217br; Kurt Krieger 256bc; Owaki - Kulla 178cr; Frans Lanting 181br, 198cl; Danny Lehman 255tl; Charles & Josette Lenars 256bl; Liu Liqun 181bl; Araldo de Luca 232bl, 232c, 232tl; Joe Macdonald 39crb; Jamed Marshall 180cr, 198clb; Leo Mason 200tl; George McCarthy 39tl; Gideon Mendel 121tr; Minden Pictures/Michael & Patricia Fogden 178bl; Momatiuk - Eastcott 180tl; NASA 177cr, 181tr; Eric Nguyen 176tr; Nightlight/zefa 176bc; James Noble 110bl; Kazuyoshi Nomachi 192tc (sand dune), 222cr; Richard Nowitz 182br; Charles O'Rear 192cr; Miyoko Oyashiki 120cr; Paul Hardy 28-29c, 257cl; PoodlesRock 160cl; Jim Reed 176tl; Reuters 160b, 189cr, 200tc (cyclists); Reuters/ Jim Ruymen 274-275tc; Quentin Rhoton 183t; Lynda Richardson 53t; Galen Rowell 204tl; Pete Saloutos 178-179tc; Kevin Schafer 37bl; Joseph Sohm; Visions of America 215bl; Paul Souders 38c; George Steinmetz 205tl; David Stoeklein 192crb; STScI/NASA 126-127c, 128tc; Jim Sugar 124-125bc, 158-159c; Paul J. Sutton 266tc; Swim Ink 2, LLC 270tl; Gustavo Tomsich 201c; Peter Turnley 243br; TWPhoto 161t; Ultimate Chase/Mike Theiss 177cl; Alessandro Della Valle/Keystone 257bc; Francesco Venturi 259fcl; Visions of America/Joseph Sohm 242bl; Philip Wallick 176br; Michele Westmorland 52t; Nik Wheeler 188cl; Dennis Whitehead 188-189c; Haruyoshi Yamaguchi 120bl; Yann Arthus-Bertrand 152-153c; zefa/Frank Krahmer 54bl; **DK Images:** Academy of Motion Picture Arts and Sciences 197tl; Angus Beare Collection 55c; James Kuether 174bl, br, 175tl; Masato Hattori 175br; Archaeological Receipts Fund (TAP) 222cl; Australian Museum, Sydney 224tr; Birmingham Buddhist Vihara 195br; British Howson/Chas Howson 248b; British Library/ Laurence Pordes 255tbc; British Museum 230-231c, 236clb, 236cr, 237tl, 249bc, 259cl, 259crb, 259tr; British Museum/Chas Howson

248br, 248c, 248cl, 248tl, 249c, 249cr, 249cra, 249fcl, 249fcr, 249fcrb; Clive Streeter / American Express (Platinum card) 249br; British Museum/Museum of Mankind 202ca; British Museum/Museum of Mankind/Kate Warren 249bl, 249tr; The British Museum 232tr; Cecil Williamson Collection/Alex WIlson 192-193c (drum); IFREMER, Paris/Tina Chambers 171tl; Charlestown Shipwreck and Heritage Centre, Cornwall/Alex Wilson 249tl; Conaculta-Inah-Mex. Authorized reproduction by the Instituto Nacional de Antropologia e Historia 236b, 236br, 236cl, 236-237b, 236-237t, 237bc, 237bl, 237br, 237cb, 237crb; Crown copyright/Gary Ombler 214c; David Edge/Geoff Dann 241bl; Based on a Crown copyright image of the British Passport (c) Crown copyright material is reproduced with the permission of the Controller of HMSO and Queen's Printer for Scotland 214 c; Dinosaur State Park, Connecticut 173bl; Eden Camp Museum 250tc; Linda Esposito 192tc (Jump Dance); Football Museum, Preston 260-261 (Futebol poster); Glasgow Museums 255tr; Gordon Museum/Guy's, King's and St. Thomas' School of Medicine 76cr; Rowan Greenwood Collection 204tr; Henry Moore Foundation (The work illustrated on page 255 is reproduced by permission of the Henry Moore Foundation) 255bl; Jamie Marshall Collection 243tr (flag detail), 258cl; Kröller-Müller Museum 255c (Van Gogh); Lindsey Stock Collection 55tr; Museum of London 260-261c, 261cr; National Maritime Museum, London/James Stevenson and Tina Chambers 239br, 239cr; National Maritime Museum, London/Tina Chambers 154-155bc, 238bl; Judith Miller / Cooper Owen / © DACS 2008 255bc; Judith Miller/Bibliophion 263cla; Judith Miller/JYP Tribal Art 202tc; Judith Miller/Lyon and Turnbull Ltd. 154-155; Judith Miller/Nigel Wright Collection 259cr; Moorfields Eye Hospital, London 82-83c; Musée du Louvre 254fcl (Mona Lisa); National Maritime Museum, London/James Stevenson 125bc; Natural History Museum, London 172bc, 172cra, 173t, 254tc (figurine); Vincent Oliver 214br; Liberto Perugi/Museum of Natural History of the University of Florence, Zoology Section 'La Specola' 66c, 66cr, 67c, 67cr; Pitts Rivers Museum, University of Oxford/Dave King 249cla; Rough Guides 223br; Courtesy Science Museum, London 244-245c; Science Museum, London 251bc; Scottish United Services Museum, Edinburgh Castle/National Museums of Scotland/Geoff Dann 241fcl, 241tc; South West Shopfittings Ltd. 212-213c; The Science Museum, London/ John Lepine 245bc; Wallace Collection/Geoff Dann 241bl; Wallis and Wallis/Judith Miller 275br (boots); Jerry Young 55br; Michel Zabe 259t; **Dreamstime.com:** Manaemedia 78cb; Grey 18 (Mars surface) 121cla; Viktorijareut 211cb; altrendo images 249br; Buurserstraat386 257bl; **FLPA:** Nigel Cattlin 151bc; Mike Lane 46-47cs; Minden Pictures/ Gerry Ellis 202c; Minden Pictures/Jim Brandenburg 163bc; Minden Pictures/Suzi Eszterhas 51bc; Sunset 267tc; **Galaxy Picture Library:** 133tl, 142cb, 142cl, 142tc, 142tr, 142-143b, 142-143c, 143br, 143cr, 143cra, 143tc; Getty Images: VCG / Visual China Group 120l; 121cr, 151c, 189br, 244tc, 250tr; AFP 150tc, 198tl, 214cra; AFP/ Martin Bernetti 215br; Bridgeman Art Library 215br; S. Brimberg & C. Coulson 163cl; Peter Dazeley 274-275c (background); David De Lossy 62-63c; Phil Degginger 200clb; DigitalGlobe 161b, 161cr; Dave Hogan 274fbl; altrendo images 195ftl; Frank Micelotta 275cl; National Geographic/ Gordon Wiltsie 163c; Dana Neely 125cr; Bob O'Connor 274-275t; Panoramic Images 178tl; Petrified Collection 251cl; Andy Ryan 176-177c; Time & Life Pictures/Nat Farbman 160cr; Time & Life Pictures/Terry Ashe 216bc, 216bl, 216br, 217bl; Time Life Pictures 246b; Untitled X-Ray/Nick Veasey 65ca, 65cb; Chumphon Wanich / EyeEm 264crb; **Hutchison

Library:** J. Wright 224tc; **Courtesy Intel Corporation Ltd:** 88-89c; **iStockphoto.com:** 274bc; Linda Bucklin 76-77c; Marc Dietrich 214crb; Eileen Hart 141l; Shaun Lowe 224cl; Gytis Mikulicius 224clb; James Steidl 215cla; **The Kobal Collection:** Dreamworks/LLC 270br; Universal 271bl; Warner Bros/DC Comics 270bc; **Leeds Library and Information Services, McKenna Collection:** 245tc; **Lumigenic Media / Marc Shargel:** Marc Shargel 37br; **Duccio Malagamba:** 257br; **Ian McKechnie:** 183cr; **Museum Of London:** 251bl; **NASA:** 90tl, 104l, JPL-Caltech 121cla, 128cb, 129tr, 130-131cl, 132bl, 132c, 132cl, 132cra, 132crb, 132l, 133bc, 133bl, 133cb, 133crb, 133tc, 133tr, 136-137c, 139clb, 146t, 146-147tc, 147br, 147cl, 147crb, 147ftr, 147tr, 151; **National Geographic Image Collection:** David Liittschwager 22-23c; **Natural Visions:** Soames Summerhays 37clb; **naturepl.com:** Juan Manuel Borrero 52br; John Cancalosi 52r; Jim Clare 52l; Hans Christoph Kappel 37cla; Kim Taylor 52c; **NHPA / Photoshot:** Bryan & Cherry Alexander 50-51c; Linda Pitkin 30tc; Andy Rouse 197crb; T.Kitchen & V.Hurst 39tr; **Photographers Direct:** Chris Stock 274cr; **Photolibrary:** Gerard Soury 37crb; **PunchStock:** Stockbyte 64c; **reggie.net:** Reggie Thompson 183br; **Courtesy of Renault:** 106c, 107l, 107r; **Richard Revels:** 37ca, 37tr; **Rex Features:** 20th Century Fox/Everett 271tr; Peter Brooker 215cb; **rogersmushrooms.com:** Roger Phillips 18-19c; **The Ronald Grant Archive:** 270bl, 270cr, 270tc, 271tc; **Science & Society Picture Library:** Science Museum 119c; Science Museum, London 119tr, 119fcra; **Science Photo Library:** Prof. P. Motta 78-79t; 63bc, 124cr; Agstocksusa/B.W. Hoffman 10-11c; Anatomical Travelogue 75bl; Andrew Lambert Photography 90bl, 90cl, 90cr, 91br; Julian Baum 105c; Chris Bjornberg 112l; Martin Bond 178-179bc; British Antarctic Survey 204-205bc; BSIP, Cavallini James 109cl; BSIP/Kretz Technik 81bl; Jean-Claude Revy, A. Carion 144c; Jean-Claude Revy, A. Carion, ISM 145tr; Lynette Cook 129b; Kevin Curtis 72-73; Custom Medical Stock Photo/Richard Rawlins 80tr; Charles D.Winters 91cl; Edelman 80bc, 80bl, 80br, 81tc, 81tl; Eurelios/Karim Agabi 204tc; Eye of Science 31tr, 60-61c, 62br; Mark Garlick 128-129t, 129l; Genesis Films/ Neil Bromhall 81tr; Pascal Goetgheluck 120tr; Steve Gschmeissner 62bl, 67clb, 67tl, 74tr; Gustoimages 112cl; Innerspace Imaging 70-71c; Mehau Kulyk 64-65b, 64-65t, 105br; Veronique Leplat 112cr; Living Art Enterprises 64-65c; Living Art Enterprises, LCC 64bl, 64tr, 65cra; Jerry Lodriguss 144l; George Mattei 65br; David McCarthy 63bl; Will McIntyre 189cl; Professors P.M. Motta, P.M. Andrews, K.R. Porter & J. Vial 63c, 67cla; Mount Stromlo and Siding Spring Observatories 132bc; Dr Yorgos Nikas 80cl; Susumu Nishinaga 63tl; NOAA 113l; David Nunuk 146l; Sam Ogden 120c, 121bl; Alfred Pasieka 64cl; Publiphoto Diffusion, P.G. Adam 112r; Victor de Schwanberg 113c, 128l; Volker Steger 120crb; Andrew Syred 75tl, 82-83bc; Richard Wehr 74br; F.S. Westmorland 113r; Charles D. Winter 91cl; **SeaPics.com:** 188cr; **Sony Pictures:** SLB 271cl; **South American Pictures:** Tony Morrison 224-225b; **Still Pictures:** Norman Benton 162c; **SuperStock:** Carmel Studios 197cra; **TopFoto.co.uk:** A©Photri 247br; 233bl; **Transport for London:** 07/1010/ LS 208clb

All other images © Dorling Kindersley

For further information see:
www.dkimages.com